A HISTORY
OF THE
RUSSIAN EMPIRE

OTHER BOOKS BY THE SAME AUTHOR:

The Economic Factors in the Growth of Russia, Philosophical Library, New York, 1957;
Old Ukraine, Its Socio-Economic History prior to 1781, Florham Park Press, Madison, N. J., 1963;
The Ukrainian Economy, Shevchenko Scientific Society, New York, 1965;
An Introduction to Russian History, Philosophical Library, New York, 1967;
Ukraine and the European Turmoil, 1917-1919, Shevchenko Scientific Society and the Ukrainian Scientific-Historical Library, New York-Scranton, 1973, (co-authored with M. Stachiv and P. Stercho), 2 volumes.
Philosophy in Economic Thought, Florham Park Press, Madison, N. J., 1972 (co-authored with V. Mott).

A HISTORY OF THE RUSSIAN EMPIRE

Volume I
Grand-ducal Vladimir and Moscow

by
Nicholas L. Fr.- Chirovsky
Seton Hall University

PHILOSOPHICAL LIBRARY, INC.
15 EAST 40th STREET, NEW YORK, N. Y. 10016

Copyright, © 1973, by Philosophical Library, Inc.,
15 East 40 Street, New York, New York 10016

All rights reserved

Library of Congress Catalog Card No. 72-78164

SBN 8022-2091-6

Printed in the United States of America

To You,

America, the Beautiful

TABLE OF CONTENTS

List of maps	ix
Preface	xi
Acknowledgments	xvi
Chapter 1: Introduction: The land — The people — The periods of the historical development	1

PART I: *The Pre-Muscovite Era*

Chapter 2: *The Historical Prologue*: The pre-historical legacy — The pre-Slavic era — The Slavic tribes in Eastern Europe — The way of life of the north-eastern Slavs — The social and political relations — The religious beliefs   19

Chapter 3: *The Political Prologue*: Novgorod the Great: its political beginnings — Novgorod's political fortunes — Its foreign trading — The city's political and social structure   46

Chapter 4: *The Political Beginnings*: The Rostov-Suzdal and Vladimir principality: its beginnings — Laying the foundations: Yurii I, Dolgorukii — Political growth: Andrei I, Bogolubskii and Vsievolod III, the Big Nest — Other north-eastern principalities   74

Chapter 5: *The Way of Life in the North-East*: The government — Social structure and social relations — The economic process — Cultural life   94

Chapter 6: *The Struggle for Independence*: Ancient Ukraine — The Kievan Rus' realm — The Kievan impact upon the Russian society   133

Chapter 7: *The Struggle for Independence* (Continuation): The Mongols — The invasion — The fortunes of the Golden Horde — The Mongol impact upon the Russian society   153

PART II: *The Muscovite Era*

Chapter 8: *The Beginnings of Muscovy*: The family of the north-eastern principalities — Alexander Nevskii and the subsequent decline of Vladimir — The ascendance of Moscow; from Daniel of Moscow to Ivan I, Kalita — The years of upheaval; from Simeon, the Proud to Dimitrii Donskoi   185

Chapter 9: *The Grand Duchy of Muscovy*: The struggle for consolidation; Vasilii I and Vasilii II — Political consolidation; Ivan III, the Great — Further growth: Vasilii III — Moscow, the Third Rome, and its international position   218

Chapter 10: *The Muscovite Society in the 14th and 15th Centuries*: The government — The judiciary, the finances and the military — The social structure — The economic process — The Church — The culture   249

Chapter 11: *The Muscovite Czarate*: Ivan IV, the Terrible or Dread, as a ruler — Ivan's reign — Domestic affairs and the *oprichnina* institution — Foreign relations and the dynastic plans — Eastern expansion   284

Chapter 12: *The Time of Troubles;* The brewing volcano; Czar Fiodor I, and Czar Boris Godunov — The social struggle; the first Pretender and Czar Vasilii Shuiskii — The national struggle; the *interregnum* and the election of Mikhail Romanov — Foreign affairs and the Eastern expansion   318

Chapter 13: *The Way of Life in the 16th Century Muscovy*: Autocracy — General government — Finances, judiciary, military — The Orthodox Church — Social changes — Economic developments — Cultural developments   357

Bibliography   405

Footnotes   417

Index of names   443

LIST OF MAPS

1. The European North-East in the 9th and 10th Centuries.
2. The Old Republic of Novgorod the Great.
3. The European North-East on the Eve of the Mongol Invasion.
4. Muscovy at the End of the 15th Century.
5. Muscovy in the 16th Century.

PREFACE

It is only natural that soon after I arrived in the United States, my new country, my attention turned to American studies of East European affairs, both past and present, as I have come from that area. I have ascertained that general knowledge of Eastern Europe has been rather inadequate in this country, and that American views concerning that part of the globe have been in some instances either distorted, or at least incorrectly based and formulated.

Hence, a desire developed on my part, on the one hand to present to the American student a new, and a more correct view of the East European countries and peoples, and on the other hand, to attempt to do justice to those peoples by clarifying the misconceptions about them, their historical past and their current socio-political problems. It seemed to me, that the best way to achieve this purpose would be to give to my fellow countrymen a history of Russia. A study of that East European nation which for centuries has been dominating the political scene in that corner of the world, would shed a great deal of light upon the political, social, economic and cultural development of all European nations such as Poland, Ukraine, Byeloruthenia, the Baltic countries, Rumania and the Caucasian and Transcaucasian peoples. These states in the course of history not only developed close contacts with the Russians, but also were for periods of time overrun by Muscovite-Russian imperialism and could reliably attest to the political, cultural and economic practices of that imperialism in their lands. They learned through first-hand experience of the messianic zeal of the Russians to conquer, to expand, and to dominate in the name of Russianism, Orthodoxy, Panslavism or Communism. One hundred years ago, Danilevskii came right to the point when he spoke of that Russian messianic complex: "The Russian people who live between two oceans, the Eastern and the Western, wash by their [human] waves two capitals, Moscow and Peking; and their history is that junction from which grow new centers of the world's history because, for the time being, we see no other possibilities of solution to modern problems." Messianic notes can be found in many Russian writers from the Medieval era on, when the myth of "Moscow — the Third Rome" was born.

The dominant position of Muscovy-Russia in East Europe in political matters and the messianic superiority complex of the Russians have produced some misconceptions concerning the history of that part of the European continent and its peoples in general. These misconceptions sometimes resulted from subjective interpretation of certain historical developments, like the so-called Normanistic theory of the political beginnings of Kievan-Rus' state or the Pogodin-Sobolevskii theory of the originally Russian settlement of Ukraine, or from directly intended and politically motivated deceit sponsored by the Russian government. The best example of such an intended deceit can be found under Peter the Great. In 1713 he renamed, by decree, his Muscovy into "Russia." So Chubaty observed: "After the Tsar's *Ukaz* giving Muscovy a new name, Russian diplomats abroad received instructions to persuade and even bribe foreign officials and journalists to use the new name exclusively." The change of the country's name had, of course, some long-range objectives.

Another intended confusion, introduced in the historical studies by Russian historiography, has been the interpretation of the Bolshevik Revolution and Russian Communism as international events and movements, and not exposing their true nature as political devices of Russian nationalism and imperialism. Kulski in his work, entitled *The Soviet Regime: Communism in Practice,* gave ample evidence of the nationalistic character of Russian Communism. It is my desire and intention to comment on these misconceptions, so much more, because these misconceptions have been skillfully transplanted in the

West and there uncritically repeated and quoted, giving a somehow twisted conception of East Europe and the past and present of its countries and peoples. The West has had little opportunity to hear any other views besides those presented by Russian historians. Bukharin, a leading communist in the early days of the Bolshevik Revolution and take-over, clearly stated in his polemics with Pavlov, the outstanding scientist who violently criticized Communism, that the mission of Russian Communism was to save and preserve Great Russia. All later developments of the Soviet era indicated that Bukharin was correct in his convictions as far as the national mission of Communism was concerned but not all Western historians and political philosophers recognized this fact. And thus these misconceptions and misunderstandings of Russian history, but a few among many others, have evolved.

The study of the Russian past is extremely interesting, and this is another reason for my enthusiastic indulgence in it. It has been almost inconceivable how the Russians, surrounded by many enemies and hindered by numerous obstacles, could have succeeded in creating an empire from such modest political beginnings as the Rostov-Suzdal-Vladimir principality in the wooden and inaccessible and economically deprived European north-east frontier. How could the paradoxical Russian "soul," by paraphrasing Dostoyevskii, on the one hand, extremely revolutionary and anarchistic, almost atheistic, very cunning, cruel, inconsiderate and irrational, and on the other hand, a slave-like subordinate to tyranny, deeply religious and mystical, primitive and straightforward, merciful and rational in action at the same time, assume the burden of empire-building? Having taken this into consideration, I have been fascinated by the political perseverance, diplomatic genius and unbridled belligerence of the Russian nation in its "master plan" of building an empire. To prove the point, the following quotations are in order. Day said that "Genghis Khan prepared the way for Ivan the Terrible, that Czar of a later century who, with ruthless ferocity, quelled all opposition and built up the autocratic state. The Russians showed in their succeeding history more persistence, more continuity of thought and action and less mobility than other Slavic peoples. The discipline they suffered under Asiatic rulers contributed to this result." And Pares admitted that "Russian history is in a broad sense more military than that of other countries." While Kuzhil put it in harsh words: "The trend of foreign policy which always in the course of Russian history had an aggressive character, was drawn. . . by geographical conditions and an insatiable psychology."

Furthermore, the Russians have always known how to use most skillfully some seemingly unrelated movements and ideologies to their political-national advantage, like those of the call for "gathering of all Russian lands," the mission of the Orthodox Church, the Pan-Slavic movement, and the doctrine of Communist internationalism. Not all these significant elements have been adequately evaluated, and after having been cumulated with certain long-accepted fallacies, they have blurred historical perspective. I intend to throw a new and perhaps unorthodox light upon these matters.

I have spent four decades of my life in research and study of the political, social and economic affairs of East Europe, including Russia, in order to make my thoughts well founded and not shallow.

In closing this preface to my work, I would like to quote some lines from the introduction to another book of mine, published a few years ago: "To those who would object to my, at times, unorthodox presentation of Russian history, I . . . suggest that this is the approach and interpretation of the Russian past by the prevailing non-Russian, East European historiographers, who cannot all be discharged as partial and subjective. Hence, in the name of scholarly objectivity *adiatur at altera pars*: listen also to the other side of the story, and not only to the prevailing presentation and interpretation (based largely on Russian sources)." Furthermore, America has always been a free market of ideas, where these ideas could be freely exchanged. I am going to take full advantage of that opportunity to present to the American reader the facts, views, and interpretations of the Russian past I consider to be sincere and true. The job of the reader will be to evaluate them.

Finally, I would like to express my great admiration for Prof. Florinsky's magnificent interpretation of Russian history. Although I have not agreed with him on all points, yet at times I was so deeply impressed by his presentation that I simply reflected his views in my work and in particular in the case of his coverage of the times of Ivan the Dread and the era of the "Time of Troubles". Also Prof. Vernadsky's analysis of the Mongol impact upon Russia and Prof. Lyashchenko's history of Russia's economy helped me greatly in developing a proper and comprehensive presentation of the respective subject matters.

Maplewood, N. J.   Nicholas L. Fr. — Chirovsky
1972

ACKNOWLEDGMENTS

The author wishes to express his deep appreciation to Messrs. Jack Stukas, Ph.D., Vincent Mott, Ph.D., Charles J. Weiss, Paul Geraci, John Deehan, Anthony D'Amato and Stanley Strand from Seton Hall University and Mrs. Jack Stukas who assisted him with valuable advice on the preparation of this publication and who have painstakingly read the entire manuscript and contributed toward its editing. He also thanks Mr. R. Koczerzuk for preparing the maps of Russia in various periods of its political development for this publication.

Many thanks are also expressed to Mrs. Norma Manigan, Katherine Dughi, Helen Dashuta, Katherine Swan, and Miss Barbara Gizzi for their tireless typing and retyping of this manuscript, which seemed endless.

N. L. Fr. — Chirovsky

Maplewood, N. J.
1972

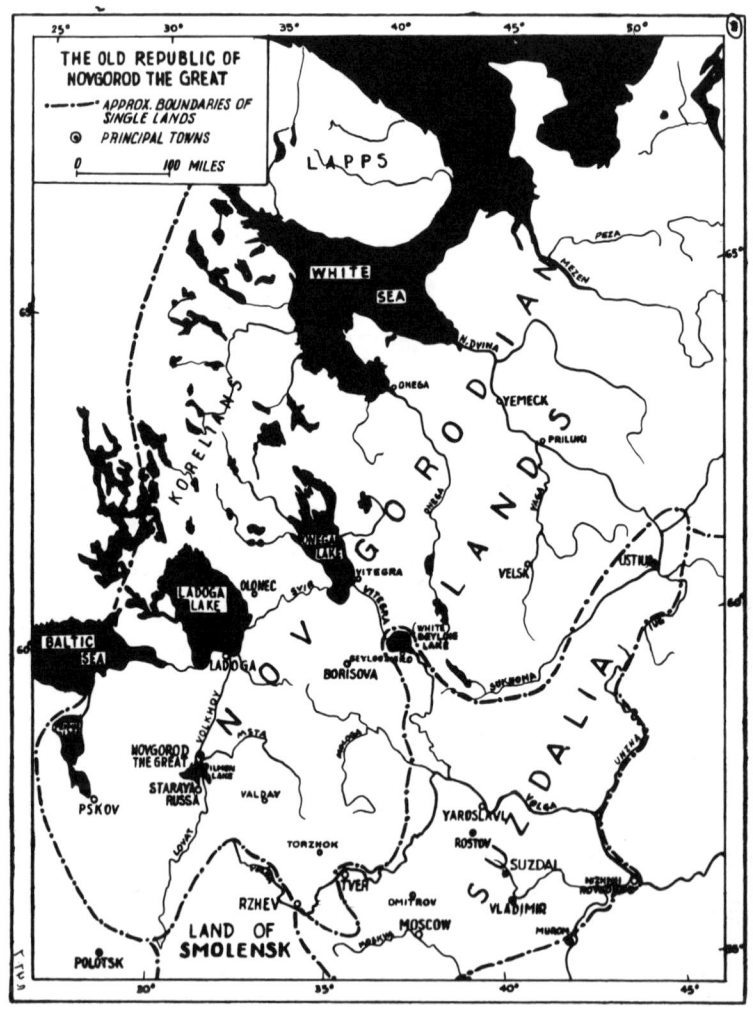

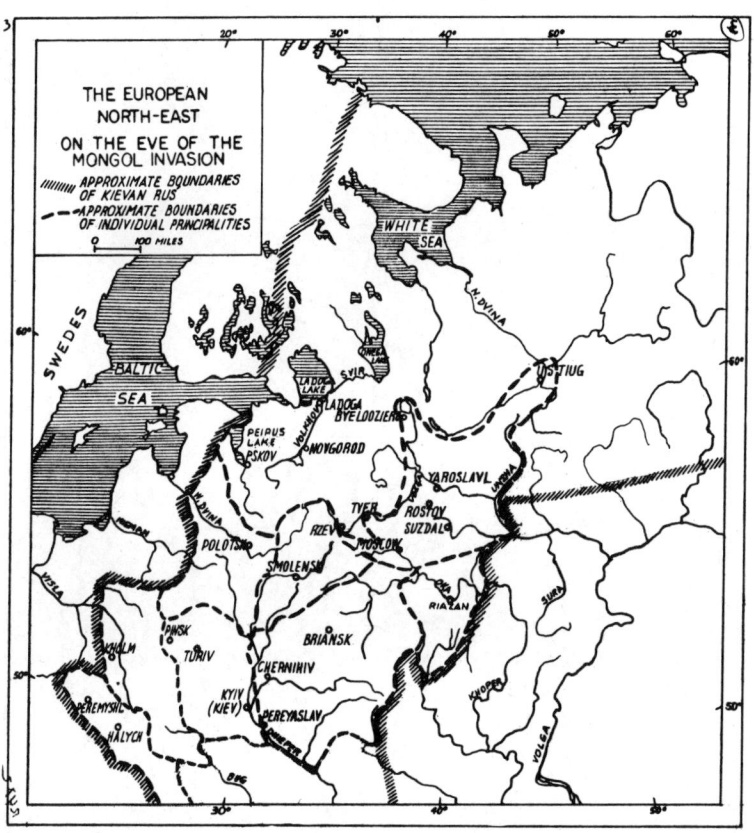

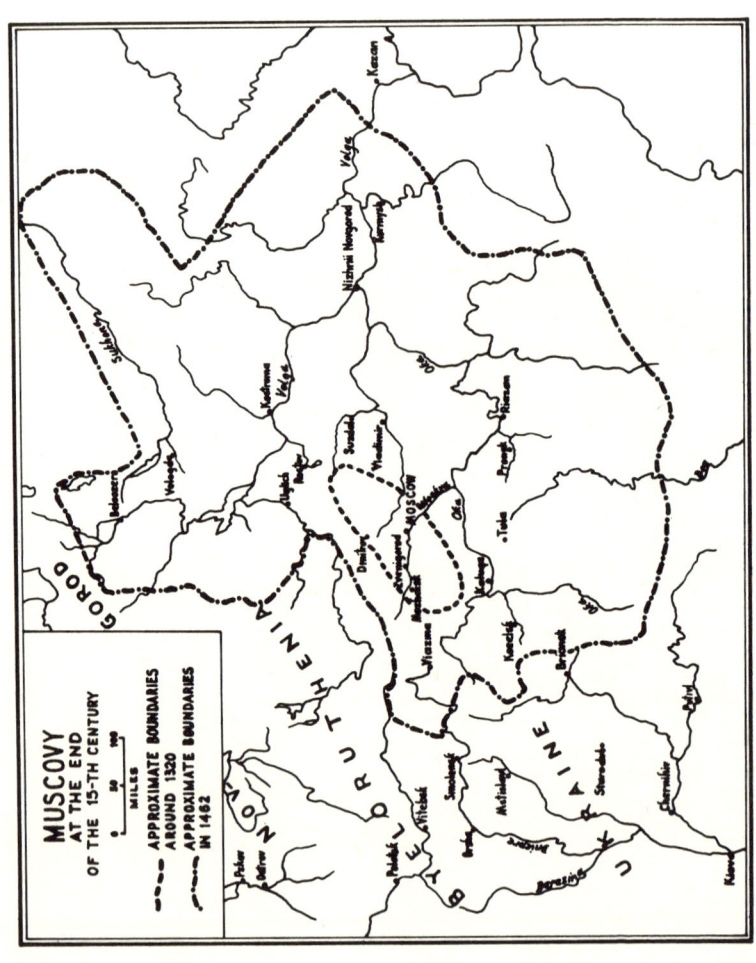

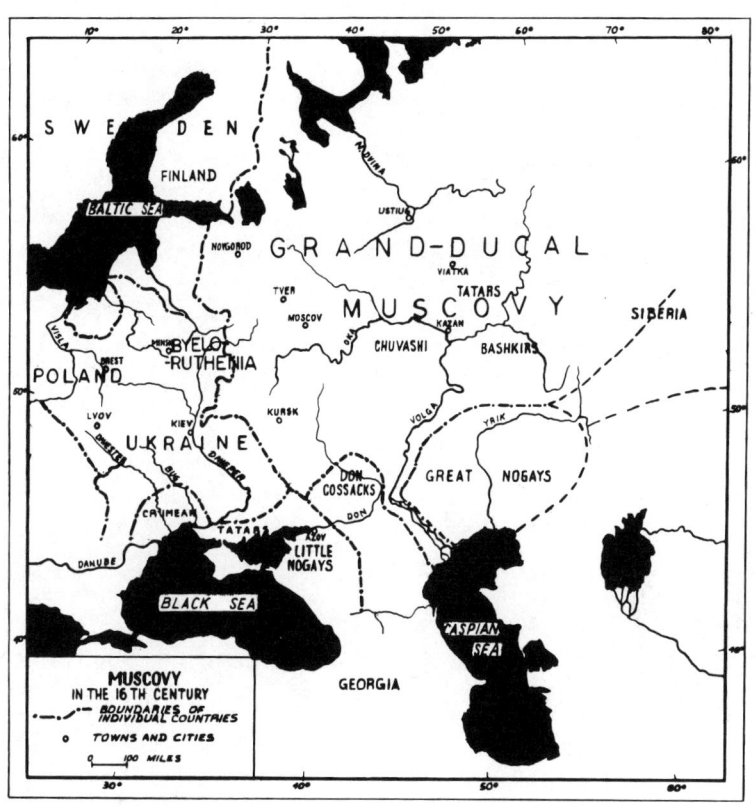

A HISTORY
OF THE
RUSSIAN EMPIRE

CHAPTER ONE

INTRODUCTION

The Land

An historical treatise on the Russian Empire must not terminate with the March Revolution of 1917 which ended the era of Imperial Russia. In fact, the March, so-called "democratic" Revolution professed the ideal of an undivided Russia as in Czarist days. The October Revolution of the Bolsheviks initially departed from that political idea, but only for a brief while. In reality, after a short political and constitutional crisis between 1917 and 1921, the Russian Empire was resurrected under the auspices of the Russian Communist party of Bolsheviks with a new and somewhat deceiving name: the Union of Soviet Socialist Republics, the USSR, or commonly identified as the Soviet Union. This new constitutional form for the new Russian Empire, the federal structure of which was from the very beginning a legal fiction, was officially established in 1922. A new constitution of the USSR was adopted in 1924.

Hence, the discussion of the territorial extent of the Russian Empire should coincide with the enormous territory of the Union of Soviet Socialist Republics. This area theoretically consists of fifteen Union republics, a number of autonomous republics and autonomous areas, which are, in fact, a variety of structural forms of territorial administrative units of a centrally ruled state.

The historical growth of Russia began in the ninth century in the European North-East from two centers, Novgorod the Great and Rostov. The republic of Novgorod was a kind of political prologue to mark a historical tie of Russia with Europe, while the tiny principality of Rostov, evolving later into the Rostov,

Suzdal and Vladimir princely political entity, was the real embryo of the future empire. Both centers were soon overrun and came under the foreign rule of a southern neighbor — Kievan Rus', a powerful state organization of the south-eastern Slavic tribes, which subsequently formed the Ukrainian nation. The south-eastern Slavs were helped by the Norsemen in building the Kievan Rus' political center. Hence, it could be accepted that the future Russian nation in the cradle of its history was exposed to the rule of two invaders, the Kievan Rus' and the Norsemen.

With the progressive decline of Rus', the principality of Rostov, Suzdal and Vladimir succeeded in emancipating itself politically and in becoming sovereign and dominant among the north-eastern Slavic political organizations which amalgamated later in a Russian nation. During the Mongol Invasions in the thirteenth and fifteenth centuries, the Rostov-Suzdal-Vladimir principality declined politically and Moscow took over as spokesman for the "Russian" cause.

The Muscovite principality began immediately to exhibit a most aggressive attitude toward neighboring lands, carrying the torch of a political mission of uniting all north-eastern Slavic and Finno-Ungric tribal and territorial communities into one powerful state. The principality of Moscow soon became the Grand Duchy of Muscovy, growing and expanding territorially very rapidly in all four directions of the world, northward, southward, westward, and eastward. Moreover, this territorial expansion of Muscovy, initiated in the fourteenth century, has uninterruptedly continued for over 600 years under imperial Russia and the Union of Soviet Socialist Republics of modern times.

Today the land called the Union of Soviet Socialist Republics extends territorially over 8,436,000 square miles, approximately 1/7 of the entire land area of the earth. It stretches for about 7000 miles from the West to the East, and for over 2,700 miles from the North to the South.[1] Geographically, the USSR is identified as being located approximately between 25 and 170 degrees of the eastern longitude, and 35 and 75 degrees of the northern latitude. It includes a variety of climatic zones, from the polar to the semi-tropical ones, being on the other hand a vast plain stretching almost from the heart of Europe, through Siberia, to the Far East, and protected in most part by the natural boundaries of oceans, seas, rivers and mountain ranges. The Ural mountains cut the country's vast plain. The mountainous regions are not over 3,000 feet high and do not represent any serious obstacle to the country's political unity, administration and economy. Many large rivers, such as the Don, Volga, Kama, Ob, Yenissey or Lena and Amur, can be used only to a limited extent for transportation and power production because of weather conditions, being in most part frozen in the winter months. Canal construction helped rather little to improve Soviet waterways.

Agriculturally, the country consists of six major zones. Tundra and taiga in the North are not adaptable for farming. The desiduous forest zone, mostly in European Russia proper and in parts of Siberia, is a source of forest wealth, but is characterized by inefficient agriculture due to the mediocre or poor fertility of soil. The wide steppe zone of the USSR is the source of its agricultural wealth. Its black soil is extremely fertile and constitutes the Soviet grain belt, extending from Ukraine, and over the Don-Volga region, deep into southern Siberia. In Central Asia and Kazakhstan desert and semi-desert lands prevail and only through irrigation some farming may partially succeed. The semitropical zone in Transcaucasia and beyond the Caspian Sea produces tropical fruit. Livestock is raised in many regions of the USSR.

Industrially, the country is extremely rich in power and mineral resources such as coal, petroleum, iron ore, manganese ore, copper, lead, bauxite, nickel, tin, chromium, gold and silver. These resources help to explain how the Soviet Union became an industrial giant in the course of some 35 years.

The population of the USSR is highly diversified. Out of some 240 million people 60 percent is Russian, while the other 40 percent is comprised of over 150 different nationalities and ethnic groups, speaking a variety of languages and dialects. The Ukrainians, Byeloruthenians, Baltic peoples, Jews and Tartars, are the largest national communities, extremely hostile toward the Russians and their dominant position in the Soviet Union. Hence, the USSR is not ethnically monolithic but highly diversified, which constitutes its internal weakness. Having realized this fact, the Soviets initiated and are systematically carrying on a large-scale forced internal recolonization and resettlement program, accompanied by an intense Russianization policy aimed at splitting up the territorially compact non-Russian national communities and producing the new breed of the Soviet-Russian man, to make the USSR internally more homogeneous and thus politically stronger.

The population distribution in the Soviet Union is very uneven. Only until recently some 45 percent of its people lived on about 7 percent of its territory, while on the other hand, some 10 percent of the people inhabited approximately 2/3 of its territorial space. The highest density of population is in Europe and the lowest is in the northern regions of the country in Asia. This uneven density of population has been mostly conditioned by climatic considerations. Taiga, tundra desert regions, though relatively rich in mineral resources, have a very harsh climate, too demanding to attract any voluntary, large-scale colonization. Hence, for political reasons and economic considerations, the Soviets have sponsored an internal resettlement program to populate the distant areas of the USSR. Of course, the uneven distribution of the population has been an obstacle in the social, economic, and political development and progress of the nation.

Some 55 percent of the Soviet population lives in the cities, towns and townships, and the other 45 in the villages and countryside. The pecentage of the urban population has been growing rapidly during the last four decades because of the intense industrialization plans of the Soviet Union under the Communist leadership.[2]

The largest of the Union Republics, the Russian Federal Soviet Socialist Republic which has exercised the leading and dominant role in the USSR, covers approximately 6.5 million square miles out of approximately 8.5 square miles of the entire Soviet Union, roughly a little more than 3/4 of the entire Soviet square mileage. However, this would not properly illustrate the relationships since the Russian FSSR includes Siberia, Far East and other, essentially non-Russian lands. Russia proper constitutes, perhaps, only some 1/8 of the total territory of the USSR, the rest being conquered lands, induced by force to join the Russian Empire in the past or the Union of Soviet Socialist Republics of the present. The position of those non-Russian lands within the USSR is essentially that of internal colonies and colonial borderlands of Russia.

The People

The Russians, the true builders and rulers of the Empire, of which the other, non-Russian peoples, nationalities and ethnic groups have been only an object and never a subject, have been commonly regarded as a Slavic nationality along with other Slavic peoples such as the Ukrainians, Byeloruthenians, Poles, Czechs, Slovaks, Serbs, Croats, Slovenians and Bulgarians. However, the ethnic origin of the Russians was more of a dual nature than that of any other Slavic national group, except, perhaps, of the Bulgarians, because of a very considerable Finno-Ungric, and Mongol ethnic impact on the formation of the Russian people since time immemorial.

The Finno-Ungric tribes inhabited the territory of Russia proper in the north-eastern corner of the European continent long before any Slavs ever arrived there. From the banks of the Baltic Sea, off the Gulf of Finland in particular, eastwards across the wide areas of the upper and middle Volga and Oka Rivers, toward the Ural Mountains and far beyond, extended the original settlements of various Finno-Ungric tribes of the Chud, Suomi, Ves, Yem, Meria, Muroma, Mordva, Komi, Cheremisia, Vogul, Ostiak, and many others, considerably differentiated in various lingual groups and branches. In later centuries the Suomi became the present-day Finns; the Chud — the present-day Estonians, while other Finno-Ungric tribes west of the Ural mountains became extinct or merged with the incoming Slavic invader, later on amalgamating and crystalizing into the future ethnic complex of the Russian people.

At the time of the arrival of the Slavs, most of the north-eastern Finno-Ungric tribes had reached the so-called "Iron Age" in development. This has been proven by excavations of ancient graves in numerous localities throughout Russia proper. In the graves iron, bronze, and stone objects such as sickles, knives, spindles, fishhooks, arrowheads and other implements were found in reasonably large quantities. Those findings proved a continuity of cultural development of the early North-East even from the Finno-Ungric era.

This was approximately the state of affairs in the European North-East (Russia proper) on the eve of the Slavic invasion. The Finno-Ungric tribes lived a primitive but relatively peaceful life, hunting, fishing, farming and trading.

After the collapse of the Empire of the Huns in the sixth century A. D., the Slavs began to leave their original settlements north of the Carpathian mountains, the Oder River in the west, and the Dnieper River in the east. They began their colonization of neighboring and distant lands. They spread their settlements westward beyond the Oder, across the wide eastern parts of Ukraine and Byeloruthenia; also south, beyond the Carpathian mountains, and over the major part of the Balkan Peninsula, while other Slavic tribes moved deep into the northeastern Finno-Ungric territory to establish new homes. In the sixth century Greek historical sources identified some Slavic tribes in East Europe. In the seventh century the Slavic ancestors of the modern Russians, the tribes of the Slovenians, Radimichians, Viatichians and, in part, the eastern branch of the Krivichians, were already settled east of the Gulf of Finland and the Dvina River. These tribes penetrated Finno-Ungric ethnic territory in the north and east.

The assimilation and amalgamation process of the two different ethnic groups continued for many years. At first it was a hostile process, accompanied by social upheavals, tribal wars and bloodshed. Later on, the assimilation became more peaceful as time progressed. Both ethnic elements got accustomed to each other; intermarriages and close social contacts facilitated the development of a new ethnic "alloy" to become the foundation of the future Russian nationality. At first, Russian historians preferred to ignore or to minimize the Finno-Ungric impact on the formation of the Russian people i.e., Kluchevsky. But more recently, a whole score of Russian historians, such as Platonov and Pokrovskii, not only admitted but even stressed the importance of that impact. They admitted the violence of the Slavic colonization. Pokrovskii wrote that the Russian state had been built on the bones of foreigners and that in the veins of the contemporary Great Russian flows at least 80 percent of Finno-Ungric blood.

The Slavic Slovenians, Viatichians and Radimichians had a higher cultural level and better arms because their original settlements were closer to the cultural centers of those days than those of the Finno-Ungric tribes. The Slavs proved to be a stronger ethnic element, absorbed the weaker Finno-Ungric populations, and together evolved into the prevailingly Slavic Russian nationality.[3]

The relative poverty in the harsh physical and topographical environment of the European North-East considerably affected the formation of the national psychology of the future Muscovites — Russians. From an economic point of view, it was really a very hard struggle for survival, since those regions were poorly endowed by nature, with marshes and massive, wild and inaccessible forests predominating. It was difficult to support a civilization barely adequate for agricultural cultivation, and too distant for efficient trading. Scarcely a subsistence minimum could have been provided by those regions to the relatively scanty population which settled there. Being great distances from the cultural centers of Europe and intermingling with the primitive Finno-Ungric tribes, were factors making the way of life and the methods of production of the North-Eastern Slavic, pre-Russian tribes so much more backward. This economic primitivism only aggravated the problem of survival. Furthermore, the natural poverty of the country in addition to the primitivism of the population were apt to retard any progress. Hence, the northern civilization centers, probably of the Finns from the Bronze and Early Iron ages, the so-called *Fatianovo* and *Ananyino* cultures developed later and to a lesser degree than the cultures of other places and peoples.

However, historians such as Kluchevsky, Struve, Chubaty,

Doroshenko and Vernadsky, have essentially agreed that "The hard struggle for survival hardened these people and prepared them for difficult living in the cold climate, hewing out of them a nation of realists, which became accustomed to living in the collectives of the hunting and fishing hordes. Physical strength was essential for survival. This was the type and kind of men diametrically different from the soft and poetic individualists, the Antic Slavs of the Kievan Rus'-Ukraine."[4] In these characteristics of the Russians the Russian historian, Struve, found the answers for the later Muscovite domination of Ukraine, whose people also developed under the influences of the Hellenic-Iranian civilization. Struve said: "The forest regions of Russia became the growth cone of that living, social, and also political force, which formed and strengthened the state. Eventually, the forests (the people of the poor wooden regions) conquered the fertile [Ukrainian] steppes."[5]

Submissive respect for authority, discipline, collectivistic inclinations in the socio-economic respect, a genius for diplomacy, an economy which necessitated conquest, annexation, exploitation of the conquered, and contiguous colonization, have been developed as conspicuous Russian traits. In the 13th century the European East was overrun by the Mongols (Tartars) and their rule was particularly lasting on the territory of Russia proper. There the North-Eastern Slavs and their rulers, having in their veins the blood and in their psychology traits related to the Mongols because of their Finno-Ungric heritage, developed very close family, social, economic and political connections with the Mongols (Tartars). Kluchevsky stated that at the end of the seventeenth century, approximately 18 percent of the Muscovite aristocracy was still of Mongol or otherwise eastern origin. Throughout the provinces of Russia proper there was an intensive assimilation of the Mongol ethnic elements into the social strata from the 14th to the 17th centuries, increasing the Mongol percentage of the ethnic "alloy" of the Russians.

Particularly useful to the Russians were their experiences under Mongol domination. Not only the Mongol influences strengthened some original traits of the Russian psychology, but because of their Finno-Ungric heritage, they were quick to learn from the Tartars and their Golden Horde. Numerous historians, such as Trubetskoi, Pokrovskii, Vernadsky, Doroshenko and others, have indicated the Mongol impact on the formation of Russian spiritual, cultural, social, political, administrative, legal, and economic institutions. As Day said, "the spirit of Genghis-Khan was definitely at work in building the huge Russian Empire."[6]

This was the ethnic process in the European North-East, culminating in the formation of a Russian nationality, distinct from others in Eastern Europe. However, in the middle of the 19th century, purely out of imperial political expediency to justify Russian rule over the Ukraine, and to satisfy Russian nationalistic feelings, a Russian historian, Pogodin, developed a theory, according to which a Russian nationality did not form in the North-East, but was formed and settled in Ukraine. At first, during the Mongol invasion, they supposedly left the Kiev and the Middle Dnieper regions and migrated north to colonize the North-East; these regions which today are identified as Russia proper. Subsequently, in the fifteenth century, Pogodin continued, the Ukrainian Dnieper regions were settled by colonists from the West, Galicia and Volhynia, who became the ancestors of modern Ukrainians. Pogodin's theory was also useful to establish the claim, that the old Kievan Rus' state was the creation of Russian genius and not of the Slavic ancestors of the Ukrainian nationality. A few years later, Sobolevskii attempted to support Pogodin's hypothesis by linguistic arguments.[7]

A score of Russian and Ukrainian historians opposed the Pogodin-Sobolevskii theory, including Antonovych, Golubiev, Vladimirskii-Budanov, Shakhmatov, and Hrushevsky, and debunked it by using linguistic, archeological and historical arguments. There have been no reliable historical evidences uncovered as yet, that there was any mass emigration from Ukraine at the time of the Mongol Invasion or thereafter to back Pogodin's assumption.

Soviet historians and linguists, in order to support the Russian claim on the creation of the Kievan-Rus' state, developed another, and, a far more fundamental theory about a pre-Rus' people, which inhabited most of Eastern Europe and were the predecessors of the modern Russians. Accordingly, in the 15th and 16th centuries, under Catholic and Polish influences, the Ukrainians and the Byeloruthenians split from the pre-Russian ethnic camp. This Soviet hypothesis was by far more comprehensive than that of Pogodin-Sobolevskii, because it applied one national identity for the Russians, the Ukrainians and the Byeloruthenians. Hence, the Soviet theory was of greater use for Russian imperial plans to affirm the logic of a Soviet federation of people's republics. Soviet scholars, however, soon recognized the artificiality and unscientific nature of the theory, and silently abandoned it.

In fact, the differentiation of the Eastern Slavic tribes into three national groups, which later formed three distinct Slavic nations: the Russians, Ukrainians and Byeloruthenians, began as early as the third century A. D. This differentiation process began within the original settlements of the Slavs, and took definite shape in the seventh century. Recent archeological and historical studies, conducted by two outstanding Russian scholars, Tretiakov, an historian, and Rybakov, an archeologist, bear this out.[8] Later developments were the continuous assimilation of the Finno-Ungric tribes by the North-Eastern Slavs, the influx of the Mongol ethnic element into the Muscovite society, and Catholic and Polish influences on the Ukrainians and Byeloruthenians which only deepened and intensified the ancient differentiation process. This is the origin of the Russian people who established a vast and lasting empire.[9]

A great Russian historian-philosopher, G. Fedotov, asserted that already at the end of the twelfth century there was a deep cleavage between the Kievan and the Suzdalian, or later Muscovite, cultural atmospheres, as far as the understanding of individual freedom, personal dignity and honor were concerned. Furthermore, he asserted: "In Kiev one cannot speak of Russian messianism in the sense of uniqueness or exclusivity of national religious calling." Hence, it logically follows that there was no direct spiritual relationship between Kiev and Moscow at any time. Then, Shulgine adds, that "... Kiev ... was a part of Europe; Moscow long remained the negation of Europe." It seems, therefore, that the attempt of identifying the Russians, Ukrainians and Byeloruthenians as of one national stock remains highly fallacious, serving rather Russian political ends than being really an objective and scholarly conclusion.[10]

The Periods Of The Historical Development

The historical development of any nation may be analyzed from various points of view. Its periodicity may be differently established depending upon the criteria applied: religious, cultural, social, economic or political. For example, the periodicity of Russian history from the economic point of view may be differentiated into four basic eras: primitive slave society, feudal society, capitalist society and communist society. This would be largely a Marxian approach to history.

The political history of a country can also be divided into different periods according to different criteria: various forms of government which constitutionally followed each other, ruling dynasties, or status in international relations. It seems logical that the history of the Russian Empire should be subject to periodicity which would reflect the successive stages in that empire's construction, indicating its growth and rise to international prestige.

From that point of view five periods of Russian history may be identified: the pre-Muscovite era, the Muscovite era, the era of early Russian Empire, the era of nineteenth century Russia, and the Soviet era.

The first *pre-Muscovite era* constitutes the political beginnings of the Russian Empire when the name "Russian" did not yet exist. It includes the historical prologue of the times of the ancient Slavs, of the rule of the Kievan-Rus' state over the European North-East, the history of the Mongols and their impact upon a future Russia, and finally, the formation of early political entities and states in the North-East of Europe, in particular the development of Novgorod the Great and the Rostov-Suzdal-Vladimir principality. The era began in the dark and rather inadequately known pre-history of the European North-East and terminated with the decline of Vladimir and rise of Moscow at the beginning of the fourteenth century. In this work, the pre-Muscovite era has been covered in Part I, Chapters Two to Seven inclusive.

The second, or *Muscovite era,* representing the initiation of the future Russian empire, lasted from the beginning of the fourteenth century, through the fifteenth and sixteenth centuries, until 1613, the year of electing Mikhail Romanov the new Czar. The Muscovite dukes and Grand Dukes began with utmost zeal and at times used most perverse means to extend their rule, having assumed a mission to unite under their scepter all provinces of future Russia-proper and beyond. Ivan the Terrible or Dread was the most outstanding from among those Muscovite rulers. The growth of the Czardom was not smooth and steady after Ivan. A downhill development followed under the name of the "Time of Troubles," which shook the emerging empire down to its foundations and its very future was made questionable. Yet, then the new dynasty of the Romanovs was called by the destiny to save the emerging empire and to assure its growth to new heights. Part II, Chapters Eight to Thirteen inclusive, discusses the developments of the Muscovite era, concluding the first volume of A *History of the Russian Empire.*

The third era of the Russian history was initiated by the election of Mikhail Romanov. The new Czar gave rise to a new ruling dynasty, which guided the fortunes of Russia, theoretically speaking, for over three hundred years. This epoch terminated with the death of Peter I, the Great, in 1725. This was mostly the seventeenth century Muscovy becoming a modern Russia. Peter established Russia as an imperial power and made himself an emperor. It was still a *Muscovite* era, though *late,* for a number of years, until Peter established his new capital of St. Petersburg and there transferred the seat of the Russian emperors and empresses. The time period which began with Peter's immediate successors to the imperial throne of Russia, and which can be rightly termed as the *St. Petersburg sub-era,* though for a short while the emperor returned to Moscow, lasted the course of the seventeenth century, until the death of Paul in 1801. That significant time of the Russian history, namely the seventeenth and eighteenth centuries, would comprise the second volume of *A History of the Russian Empire*, to be entitled *Imperial Russia*, in two parts: Part I, from Mikhail Romanov to Peter's death and Part II, from Peter's death to the assassination of Paul I. It was the time of the Romanovs on the Russian throne.

The next, or fourth, era would comprise the nineteenth century in Russian history. Theoretically, it was still the age of the Romanovs, but in reality the Russian emperors of the nineteenth century were very loosely related to the original house of the Romanovs, and it would be much more realistic to call them the *Pavlovichs*, the descendants of Czar Pavel or Paul I. The time lasting through the reigns of Czars Alexander I and Nicholas I, can be termed as the sub-era of the Russia's being on the *Top of the World*, Russia was truly a first class world power with tremendous impact upon the world's political scene. The sub-era comprising the reigns of Alexander II, Alexander III and Nicholas II, ran over into the twentieth century. It was the period of *Downhill* developments, which prognosticated some troubles for the empire. It was terminated by one of the bloodiest revolutions in the world's history, the so-called Bolshevik Revolution, headed by Vladimir Ulianov, party-name – Lenin. The whole nineteenth century, including 17 years of the twentieth century until the Revolution, will comprise the third volume of the above work, still having the subtitle *Imperial Russia*, and consisting of two parts: Part I, *On Top of the World*, and Part II, *Downhill*, corresponding with the respective historical eras of Russia.

The fifth and last era of the Russian past, contemporary Russia, will cover Soviet times. Its first sub-era lasted from the Bolshevik Revolution to Stalin's death, having represented a *Communist struggle for survival* through the early days of the collective experimentation, the Second World War and the post-war period of reconstruction. Soviet Russia was emerging as the second greatest power in the world. The next sub-era, the *post-Stalinist* one, of Russian history would carry the accounts of the latest developments under Khrushchev and then, under Brezhnev and Kosygin, as the present Communist leaders of the U.S.S.R. As the second largest power in the world, the U.S.S.R. had its problems after all. The fifth or last era of the Soviet rule will comprise the fourth volume of *A History of the Russian Empire*, with the subtitle *Soviet Russia*: Part I, the *Struggle for Survival* and Part II, the *Challenge to the World*, corresponding to the respective sub-eras of the Soviet period of contemporary Russia.

Of course, in most cases there have been no clear-cut demarcation lines between the individual historical eras or periods of the Russian past. Sometimes the transitions from one period to another were slow and lasting; other times the separation between two eras was sharp and clear-cut. For instance, the decline of the political role of Vladimir and the rise of Moscow to mark the closing of the first and the beginning of the second period of the Russian history lasted a couple of decades, while the Bolshevik Revolution rapidly changed the course of history by abruptly ending the era of imperial Russia and initiating the Soviet era. But in most cases the transition was rather slow and gradual.

Nor were any of these historical eras that homogeneous that they could not have been broken down into a number of sub-periods of a shorter duration and specific characteristics. Nevertheless, they all together, each of different duration, different pace of development and specific characteristics, as component parts of a whole, constitute the mosaics of the Russian historical past. The last Soviet era, for example, could be easily divided into five sub-periods, such as the Revolution and War Communism, the era of the New Economic Policy, the Stalinist planning era, the period of coexistence and era of competition with the United States. Generally speaking, each individual chapter of this work actually represents and discusses in most cases a certain sub-period of the Muscovite-Russian history.

The periods of Russian history are not homogeneous politically socially, or economically. None of these aspects was sharply separated from the preceding and succeeding eras in most of the cases, yet each represents a specific stage in the political, social and economic development or evolution of the Russian nation. The identification of these stages can be very helpful in learning and understanding the Russian past. The writing of history of any meaning cannot be done otherwise.

PART I

THE PRE-MUSCOVITE ERA

CHAPTER TWO

THE HISTORICAL PROLOGUE

The Prehistorical Legacy

The cultural, social, economic and political development of any society is "organic" to the extent that any new link in that development arises on the basis of past mistakes or achievements. Nothing comes from nothing. Past developments built the foundations of the present, and the present predetermines the future in a continuous evolution. However, evolutionary development does not only mean a permanent growth; evolutionary ups and downs are historically interdependent, ever causes and consequences of each other. Hence, in retrospect the remote prehistory of the European North-East predetermined the developments in medieval Muscovy, and the growth of the Muscovite state laid the foundations for the spectacular political expansion of modern Russia. The political and social legacy of modern imperial Russia to some extent predetermined developments in the present-day Soviet Union.

This should explain and justify the need of going deep into the past thousands of years, when studying the history of a country. Russian history is no exception. In fact, a prehistorian should go back some 40 thousand years, looking for traces of human existence in the territory of Russia proper.

The prehistoric legacy of the Russian people can be learned from archeological excavations and the comparative archeology of peoples living on similar cultural levels in different times. At times, especially in the very remote and distant past, archeology and archeological interpretations are the only sources of historical information, while written sources can often be used to supplement the findings of the later periods of prehistory. In many cases, ancient documents were too poetic, too biased, and clouded by guesswork and myths. Only parts of them are reliable historical material, supported by archeological findings.

For instance, the ancient Greek and other chroniclers who hated Slavs called them "man-beasts, living like animals, eating all sorts of dirt." This did not properly reflect either the Slavic cultural level or way of life. As Lyashchenko said: "It would be, of course, entirely erroneous to see in this depiction of the Slavs ... the reality of that low stage of social development...."[1] Archeology is a much more objective witness to the prehistoric past than written source materials. History has become more and more useful as time progressed. Its reliability increased, with greater competence in writing, the increasing objectivity of the writers, and the accumulation of a literature enabling comparison and evaluation by discriminating historians.

Nevertheless, to learn about the dawn of our earth and the beginnings of mankind on it, even archeology is inadequate, and the historian must turn for help to geology. The findings of geology in this respect have been much more trustworthy and reliable than those of archeology, since the former have been established on a much more scientific basis and on an international scale. Furthermore, geological explorations and research were started much earlier than archeological studies of man's ancient past, hence their findings were already available to aid emerging archeology in its interpretations.[2]

Archeology revealed the existence of prehistoric man, his characteristics and ways of life, through the excavation of his tools, appliances, weapons, religious articles and ornaments. However, geology provided a framework for the prehistory of the earth by dividing it into a number of evolutionary stages according to its geological development. Each age of that development lasted tens of thousands of years. Then, within that geological evolutionary framework, archeology succeeded in placing the first man on earth, and, following its own requirements and criteria, suggested its own theoretical system of bronze, or iron appliances in his struggle for survival and his attainment of higher stages of civilization. Hence, according to studying man's changing mode of life and his use of stone, bone, archeological and historical findings, man's prehistoric past is divided into the Old Stone or Paleolithic age, the New Stone or Neolithic, the Copper and Bronze and Iron or Paleometalic and Neometalic ages. Each stage constitutes a number of eras in man's cultural evolution. Each era had its impact on the prehistory of Russia.[3]

Traces of man's existence on the globe go back as far as the so-called Lower Old Stone or Lower Paleolithic age some 30-40 thousand years before our era. The Old Stone or Paleolithic age of man's history can be divided into three eras: The Lower, the Middle, and the Upper Old Stone or Paleolithic eras. During the early Lower Paleolithic age, Europe experienced its interglacial period, with its mild and humid climate, a Mediterranean-like vegetation and large animals, like the elephant, the hippopotamus, and the mammoth. At that time the earliest traces of man in Europe, the so-called Heidelberg man, were scientifically established. But there are no evidences of man inhabiting the European North-East or Russia proper, according to modern terminology, during that era. The Heidelberg man lived at the lower stage of savagery in primitive herds. Tribes were yet unknown. Since the climate was mild, it seemed that the Heidelberg man did not know how to build dwellings or even how to use caves for protection against changing weather conditions. He used extremely crude stone tools, as, for example, a crude hand-cleaver for hunting, which, perhaps, took a lifetime to make.

Then, advances of glaciers changed the European climate severely, substantially changing the way of life of prehistoric man. Cold weather forced him to invent or perish. It forced him to advance "culturally." This new era in man's material evolution is called the Middle Stone Age. The more advanced prehistoric man of this age is called the Neanderthal type. He learned to seek cover in caves and dugouts and to dress in animal skins to protect himself against the cold and other dangers and inconveniences. Of course, hunting, trapping and fishing were still his main occupations and sources of livelihood, but his stone and bone appliances were improved, sharpened at the top, as, for example, spearheads and hand-cleavers. Economically, he advanced to some division of labor. He hunted for mammoth, bear and deer.

The Neanderthal man lived in large families of the pre-tribal stage, developed some religious beliefs and burial rituals, indicating perhaps an awareness of the immortality of the soul. This stage of man's evolution has been also termed as the second era of savagery.

Since no traces of the Neanderthal man were as yet found on the territory of Russia proper, this might indicate that man had not arrived there by the Middle-Paleolith age, perhaps discouraged by harsh climate prevailing there at the time. There is strong archeological and historical evidence available, however, of human settlements in Ukraine, along the rivers Dnieper and Donets and in the Crimea during that period. This might have explained (at least, to some extent, and along with other contributory factors, like the impact of Greek culture upon Ukraine), why the cultural development of Ukraine was earlier and faster than that of Russia during the ancient era. Man arrived earlier in Ukraine and began earlier to cultivate the area.[4]

The retreat of the glaciers brought to Eastern Europe a moderation of climate, initiating a new era. This was called the Upper Old Stone age: The era of *Homo Sapiens*, a rational, though savage, human being. Although *Homo Sapiens* continued to use stone, bone and horn weapons and appliances, his workmanship was far better and the articles much improved. He began to build permanent dwellings, huts, which sometimes were even equipped with heated chambers for cold seasons. His technique of division of labor and specialization was, for the times, quite advanced.

Socially, this man of the Upper Paleolith lived in tribes, while matriarchy prevailed in the family, which was rather sedentary and less nomadic in any case. Religious life was more elaborate and deeper. This was apparently the era when man, taking advantage of improvement of climate in Europe in general and its North-East corner in particular, arrived and settled on the territory of future Russia proper. The traces of his existence in these ancient times have been found on the banks of the Oka River, in the very center of later Muscovy.

Then, sometime between 10,000 to 3,000 B. C., the transition to a higher cultural stage was accomplished by man; differently in different parts of Eurasia. Man overcame at that time his savagery and reached the age of barbarism; he developed his civilization considerably when compared with previous eras. Hence, the new era was termed by archeology as a new Stone or Neolithic age.

During this period the climate further improved. This apparently facilitated population growth, while that growing density of population in relation to primitive methods of production of means of survival, induced more advanced economic life. The Neolithic man began to domesticate animals, like dogs, cats and horses; raise cattle, sheep and hogs; initiate farming by raising wheat, oats and flax. He already drilled wells for water supply; improved production of appliances and weapons by polishing stone and boring holes, which took him many years of work. Horn and bone were still used to make useful things, but at the same time man began also to manufacture pottery and dishes from clay and beautify them with simple designs. Production was done collectively in primitive "shops." Simple trading and merchandise exchange by barter began to develop along the water routes.

Blood relation and tribal system became the foundation of the socio-economic organization in the Neolithic age; villages replaced the isolated settlements. Social differentiation into wealthy "nobility," free and unfree (slave) members of the tribal society had already come into being. Religious life further developed and burial rituals became complex.

The Neolithic man occasionally lived in various parts of the European North-East, in the Volga-Oka River basin, in the region of the Lake Ladoga and other areas, even in the direction of the Ural Mountains. The warming of the climate there was the chief, although not the only explanation of the extensive distribution of human settlements in those regions during the Neolithic age. It seems, however, rational to assume that the increase of population at that time made the struggle for survival the cause of some tribal strife and warfare, and that, as a result, some clans and tribes were driven North in search of more peaceful surroundings.[5]

However, man permanently settled in the European North-East sometime during the Upper Paleolithic age, and there the historian was to look for the very beginning of human history on the territory which today is called Russia proper. According to the archeological findings, various types of long-headed men inhabited the North-Eastern plain of Europe already during the late Paleolithic age. Then a broad-headed race, perhaps of Mongol extraction, emigrated there from Eurasia and pressed westward, toward the Baltic Sea. These were perhaps the predecessors or ancestors of the historical Finno-Ungric tribes, who occupied the European North-East before the dawn of Russian nationality.

Nevertheless, the cultural development in the North-East was much slower than in other parts of Europe for various reasons: climate there was more severe; man came there substantially later; water routes, essential for transportation, were frozen for long months, stopping all traffic. As a result, first on the demarcation between the New Stone and the Old Metal (Copper and Bronze) ages a certain cultural identity in the North-East began to evolve, and later became the *Fatianovo culture* from the village Fatianovo, in the Yaroslav region. It extended over the entire basin of the Oka and Volga Rivers, reaching, at its peak, as far as Smolensk, Tver, Kostroma and Kozlov (Michurinsk). Carefully polished stone axes, ornamented vases and some copper and bronze objects testify to the level of *Fatianovo culture* which continued into the Old Metal era. Hunting, fishing and some farming, but on a very limited scale, constituted the material basis of the Fatianovo civilization.

The Pre-Slavic Era

The Stone Age was over and the Metal Age had begun. Already at the end of the Neolithic era man learned how to extract metal from ore and how to make and use some metallic appliances and weapons, although stone and bone utensils still remained popular.

The Old Metallic or Paleometallic era of Copper and Bronze, about 3,000 to 1,000 B.C., was subsequently replaced by the New Metallic or Neometallic era of Iron, somewhat between 1,200 B.C., on Russian territory. These transitions were completed earlier in the South, in Ukraine and Caucasia.

The North-Eastern plain of Europe was occupied in the meantime and inhabited by the Ugro-Finns, who in due time and process formed numerous tribes of Mongol extraction: the Ves, Meria, Chud, Mordva, Muroma, and further east, the Cheremisians, Permians and other somewhat related tribes like the Voguls and Ostiaks, who migrated and extended their settlements far beyond the Ural mountains. Later, the Bulgars of Turkish extraction arrived and settled in the middle Volga Basin to effect the history of the North-Eastern plain.

The Metallic age was marked by the use of copper, bronze, and finally iron to manufacture various utensils, appliances and weapons, and represented great progress toward the highest stage of "barbarism," leading directly to the epoch of "civilization," as Engels pointed out. Although the copper and bronze era was of minor historical importance for the Russian past, most historians agree that it was marked by two distinct cultural developments in Russian-Eurasian regions: (1) by the further evolution of the *Fatianovo culture*, which connected the Neolithic and Paleometallic eras, and (2) by the so-called *Ananyino culture*, which developed from the Bronze into the Iron eras. Skillfully ornamented vases, copper and bronze axes, some with curved ends, spearheads, arrowheads, knives, sickles, awls, silver articles, ornamented dagger handles, and pottery evidencing skilled craftsmanship, were found in the ancient graves of that epoch in the Oka-Volga basin, near Fatianovo, Borodino, Murom and Seima, to testify about the cultural level attained by what was identified as the *Fatianovo culture*. Even some iron was found, indicating slow progress toward the subsequent evolutionary stage. Also bronze and copper articles made in the South, in the Caspian and North-Caucasian regions, were found in these grave sites, indicating some commercial intercourse between the people of the Oka-Volga basin with the peoples of the South, who had already attained a higher cultural development.

The *Ananyino culture* evolved later in the Middle Volga and Kama area, between the seventh and second centuries B.C. It was designated by the village of that name in the Viatka region, where its typical burial sites were first located. The Finnic, Ugrian or Turkish tribes, who developed the culture, still lived in the hunting and fishing stage, with a little supplementary farming. Hunting and fishing tools, made of bone, stone, bronze and iron, knives, bracelets, leather belts with bronze buckles, hemp seeds, and other remnants of the ancient culture were discovered there. The ornamental designs of the Ananyino era indicate some relation to Greco-Scythian and Caucasian artifacts. The archeological findings, furthermore, indicate that the *Ananyino* people were busily engaged in foreign trade via the Volga river and also overland. Perhaps even Greek merchants from the Black sea shores visited the Middle Volga regions for commercial reasons.[6]

Bronze and then iron came into use among the Ugro-Finnic tribes, where copper and tin, and subsequently iron ore deposits, were already discovered in remote prehistoric times, in the Northern Ladoga and Onega Lake regions, the Oka and upper Volga basin and Peckora basin, as far as Siberia and Turkestan.

The Ugro-Finnic tribes advanced their over-all social and political organization along with their cultural progress. Their centers were as a rule, located along the water routes rendering opportunity for transportation, communication and commerce, and facilitating contacts with other peoples. Sometime during the Paleometallic era they overcame the matriarchal system of family structure and adopted patriarchy. They began to create tribal political organizations to better resist external and internal threats and dangers. By the third and fourth century A.D., some of the tribes, such as the Chud, Mordva, Muroma, and Meria, were conquered by the East-Goths, who succeeded in suppressing, in Ukraine, the people of the Antes, ancestors of the contemporary Ukrainians, and in establishing there a strong though short-lived state. The Ugro-Finns even organized some supertribal political unions either by mutual agreement or by force. They sought to defend their common interests against the threat of invasion by Goths, Bulgars and others. Some Gothic and other historians, such as Saxo-Grammaticus, a Dane, mention a number of Ugrian and Finnic Tribes, who lived in the Volga and Oka basin and the Northern Lakes regions.[7] The Finns living close to the Baltic shores (the Suomi, Karelians and Biarmia), achieved a political, social, and commercial stability and prominence due to their fortunate geographical location. These tribes participated only slightly and indirectly in the development of the Russian nationality.

In almost all provinces of the North-East or Russia proper, in the Pskov, Tver, Novgorod the Great, Vologda, Moscow, Yaroslav, Vladimir, Riazan, Perm, Nizhnii Novgorod and other regions the remnants of the ancient Ugro-Finnic settlements, castle-like *gorodishcha* were found. These settlements were sanctuaries or forts for defense against foreign enemies, or centers of Finnic political, semi-state, tribal or super-tribal organization, around which substantial trading developed. They were always strategically located on steep hills or steep river banks, and protected by man-made moats and ramparts, as noted by Vernadsky. A typical example of these settlements has been the *Diakovo* settlements on the banks of the Moskva river, some five miles from the city of Moscow.

The Finns lived in poorly constructed wooden shacks mostly without chimneys, widely scattered in inaccessible forest areas. They were clothed in burlap, rough woolen materials and skins. Men and women wore metal ornaments, neck rings, earrings, and belt buckles, made from bronze and silver. Female headdresses were elaborate.

The economy of the Ugro-Finnic tribes was primitive, based on hunting, trapping and fishing with modest farming as a subsidiary activity. In a few instances commerce prospered. Food was supplied by fishing and hunting while trapping and hunting supplied skins and furs for substantial trade with the Volga Bulgars and Khazars from whom they received metal tools, weapon and luxury items. From the Southern Slavs in Ukraine, they obtained goods made in Greece or the Near East.

The religious life of the Ugro-Finns was rather primitive and not very imaginative. But it must be noted, to their credit, that it was monotheistically oriented. They believed in a Supreme Being called Yen, Yuma or Yumala. They believed in a score of spirits; some good, but mostly evil. These could assume the shapes of animals and birds. The Ugro-Finns revered some animals and birds as sacred. The priest-magicians, called *Volkhvi*, directed religious practices which at times included human sacrifice. The belief in life after death in another spiritual world was common. The dead were revered and buried with elaborate ceremonials dating since prehistoric times, as has been noted before.[8]

In the seventh century A.D. a powerful state organization of the Great Bulgars, a people of Turkish extraction, in the Black and Azov Sea steppes broke down under the pressure of Khazar expansionism. The Khazars were of a mixed, Finnic and Turkish origin, and soon succeeded in creating a powerful empire in the Don-Volga steppes, and in conquering many lands and peoples. As a result, the Bulgars emigrated. Some went to the Balkans and there originated the modern Bulgarian nation. Others migrated and settled in the middle Volga regions, there establishing a new, so-called "Volga Bulgar state," with the city of Bulgar on Volga, as its capital. Soon, the Volga Bulgars extended their domination over a number of the Ugro-Finnic tribes, including the Mordva, Burtasy, Cheremisians and others. The Bulgars, located on commercial crossroads from the West to the East and South through the Volga and Kama rivers to the Caspian Sea and the Don-Volga basin, developed commercially with much success, and became market-minded middlemen for the Ugro-Finnic-Khazar-Slavic trade. They extended their trading activities to Turkestan and beyond the Ural mountains by way of the Yaik river and other waterways, also to Ukraine, and as far as the Byzantinian possessions on the Northern shores of the Black Sea. It certainly was not just a simple coincidence, therefore, that the Volga Bulgars succeeded in establishing a strong state and in achieving a high level of commercial civilization, where once the *Ananyino culture* flourished. The geography of the middle Volga region, and its strategic location in Eurasia repeatedly stimulated cultural development there, although political odds were against it.

The Bulgar trade consisted of furs, skins, and burlap coming from the Ugro-Finnic territories, and appliances, footwear, cloth and ornamental articles from other areas. The Bulgars themselves were skilled farmers and craftsmen, widely supplying a variety of goods for trade and thus showing the Ugro-Finns how to develop their primitive economies. These efforts were not very successful.

In the course of the seventh and eighth centuries, the Slavs invaded and penetrated deeply into the Ugro-Finnic territories of the Russian North-East, establishing permanent settlements there. As they conquered, they either forced the natives to submit, or to leave for more tranquil homes in the distant north. Oppression, bloodshed, and social upheavals accompanied the process of Slavic colonization of the Volga-Oka-Klazma basin and the Northern Lakes regions. Later, peaceful assimilation through social contacts, intermarriages and other ways amalgamated the new ethnic alloy of Ugro-Finnic and Slavic elements into the Russian (sometimes called "Great Russian") nationality.

The Ugro-Finnic influence on the formation of the Russian nationality was paramount. In the tenth century, when the states of the Volga Bulgars and the Khazars were destroyed by the power of the Kievan Rus', and most of the Ugro-Finns were forced into submission to Kiev, their assimilation into the new nationality was advanved and then completed. The Finnic influence has been evident in the anthropology of the contemporary Russian as evidenced by his body structure, facial features, many character traits, his language, his customs, and even in his interpretation of events.[9]

The Slavic Tribes in Eastern Europe

Leaving their original habitations between the Oder and the Dnieper Rivers in the sixth century, the Slavs continued to migrate east, northeast and south under the pressures of incoming nomadic hordes from Asia. At that time, Procopius, an historian, differentiated two groups of Slavs, the Sclaveni and the Antes. Both groups, especially the Antes, were composed of a number of smaller tribal communities. Jordanis, the sixth century historian of the state of the Eastern Goths, identified three Slavic groups, the Venedi, the Sclaveni and the Antes, comprised of various tribes of different names as well.[10] Neither of these two historians, however, undertook the giving of a detailed account of the Slavic ethnography of that time. Later, various Byzantinian, Arabic and Jewish travelers and writers reported various details about the Slavs, their clans and tribes, and their ways of life, and on that basis history can attempt a somewhat more systematic presentation of the early Slavic era in East Europe.[11] The Antes lived in Ukraine and there they established a strong state organization of their own as early as the fifth or sixth century, which collapsed under the invasion from Asia by the Avars, another people of Turkish extraction. The "Sclaveni" at that time inhabited the regions north of the Danube, and further north beyond the Carpathian mountains while the Venedi were settled in the area between the Vistula (Wisla) and Elba (Laba) Rivers, all having reached tribal semi-states and even supertribal unions in their political development.

Large-scale migrations of the Slavs continued, and around the eighth and ninth centuries the old terminology and classification of the Slavs disappeared from historical sources. New Slavic tribes with new names developed. Some of them in the West later became the Polish, the Slovak and the Czech nationalities. The southern branch of the Slavic tribes merged into the Serb, Croat and the Slovenian, and still others, amalgamating with the Bulgars, created the Bulgarian nationality, which has since inhabited the Balkan Peninsula.

The Slavic tribes which extended their settlements throughout Eastern Europe, were designated in the chronicle, *The Story of Ancient Years*, (also called *Primary Chronicle*) from the twelfth century. The authorship has been attributed to a Ukrainian monk, Nestor. Other written sources, either East-European or foreign, also mention these peoples.[12]

The ethnic process in East Europe crystallized into three Slavic nationalities, the Russians, Ukrainians, and Byeloruthenians. The Slavic tribes of the eighth and ninth centuries were later also classified. The North-Eastern group of the Viatichians, Radimichians, Slovenians, and partially, the eastern segment of Krivichians merging with the Ugro-Finnic Chud, Ves, Meria, Muron and others, amalgamated into the future Russian nationality, as already stated.

The Viatichians inhabited at that time the southern Oka and upper Don regions. At first they penetrated deeply into the Volga-Don steppes, but then, evidently, were pushed back to the Oka-Don section by recurring waves of nomadic invasions from Asia: by the Pechengs or Patzinaks and others.

West of the Viatichian territory the Radimichians, closely related to that tribe, occupied the region between the upper Dnieper and Desna Rivers. This was a rather small area, compactly surrounded by tribal areas of other Slavs, the Ukrainian Severians and Polyanians from the South, the Byeloruthenian Dregovichians from the West, and the Krivichians from the North. The ancient legend about two brothers of Polish descent, Radim and Viatko, related by the Nestor chronicle, from whom presumably the respective tribes descended and derived their names, clearly indicates the ancient agnatic relationship among the Slavic tribes in general. Although the credibility of that particular legend is doubtful.

The Krivichians settled north of the Radimichian and Viatichian territories, the eastern segment of which occupied the area of the upper Dnieper and upper Dvina Rivers. Having merged with the Ves, Chud, Meria and other Finns, they joined the Russian ethnic process, while their eastern segment amalgamated with the Dregovichians and Polotsians, the latter being their branch, into the Byeloruthenian nationality.

Further north of the Krivichian settlements, in the Northern Lakes regions, the Ilmen and Onega Lakes, and close to the shores of the Baltic Sea, the tribe of the Slovenians closely related to the Krivichians settled, bordering on the Ves, Chud, and Meria. The Slovenians attained important historical prominence over all North-Eastern Slavs because of their commercial activities aided by their strategic geographical location close to the Baltic Sea. They soon became market middlemen between the Scandinavian and West European lands on the one hand and the Eurasian North-East on the other. Their capital, the city of Novgorod the Great, was to perform a significant political and economic mission in that part of the European continent in the near future as an historical prologue to the development of the Muscovite-Russian Empire. That process did not originate in Novgorod itself, but east of it, in the Volga-Oka-Klazma basin.

These Slavic tribes invaded and at first dominated the original Ugro-Finnic territories as far as the Oka-Volga and Klazma river basin and the northern lakes region. They established themselves there by subjugating the Finnic natives. There the assimilation process of the two ethnic elements, Slavic and Finnic, as described above, also began and continued for many decades, continuously extending ever deeper into the East and North-East, toward the Ural mountains and the Arctic Ocean. The political power of the Rostov-Suzdal-Vladimir principality and other pre-Muscovite principalities of the European North-East at first, and later on, of the Muscovite Grand Duchy, constantly grew and continuously seized more territory, subjugating new areas and new peoples and forcing them into the Muscovite-Russian ethnic melting pot. In later centuries, Russian government continued to facilitate the assimilation process by means of Russianization and denationalization of non-Russian nationalities throughout the Empire, aimed at strengthening its Russian character and eliminating its original multi-cultural ethnic conglomerate.

In the southern part of the European East, seven Slavic tribes settled to build the Ukrainian nationality: the Polyanians in the middle Dnieper, Severians in the upper Seim and Donets basin east of the Polyanian territory, the Derevlianians west of the Polyanians and south of the Pripet River, further west of the Derevlianian territory, the tribe of the Dulebians in the region of upper Bug, Styr and Horyn Rivers, the Khorvatsians north of the Carpathian mountains and on the banks of the Dniester River, and finally, the Ulichians and Tiverians on the banks of the lower Dniester River, between the Pruth River in the West and the Bug River in the East. The Ukrainian tribes reached with their settlements as far as the Danube River. The tribes of the Dregovichians, between the Pripet and Berezina Rivers, the Polotsians, on the banks of the middle West Dvina, and the western segment of the Krivichians, who were less affected by the Finnic impact, made up the Byeloruthenian nationality, as already mentioned.

These were the Slavic tribes in East Europe. The Ukrainian and Byeloruthenian tribes, although having amalgamated in the course of centuries with numerous historical inhabitants of those areas, have not been as deeply affected by the significant ethnic Ugro-Finnic component as the Russians have been for various reasons. The Ukrainians were nationally crystallizing under the impact of Hellenic and Iranian cultures, while the Russians were influenced only indirectly by those civilizations.[13]

The Way of Life of the North-Eastern Slavs

At the time of the Slavic invasion and domination of North-East Europe, the Oka-Volga-Klazma basin and the Northern Lakes regions, the respective Slavic tribes must have been culturally, socially and organizationally somewhat superior to the conquered Ugro-Finns. This may be the reason why the Slavs absorbed Ugro-Finnic ethnic elements and then developed into a predominantly Slavic, Russian nationality. The Slavic tribes had reached at that time a higher level of economic evolution, the pastoral or cattle raising stage. There was also subtantial farming, trapping, hunting and fishing as supplementary industries, although the Finns have still relied on these latter occupations, with a little cattle raising and farming. The Slavs, furthermore, had already reached the stage of iron culture, having used such iron articles as sickles, spindles for weaving, knives, spearheads, swords and other iron appliances and weapons, while the Finns, with a limited number of articles of iron, chiefly used bronze. The Slavs continued to use bronze along with silver for ornaments, rings, bracelets and other jewelry. The Slavic crafts and industries were also much more advanced, especially furriery, blacksmithy and home building.[14]

There were two major reasons for the Slavic cultural superiority over the Finns. First of all, the Slavs in their original settlements were geographically much closer to the centers of the contemporary civilization, Rome and Constantinople, from which civilization radiated. Secondly, the far-distant European North-East was poor in natural resources, being predominantly forest (farmland and ores were scarce). This substantially delayed the economic progress of the Finns, and later on also of the Northern Slavs, when compared with the southern Ukrainian Slavic tribes.

The Slavs, coming to the Oka-Volga-Klazma basin, were already acquainted with land and cultivation and farming on a limited scale, including vegetable and fruit raising. They also began to practice bee-hiving along with traditional Northern forest activities: animal trapping, hunting and fishing for their supply of necessities such as meat, skins and furs. How profoundly important furs were for the man of that time can easily be seen in the early use of fur as a kind of commodity-money for limited trade and exchange among the eastern Slavs. Furthermore, fur was the major commodity used for paying tribute and other tax-like contributions either to invaders and conquerors or to the Slavic rulers themselves. It was also the chief item of northern export.[15] Bee-hiving, another branch of the northern forest economy, supplied important honey and wax. It was concentrated rather toward the South. Honey served as food, and wax was used to make candles. Both articles were also exported.

Cattle raising known by the Slavs moved northward very slowly, and horses as draft animals were virtually unknown there for a long time.

At first, all production and consumption was done collectively and without any division of labor (specialization), in the framework of the self-sufficient household economy of the ancient patriarchal family, which comprised many free and unfree members. The family business affairs were managed by the patriarch. Later on, however, the clan community began to collectively attend to various phases of the economic process. While having been a superordinate social cell to the family, the clan for efficiency reasons, somewhat restricted the business autonomy of the family. Later, some crude work specialization according to sex, age and social status was initiated. Men hunted, fished, tailored clothes, and twisted ropes for nets. Women spun and wove the cloth, prepared meals and did housework. Slaves performed menial tasks: taking care of cattle, doing a little farming and other odd jobs.

Eventually all kinds of crafts developed, such as weaving, spinning, tailoring, furriery, tanning, carpentry, building and some ceramics, and rational division of labor progressed to assure greater economic efficiency.

Trading was known in the North-East of Europe since the *Fatianovo* era because of the key commercial position of the Oka-Volga and Klazma basin between the Orient and the Occident. The Slavs advanced trading activities because of their better knowledge of the outside world. Domestic trading had rather a "local" character. It was chiefly barter between the ancient "town," the *"gorodishche"* and the countryside, and among the specialized crafts and occupations. The exchange among various regions of the Russian North-East was limited, since their economies were similar and they had little to offer to each other in the way of specialization. Coins were little used in that trading, while fur as a means of exchange was growing in importance.

On the other hand, numerous findings of foreign, Roman, Greek, and Arabic coins in the territory of Russia proper evidenced extensive trade relations of the European North-East with distant foreign countries via water routes of Volga, Dnieper and Dvina, as well as overland. Russian areas exported the products of their forest economy: wood, wooden articles, furs, skins, honey, wax and slaves. They imported manufactured goods, fine cloth, garments, metal appliances and some luxuries, like jewelry, wines, salt, and arms. Foreign trade was centered in such towns as Novgorod the Great, Bielooziero, Izborsk, Rostov, and Murom and others.[16]

These "towns" or "fortresses" were sometimes very ancient, dating from the long-past Finnic era when inaccessible religious sanctuaries were built. *Diakovo gorodishche,* near Moscow, was an example. They were the centers of the political, state-like organizations of the Slavs as well. They were usually built either on river banks to facilitate commercial activities by accessible transportation, or on hills or in other defensible places to provide some protection for the tribe against its enemies. In all cases, however, their construction was rather strong, protected traditionally by moats, earth ramparts and high wooden walls. Slavic religious life began to concentrate a little later in these places. Originally the Slavs worshipped under the open sky, in the woods or on the river banks.

As the clans grew and slowly disintegrated, additional premises were needed for a growing population and larger families. As a result, villages began to develop in the Russian North. New huts and household buildings were constructed. Villages were built in various ways, at first at random, later, some sort of pattern was followed. Huts were built along the main road or central plaza, or according to some other plan. In most cases building was done with protection against external dangers or enemies in mind.

As time passed the clan community (which continued to exist much longer in the Russian North-East, than in any other Slavic lands) began to be replaced by a new territorial village, or *very* community, usually larger than a village. In either case, in the framework of these territorial-administrative communities, social and economic collectivism persisted longer and more intensely than among other Slavs. Harsh climatic conditions and dangers of the unfriendly environment, which made survival difficult, might have been responsible for strong collectivistic inclinations of the forefathers of the modern Russians.[17]

The Slavic invaders at first lived, as many native Finns still did, in dugouts in the earth. Later they started to build wooden huts, protected by a coat of clay from the outside to resist cold and wintry weather. Along with living quarters (for a long time in old Muscovy without chimneys), stables, storage rooms and other farm buildings were constructed. The wealthy began very early to construct "palaces" and "mansions," sometimes with two floors.

Consumption of the ancient Slavs was as simple as was their economy, related to trapping, hunting, fishing, a little agriculture and primitive crafts. Hence, meat, fish, poultry, wild fruits, vegetables and berries, honey and some cultivated produce of supplementary farming constituted the diet, which differed, of course, with the social status. The wealthy could afford more substantial and more diversified consumption, including imported luxuries.

In general, ancient Slavic clothing consisted of a shirt, which could be long or short, wide trousers and a coat for men. In the Russian North-East skins and furs were used longer and to a greater extent than in other parts of Eastern Europe because of the severe climate and economic backwardness. Linen and textiles were rare and costly for a long time. The manner in which the parts of clothing were cut and tailored differed from one tribal area to the other. Women dressed differently from men; the wealthy wore better, frequently imported, woolen or silk clothing, while the poor were simply dressed.[18]

Social and Political Relations

Socially, the Slavic clan and tribal system, based on the agnatic principle, because it originally developed out of the family cell, was already well developed in the ninth century, as historical sources indicate. Blood relationship as the origin of the tribal organization is evident from various legends, which partially reflected the immemorable-distant past. For example, the two brothers Viatko and Radim, presumably of Polish origin, were the alleged forebears of the Viatichians and Radimichians; the three brothers, Lekh, Czech and Rus, were the supposed forebears of the three future nationalities of the Poles, Czechs and Ukrainians; and the three brothers Kyi, Shchek and Khoryv, with their sister

Lebed, were connected with the legend concerning the political beginnings of the Kievan state in Ukraine.

Patriarchy was predominant among the Eastern Slavs by the ninth century as was social stratification into aristocratic grandees, free commoners and slaves. Slavic families at first developed into clans, then clans formed tribes, and later various clans began to join tribal organizations on a territorial rather than agnatic basis.

The ancient Slavic family, composed of free and unfree members, lived in a self-sufficient household community, under the authority of its head the patriarch of the family, usually its oldest male. The clan, populating a village or a section of a village, was governed by an elected *starosta* (clan chieftain), and advised by an influential clan council.

After tribes were formed, they began to develop certain specific characteristics of their own, in order to assure their identity, unity and distinction from other tribal communities. Among these were: the memory of common-ancestry, a territorial community of interest (village or *verv* territorial-administrative union), common tribal customs and rituals with strong religious and social undertones, unwritten tribal laws and folkways, subtle differences in tribal religious beliefs, deviating from Slavic paganism due to various outside influences, tribal manners in female and male clothing, and slight language differences. In the Russian North-East, Slavic tribal characteristics from the very beginning were heavily exposed to Finnic influences in the areas of religion, customs, language and the over-all way of life, in the course of ethnic assimilation.

It seems that the Slavs were socially differentiated in their original settlements, before they arrived in the eastern and northern regions of Europe. Later developments only deepened the differentiation.[19]

Essentially, three social strata were formed: the tribal aristocracy of grandees, the free commoners and the unfree servants or slaves. Further social evolution established a number of subgroupings within each class. The tribal aristocracy or nobility developed either as a result of the personal leadership abilities of individuals who acquired influence, prestige and higher material standing, or as a result of their business, and in particular, of their commercial abilities and activities. At that time these abilities were the surest way to amass fortunes, and by so doing, to raise social prestige and influence in the tribe.[20] The Slavic conquerors constituted the stratum of the free commoners, while the conquered native Finns, as war prisoners, were partially turned into slaves, along with other elements, such as common criminals, insolvent debtors or purchased servants, who by the law of tradition lost their personal freedom and right to own property. Originally, as Kluchevsky noted, war and conquest were the only means for providing slaves; the others were added later. It is important, however, to note that the social and economic role of slavery in the Russian north was less than in the Ukrainian south. Although the conquered Ugro-Finns were partially made slaves or joined the ranks of the commoners, frequently some of them, due to their ability and wealth, climbed the social ladder, and, joined the ranks of nobles. Eventually there was ethnic fusion of the Finnic and Slavic populations on all levels.

The tribes developed as a natural process, out of social, political and economic needs to provide order and defense on a broader base. They were, as pointed out before, a natural continuation of man's gradual need to live in a broader community, superseding original family and then clan ties which were no longer able to provide the necessary framework for orderly, peaceful and safe existence under changing conditions and an increasingly difficult environment. The tribe therefore was a semistate organization which predated the nation-state. The latter evolved through the merging of a number of tribes for reasons of order, defense and security, just as the confederation of a number of clans into a tribe took place in the distant prehistory.[21]

According to Procopius, the Greek historian, and other writers of that period, the people's meeting, a democratic body, a gathering of all adults of the tribe, called *vieche,* was the supreme governing agency. The hardships of survival under the adverse and highly demanding, geo-political environment of the European North-East soon induced a partial departure from the democratic tradition of the Slavs. At first this was done for practical reasons and in the name of expediency to improve order and increase security. Some outstanding individuals either usurped or were entrusted with a dominant, leading or even ruling position in the tribes.[22] They were called *Voyevods* (warrior leaders) at first and then, *Kniazes* (princes). With the passage of time the office of the prince acquired a permanent and constitutional status and became another chief agency in the tribe, along with the people's meeting.

Originally, the princes were, without doubt, elected by the people, but in time, strong princely individualities began to press for a hereditary system of princely succession. The oposition to this one-sided trend was intense. In many cases the institution of the people's meeting was even more influential than the prince, and whenever the prince did not meet with the approval of the people's meeting, he could have been deposed, expelled or even killed. However, in most cases the individuality, the strength of will and the character of the prince or of the leaders of the community as expressed in the meetings and during the whole power struggle, were the deciding forces in such constitutional disputes.

Constitutional troubles were reported in early chronicles as having occurred among the Slovenians, who could not agree among themselves and did not want to submit to the authority, presumably, of their prince. They finally called the Norsemen in to rule over them.[23] Whether the passage in the chronicle about the invitation to the Norsemen deserves credibility or not, is irrelevant at this point. It may correctly reflect, however, the chronic and persistent constitutional conflicts between the authority of the tribal prince and that of the people's meeting, which had deep roots in the earliest days of the Slavs in the North-East of Europe, much earlier than the arrival of the Norsemen at Novgorod the Great and other towns of old Russia proper.

The harsh environment and difficulties of survival in the North-Eastern borderlands of Europe demanded strong leadership to overcome upheavals due to continuous invasions and wars. The Oriental traditions of despotism were another contributory factor. As time passed, therefore, the tribal princes aspired more and more to assume absolute power. Displaying their despotic tendencies, they attempted to push the people's meetings aside, to strip them of their traditional rights and authority. Obviously, the people did not like this, and the struggle for power continued, having received its full expression in the eleventh and twelfth centuries in the Rostov-Suzdal-Vladimir principality. The result there was a complete victory of the prince which ultimately gave rise to the growth of Russian absolutism.[24]

The names Viatko, Radimko, Gostomysl, Mal, Kyi, Shchek and Khoryv do indicate that in the remote prehistory of the Slavs there were some outstanding princes whose deeds made them great in the eyes of their own contemporaries. Their names in the way of legends have been transmitted by oral tradition to posterity, and retained in the memory of the later generations.

The *gorodishcha* or "towns," like Novgorod the Great, Bielo-oziero, Rostov, Izborsk or others mentioned were not only economic centers of the old Slavs in the North-East, but, without doubt, also centers of tribal political life. Evidently, people's meetings may have taken place and the princes usually resided in the "towns" from which they ruled. The "towns" may have also been the centers of some super-tribal unions, created for mutual defense by all tribes concerned, or some super-tribal state-like organizations, created by some outstanding princes who were motivated by political ambitions or hunger for power. Although there have been no direct historical references to such super-tribal political creations among North Eastern Slavs (with the exception of Novgorod the Great in the land of the Slovenians), they certainly must have existed, necessitated by the upheavals of the Finnic-Slavic assimilation process, the threat of political power of the Volga Bulgars and other menacing developments. Such political unions and confederations of the tribes, furthermore, were organized among Ukrainians, Polish, or Czech Slavs, and Russian Slavs were not an exception.[25] As a rule, however, such super-tribal political creations were short-lived. Tribal differences were too great, the over-all environmental conditions changed too much and too often, and the art of state building was still in its infancy among the Russian Slavs.

The only important exception was the state or commonwealth of Novgorod the Great. Already before the arrival of the Norsemen to Novgorod between 852 and 854, the city dominated extensive territories, including the Chud, Meria and Ves lands, extending its domain as far as the White Lake (Bieloe Oziero).

Under the impact of the organizational skills of the Norsemen and after having experienced conquest by the Ukrainian-Kievan Rus' state, the Russian tribes mastered the art of state building. In the twelfth century they began the construction of the powerful Muscovite-Russian Empire. The Mongol conqueror of Muscovy-Russia in the thirteenth century greatly contributed toward the perfection of their political acumen during his rule.

Religious Beliefs

In order to learn at least in broad outlines the way of life of the North-Eastern Slavs as a basis for the historical growth of Russia, it is necessary to cover briefly the religious beliefs, which were the expression of their spiritual and cultural life. These had a significant bearing on their history.

The Slavs were pagans whose body of beliefs was still immature and on a much lower level of spiritual evolution than that of such civilized people as the Hindus, Greeks, Romans and Germans. At the time of the introduction of Christianity to Russia, furthermore, Slavic paganism there had assimilated Finnic and Scandinavian religious elements.

Slavic paganism was polytheistic, it was based on belief in a plurality of gods. In this respect, it represented a religious regression when compared to the old monotheistic Finnic religion. This was, however, a normal course of spiritual evolution of ancient man from his original belief in one Supreme Being to a polytheistic religion of many gods, lesser gods, demons, fairies and nymphs, living in the woods, on the mountains and in the seas. Christianity reintroduced belief in one God to the European continent.

The Slavs then believed in a number of gods, related to various forces of nature, the marvel of which they could explain only through the intercession of a supernatural power. In their pantheon the leading gods were Svarog, Dazhbog, Khor, Stribog, and then Perun, Volos (Veles), Mokosh and Thor. References to these deities have been scattered throughout various historical source materials, such as chronicles and travel descriptions, writings about the lives of saints and old poems, originated however, a little later, in the Christianized Kievan state of the tenth century.[26] It is highly possible that this pantheon of gods may represent a later fusion of the two different religious systems of the Sclavenis and Antes, since it seems that there was no logical connection between Svarog, Dazhbog, Khor and Stribog, who were related to each other in Slavic beliefs, on the one hand, and Perun and Volos, on the other. Mokosh, apparently, was a female deity, a lesser goddess of Finnic origin, whose meaning in the cult is not clear. Thor, whose divine capacities were similar to those of Perun, was introduced into the northern Slavic religious body by the Scandinavians. The adoration of Mother Earth for her fertility had an Indo-Iranian background, and was absorbed into the paganism of the Slavs.

Svarog, apparently the chief deity among the Slavs, was the god of the heavens and of light and fire. It can be assumed on the basis of historical references that three other gods, Dazhbog, Khor and Stribog, were related to Svarog, presumably having been his sons or embodiments of his specific qualities. Dazhbog was the creative god of the sun, a living deity, who blessed nature with fertility. He was definitely a helping god and friendly to man. Stribog was the god of winds, while Khor was considered the god of sunlight, akin to Svarog. These three gods were sometimes referred to as the *Svarozhichi*, being in Svarog's family.

Perun and Volos were not in Svarog's family. Perun, a powerful and widely adored deity, was the god of storms, thunder and lightning, while Volos was the divine protector of cattle, money and commerce. It has been suggested by some students of Slavic history, that even the cult of Volos developed under Scandinavian influence.

Along with these major deities the old Slavs revered rivers, trees, nymphs, fairies, and other spirits or the reincarnation of spirits. Their belief in evil spirits or demons was definitely of foreign, primarily Oriental, origin.[27]

The religion of the Slavs was closely related to nature. This is illustrated by its rituals and festivities with a yearly and seasonal cyclic character. Those rituals and festivities survived much longer than paganism in Eastern Europe. After the introduction of Christianity, for more than two centuries a form of religious dualism prevailed, a religious mixture of paganism and Christianity. During that era, the people, having kept their traditional customs and rituals, gave them a Christian counterpart: they identified St. Ellias with Perun and St. Vlasius with Volos; they celebrated Christian holydays with paganistic festivities. Some remnants of Slavic pagan rituals and customs can be found even today among the village folk throughout the European part of the Soviet Union.

The old Slavs evidently did not build temples and had no priests. Later, however, perhaps under foreign influence as well as Finnic influence, and due to a further evolution of their religion, temples were constructed and priests, called *Volkhvi*, took charge of religious rites.

Idols, however, mostly made from wood and sometimes from stone, and pictures of deities were known among the Slavs. The remnants of those idols have been found in various places.

The Slavs must have believed in, or at least subconsciously admitted the immortality of the human soul. First of all, they had elaborate burial rituals either by inhumation or by cremation. Vernadsky states that the cult of Perun, as God of lightning, must have been connected with cremation, while inhumation of the dead must have been the ritual of the Svarog cult.[28] Secondly, the worship and adoration of clan ancestors, bringing them milk, bread, meat and honey as offerings on certain religious days, to invoke their protection for the clan, was an ancient custom among the Slavs. These customs persisted beyond the pagan era, deep into the thirteenth century. These two facts indicate the Slavic belief in a life after death. The burial rituals among the Slavic tribes were described at length by the Arabic travellers, Ibn-Fadlan and Ibn-Dasta.[29]

To be sure, those religious beliefs of the North-Eastern (Russian) Slavs were, during the latter period, considerably different from those of the South-Eastern (Ukrainian) Slavs, since the former were affected by Finno-Ungric and the latter — by Hellenic and Iranian religious and spiritual trends, as indicated before.

This, then, was the Finnic-Slavic spiritual, social-political and economic background of the European North-East on the eve of an already traceable historical era, building the foundations for the development of the powerful Russian Empire which was soon to appear.

CHAPTER THREE

THE POLITICAL PROLOGUE

Novgorod The Great: Its Political Beginnings.

The political origins and beginnings of Novgorod the Great in the land of the Slovenians are not known since they are rooted in the remote and unrecorded centuries of the pre-historic era. At the time when the first historic reference was made about Novgorod, it was already a rich and economically strong city, a capital of an aristocratic republic where the prince had a secondary role to perform. It dominated a vast territory, from the shores of the Gulf of Finland in the West to the White Sea and beyond the Northern Dvina River in the North-East. Included in the sphere of its political influence was the Volga-Oka basin in the South-East. It was a colonial empire, existing for the benefit of the city and its small mercantile and neighborhood landed-aristocratic clique, which also ran its political and economic affairs.

The colonial empire of Novgorod the Great may have been the creation of the Slovenians; its political origin could have gone even further back to the Finnic era. The arrival of the Slavs should have substantially contributed to the splendid commercial growth of the city and its political dominance over the more primitive Finns. Moreover, early commercial and social contacts of the Slovenians with the Scandinavians (already at the end of the seventh and the beginning of the eighth centuries) might have facilitated that growth. Tikhomirov and Smirnov have suggested that the Scandinavian adventurers, warriors, and traders, later called the Varengians, penetrated as far as the Volga-Oka at that early date.[1] Therefore, they must have been well known in Novgorod even before that time.

Novgorod's achievement of commercial and also political prominence in the European North-East, ahead of any other tribal community with its capital there, was due to the city's extremely favorable geographical location, making possible large-scale trading for which the Slovenians apparently had exceptional ability. It has been pointed out that convenient water or overland trade routes have since time immemorial stimulated development of commercial, political and cultural centers. The land of the Slovenians had the advantage of a very favorable geographical location, with good waterways in all directions. Situated on the banks of the Volkhov River, which connected Lake Ilmen with Lake Ladoga (the latter being connected by the Neva River with the Gulf of Finland and the Baltic Sea), Novgorod the Great possessed a natural, open route to the Scandinavian Peninsula and Germany in the West. Access, furthermore, to the Dnieper River, to convey the city's trading activities to Ukraine and her commercial center of the city of Kiev in the land of the Polianians, and Greece with her commercial capital of Constantinople, was rather easy from Novgorod the Great. This constituted the old commercial route "from the Varengians to the Greeks," in the old terminology of the *Primary Chronicle*, making the city a kind of a market middleman for Scandinavian-Greek trade. Novgorod was also close to the Volga-Oka basin which enabled the city to contact by way of the Volga River route and its tributaries, the Caspian Sea, Transcaucasia, the Middle East, and above all, the commercially strong state on the Volga River banks, the State of the Volga Bulgars, with their mercantile capital, the city of Bulgar. By way of Ityl and Bulgar even Central Asia may have been known to the Novgordian merchants. Having dominated the areas up to the North Dvina River, Novgorod received access to almost inexhaustible fur-bearing animal resources of the northern forestland reaching the Ural Mountains and beyond, fur being at that time the chief trading item in the vast Eurasian regions.

Due, chiefly, to its commercial importance, Novgorod the Great established itself as a colonial empire of Slavic stock of the Slovenian tribe, and incorporated into its huge political body the tribes of the Chud, Ves, Meria, Iam and Biarmia of Ugro-Finnic stock. The rule of Novgorod over these tribes was in most cases of an economic nature, visible in the institution of annual tribute collection and unrestricted fur trading activities. Their political dependence upon the city was weak. However, Novgorod with its aristocratic democracy did not originate Muscovy-Russia and her future absolute monarchy. That Muscovite-Russian absolutist state originated in the Rostov-Suzdal and Vladimir principality east of Novgorod, which came later. The Novgordian commercialized democracy was only a political prologue to the dramatic development of a future Russian imperialist growth so vastly different in its nature from what had taken place in the land of the Slovenians. The town of Rostov itself was at first in the orbit of political and economic influences of Novgorod in the seventh century. Namely, Roric of Jutland, having established himself as the ruler of Novgorod, appointed his viceroy to Rostov in 862 A.D.

The wealth and fame of the land of the Slovenians with its capital, Novgorod the Great, very early began to attract the attention of foreigners, most probably at the end of the sixth century, as mentioned above. In 852 a large naval force of Danish warriors sailed across the Baltic Sea and landed in Slovenian country, no doubt looking for booty. They were motivated by their inborn spirit of Norse adventurism which made Norsemen travel to West and South Europe, to Iceland and to America. Evidently they seized the city of Novgorod and a large part of surrounding territory and demanded a ransom.

The Slovenians did not like the invasion. They organized an armed resistance and forced the Danes to leave their country. An *Hypatian Chronicle* related the above event as follows: "... And they [the Slovenians] chased the Varengians away and did not give them tribute and set out to govern themselves."[2]

According to the legend, related by Tatishchev, the Slovenian prince who defeated and chased the Danes away was presumably called Gostomisl. However, troubles soon developed among the Slovenians and other tribes, and the same *Hypatian Chronicle* notes: "... and there was no justice in the administration, and clan rose against clan, and a civil war started. Then, the Chud, the Slovenians, the Krivichians and the Ves said to the Rus' people: 'Our land is great and abundant, but there is no order in it: come to rule and reign over us.' "[3]

This was the famous, perhaps only legendary or perhaps only a symbolic relation to factual developments, identified in historical writings as the "calling of the Varengians." Whether it was really a friendly invitation extended in 854-855 by the Eastern Slavs and their Finnic neighbors to the Norsemen to help them in their domestic and foreign affairs, or whether it was another Danish invasion of Slovenian and neighboring lands led by the Danish feudal Lord Roric of Jutland, historians have never agreed since they had reasons to doubt the credibility of the *Chronicle*. The fact is that Roric of Jutland had to leave Denmark at that time because of political strife. After numerous military and seafaring adventures earlier, Roric eventually turned his attention to the wealthy city of Novgorod, well known to the Danes from their earlier experiences. Once again the Danes crossed the Baltic Sea. Their leader, Roric, soon established himself in Novgorod as ruler, and became known among the Slavs under the name "Rurik." This was the beginning of the Rurik dynasty, the branches of which ruled for centuries in Muscovy-Russia, Ukraine and Byeloruthenia. It resembled the dynasty of the Hapsburgs, branches of which reigned in various European countries.[4]

The story in the *Chronicle* about the "calling of the Varengians" has presented much difficulty to Russian and Ukrainian historians in their attempts to correctly interpret the political beginnings of Russia and Ukraine. As a result, two schools of thought, the Normanistic and the anti-Normanistic, have developed to shed light upon this controversial question. The Normanistic interpretation of the origin of Russia has been an older one, holding strictly to a literal acceptance of the report in the *Primary Chronicle* as already quoted. It was initiated by three eighteenth century historians of German descent, Bayer, Schloezer and Mueller, who, in their historical works, insisted on a Germanic or Normanic political origin of Muscovy-Russia. Taking into consideration the account of the events in the *Chronicle,* the ancient presence of a relatively large number of Norsemen-Varengians in Novgorod, Rostov, and then Kiev, and some old documents of early princes about their relations with foreign countries, Greece in particular, these historians concluded, that actually the Norsemen initiated, organized and maintained early political organizations (states) in Eastern Europe. The Slavs were unable to rule themselves, as the wording of the cited *Chronicle* admitted. The theory has certain elements of inborn German national pride and contempt for the Slavs, hence it was mainly originated by the Germans, residing in Russia. At first, the Normanistic interpretation of the origins of Russia was accepted by a score of Russian, Ukrainian and other historians. But there soon came another interpretation.

Historical source materials clearly evidenced the fact that for a prolonged period of time, some 250 years, small bands of Norsemen migrated to the European North-East, as a continuous flow of varriors, adventurers and merchants, settling there and entering the services of local princes, first as members of their retinues, and later in their administration systems. Since the Norsemen arrived in rather small parties, they were quickly assimilated along with the Ugro-Finns by the more numerous and predominant Slavic ethnic groups. Therefore, although Rurik, Ihor, and Oleh could have been considered as Normanic warriors who acquired princely authority among the Slavs either by conquest or election, later rulers of the Scandinavian dynasty in the Ukrainian south, like Volodymyr and Yaroslav, were already thoroughly Ukrainianized, while those in the Russian north, like Yurii Dolgorukii and Andrei Bogolubskii, were quickly and thoroughly Russianized.[5] The Norsemen no doubt influenced the course of events, more in the North-East, where the Normanic immigration had been continuing much longer and from a much earlier date, than in the South-East, by way of customs, religious beliefs and state-building techniques. Normanic discipline, strong military organization and even its

Germanic "herd" instinct, were welcome contributions which accelerated the political maturity of the North-Eastern Slavs.

The Normanistic theory soon provoked a reaction. Above all, it was a direct insult to the national and patriotic sentiments of the Russians and Ukrainians, instigated by German-originated insinuations, attempting to prove that the Norsemen were the only state-building force in the East, the Slavs having lacked such qualities. Prominent Russian and Ukrainian historians, like Lamanskii, Gedeonov, Ilovaiskii and Hrushevsky, who uncovered several weak points in the Normanistic interpretation, opposed it. First of all, they came to the conclusion that the wording of the *Primary Chronicle* cannot be taken at its full face value. However, most important was the historical fact of an ancient existence of a strong and wealthy political organization of Slavic Rus' in the Ukrainian South, well known to neighboring peoples long before the Varengian arrival in Kiev, attesting to the state-building qualities of the Slavs. Obviously, the North-Eastern Slavs, the Slovenians or Krivichians, must have possessed similar abilities and similar organizations. Furthermore, some Normanists associated the name Rus' with the Norsemen and thought it was of Normanic origin, while the Anti-Normanists proved, as mentioned before, that Rus' was known in the South prior to "calling the Varengians" and that it was most probably of Slavic origin. The Norsemen may have helped the political evolution of the pre-Russian and Rus' Slavic communities at a later stage, but they were not the only state-constructing force, as the German originators of the Normanistic theory preferred to see.[6]

In the development of Novgorod the Great in the land of the Slovenians, as well as in the later growth of the Rostov-Suzdal-Vladimir principality (the embryo of the Russian Empire), Finnic elements, the echo of the *Fatianovo culture*, and Norse elements, with the predominance of Slavic socio-political creativity, were at work. At the time of Rurik (854-873), Novgorod already dominated vast areas, reaching the White Sea and far beyond the Northern Dvina River, to the foot of the Ural, and including different peoples, the Slavs, the Ugro-

Finns and the Scandinavians, imposing on them its mild and commercially motivated tyranny. In 862, Rurik appointed his governors and viceroys from among the members of his Norman retinue, the normal Viking-Varengian practice whenever the Norsemen dominated the lands, as in England, Normandy, and Southern Italy. The viceroys were installed in various cities of the realm, including Rostov which must have been within the political influence of Novgorod, and which soon was to acquire political prominence of its own.

However, the Vikings-Varengians, being adventurers and booty-seekers by nature, were soon attracted by even more lucrative opportunities in the Ukrainian South-East, than those available in Novgorod. To that area they shifted their interest. Many military and mercantile incursions by the Varengians went south by the Dnieper River in several waves to the mighty and wealthy city of Kiev in the land of the Polyanians, the capital of the Rus' state. One of those incursions was led perhaps by two Norse warriors, Askold and Dir, and another one was certainly under the leadership of Oleg or Oleh, the tutor of Rurik's son, prince Igor or Ihor. The Varengians helped the seven Ukrainian tribes to organize and to enlarge a powerful Kievan Rus' realm, which, in turn, in the course of some hundred and fifty years (860-1015) succeeded in conquering and dominating almost the entire eastern part of the European continent, including Novgorod the Great, Rostov, Suzdal and other Russian and Finnic territories, and reducing them to administrative units of colonial possessions. Novgorod and its lands and dominions came under Kievan rule in a rather peaceful manner, by way of the gradual shifting of interests of the princes of the Rurik dynasty from the North to the South, and the transfer of the capital of their new empire from the city of Novgorod to the city of Kiev in Ukraine, retaining the Northern possessions as integral parts of the realm and property of the dynasty. Oleh, Ihor, Volodymyr or Vladimir and Yaroslav at first resided and ruled in Novgorod as princes or viceroys, before they became solely Kievan rulers. They could be referred to as Grand Dukes, although they actually did not use that title.[7]

Political Fortunes

The Novgorodians did not like Kievan-Ukrainian supremacy and continually exhibited separatist tendencies. For example, in 1014 they stopped payment of tribute to the Kievan suzerain, thus attempting to free themselves from foreign rule. The Novgorod-Kiev conflict had from its very beginning national, political and economic implications. The Novgorodians-Slovenians were crystallizing into Russians. It was their ambition to rule the north-eastern territories and to maintain their position as the commercial center of East-West and North-East trading, in the city of Novgorod the Great. Kiev was the Ukrainian capital, and dominated South-Eastern Europe. It was located in the land of the Polyanians, who with other Ukrainian tribes were evolving into a Ukrainian nationality with different characteristics from the future Russians. As a result, the seed of ethnic antagonism was sown there. Kiev was also very significant, perhaps even more important than Novgorod, as a commercial center for similar East-European mercantile and trading currents from East to West and from North to South. The rivalry was open and acute, and growing in intensity as Kiev attempted to impose its will upon its Northern competitor by political means.

After Novgorod discontinued paying tribute, the Kievan prince, Volodymyr the Great, began to prepare a war against that city, but he died in the meantime. An open break between Kiev and Novgorod did not come at that time, because Volodymyr's son, Yaroslav, prince of Novgorod, who was actually behind the refusal to pay the tribute, succeeded his father to the Kievan throne after a bloody dynastic war. Being popular among the Slovenians, who hoped for more reasonable relations with Kiev under his scepter, Yaroslov was able to retain the Ilmen and Onega Lake territories within the realm and under Kievan-Ukrainian supremacy. Nevertheless, the Novgorodians did not give up their struggle for independence and soon resumed their opposition to Kiev.

In order to strengthen its political position, Novgorod continued to expand into the North and North-East, increasing its commercial ties and building up its economic power. Having been in Kiev, Yaroslav waged a war against the Chud in Estonia to protect Novgorodian interests. In 1030, the city of Yuriev, (from Yaroslav's Christian name Yurii), on the western side of Lake Peipus, was founded to keep the Chud, later on called the Ests, in check. In 1042, his son, prince Volodymyr, the Viceroy of Novgorod, subjugated the Finnic tribe of Yam to secure Novgorod's control over the Gulf of Finland. Later princes of Novgorod further enlarged their land and their possessions. Prince Vsievolod in 1132-33 conquered and dominated most of Estonia, recaptured the city of Yuriev and strengthened Novgorodian commercial interests. During most of this time the city was in a close alliance with Kiev.

In 1136, the Novgorodians successfully revolted against Kiev's supremacy. Prince Vsievolod, with full princely authority and still Kievan viceroy, was expelled, and the city became an independent community. From that time on, ignoring Kiev entirely, the Novgorodians elected their own princes, whose authority was greatly reduced to the position of high-level, hired officials of the city. From then on the authority of the Council of Nobles greatly expanded having been superimposed over that of the prince. In 1156, Novgorod became ecclesiastically independent and elected its own bishop, who was only indirectly connected with the Kievan metropolitan.

Meanwhile, another political power was emerging in the neighborhood of Novgorod — the principality of Rostov-Suzdal and Vladimir. Its policies increasingly affected the political affairs of the city. Following the events of 1136, Yurii Dologrukii of Rostov-Suzdal acted immediately and suggested that the city elect a prince, who would meet with Rostov-Suzdal approval. Novgorod had done so. In that way and for the first time it accepted *de facto*, although initially in a loose form only, allegiance to the Northern principality which was to be the growth cone of the future Russian Empire. In 1170, after the pillage of Kiev by the Suzdalians, Andrei Bogolubskii, Dolgorukii's son, prince of Rostov-Suzdal and Vladimir, also attacked Novgorod with his armies. He wanted to force it into complete subjugation, but was repulsed. Due to Novgorod's dependence upon foreign food supplies, for which the Volga-Oka Basin in the Rostov-Suzdal and Vladimir principality was a channel, the situation of loose allegiance to Suzdal remained in force for many decades. Vsievolod III, the Grand Duke of Vladimir, forced Novgorod to submit to his leadership and authority.[8]

Nevertheless, the degree of allegiance of Novgorod to Vladimir varied constantly. Novgorod and Vladimir differed on several accounts. The first was a traditional commercial center and the latter — a new and emerging one. Actually, Andrei Bogulubskii planned to destroy the economic power of Novgorod, as he did with Kiev's. Novgorod, furthermore, controlled vast North-Eastern regions of Europe, even beyond the Urals, and extending into Asia, from where it obtained valuable articles for its lucrative trading activities. The expansion of Vladimir's political and economic influences there was in direct conflict with Novgorod's interests. At times, certain North-Eastern forest regions were in allegiance to both Novgorod and Vladimir. Occasionally even open warfare broke out between the Novgorodian "republic" and the authoritarian Vladimir principality. In 1216, the Novgorodian prince, Mstislav, scored a victory over Vladimirian troops in the battle of Lipitsa, in order to defend Novgorodian autonomy and commerce.

With the disintegration of the Kievan realm, various North-Eastern principalities increased their autonomy and expanded territorially. Novgorod increased its relationships with Sweden, Norway, Denmark, Lithuania and the Teutonic Knights. These relations were not always friendly and peaceful, and were frequently accompanied by warfare. The Novgorodians were relatively successful in defending their interests against the Western adversaries, for three reasons. First of all, the Western foes faced Novgorod at a later historical stage, after the republic was politically and economically established and, therefore, able to accept any challenge. Secondly, the Vladimir principality was soon weakened by the Mongol invasion and almost fully absorbed in its relations with Sarai, the Mongol capital, of which it was a vassal, and it therefore could not continue the policy of Andrei Bogolubskii. The Muscovite state did not become powerful until much later. Third, the Mongols, who virtually invaded all of Eastern Europe, pillaging and having brought destruction and ruin to most North-Eastern principalities, spared Novgorod the Great. Novgorod accepted a vassal relationship to the Mongol Suzerain in a submissive manner and agreed to pay annual tribute to Sarai, never opposing the Khan in any flagrant way. The Mongols therefore not only left the city and its republic alone, but were even disposed to it in a friendly manner. Its trading activities enjoyed Sarai's utmost protection. This enabled Novgorod to actively oppose its Western foes, although it had accepted a nominal vassalage to its Eastern ruler. In the fifteenth century, as Mongol power progressively disintegrated and the Muscovite Grand Duchy became a leading power in the Russian North-East, the political and economic safety of Novgorod the Great became increasingly problematical.

Meanwhile, as Novgorodian influences widened along the White Sea and the Arctic Ocean littorals in the twelfth and thirteenth centuries, Novgorodian fishing and commercial interests clashed with those of the Norwegians. The conflict was never settled. The Novgorodians and Norwegians fought each other several times. The conflict with Sweden was even graver. Novgorod had some twenty-six larger and smaller wars or military clashes with the Swedes over the question of supremacy over some Finnish territories and the littorals of the Gulf of Finland. Most notorious was the war with Sweden in 1240, when Alexander Nevskii, prince of Novgorod and Grand Duke of Vladimir, defeated the Swedish troops in a smashing victory on the banks of the Neva River. Novgorod had defended its right to trade with the West.

In the thirteenth century Novgorod was involved in a series of wars, some fourteen of them, with the Lithuanians over some Byeloruthenian regions, and with the Letts and Ests over some Livonian and Estonian territories. In 1212, Prince Mstislav conquered additional Livonian regions, south of Yuriev, and imposed tribute upon them.

In the meantime, a real threat developed for Novgorod and Pskov in the Baltic area, and things became politically more serious for both cities, after the Order of Sword Bearers of German Knights (the Teutonic Order) established itself in Livonia after 1207. The Order began to exhibit strong imperialistic tendencies disguised under the pretext of Christian missionary work in the pagan and Orthodox lands. The Novgorodians and Pskovians soon became aware of the German danger and waged twelve battles with the German Knights. Between 1212 and 1221, several attacks and raids, initiated by either side, were carried out. The warfare was prolonged, bitter and bloody, with heavy losses for the Novgorodians, Pskovians, and German Knights, as well as for the Letts and Lithuanians, who allied themselves either with Novgorod or the Order. Churches were destroyed; the grain in the fields burned; men, women, and children mercilessly killed or taken into captivity.[9] Complete annihilation of the other side was the end purpose of either fighting force. In 1224, the Germans conquered and annexed the city of Yuriev, which was a serious blow to Novgorod's political prestige. The city was renamed Dorpat. (In the twentieth century its name was changed again to Tartu.) In most of these wars the Letts and Ests allied themselves with the Teutonic Knights, while the Lithuanians supported the Novgorodians, Pskovians and Byeloruthenians. In some cases, the Lithuanians were bitter adversaries of Novgorod the Great because of German instigations. Later, in the fourteenth and fifteenth centuries, during the era of great political expansion of the Lithuanian Grand Duchy, Novgorodian-Lithuanian antagonism was intensified because of the Lithuanian conquest of all of Byeloruthenia and due to Novgorod's fear of Lithuania's imperialism and growth.

The German menace, however, was most acute. Yet, in 1242, the Novgorodian troops under the command of Prince Alexander Nevskii defeated and completely routed the invading German Knights and their Finnish allies in a battle on the ice of Lake Peipus in Estonia.

In early 1200 Denmark also atempted to get hold of Estonia.

In 1219, the Danes built the fortress of Reval as their bridgehead. Some twenty years later, in 1237, Estonia became a Danish possession. This event had an impact on Novgorodian affairs. As Riasanovsky asserted on the basis of Soviet research: "... between 1142 and 1446 Novgorod fought the Swedes twenty-six times, the German Knights eleven times, the Lithuanians fourteen times, and the Norwegians five times."[10]

In the fifteenth century, Mongol domination over East Europe began to show signs of disintegration. In the meantime, the Grand Duchy also declined, and the new power of the Muscovite Duchy began to grow, assuming the mission of uniting all Russian lands and principalities in one giant political organism. Novgorod the Great, with its wealth and power, its trading and well-developed commercial relations, and its semi-republican and self-governing constitution, irked the economically poor and despotically ruled Muscovites, and induced them to undertake conquests. During the turmoil under Mongol domination, the Muscovite Dukes adhered to patrimonial succession, a constitutional system which promised greater stability in domestic and foreign affairs. Novgorod the Great, always threatened by its western neighbors, looked toward Moscow as a possible ally. After Sarai declined as a powerful protector, it transferred its vassal-like loyalty from Sarai to the capital of the newly emerging empire. The choice was a poor one.

Antagonized by Novgorod's political dealings with the Lithuanians to secure its independence upon Moscow, and using these dealings as an excuse, Vasilii II, Grand Duke of Muscovy, in 1456 sent a punitive expedition against the city. The Novgorodians were unable to militarily face their powerful adversary and accepted harsh peace terms. In exchange for preserving its traditional liberties and self-government, Novgorod became a territorial part of the Grand Duchy of Muscovy, paid a large indemnity and pledged loyalty to the Grand Dukes. Moscow's interference in Novgorod's internal affairs gradually increased.

Infringement of their traditional liberty and territorial integrity by Moscow embittered the Novgorodians. The old pro-Lithuanian party, under the leadership of the ancient noble family

Boretskii, gained strength and influence, and resumed negotiations with the Grand Duke of Lithuania for assistance in ridding Novgorod of Moscow's interference. Pro-Muscovite and pro-Lithuanian factions in Novgorod intensely fought each other.

Ivan III of Moscow, Vasilii's son, arranged a "holy war" to defend Russia and Orthodoxy "against the traitors" and invaded Novgorod in 1470. Novgorod yielded, paid a large indemnity, but still preserved its ancient autonomy by the agreement of 1471. Most of the leaders of the pro-Lithuanian party were executed. The Lithuanian Grand Duke, who had promised assistance, did not move to help the Novgorodians resist the Muscovite aggression.

The Novgorodians lived under the illusion that Moscow would stop at this point, and would not dare crush their accustomed way of life. But Muscovite demands increased, clearly aiming at the liquidation of traditional liberties. The popularity of pro-Lithuanian orientation widened. Ivan was waiting for this. He moved with a large army and besieged the city in 1477. Novgorod's defense was too weak, and the city yielded to Ivan's uncompromising demands.

The year 1478 marks the end of Novgorod's autonomous political existence. The city and its huge lands were to be governed as any other regions of the Muscovite Grand Duchy. The old constitution of the republic, its people's meeting, the Council of Nobles, the mayoralty and other elected offices were abolished. The bell, which called the people to meetings and was the symbol of traditional liberties in the city, was taken to Moscow. Unreliable Novgorodians, for example, the leaders of the pro-Lithuanian party, were deported.

Ivan III was determined to make Novgorod a part of Muscovy and to prevent rivalry within the city. Deportations of leading Novgorodian citizens, like Archbishop Theophilus and Martha Boretskii, continued for many years. In the years from 1484 to 1489 a large-scale resettlement project was carried out by Moscow. A large number of Novgorodian noble families was resettled on estates in service-tenure throughout Muscovy. Many Muscovite noble families, to whom Novgorod's traditions were alien and hostile, received landed estates in Novgorodian lands, also on service-tenure terms. In 1494, the German conclave, an important commercial center of Novgorod, was closed by the Muscovites and its merchandise confiscated. After its political autonomy was crushed, the mercantile greatness of Novgorod never recovered. Another page in the history of the Russian political prologue was turned and closed.[11]

The story of Novgorod the Great would not be complete without including some historical events around Pskov. Originally having been Novgorod's branch-town, *prigorod*, it developed later into a separate, autonomous and self-governing community. It become Novgorod's "junior" or sister-city with a similar constitutional structure. Initially, having been closely dependent upon the mother-city, Pskov shared all of Novgorod's fortunes and misfortunes. From earliest times, the branch-towns, *prigoroda*, with their territorial districts, *volosti*, have enjoyed some degree of local autonomy, Pskov, being a wealthier and more important branch-city due to its location, exhibited a stronger autonomous tendency than any other town. In the sixties of the thirteenth century it succeeded in separating itself to a great extent from Novgorod. A few decades later, Pskov had its own people's meeting and its own mayor and other elected officials. This gave rise to permanent frictions with Novgorod, until a treaty was concluded between the two cities in 1347, in which Pskov and its adjoining territory acquired Novgorod's recognition of their independence. Novgorod ceased interfering with Pskov's internal affairs and the latter became Novgorod's "junior sister-city" with a similar constitution.

Having freed itself from the influence of Novgorod, Pskov, territorially close to the Grand Duchy of Lithuania, was increasingly influenced by Lithuanian political affairs. Lithuanian backing and support, furthermore, enabled Pskov to show more resoluteness and more of an independent spirit in its dealings with the Grand Duchy of Vladimir, and, later on, with the Grand Duchy of Moscow, toward the preservation of its political autonomy.

Although the Pskovians were involved in dealings and warfare with Novgorod, Vladimir, Moscow, some Byeloruthenian territories, Lithuania, Sweden, the Germanic Knights and the Tartars, and although there were internal social frictions in Pskov, it seems that their political affairs were a little more peaceful than those of Novgorod the Great.

In the middle of the fifteenth century, the Muscovite Grand Dukes began to press more aggressively upon Pskov in their stated mission of "gathering all Russian lands." At first Moscow demanded that the Pskovians accept its representatives without any infringement of their autonomy. Internal dissensions and frictions among opposing political parties of the city helped Muscovite interference to grow. Finally, some two decades after Novgorod's self-government had been liquidated in 1510, the Pskovian autonomous status was crushed by Moscow's absolutism. The Pskovian "elders" were summoned to Novgorod and forced to accept Moscow's ultimatum. The people's meeting, and city's elected offices, including that of the mayor, were abolished. The bell, to call the people to meetings, was silenced. Pskov and its territories became an administrative unit of the Muscovite Grand Duchy. Soon a large-scale resettlement project was arranged. Many Pskovian nobles were settled throughout Muscovy and Muscovites were brought to Pskov, all having been given landed properties in their new homes on service-tenure terms set forth by the Grand Dukes of Muscovy. Another self-governing community was liquidated as an obstacle in the victorious path of the Muscovite Grand Dukes toward building an absolutist empire which was to come later.

Some historians have made the observation that in Novgorod actually a fourth Slavic nationality could have developed along with the Russians, Ukrainians, and Byeloruthenians, if that autonomous community had not been conquered, crushed and annexed by Muscovy in 1478. This seems a too far-fetched hypothesis for two obvious reasons. First, according to linguistic studies, the differentiation of the Eastern Slavs into future Russians, Ukrainians and Byeloruthenians was already established by the linguistic process as early as the seventh and eighth centuries. It began much earlier, most probably in the original settlements of the Slavs, before they were forced to expand their colonization to the Russian North-East.[12] Secondly, the ethnic and linguistic similarities existing between the Slovenians and the other pre-Russian tribes were made distinct from the very beginning. It was only natural, therefore, for these tribes to merge later into one Russian nationality. The conquest of Novgorod by Muscovy in the fifteenth century could not have had any impact upon this earlier evolution of an ethnic and linguistic differentiation.[13] Novgorod the Great, would it have had the power to withstand the Muscovite assault, could have developed into a second permanent but democratic Russian state, counterbalancing the ruthless and absolutist tendencies of Moscow.

Foreign Trade

Novgorod the Great occupied a very singular position in the medieval Russian North-East among other Russian lands and principalities, largely because of its commercial activities. Its developed trade deeply affected its social and political fortunes. No other Russian town of that time was able to match Novgorod's commercial status; its thriving trade and preoccupation with commerce made the city wealthy and famous. On the other hand, it also proved to be the source of its political weakness at a later stage of its development. First of all, the Novgorodian townsmen were poor soldiers. Clarkson quotes two instances. At one time, 5,000 Novgorodian militiamen on horseback were beaten by 200 Muscovite foot soldiers; at another time, a crowd of 40,000 townsmen on foot were beaten and slain by 4,500 Muscovite cavalrymen.[14] The Novgorodians, therefore, were always looking for a strong military protector, from the Grand Dukes of Kiev, of Vladimir, of Moscow or Lithuania. Secondly, Novgorod's wealth provoked the jealousy of stronger neighbors, who at one time or another were tempted to completely dominate the city. This was bound to bring trouble for the city. Furthermore, the commercial character of the city advanced its semi-democratic and semi-republican constitutional structure, making it too weak to oppose the military absolutism of Muscovy.

The trading radius of Novgorod at the peak of its development was vast, extending from the European West coast, far beyond the Urals in the East, and reaching the Caspian Sea in the South-East. Of course, the territorial coverage of that trade had changed during the centuries. At first, Novgorod was a market middleman more for North-South commercial currents, between Scandinavia and its possessions in the North, and Ukraine, Constantinople and the Near East in the South, including also the Volga water route and the Caspian Sea shores and some contacts with Central Asia. In particular after the fall of Kiev, Novgorod became a trade center for East-West commercial currents by waterways and overland routes. By waterway, through the Volkhov River, Lake Ladoga, Narva River, the Gulf of Finland and the Baltic Sea, Novgorod traded with the Island of Gotland and the towns of Danzig, Viborg, Abo, and Luebeck, in this way contacting Scandinavia, Germany, Flanders and even England. In its immediate neighborhood, the city maintained vital mercantile relations with Dorpat, Reval, Riga, Pskov and Narva. Along the distant north overland routes, Novgorod became a trade artery for the Russian North-East with its leading towns of Moscow, Tver, Riazan, Viatka, Luga and others. The ancient Volga-Caspian route, once a channel for the Arabian trade via Ityl and Bulgar, continued to connect Novgorod with Central Asia and the Caucasian lands. Its northern possessions for the purpose of foreign trade, contacted Novgorod the Great by overland expeditions, as well as by waterway through the Northern Dvina, Sukhona, Pechora and Onega Rivers.

Novgorod not only succeeded in capturing a key market position in the Russian North-East, but it also managed to establish market exclusivity or a monopoly for itself. Foreign merchants were confined to their settlements and could not indulge directly in retail trade in the city itself, or direct trade with other nationals or Russian merchants from other towns. Foreign ships were not admitted to the city, and all foreign imports had to be reloaded on Novgorodian vessels at a certain point on the Volkhov River.

Obviously, neither the foreign merchants, nor the Russian merchants from other regions, nor the Novgorodian princes and landed nobles, the *boyars*, liked these arrangements. As a result, continuous abuses, evasions, frictions, quarrels and court procedures marred the mercantile life of Novgorod the Great and hurt its economic interest. The confinement of foreign merchants to their *ghetto* settlement, for example, as Florinsky remarked, deprived the people of Novgorod of such legitimate earnings as renting of lodgings, warehousing and innkeeping. Some of the regulations were unreasonable in this respect and provoked numerous violations on the part of the foreigners and of the Novgorodians themselves.

In order to preserve to the utmost monopoly gains of the Novgorodian merchants in foreign trading, the legal status of foreigners was strictly circumscribed. Germans and other foreigners could not freely enter the city of Novgorod, but were confined to their national settlements. Gates were locked at certain hours and guards were stationed to enforce the rules. Mercantile transactions were carried out within certain definite time periods; imported merchandise was stored in prescribed warehouses.

On the other hand, Novgorod, as a member-city of the Hanseatic League, granted foreign merchants home rule — the status of an autonomous self-governing community, and made them exempt from the local jurisdiction of the prince, people's meeting, or other agencies or officials. The legal status of the majority of foreign merchants, the Germans, in Novgorod, was established in the book of statutes, called *Skra*, and regulated such matters as self-government, the judiciary, election of officers, penalty code, rights and terms of trade, including the use of currency and credit, and other problems. The *Skra* developed out of the trade agreements of the Novgorodians with the German merchants, going as far back as the middle of the twelfth century, while its first general adoption dates from the thirteenth century. Agreements with Swedish merchants from Visby on the Island of Gotland were concluded during the latter part of the twelfth century.[15]

German merchants were organized as a corporation or a guild, under the authority of an elected elderman, his council and the general meeting of the merchants. Crimes, abuses, violations and frictions among the members of the self-governing community were dealt with by the elderman and his court, while violations and grievances which involved the Germans and the Novgorodians were dealt with jointly by the elderman and local Novgorodian officials. The cases could have been appealed to the higher courts of the Hanseatic League in Gotland and Luebeck.

German merchants (or other foreigners) were not allowed to settle in Novgorod permanently, but only temporarily for the time needed to transact business. According to regulations, business transactions were supposed to be carried out on the basis of commodity or merchandise barter exchange. Currency and credit operations were prohibited, but this prohibition was frequently ignored. Foreigners were not allowed to deal commercially with other foreigners and serve as market middlemen or charge commisions for services rendered on Novgorod's territory. Only the Novgorodian merchants could serve as trade intermediaries.

Novgorod the Great was a large trading center, an advanced urban community of contemporary western style, like Visby, Luebeck, Danzig or Venice, and far ahead of the primitive feudal "towns" of the North-East of that time. It was involved in large-scale international commercial relations. The Novgorodians did not travel abroad and did not maintain any large seagoing maritime fleet. They confined themselves to the European North-East, operated cargo vessels on the Volkhov River, and did not go farther west than Gotland. The foreign merchants controlled the lucrative business of physically importing foreign-originated goods to the Russian territories. They exported Russian products abroad, denying a great deal of potential earnings to the

Novgorodians, who in turn did not admit foreigners into the Russian mercantile process.

Because of that traditional arrangement, the Novgorodians pushed for further annexations and penetrations of the North-Eastern regions beyond the Pechora River and the Ural Mountains in order to expand their trading radius and earning opportunities. They continually sent armed expeditions, subjugated primitive tribes and levied tributes, traded with them and sometimes plundered their settlements, constantly looking for furs as the most important Russian export of that time. At the same time, Novgorod jealously guarded its position as market middleman with respect to other Russian principalities and towns, attempting to keep in its exclusive hands the channeling of foreign-originated goods to those areas. Only at a later time, in the fourteenth and fifteenth centuries, Pskov, Polots, Vitebsk and Smolensk developed additional direct trade relations with foreign commercial centers. They never reached, however, the level of Novgorodian mercantile development.

The articles comprising Novgorod's foreign trade were numerous for those times. Its exports included all kinds of raw materials of the North-Eastern forest economy, especially furs, and valuable furs, above all: sable, beaver, mink, silver fox, ermine, marten, muskrat, bear, and fox. Also on the list were skins, wax, honey, and later on, timber. The products of the fishing industry were: fish and cod-liver oil, and produce of primitive North-Eastern agriculture included: hemp, flax and a few other products. All goods and commodities came either from Novgorod and its possessions or other distant regions of the Russian North-East.

Novgorod's imports were even more diversified. From the West, the city imported woolen materials, industrial products, iron, metal processing items, copper, tin, lead, gold, silver, linen fabrics, salt, wine, beer, herring, luxury items, as well as goods for mass consumption, sweets, needles, thread, and yarn. At first, grain was imported largely from Ukraine, but later on from Poland, and other countries as well. Grain and flour constituted a very necessary import since the Novgorodian economy could not produce enough food for its own consumption. As long as the

Mongols maintained indisputable control over East Europe, under conditions of the so-called *Pax Mongolica,* Novgorod imported considerably from the Orient, especially spices and fine fabrics.[16] All these items Novgorod imported either for its own use or for a large distribution throughout the Russian North-East, with the exception of grain, which it also purchased from other Russian regions. Novgorod's dependence upon the food supply from abroad (Ukraine, Poland) and from other Russian principalities was actually the primary reason for the ultimately fatal political outcome of events. It could not satisfactorily feed its growing urban population, and in order to get grain and flour, it continually had to appease the Grand Dukes of Vladimir and Moscow through whose territories the grain supplies were shipped. As a result, eventually Muscovy wiped out its independence.[17]

The City's Political and Social Structure

Constitutionally, as well as economically, Novgorod the Great presented an entirely different picture from the other North-Eastern regions. In prehistoric time, the ancient Slavs ruled themselves by means of two agencies, the people's meeting or *vieche* and the prince or *kniaz*. The office of the prince evolved out of the original tribal institution of the thousandler or *tysiatski* and the leader or *voyevoda,* the elected officials of the tribe. The people's meeting represented the democratic and self-governing element while the prince was the monarchistic and authoritarian element in ancient Slavic organized life. The conflict between these two constitutional elements, the democratic and monarchistic, developed very early and persisted for centuries with mixed results. In remote antiquity the people's meeting was without doubt predominant as long as the thousandler or the leader was the chief executive power in the tribe. Later on, because of the personal qualities, wealth or prestige of the leader, *voyevoda,* more authority was attributed to him. The leader began to assume the name or the title of prince, ruling over his entire tribe, while to some of his chief official and military commanders the name of *voyevoda* was given. Theoretically, the prince was still second to the *vieche*. Even the old Scandinavian princes were considered by the Norsemen to be hired leaders of their people. Among the Eastern Slavs, mostly under the impact of the prestige of the Rurik dynasty, the power of the prince began to outweigh that of the people's meeting. In the Ukrainian Rus', the balance of authority between the *vieche* and the *kniaz* was partially preserved, although the prince was the supreme authority who was not supposed to ignore the people's will. In the real growth cone of Russia, the Rostov-Suzdal and Vladimir principality, the democratic element of the *vieche* was soon completely wiped out, and unrestrained princely absolutism unquestionably took over, while in Novgorod the Great, the process was reversed. There the power of the prince was reduced to the position of a hired official of the urban community and the status of the *vieche* established as the supreme agency of the people's will, at least in theory. The constitutional evolution in Novgorod was different from that in most of the Russian North-East, having been dominated or influenced by constitutional development in Vladimir and, then, Moscow. In Novgorod the principle of semi-democratic self-government was victorious, while the principle of authoritarian or absolutist monarchism overpowered the rest of Russia.[18]

The *Primary Chronicle* singled out the event when the Slovenians invited the Varengian prince to rule over them. This soon changed under Kievan supremacy. There, the whole empire was considered largely as the *patrimonium,* family property of the Rurik house. The Grand Duke of Kiev usually appointed or delegated junior members of the House to rule various assigned territories or principalities, theoretically in the interest of the whole imperial *patrimonium*. The appointed person was quasi-sovereign over the region. He usually tolerated local people's meetings. These, however, had no decisive powers and were secondary constitutional institutions.

This constitutional structure prevailed in Novgorod the Great, as long as the Kievan supremacy was a factual one. The Novgorodian prince appointed at that time the city's mayor, *posadnik,* the thousandlers and other municipal officials, without asking the *vieche* for approval. Even with the decline of Kievan centralist power and increasing separatism in various territories and principalities, (Rostov-Suzdal-Vladimir's in particular), Novgorod still adhered for some time to its allegiance to the Kievan throne, having been dependent upon Ukrainian food supplies and looking for political support and protection in managing its domestic and foreign affairs. In the meantime, Novgorodian princes, the Kievan appointees, ruled but briefly and changed frequently like the Kievan throne, which often changed hands and showed signs of the Empire's disintegration. Princely power and authority and the authority of princely official appointees, mayors and thousandlers, gradually declined and the power of the Novgorodian people's meeting gradually increased.

Soon the Novgorodian *vieche*, began to elect the city's mayor, thousandlers and other municipal officials, who began to administer the urban affairs independently of the prince's will and authority. The first elected mayor assumed office in 1126, while in 1156 the people's meeting for the first time elected its own bishop, who only needed formal approval from the Kievan metropolitan. In this way the *vieche* acquired jurisdiction over the city's ecclesiastical and civic administration. Defending existing rights, and demanding or acquiring new rights, the people of Novgorod always referred to their ancient privileges and liberties, assumingly granted to them by a charter of Yaroslav the Wise, the Grand Duke of Kiev, from the eleventh century, the original of which has been lost.

The people's meeting at first pressed for official restrictions on princely authority, negotiating agreements with each new prince on taxes and tributes to be paid to his treasury. Later on, these financial stipulations extended over other affairs, especially after the expulsion of the Kievan viceroy in 1136. Having exercised some will of its own in electing a new prince, the *vieche* definitely placed itself over the prince, and gradually restricted his power, making him a constitutional monarch. By the middle of the thirteenth century the prince could not perform his judicial duties without the major's participation; his power to appoint provincial officials was limited, and he could not remove them at will without the *vieche's* approval. The sources of his income were circumscribed in detail and the scope of his economic activities strictly restricted; he could not trade directly with foreigners but only through a local middleman. His fishing, hunting and beehiving rights were limited, and he could not conduct direct business deals with natives of Novgorod conquered lands and regions of the North-East. The prince was housed in a castle outside the city limits.

Weakening the status and power of the prince was not only in the interest of the people of Novgorod, jealous of their liberties, but it might have been in the interest of Vladimir and Moscow, the two military protectors of the city and its realm. Both these political centers nursed plans for an eventual absorption of Novgorod the Great, its possesions and its trade. This was to have been more easily accomplished with a weak princely rule and an unruly and unwieldy *vieche*.

The people's meeting, although a supreme authority in Novgorod the Great, which frequently expelled the princes and elected new ones, was never a well-developed and matured institution. Its jurisdiction was indefinite and its procedures were not well established. It was basically a constitutional gathering of the free adult city population. Rarely and inadequately did it represent the population of the vast territories of that "republican" realm. Although in most cases the meetings were convened by the prince, the mayor or another high official by simply striking the meeting bell could call the meeting to convene. Yet many times private citizens initiated the "wildcat" *vieche* for this or other purpose in the same way. The jurisdiction of the people's meeting usually extended over legislation, leading administrative questions, sentencing for most serious crimes and offenses, foreign relations, and dealing with the prince. At a later date, the *vieche* became so independent that it acted upon matters which constitutionally were reserved for mutual decision of the prince, the mayor and the meeting.

There was no orderly procedure for *vieche* deliberations. Raw force, frequently a foreign one, and all-out fights among the opposing parties, decided the issues. Anarchistic elements were often present at these meetings, making them a very ineffective tool of rule. Another government agency developed in Novgorod, the Council of the Nobles or *boyars*.

Real political leadership and governmental power in Novgorod rested with the Council of Nobles (*Soviet Gaspod*), a relatively small body of fifty or more men of aristocratic origin from the city and its immediate possessions. With the archbishop as its chairman, and including municipal high officials, those in and out of office, the Novgorodian council was oligarchical rather than democratic. The Council originally included the prince and his retinue, but later on they were excluded from its scope to make it an autonomous ruling agency.

The jurisdiction of the Council was broad, indefinite and procedurally not well established as of the *vieche* itself. It was also an arena for political and personal strife. Theoretically speaking, it was subordinate to the people's meeting. Actually it was above it, functioning as an independent legislative and top administrative organ of the city and its realm. In most cases, and for all practical reasons (especially at a later date) the people's meeting was convened to give approval for the Council's plans and decisions. Sometimes the *vieche* was ignored by the Council.

The Novgorodian judicial system was well developed for its time. The prince, the mayor, the thousandlers and the archbishop held their own courts, each with different jurisdiction, for specific cases. The *vieche* also functioned as a court for serious offenses. In the higher courts there was a system of jurymen, ten in number, one noble and one commoner from each borough (*konets*) of the city. Penalties were mild, tortures were almost never applied and the death penalty rarely given.

Administratively, the city was divided into five boroughs or *kontsy*, each borough with its elder or *starosta* and its own *vieche*. It was subdivided into hundreds or *sotnii* and streets or *ulitsy*, the smallest administrative units each enjoyed a certain degree of autonomous self-government. Each city borough or quarter managed certain parts of landed possessions in the neighborhood of the city, the so-called *piatiny*, while distant and vast regions of the realm were managed by the city. For military purposes, the urban territory was subdivided into thousands, or regiments and hundreds, or companies with elected military leaders. The Novgorodian townsfolk were not warriors and this was the reason why the city always sought a military protector, at first the Kievan empire, and then the Rostov- Suzdal-Vladimir and Moscow Grand Duchies.

Novgorod the Great was a well-developed commercial community, wealthy and ambitious, and economically far ahead of other Russian territories. It also had a more complicated social structure. On top of the Novgorodian social stratification were the nobles or *boyars*. They owned landed estates, held the highest offices in service tenure, controlled money and banking, and enjoyed a privileged social and legal status over and above the other classes.[19] The second social stratum were the so-called "men of substance" or *zhitii liudi*. They were not of noble birth but owned landed estates and were engaged in commercial and financial (money and credit) business.

The third class, next to the men of substance, were the merchants of an upper level, an upper segment of the city populace. They were organized into guilds, operating the city's mercantile business activity, largely as agents of the nobles and men of substance, borrowing from them or using their financial resource. Their social and political position, for example, when participating in the people's meetings, was substantially weakened due to their financial and business dependence upon the two upper strata. The lower stratum of the Novgorodian townsfolk was the actual city proletariat, small tradesmen, craftsmen, artisans and workers for hire. They were without wealth and power, and without any political influence. They were used by the nobles and men of substance for their own political ends and interests.

Initially, the rural population of the Novgorodian realm was divided into two social strata: the free peasants with full property rights on land and with personal freedom, the so-called *smerdi*; and the slaves or bondsmen, without property rights and personal freedom, the so-called *kholopi*. Later, a third class evolved. This class kept its personal freedom, but lost its land properties and cultivated the soil as tenants so-called *polovniki,* the share-croppers. The land was owned by nobles or men of substance. Small and unique was the category of peasants, who owned land, combined into communal associations, and were personally free as well. They were jurisdictionally considered to be a segment of the urban population rather than a rural one, presumably because of their historical origins as small tradesmen or artisans who acquired land either for commercial purpose or as a supplementary means to make a living.

As time passed, the share-croppers gradually lost their personal freedom under pressure from the upper classmen, and eventually became a part of the unfree rural population.

There was no social justice in Novgorod, although the law theoretically proclaimed the equality of all citizens. The reduction of the social status of the peasantry, in particular, of the *polovniki,* was progressing even with greater energy in Novgorod than in other parts of the North-East. It was accomplished at the very time, as Florinsky noted, when the city increased the competence of its self-government by limiting the powers of the prince and extending those of the people's meeting to the point of becoming its supreme authority. The exploitation of the lower classes, abuses and injustices, were great under the oligarchic rule of the upper classmen. As a matter of fact, the political turmoil and social inequalities were used as a pretext by the Muscovite rulers in their ruthless project to conquer Novgorod, although conditions in their own Grand Duchy were not better in this respect under their absolutist system.

In north-eastern Europe there was little social justice at that time. There has been no doubt, that the abuses of mob rule, brute force and demagoguery at the people's meetings, contributed to the downfall of that self-governing community. Yet it had excellent qualities with great potentials for developing into a truly democratic Novgorodian society. Muscovite despotism, afraid of freedom, did not allow that to happen.[20]

CHAPTER FOUR

THE POLITICAL BEGINNINGS

The Rostov-Suzdal and Vladimir Principality: Its Beginnings

The ancient town of Rostov, located in the Volga-Oka and Klazma river basin, was far away from the commercial, political and cultural centers of Eastern Europe — the cities of Novgorod the Great, Kiev, Bulgar and Ityl. Perhaps, the geographical factor of Rostov's location in a commercially strategic site between the centers resulted in its gaining greater historical importance sooner than any other settlement in that area. There the ethnic process of mixing Slavic and Ugro-Finnic elements into the new and distinct ethnic alloy of the future, a Russian nationality, continued for a couple of centuries. Then, Rostov became a kind of comercial station, through which traffic was moving in all directions: to Novgorod, capital of the Slovenians and the center for the western trade of the Russian North-East, to Bulgar, capital of the land of the Volga Bulgars, and to Ityl, capital of the land of the Khazars, both on the banks of the Volga River, and centers for the commercial intercourses of East Europe with the vast lands of Asia, and finally, Kiev, the capital of the land of the Polyanians and the center of the cultural and commercial ties of Ukraine with Byzantium and the Near East. The significance of Rostov's location in the growth of the principality may be historically substantiated by the fact that the city had been sited in the immediate neighborhood of the prehistoric centers of the ancient *Fatianovo culture*. The instance may prove the relevance of the central location of the Volga-Oka-Klazma river basin for the favorable evolutionary processes of the communities living there at different historical periods.[1]

The settlement-town or *gorodishche* of Rostov was first mentioned by the *Primary Chronicle* in the year 862. In that year, Rurik, after having settled himself in Novgorod the Great, proceeded to appoint his viceroys for various towns and regions, among them, Rostov. Its allegiance to Novgorod must have been from a much earlier era, however. Rurik's viceroy arrived in Rostov with a Varengian retinue to enforce its allegiance. The Norsemen were known there already in the seventh or eighth centuries as was pointed out before, from their commercial and adventurous exploits in the North-East.

Following Prince Oleh's (Oleg's) transfer of the capital of the young Rurik empire from Novgorod to Kiev, Rostov's allegiance to that southern capital followed somewhat automatically. Oleh, Ihor (Igor), and Sviatoslav, dukes of Kiev, continued a similar administrative scheme in ruling over their vast colonial possesions, by maintaining in all distant towns, including Rostov, their usually Varengian-Norse governors. With their prevailingly Varengian retinues, they enforced order and allegiance to Kiev. By the end of the tenth century, in the patrimonial structure of the Kievan realm, Rostov acquired the status of a semi-autonomous territory, ruled by a junior prince of the Rurik dynasty. According to the *Chronicle,* Volodymyr the Great, Duke of Kiev, put his sons in as viceroys. Prince Boris was to rule in Rostov, and prince Hlib, merely a child, to rule in Murom on the banks of the Moskva River, southeast of Rostov. Prince Hlib or Gleb, being a child, resided temporarily with his half brother, Boris, in the latter's capital. During the dynastic warfare after Volodymyr's death for the succession of the Kievan throne, both these viceroys of the northern territories of the realm were assassinated in 1015.

The territorial expansion of the vast and multinational Kievan state of the Ukrainian-Norse (Varengian) origin continued in the north-east after Oleh's reign, where later on the Rostov, Suzdal and Vladimir principality, already a Russian national state, had to take over. In 885 Oleh conquered the land of the Radimichians. The Kievan Duke Sviatoslav, in order to develop a strategic bridgehead of his planned attacks against the Volga Bulgars and Khazars, conquered the land of the Viatichians. Their land for a long time was in allegiance to Khazars and had suffered a "mild" oppression. The Kievan rule, however, was not very pleasant to the Viatichians, hence they revolted against Kiev at the first opportunity in order to rid themselves of their southern master. This happened immediately after Sviatoslav's death. In the years 964-968, Sviatoslav conquered the entire middle Volga area by defeating the Volga Bulgars and the Khazars, by taking their commercial centers, the cities of Bulgar, Sarkel and Ityl. At that time, almost all of East Europe was under the Kievan rule, but this was not for long.

In the course of the dynastic war, following Prince Sviatoslav's death, the centrifugal and separatist tendencies of the Viatichian and Bulgar middle Volga regions expressed themselves distinctly in their refusal to give allegiance to Kiev. Also the Byeloruthenian Radimichians gradually freed themselves from Kievan centralist power. Therefore the next Grand Duke of Kiev, Volodymyr the Great, campaigned extensively to bring the rebels back to allegiance and to recover the lost territories. He waged two wars against the Viatichians, in 981 and then in 982, after their renewed refusal to submit and to pay tribute. In 983, he defeated the Lithuanian tribe of the Yatvingians and recovered the city and the region of Polotsk. In 984, he brought back into the Kievan allegiance the land of the Radimichians. The expedition was led by *Voyevoda* Vuiefast, apparently a Norman. In 985, Volodymyr attempted to reconquer the middle Volga country of the Bulgars, who had recovered from the earlier Kievan military blow and refused to submit further. Volodymyr's commander of the Kievan armed forces, Dobrynia, after having appraised the wealth and power of the Volga Bulgars, induced the Duke to make peace with them rather than risk an uncertain military adventure. As a result, the middle Volga regions remained outside the political influence of the Kievan realm.

When Yaroslav the Wise, Grand Duke of Kiev, divided his empire among his sons, he established seniority rule in 1054, according to which the realm was to be ruled jointly by the Rurik dynasty. The eldest of the clan was to reign in Kiev, while the junior members of the family were to govern their territorial appanages, *udily*, temporarily. The common good of the whole realm was to be foremost for all princes of the house. With that constitutional set-up, Rostov and Pereyaslav, together with the entire Volga-Oka- and Klazma river basin, including the region of Bielooziero, were given to Prince Vsievolod. The lands of the Viatichians and Radimichians and the Murom region were given, along with other provinces of the realm, to Prince Sviatoslav, another of Yaroslav's sons. Having started with the oldest son, Iziaslav, and down the line, each member of the Rurik house received a part or parts of the patrimony of the princely family. Most probably Iziaslav, as the eldest and the one who was supposed to take his father's place among the Rurik clan, having received the Kievan throne, was also given Novgorod the Great and Pskov.[2]

Although at that time antagonism toward Kievan rule and the separatist tendencies of the Russian North-East in general, and of the Rostov-Suzdal regions, in particular, were strong, the dynastic ambitions of the members of the Rurik house still prevailed for the next hundred years. This did not permit the Russian territories to renounce their allegiance to Kiev. Moreover, the power of the Kievan empire was at its peak in the middle of the eleventh century, therefore any attempts at separation on the part of the North-East or Rostov only, or any other vassal land of the realm would have been crushed. At any rate, the southern Ukrainian intruders, who came from Kiev as members of the princely retinue, church or administration, were hated and despised in Rostov, Suzdal and other Northestern towns and provinces, as Shelukhin stated on the basis of old historical records.[3]

Vsievolod, prince of Rostov and Pereyaslavl, soon became involved in dynastic warfare among the members of the Rurik clan, and left his northern province to rule in Kiev. He apparently had no allegiance to Rostov. His son Volodymyr Monomakh, successor to Vsievolod's Rostov rights, was also more absorbed with the Kievan throne, although, as Kievan Grand Duke, he paid considerable attention to the northern borderlands of his vast realm. He built several castles and established a number of towns there for strategic reasons, including the city of Vladimir on the banks of the Klazma River. The city of Vladimir was soon to assume leadership in championing the cause of Russian independence and sovereignty, and then of Russian leadership in the East of Europe. Monomakh as Kievan ruler also visited Rostov, Suzdal and other northern centers on occasion, but was primarily concerned with the Ukrainian South and Kiev, for their defense against the permanent threat of the Cuman raids and invasions, which he successfully suppressed. Rostov, Suzdal and Murom in the Russian North participated but little in the dynastic strife of the Rurik house, which was mostly concerned with southern affairs, and not with the colonial borderlands of the North-East. Only a few shifts of ruling princes took place there. After Vsievolod's reign (1054-1076), Volodymyr Monomakh occupied Rostov's throne, at first only for two years. Then he went to Smolensk, Chernyhiv and Novhorod Siversky to rule there, and returned to his northern principality in 1094. Meanwhile, Prince Rostislav reigned in Rostov for some fifteen years rather uneventfully. Only the Slavic-Finnic assimilation process continued to go on there. The principality of Rostov remained under Monomakh's rule from 1094 until his death, although since 1113, he was also the Kievan suzerain.

Only once, in 1096, was Rostov drafted into the dynastic strife. In that year, Prince Oleh (Oleg) of Chernyhiv, Ukraine, in the course of those clannish warfares, attempted to capture Rostov, Suzdal, and then, Murom. Having been persecuted by the armed forces of prince Mstislav, the powerful Kievan viceroy of Novgorod the Great, Prince Oleh finally withdrew to Riazan, gave up fighting, and accepted the compromise with the senior princes of the dynasty.

With Volodymyr Monomakh's death in 1125 the Kievan empire began to disintegrate rapidly. Rostov and other northeastern principalities and lands were now able to sustain their separatist and autonomous ambitions. Kiev had no power to enforce its will upon these borderlands. Furthermore, Kiev's declining power also diminished respect for the Kievan throne and desires of individual princes to possess it. From that time on, they cared more for their own patrimonial principalities (appanages), than for the welfare of the entire Kievan-Rus' realm, as was intended by Yaroslav's testament in 1054.

Laying the Foundations: Yurii I, Dolgorukii

The Rostov-Suzdal principality was inherited and actually taken over by Prince Yurii (George) I, called Dolgorukii (the Long Arm), who ruled there from 1120-1157. He was more intensely interested in his northern lands and possessions than were his father and grandfather, although he still paid some attention to Kiev, as was deemed by tradition. Differing from his predecessors, Yurii Dolgorukii considered Rostov and Suzdal the very basis of his power and his political moves and operations. Possession of the Kievan throne, he thought, could only add to his prestige. The era of Yurii I, Dolgorukii, represented in fact the very beginning of the Rostov-Suzdal principality as an independent political entity. The era of Kievan rule over the Russian northeast was definitely over.

The princes of Rostov, then of Suzdal and Vladimir, began to take care of their northern principality, the character of which was entirely different from their southern master. It was a forest borderland, ethnically Russian, with poor economic resources, severe climate, and disinterested in the dynastic strife in Kiev. The conditions for physical and political survival in the North were much more severe than in the south, hence the Rostov-Suzdal princes and all segments of the northern population were more interested in local problems. They became potentially egoistic and separatistic and largely disconcerned with the affairs of the multinational Kievan empire, of which, for a long time, they were only an ethnically alien, colonial possession.

Initially, as Platonov said: "The forests offered various kinds of employment, such as apiculture, tar distillation, bast and fiber gathering, and hunting. But neither agriculture nor the forest industries, as pursued there encouraged the growth of large cities, and for the most part the inhabitants lived in villages and hamlets."[4] In order to strengthen their lands, the princes of Rostov-

Suzdal promoted large scale colonization, built towns, castles, roads, highways, bridges and made other internal improvements. According to the old Kievan tradition, the princes owned their principalities, and especially the virgin lands where there were no settlers. The princes settled the newcomers there and provided them with protection. In return, the tenants on princely soil and forest land had the obligation of paying tribute and taxes to the princely treasury. This, Platonov continued, enormously strengthened the political position of the Suzdalian princes, who were not only constitutional sovereigns but landlords too. The settlers were greatly indebted to them and dependent upon them.[5] These conditions substantially fostered the growth of princely absolutism in Rostov-Suzdal lands and other northeastern territories, a virtually unknown form of government in other parts of the earlier Kievan realm. The countryside settlers were fully dependent upon the prince, either because of their contractual rent-lease obligations or because of the people's need to rely completely upon the prince's protection in their struggle for survival in these difficult forest borderlands, where even the assimilation process of the hostile Finnic native was not yet completed. On the other hand, the old towns of the North-East, such as Rostov, Suzdal, Yaroslavl, Bielooziero and Murom, were not sufficiently developed commercially or strong enough (in contrast to the mercantile centers of Novgorod and Kiev) to effectively oppose the prince by their people's meetings.

In order to establish themselves as the senior princes of the North-East, the princes of Rostov, Suzdal and then Vladimir promoted the industrial and commercial growth of their cities. They looked with envy upon the mercantile greatness of Novgorod and particularly, Kiev. On the other hand, Rostov had some tradition as a market middleman for East-West trade. Before long, the Rostov-Suzdalian rulers began to nurse plans for destroying both commercial metropolises, Novgorod in the west and Kiev in the south. They wanted to make the Volga-Oka-Klazma river basin the only center for East European commerce between the Occident and the Orient and between Europe and Asia. In doing so, those princes thought they would achieve two ends. First, after having destroyed the commercial wealth and significance of the hated rival cities, their political power would diminish as well. Second, after having concentrated East European trade in their own country they would increase their own wealth and they would build the basis for their own political leadership to replace Kiev as the center of the realm. Constant Cuman warfare and raids, harrassing the Kievan Ukraine to the utmost during the twelfth century, and especially during its latter part, fitted all too well into Rostov-Suzdalian plans since they gravely damaged Ukrainian commercial interests, although they alone could not knock out Kiev altogether. Hence, the Rostov-Suzdalian princes decided on their own to contribute actively to Kiev's eventual downfall.

In conclusion, it must be accepted that there already were several forces at work in the first half of the twelfth century, which have been responsible for separatism and growth, and later on, for the political leadership of the Rostov-Suzdal principality in the Russian North-East. First, the geography and topography of the Volga-Oka-Klazma basin as a borderland of an old realm forced it to concern itself with its own immediate needs and problem rather than with the welfare of all Rus'. Second, the Russian ethnic character of the European North-East was opposed to the Slavic Ukrainian South. Third, the commercial rivalry of the new center of Rostov-Suzdal was opposed to the old Kievan commercial metropolis. And fourth, the ambition of the despotic rulers of the North-East was opposed to the rather constitutional-monarchistic system of Kiev. They attempted to shift the center of East-European political power from that city to their own principality. The divergencies in their social and cultural processes also contributed to the conflict. This culminated in 1169 in the dramatic pillage of Kiev by prince Andrei Bogolubskii of Suzdal to end Kievan-Ukrainian sovereignty and to start the future Muscovite-Russian supremacy in East-Europe.

Yurii I, Dolgorukii planned to increase his power and to

expand his principality, and he thought that he should establish himself as a more absolute monarch. Therefore, in order to weaken the role of the people's meeting and the Council of Nobles in the old city of Rostov, and to make himself constitutionally freer from any restrictions, he moved the capital of his principality from Rostov to the less important Suzdal, where the *vieche* initially had little importance.

After having strengthened his princely position, and also having increased the power and prestige of his principality, he moved ahead with his long-range plans for Kiev and willingly became involved in the continuous dynastic warfare. Several times he tried to dominate the Kievan throne, each time in alliance with the hordes of the Cumans, the traditional enemy of the Ukrainian South. This instance may have been indicative of his motives. His intention was not the defense of Kiev against a nomadic adversary like his father and grandfather and other princes of the Rurik clan had in mind, but an alliance with them to superimpose Suzdal over Kiev.

Yurii's first attempt, leading the allied Cuman hordes to occupy Kiev, came in 1149. A year later he actually seized the Kievan throne, but not for long. He was forced to leave the capital in a hurry, by the princes of the Ukrainian branch of the Rurik dynasty. In 1152, Yurii again tried his luck, aided by the Cumans, without much success. He had to surrender Kiev. A year later Yurii led a huge army against the old capital, assisted by Cuman armies "from all Cuman lands, extending from the Dnieper to the Volga river" the chronicler said. He did not even reach Kiev. After pillaging the Kiev and Pereyaslav regions, he finally withdrew.

Finally in 1155, Dolgorukii seized the Kievan throne and remained there for a while as the dynasty's senior prince. However, his presence was not appreciated. The Kievan population did not like the northern invader, nor did they like his Suzdalian aides and lieutenants, who were so different ethnically and psychologically and who had alien views and concepts. Their behavior was arrogant and insulting to the culturally superior Kievans. No wonder, therefore, that Yurii's sudden death in May 1157 provoked an outbreak of violence in Kiev and its vicinity. The houses and residences of the prince, his son and his Suzdalian lieutenants were pillaged and burned; the Suzdalians were abused and beaten.[6]

With the death of Yurii I, Dolgorukii, there came a definite break with tradition. His son, Andrei, was already a Suzdalian ruler *par excellence,* who was in no way interested in the Kievan-Ukrainian throne, other than its complete destruction, which he considered a stepping stone in the elevation of Suzdal and Vladimir. He was to end the project his father was either unable or unwilling to complete, being to some extent under the spell of the old Kievan splendor, and having, therefore, put his dynastic ambitions before the national interests of his Russian lands.

However, Yurii's other actions have shown that he was a Suzdalian rather than a Kievan patriot. He tried and succeeded in getting Novgorod the Great out of Kievan control, and drawing the city into the Rostov-Suzdal orbit of political influence. By intrigues and extortion, he forced the Novgorodians to accept his sons as princes of the northern metropolis. Later he involved the city in several political conflicts and strifes, intending to undermine its political autonomy and to subordinate its foreign trading to the long run economic and political interests of the Suzdalians.

Prince Yurii, planning to acquire the position of a capital of east Europe for Rostov-Suzdal and to concentrate there the Occident-Orient trade, waged a war against the Kama Bulgars in 1120. By doing this he could free the routes for eastern commerce via the Volga-Kama watershed toward the Caspian Sea.

Yurii I, Dolgorukii has established himself in the early period of Russian history (the so-called Pre-Muscovite era), as the ruler who began to lay the foundations for the construction of a future empire. His political legacy was taken over and forcefully continued by his able successors, Andrei I, Bogoliubskii (1157-1174) and Vsievolod III, the Big Nest (1176-1212).

*Political Growth: Andrei I, Bogoliubskii
and Vsievolod III, the Big Nest*

Prince Andrei (Andrew) was trained by his father to attend the iron hand of a despot, even though he was involved in Volga region and became a true Suzdalian. Because of this the Ukrainian South with all its dynastic strife was alien to him, a different and unpleasant world to which he was not accustomed. During his father's lifetime he received as a junior prince the city Vladimir on Klazma, and he ruled there with the iron hand of a despot, even though he was involved in conflicts with the local people's meeting and Council of Nobles. He soon established his absolute princely position and began to nurse plans for future expansionism.

During Yurii's quest for Kiev, 1149-1157, Andrei was compelled to go south. At that time he clearly showed his hostile attitude toward the Ukrainians and the Ukrainian branch of the Rurik house. He was deeply despised by them as well. In 1154, Yurii made him prince of Vyshhorod, a city in the vicinity of Kiev. Andrei could not stand the conditions there and soon left the place secretly, without his father's knowledge, and went back to Vladimir on Klazma. He took with him a few treasured holy pictures, *icons,* including the picture of the Holy Mother which was later greatly revered in all Russia.

After Yurii's death, Rostov and Suzdal asked Andrei to become their prince. He immediately assumed his father's throne and began to realize his political ambitions. First, he forced his brothers and nephews out of their junior principalities in various parts of the Russian North-East, and got rid of the powerful *boyar* nobles, who previously served his princely rivals in various cities and who could have threatened his unification measures in building an absolutist princedom. Second, in order to avoid the unpleasant opposition of a strong people's meeting and Council of Nobles in Suzdal, (which meanwhile, during Yurii's struggle for the Kievan throne, had grown in importance and power,) Andrei followed his father's example by transferring the capital of his principality from

Suzdal to Vladimir, his original princely seat. The institutions of people's rule were practically nonexistent there. He went further and built himself a residence in the newly established township of Bogoliubovo, in the vicinity of Vladimir to keep away from the populace. That is how he got his surname Bogoliubskii. He still viewed Vladimir as the capital of his lands and he invested much effort in raising its splendor. Since the capital of the Volga-Oka-and Klazma river shed country had been moved several times (from Rostov to Suzdal to Vladimir), the historical-political name of it, as a result, has been the Rostov-Suzdal and Vladimir principality.

The political blueprint for Vladimir's expansion, set up by Yurii Dolgorukii, was faithfully followed by Andrei, who dreamed of its greatness and "senior" position among the Russian cities, paraphrasing and changing the old myth of Kiev. Having suppressed democratic institutions in his lands and having established himself as an autocrat, he decided to destroy Kiev and to knock out its power for several reasons. First, Andrei intended to ruin Kiev so severely that it would lose any attraction as a "senior" city of the realm. In this way he would elevate Vladimir as its political successor because of the latter's factual power. Andrei's later action in 1169 proved that to be his original intention. Second, Kiev's ruin would force its flourishing trade to disappear and East-European commerce would necessarily establish its center in politically safe Vladimir. The prince thought, of course, he would be helpful in relocating that trade center. Thirdly, damaging Kiev's power and prestige would eliminate it as Vladimir's rival and as a contender with respect to political supremacy over Novgorod the Great. This domination seemed to Yurii and Andrei to be a necessary prerequisite for strengthening Vladimir's position in developing the Occident-Orient commerce, Novgorod being somewhat a "window to Europe." The Kievan and Novgorodian questions were linked inseparably in Andrei's mind. Finally, the fourth reason for Andrei's animosity to Kiev was, of course, anchored in its Ukrainian ethnic character as opposed to Vladimir's Russian one.

To carry out these motives and without any historically clear *casus belli*, Andrei sent his armies under his son's command against Kiev at the beginning of 1169. Some princes of the Ukrainian and Byeloruthenian branches joined the Suzdalians in the siege, and eventual conquest, pillaging and looting the old city of Kiev. The *Chronicle* stated that such merciless destruction and looting had never been witnessed before.[7] For many decades many contenders to the Kievan throne fought for the city, conquered or left it. However, they had rather intended to preserve its splendor. Andrei meant to destroy it once and for all. Andrei's invasion and pillaging left a permanent scar; Kiev never recovered. The era of Russian supremacy had begun in East Europe. From that time on Andrei considered himself to be the senior prince in the Rurik dynasty, with his capital in Vladimir on the Klazma in the Russian North-East. In that self-styled capacity of "Grand Duke," he began to dispose of Kiev and other Ukrainian towns and principalities as his vassal possessions. He placed his candidates as junior princes there or ordered them out at will, and he continued to interfere in Ukrainian affairs from his northern Russian capital, causing more chaos, confusion and dynastic strife. He invited Cumans raids which aimed at the further weakening of Kiev. Andrei's sudden death in 1174 stopped Vladimir's interference in Kievan matters for a while. This lull lasted until his younger brother Vsievolod emerged from the Rostov-Suzdal-Vladimir dynastic wars as a victorious contender, and placed himself on the Vladimir's throne.

No less active was Andrei Bogoliubskii in the other, Novgorodian section of Vladimirian politics. Like his father, Prince Yurii, Andrei tried to force his sons and nephews on Novgorod as its princes. He clashed with Kievan princes, who did not want to give up their traditional seniority rights for placing their candidates on the Novgorodian princely throne. This rivalry without doubt contributed to the dramatic epilogue of the pillage of Kiev in 1169. In 1170, Andrei moved his armies on Novgorod in order to force it into complete submission, but he was repulsed. Later he used economic sanctions to enforce the city's allegiance.⁸ Novgorod's food supply, necessary for its survival, was dependent upon trade with other areas. By interrupting these supplies and threatening to bottleneck commerce, Andrei won the contest and the Novgorodians asked him to appoint a prince for them. They continued to do so, in this way acknowledging their loose allegiance to Vladimir, since Kiev's power was gone for all time.

Commerce and politics motivated Andrei's wars against the Kama Bulgars, who still made trouble despite Yurii's campaign to clear the middle Volga basin and to open wide the fur trade routes to the Urals.

In domestic affairs, Bogoliubskii acted as a benevolent despot. He fortified and enlarged the city of Vladimir and built fine stone churches to raise the capital's fame and prestige. He also tried to increase wealth and foster culture in his land. More than any other northeastern prince, Andrei wanted colonization of his lands. He built new villages, townships and towns, erected churches, doing whatever was possible to improve the economic potential of the Vladimir princedom. In his campaigns, especially in Ukraine, he looted and sacked cities, castles and churches, gathering pictures of saints (icons), ecclesiastical books, garments, vestments, bells, golden and silver vessels and other objects of value which belonged to foreign princes, and brought them home to enrich his northern capital both materially and culturally, at the expense of other lands.

In order to elevate his capital's prestige and to control ecclesiastical matters in the Russian North-East, he made a considerable effort to establish in Vladimir, apart from Kiev, a metropolitan province with its own metropolitan of the Orthodox Church. Although he failed in this respect, he nevertheless strengthened his power over the church, disciplining, appointing and dismissing bishops at will.⁹

Because of his autocratic methods and despotic leanings, Andrei was continually involved in strife with the nobles and the people's meeting. Blood was freely shed in these constitutional struggles. Some who profited through Andrei's protection, and also favored a strong and united land, admired and supported him, while others hated him deeply and did not miss any opportunity to try to get rid of him. Plots were organized and intrigues arranged with other princes, mostly initiated and sponsored by the *boyars* to remove the tyrant. Finally a *boyar* conspiracy resulted in the assassination of Andrei in June, 1174. The assassination provoked an outburst of hatred, giving rise to a massacre of his lieutenants and favorites and the pillaging and burning of their residences. The *boyars*, whose wealth and prestige were on the rise, thirsted for the restoration of their political influence.[10]

After Andrei's death, since none of his sons was alive, there was no immediate succession to the Vladimir throne. For two years a dynastic war raged among various princely pretenders, Andrei's brother and relatives for succession, and among the cities, Rostov, Suzdal and Vladimir, in particular, for supremacy in the North-East. Finally, Vsievolod III, the Big Nest (called because of his large family), emerged victoriously from the bloody struggle. He established himself at Vladimir, having secured the city's supremacy and the principality's unity for the next three and a half decades. His domestic and foreign politics were analogous to those of Andrei's and along the principles drawn by Yurii Dolgorukii.

In order to establish his supremacy over other Russian principalities and lands, Vsievolod III assumed the title of "Grand Duke," which claimed undisputed seniority rights. He really meant business as the Grand Duke of Vladimir, ruling in a despotic manner and ordering other princes from Riazan, Novgorod, Smolenski, Tver, and even the senior prince of Kiev, to obey his commands. Only with Vsievolod's consent could they ascend their princely thrones, or be deposed from their seats. The cases of Riazan and Novgorod are the most classical examples. The princes of Riazan at first were faithful followers of the Grand Duke: "They walked always in his will" said the *Chronicle*. In 1207, however, Vsievolod learned that some of them were enmeshed in intrigues and plotting against Vladimir's supremacy. He immediately reacted in an autocratic fashion by arresting and confining all members of the Riazan princely branch. He then placed his son there as a governor and appointed his own mayor for the town. When the people of Riazan refused to accept his son as viceroy and banished him, Vsievolod conquered the principality and annexed it. The city was burned to the ground. Townspeople, nobles, and the bishop were seized and then relocated throughout the Grand Duchy of Vladimir. It was perhaps the first case of genocide, so often to be repeated in the policies of the later Muscovite Grand Dukes and Russian Czars.

Vsievolod directed his attention to the developments in Novgorod the Great, which had desperately tried to save its autonomous self-government against the repeated assaults of its eastern neighbor. Novgorod allied itself with Smolensk and Chernyhiv to resist Suzdalian-Vladimirian pressure, but to no avail. Vsievolod used political and economic measures to force acceptance of the supremacy of the Grand Duke of Vladimir, and his appointees as Novgorodian princes, whose authority was *nota bene* very limited. Vsievolod did not dare to completely crush the city's autonomy. For the next hundred years a strange alliance between Novgorod and Vladimir continued. Within this framework Novgorod was often unfaithful and often tried to rid itself of Vladimir's "leadership." Vladimir continually tried to extend its protection over the self-governing city and to limit its cherished liberties.

Grand Duke Vsievolod III, although interested in Kievan and southern political affairs, never intended to visit there or to become militarily involved in Ukrainian dynastic warfare, as his father Yurii or his brother Andrei had done. He simply used political and diplomatic intrigues to stimulate and to intensify this warfare by setting one senior prince of the Ukrainian-Kievan branch against the other and by encouraging the Cumans to raid the Ukrainian provinces. He utilized the resulting chaos to enforce his grandducal will in Kiev, without openly placing in doubt the seniority rights of the Kievan dukes.[11] By this or other means Vsievolod's influence was widely felt.

Vsievolod also campaigned, in 1184-1186, against the stubborn Kama Bulgars. He followed the political blueprint of his predecessors, having the same reasons for expanding eastward trading, especially fur trading opportunities, to widen the avenues for contacts with Asia. The continuity of political and state building policies in the foreign and domestic sectors of the Rostov-Suzdal-Vladimir dukes was amazing, and extremely successful.

On the domestic scene, Vsievolod III continued to foster colonization, build towns, castles, fortresses and churches, suppress the noble opposition and make people's meetings almost nonexistent. He administered his lands very effectively.

Vsievolod's death ended a magnificent era of undivided authority in the Vladimir's Grand Duchy. A war of succession shattered the land and ended in breaking up the duchy into a number of appanage principalities. Vsievolod disliked his oldest son Constantine and gave Vladimir to Yurii (called the Second), who struggled against Constantine and other candidates, but who was not strong enough to dominate the political scene of the upper Volga region. Although he retained the Vladimirian grandducal title after Constantine's death, his actual power, however, had been greatly reduced, because his actual brothers, uncles and nephews succeeded in acquiring virtual independence of their principalities. Shortly, as Platonov characterized the situation: "The old clannish system of succession, with brother following brother and nephew succeeding uncle, was restored."[12]

The rule of Yurii II, which theoretically lasted from 1212 to 1238, did not belong to a glamorous period of Russian history. Princely quarrels and dynastic warfare continued, reducing the political power of the North-East, and this lack of unity was the major weakness of the Russian lands on the eve of the Mongol invasion. As a result, there was no strength to resist the impact of Batu's hordes, and the invasion swept over almost all of Russia, beginning some 250 years of Mongol rule over north-eastern Europe. Yurii II was killed resisting the invasion. Meanwhile, the political prestige of Vladimir declined and Moscow came into political prominence.

Other North-Eastern Principalities

After Yaroslav the Wise established the seniority principle and divided his realm into several territories or principalities among his sons, the kingdom continued to split further into ever smaller junior princely possessions as the Rurik clan multiplied. The struggle for the senior princely seat in Kiev ruined and weakened the country. Of course, Yaroslav had neither this strife nor the ruination of the whole land in mind. The situation considerably worsened, also, because of two developments. First, not all members of the Rurik clan had the opportunity of becoming Kievan senior dukes. Therefore, embitterment among some of them developed. Second, in the process of princely warfare for seniority, a new phenomenon appeared: the institution of the *izgoi*-princes had evolved. *Izgoi*-princes were princely orphans without lands, who were forced from the principalities of their fathers by ambitious and greedy relatives. The *izgois* tried to regain their lands at any price, causing ever-growing unrest and rising strife. Three older sons of Yaroslav, Vsievolod in particular, were largely responsible for the growing number of the princely *izgois*.[13] Finally, all important members of the Rurik house held a meeting in 1097 at Lubech (near Kiev), to relieve this awful political strain. The meeting at Lubech produced an important constitutional changes in the Kievan realm. It established the specific right of each branch of the Rurik clan to hold its patrimonial (appanage) lands. The meeting did not abrogate Yaroslav's seniority rule, but considerably weakened it.

Lubech did not essentially affect the principality of Rostov as such, which, at that time, enjoyed already a large degree of independence. It did stimulate the growth of the independent appanage idea among several sub-branches of the north-eastern branch of the Rurik clan, occupying various towns and regions of the Kievan realm. Throughout the twelfth century more or less autonomous principalities existed for a longer or shorter period in the North-East: Rostov, Suzdal, Vladimir, Tver, Riazan, Pereyaslavl, Yaroslavl, Bielooziero, Torzhok, Gorodets,

Murom, Kostroma, Kolomna, Pronsk, Kozelsk, Yuriev, Novgorod, Pskov, Viatka, Polotsk, Izborsk and others. This constitutional arrangement in the Russian North-East prevailed later on under Mongol supremacy during the thirteenth and fifteenth centuries, until they were all eventually liquidated and annexed by the Grand Duchy of Muscovy at the beginning of the sixteenth century.

The number of territorial boundaries, and the degree of political autonomy of the principalities were constantly changing, due to petty dynastic quarrels and fluctuations in power and authority, at first, of the Kievan and later of the Rostov-Suzdal and Vladimirian senior princes, and then, of the Grand Dukes. The Lubech agreement, largely the legal justification of the locally egoistic, centrifugal and separatist tendencies of those northern lands and principalities, was soon forgotten as an important event pertaining to the past of the Ukrainian South. In the Russian North-East raw force decided the issues of political fluctuations.

Soon after Yaroslav's death in 1054, there was an extension of the authority and power of the petty princes, which were then greatly reduced at the time of Andrei Bogoliubskii and Vsievolod III, because of the despotic ruthlessness of the two rulers. The princes of Riazan had made serious trouble for Yurii I, Dolgorukii, by delaying some of his actions in his quest for Kiev, associating themselves with Yurii's enemies and raiding the Suzdalian lands alone or together with the Novgorodians, such as in 1146 or later. Andrei also quarreled with Riazan, while Vsievolod cut the Riazan princes down to size by placing all of them under arrest. Their subjects from the city itself had been resettled into various regions of the grand duchy. Andrei, and especially Vsievolod, had increased their own authority to such a point that the petty princes of Riazan, Promsk, or Kostroma had "to walk in Vladimir's will," paraphrasing the chronicler's words. Both these grand dukes arranged punitive actions to bring their disobedient "viceroys" back into allegiance. Novgorod, constantly reprimanded and forced into obedience, was another example of the permanent constitutional upheavals in the Russian North-East.

After Vsievolod's death, the degree of political independence of the petty princely appendages rose rapidly. Dynastic quarrels and chaos intensified, because the central grandducal authority had faded away and the old clannish system of succession had been reintroduced. The princes and their lands were not equal either, smaller lands being dependent upon larger and junior or weaker princes being dependent upon stronger or abler princely personalities. Their main political interest was concentrated exclusively in the ethnically and nationally Russian North-East, while any ties with the Ukrainian South were forgotten as being too distant territorially and too alien ethnically.[14]

CHAPTER FIVE

THE WAY OF LIFE IN THE NORTH-EAST

The Government

Originally, the Volga-Oka-Klazma river shed basin, with its capital, the city of Rostov, was a province or principality within the patrimonial Kievan-Rus' realm of the Rurik house. Various historians have viewed the constitution of the realm differently, focusing their attention on assorted aspects or different stages of its evolution. Soloviov believed that the Kievan realm was a clan community of the Rurik dynasty with an hereditary character, more of the civil law, than a political body of public law. Kostomarov stressed its rather constitutional character in the sense of public law, as a state federation of a number of individual territorial political entities, of which the Rostov-Suzdal territory was one, along with Novgorod and Pskov. But he did not deny that the ruling dynasty considered the entire realm as exclusive property of the family. The private law characteristics of the Kievan state as a patrimonial commonwealth of the Rurik house, have also been stressed by Pogodin and Presniakov, while Kluchevsky has expressed a completely opposite view. He believed that the individual lands, including Rostov-Suzdal, were only administrative units of the realm, and that the individual princes were merely the deputies of Kiev. It was their sworn duty to preserve law and order.[1]

None of these interpretations are fully correct, since none have properly evaluated the constitutional changes during the historical process of the Kievan realm, continuing from the ninth to the thirteenth century. The patrimonial-commonwealth nature of the Rurik realm, owned by the clan and ruled centrally from Kiev by means of its viceroys who preserved law and order in various territories and colonial borderlands, (including the Rostov-Suzdal principality), was, perhaps, the constitutional structure of Kievan-Rus' until the death of Yaroslav the Wise in 1054. Thereafter, however, having retained the patrimonial characteristics of the property of the Rurik clan, the Kievan realm gradually became a federation. After the Lubech agreement in 1097, it soon developed into a confederation of nearly sovereign lands, where the primogeniture of succession to the throne, with some irregularities, prevailed.

Yurii Dolgorukii's Rostov-Suzdal principality was such a sovereign land within the Rurik confederation, while under Andrei Bogoliubskii and Vsievolod III, a new state of affairs slowly began to develop. Namely, the Rostov-Suzdal-Vladimir principality gradually assumed a suzerain position among the vassal lands and principalities of the Russian North-East and even other parts of Eastern Europe. After Vsievolod III assumed the title of Grand Duke, his Grand Duchy of Vladimir became a centrally ruled patrimonium of the Grand Duke and his Rurik family branch of descendants of Monomakh. It was administered by means of junior vassal princes as viceroys or lieutenants of the Grand Duke himself.

The Grand Duchy of Vladimir was similar to some extent to the old constitutional structure of the Kievan realm, prior to 1054, being centrally ruled (in the sense of Kluchevsky's interpretation) but with a much more intense, absolute and despotic power of the Grand Duke, which the senior princes of Kiev never had. Also, it had all the characteristics of political feudalism: a lord-vassal relationship, which had never prevailed in the Ukrainian South. The suzerain position of the Grand Duke of Vladimir, as in Western European political feudalism, had him hold supreme authority over his vassals, junior princes and boyars. This was already asserted by Andrei, as Vernadsky points out, while Vsievolod's suzerainty was acknowledged publicly by Riazan in 1180, also by Novgorod and other smaller principalities as well.[2] The vassal princes exerted their "feudal" authority over their subordinate *boyars*, and so on down the line, to the social level of the peasantry.

From the very early days of the assertion of Rurik's authority over the European East, the princely court was the center of administration of the land. As a result, a complete fusion of public administration with the administration of princely affairs followed. Initially, three constitutional elements: monarchy (the prince), oligarchy (the Council of Nobles), and democracy (the people's meeting), were present and visible in the Rostov-Suzdal-Vladimir principality. However, the democratic element was soon completely eliminated, the oligarchic greatly suppressed, leaving the monarchistic element fully victorious in the form of the absolute power of the Grand Duke. Vsievolod III, as a sovereign, apparently was ready to assume the title of "autocrat" or "Czar."

The prince or Grand Duke always a member of the Rurik clan, was the central authority. He was the chief justice, legislator, supreme commander of the military, and the chief executive, in his land. Especially in a later era, under Andrei and Vsievolod, there were no limits to grandducal authority. Lesser princes, still classified as senior and junior ones according to the old tradition, were grandducal subordinates and vassals, whether they resided in lesser towns and principalities or simply were grandducal lieutenants or officials. The old Kievan concept of all princes of the Rurik house being equal "grandchildren of the same grandfather" was largely lost in the Grand Duchy of Vladimir. The heraldic emblem of the Grand Dukes and the Grand Duchy was a lion, not a trident as once utilized in Kiev, indicating that it was another country and another nation.

The Council of Nobles, *boyarskaia duma*, the oligarchic element of government, was of ancient origin, with no set composition or competence. Its membership and power were exposed to wide variations. It was, of course, an advisory body. At first, in the most North-Eastern Russian regions, the prince, according to Slavic and Norse traditions, could not make any decisions of importance without consulting the Council of Nobles, although he was not really bound by its advice. The Council participated in legislation, international affairs, and the judiciary, by functioning at times, together with the prince, as a supreme court in matters of importance, like the murder of a grand *boyar* or high treason. In domestic administration, it could participate in levying new taxes. But in the Rostov-Suzdal principality the absolutist princes soon suppressed the meaning and significance of the council, and in most cases did not even bother to listen to its deliberations and advice. It almost ceased to exist under Andrei and Vsievolod. Florinsky gives this reason for the attitude of the Rostov-Suzdal rulers: "The princes of Rostov-Suzdal were 'frontiersmen'; they looked upon the domain they had built for themselves by the sweat of their brow as their private property, their patrimony, *otchina*, and felt they could dispose of it as they pleased."[3] Of course, the *boyars* did not like it at all and were deeply antagonized by the Grand Dukes. This precipitated a fierce power struggle between these two constitutional elements, the monarchistic and oligarchic, which culminated in the assassination of Andrei Bogoliubskii and the outburst of hatred against his lieutenants in 1174. During the rule of Vsievolod III, the full importance of the Council was not regained, but it certainly gained more authority later, when the country was again divided into several weak principalities.

The Council of Nobles functioned in two ways: as a plenary assembly and an inner circle of a princely "cabinet." The plenary assembly was called to session to discuss major state affairs, and it included the members of the princely retinue, the city and countryside *boyars* and some city elders, representatives of the commercial aristocracy. This plenary assembly of the *boyars* was called less frequently to meet and advise, and its members felt they had been discriminated against and neglected. On the other hand, the small body of a few members of the princely "cabinet" included only three, five or seven outstanding people, *muzhi perednie*, who were especially trusted by the prince and were permanently consulted even by such despots as Vsievolod III.[4]

The people's meeting, *vieche*, was a permanent institution

in every Slavic community in ancient times. Almost every village or a group of villages, township, town, city, or city borough had their own meetings, attended by all family heads and other male adults, to deliberate and decide the community's affairs. The people's meetings of capital cities, like Rostov, Suzdal, Pronsk or Pereyaslav, where the princes resided at first acquired a political significance along with their social or judicial responsibilities. Unanimity of decision was the rule of the *vieche,* where the minority had to accept the will of the majority. If there was no clear-cut majority, fighting among dissenting factions usually decided the issues. It was presided over by the mayor, chiliarch, or bishop.

The competence of the people's meeting extended over local administrative, legislatory and judiciary matters, while in the capital cities it also included advice to the prince in matters of importance. It even had a role in princely succession. In certain instances, various cities called princes, or ousted them. Nevertheless, in the Russian North-East, and in particular in the Rostov-Suzdal and Vladimir lands, that right was taken away from the cities and towns very early. Yurii, Andrei and Vsievolod moved their capitals from the cities where the people's meetings were strong, to the cities, where they were weak, in order to rid themselves of this embarrassing democratic institution. There they fully succeeded in establishing their autocracy, the foundation of a future empire. Only in Novgorod and Pskov did the institution survive much longer. The scope of the *vieche* varied in different regions, depending largely upon the personality and power of the prince.[5]

Vsievolod III, who largely eliminated the role of the people's meeting from the political life of his Grand Duchy, temporarily introduced, however, a constitutional novelty of people's representation. He invited to it the bishop, the abbots, priests, the urban and rural *boyars,* his court, the merchants, and perhaps even some peasants.[6] The move may be considered a prototype of the future landed council or *ziemskii sobor* of later Muscovy, first convened by Ivan IV (the Dread) either in 1550 or 1556.

The princely or grandducal court was the center of the country's administration. A number of princely officials, lieutenants and appointees performed various functions, such as financial, judicial, military, foreign relations, general office and court, and over-all administration management. There was a complete fusion of a strictly public and princely private administration process in the Rostov-Suzdal-Vladimir Grand Duchy, where the Grand Duke held absolute power and considered the state his private property.

The major-domo or *dvoretskii* was in charge of financial affairs and court administration; the chancellor or *piechatnik* ran the princely office; the judicial clerks or *tivuns* administered judiciary and general affairs, being partially involved in the central and partially in the provincial administrative schemes. For the purpose of maintaining peace and order in various towns and regions of the Grand Duchy, the Grand Duke appointed his viceroys or *posadniki* from the junior princes or from the *boyar* nobles. *Posadnik* meant an appointed one. It must be borne in mind also, that various communities, especially the urban ones, elected and appointed their own *posadniki*, whose position was that of mayors. Therefore, there were two kinds of *posadniki*.

The territorial administration was operated by officers, called chiliarchs or thousandlers, *tysiatskii*, centurions or hundrenders, *sotskii*, and decurions or teniors, *desiatnikii*. The origin of these offices was electoral, and very ancient, derived from the primitive decimal-type military organization of the old Slavs. The electoral and military character of these offices was largely lost. Eventually the offices were staffed by appointess of the provincial administration. Later, under the pressure of Vladimirian and Muscovite absolutism and changing conditions, these ancient offices became anachronistic and entirely disappeared. The last Muscovite Chiliarch Veliaminov, died in 1374 and his office was abolished. The elder or *starosta* was the elected officer of local communities, villages or individual borough of a city or town. These local communities called *mirs* formed the basic cells of administration, and were burdened with fiscal, criminal, civic and social responsibilities on a collective basis. The institution of the Russian *mir* survived in some form even to the communist revolution of 1917.[7]

The three major branches of the country's administration in the Vladimir Grand Duchy were finance, the judiciary and the military. In the field of finance, in the grand Duchy, there was a fusion of public and princely private fiscal matters. The sources of revenue were many, some regular, such as tribute and capitation, others irregular, such as booty and fines.

Booty and plunder constituted a considerable source of revenue, coming from the raids on the Finnic or Bulgar territories and the wars against Kiev, Novgorod and other lands and principalities. The pillage of Kiev was an outstanding example. This source of public revenue continued in importance throughout the Mongol era and later on, as well. Tribute and other direct taxes, indirect taxes, fees, fines and income from public estates (domains) constituted the revenue sources of the Grand Duchy.

The tribute at first was collected from conquered and subjugated peoples and regions. Later, it developed into a direct tax levy, called capitation, charged against each homestead in the non-farm regions, and against each tilling unit (plow) in the farming areas. In the course of further development, the capitation was collected from each "hearth," while the local communes, *mirs*, were largely responsible for meeting the tax obligation of all their members. The *boyars* and large cities were, by rule, exempt from the capitation levy. Small towns and townships paid a special town contribution, the financial burden of which was somewhat lighter than that of the general capitation.

The first princes traveled personally from October through April of each year to collect the capitation. Later, a tax collection system was developed with special tax officials, called *virniki*, doing the collecting. The capitation and the town contribution were paid mostly in produce, such as fur, skins, honey, wax, meat, fruit, or grain, and to a minor extent, in currency.

Another type of direct tax was the service obligation borne by the peasantry and townsfolk, who were bound to labor on public projects, such as building and maintenance of bridges, roads, castles, forts and city walls. The princes frequently attempted to abuse the customary obligation, forcing people to work on jobs not authorized by tradition. In a later period, the obligation extended so far as to compel the peasants to work a few days in the princely fields without any compensation. In general, the population tried to avoid and to evade these service obligations in various ways. Among the service obligations, was the duty to transport, feed and shelter the prince and his retinue on their journeys. This subsequently evolved into a new and separate form of burdensome taxation.

Business taxes and indirect excises were numerous. Among these were taxes on storehouses and storage services, market places and market operations, taverns, shipments across rivers, sales of salt, honey and other articles, portage and other mercantile functions, like weighing and measuring merchandise in the market places by public officials. Also prevalent were tolls and duties charged at the approaches to towns and cities, at the entrances to bridges and river crossings and for the use of ferries, boats and portages, all collected by special officials, the *mitniki*.

Another and a very considerable source of princely and public revenue were the various types of court fees and penalty charges, such as death money or compensations for thefts and damages, collected by court clerks. The death or blood money varied in amount according to the social status of the victim: for the murder or killing of a *boyar* – double money, *vira*; for a commoner – the regular amount, while for an unfree princely hearth-friend again a doubled death money was charged by the court. Court fees and charges, imposed for different reasons, were frequently abusive in percentage rates to the extent that in some cases, by filling the princely treasury, they were contributing to the pauperization of the people.

The public and princely domains also provided the necessary funds for public needs. The princely property included, first of all, large landed estates, which in most cases were well administered. On them, grain was produced and cattle, horses, hogs and sheep were raised. It may be interesting to note that a prince could own land in other principalities under the sovereignty of other princes. This could have indicated a slight differentiation between the concepts of strictly public affairs and the private property of the princes. Over-all, however, especially in the Russian North-East a fusion of public and princely matters prevailed as previously mentioned. By the same token, predominance of the patrimonial principle of the whole land being owned by the Rurik clan, fostered the absolutist trend in the Rostov-Suzdal principality.[8] The prince also owned certain "rights" such as mining, fishing, hunting, and bee raising, which constituted his exclusive privilege to derive revenue from them. In addition, the princes participated either secretly or openly in profitable commercial ventures, and sometimes attempted to establish monopolies.

Public expenditures included, first of all, the maintenance of the princely court, the princely retinue and the armed forces, particularly in times of national emergencies. Since the political life of the Rostov-Suzdal-Vladimir principality as a borderland was more militaristic than any of the other North-Eastern lands, maintenance of armed forces, including mercenaries, constituted a very considerable portion of the public expenditures.

The prince himself, his wife, adult children and other members of the family were usually assigned certain shares out of public revenue. Sometimes tributes from certain territories or contributions from certain towns were given to various members of the princely family for their sustenance or comfort.

A portion of public revenue was spent on the judicial system. Policing was inadequately financed by public funds and unsatisfactorally provided by the junior members of the princely retinue as a secondary function. Policing was also organized on a local, municipal or communal basis. The chiliarch or *thousandler* and his agents protected life and property in the urban areas, while local communes, *mirs*, were responsible for the apprehension of criminals.

Officials of general administration, the judiciary, the police, and the armed forces were compensated out of public funds, but in most cases they were given landed estates or hunting and fishing rights for their subsistence. Welfare, charities and assitance to the Orthodox Church were partially financed out of public revenues.[9]

Out of the primitive judiciary of the people's meeting of the ancient Slavs, with the passage of time a very complicated judicial system developed in the Russian North-East. The court of the people's meeting, initially responsible for all cases, later on, only considered heavy offenses: murder, manslaughter, robbery and high treason. Lesser crimes were tried by other courts, mostly the minor princely ones. These were presided over only by princely officials, the *posadnik* or the *tivun*. Even the princely court, presided over by the prince himself, during the early days of the formation of the Kievan realm, had still less significance than that of the *vieche*. However, the situation was changing rapidly because of the growing prestige of the Rurik house, particularly in the Russian North-East, because of its absolutist constitutional development as opposed to the more democratic Ukrainian South.

With the disappearance of the institution of the people's meeting in the Grand Duchy of Vladimir, that phase of the old Slavic judiciary also faded away. It remained only partially in the form of local communal court proceedings, competent for minor cases of property damages, field boundaries, thefts, and personal insults. They were held in the villages, towns and city boroughs, attended by community elders, and enforced by communal officials, the *starosta* and his assistants.

The princely judiciary developed gradually and became the only body for hearing and sentencing major crimes. Initially, the prince himself travelled throughout his land and held court proceedings in various places. Later on, with the increase of social complications and the growth of the state machine, the princely appointees, the lieutenants, *posadniki*, chiliarchs, *tysiatskii*, and clerks, *tivuni*, were entrusted to hold court proceedings in the prince's name. At first these appointees were sent into the field to hold the proceedings irregularly. Later they began to hold them on a permanent basis.

When the prince himself presided at the court, only then did it have supreme and appellate jurisdiction. Although the sentences passed by the princely appointees could not be appealed in principle, in some instances, especially the court clerks, *tivuni*, could be taken before the princely court for irregularities in judicial procedures headed by them.

The princely courts, along with being competent for major crimes and offenses, were the only courts having jurisdiction over sentencing *boyar* nobles and operated as appellate courts for the communal and manorial courts.

Only the princely courts were permitted to use the ordeals, *ordalia,* or God's judgments to prove by water and fire tests the innocence of the defendant. It meant that a person who could not swim was thrown into deep water, if he or she did not drown, then it was thought they were innocent. Or if the hand of the defendant, put into fire, did not get burned, then he or she was also assumed innocent. Witnesses to the case, deeds and documents certified by authorities, and even duels were later admitted into court procedures.

Manorial or domicial courts were held by the *boyar* nobles on their landed estates to provide peace and justice. Their jurisdiction extended over the rural population, the free peasants, the bonded tenants and the unfree, who either legally or economically were dependent upon their landed lords. At first, the jurisdiction of the manorial lords was limited to minor cases and offenses, and the rural population had the right to appeal to the princely courts. With the growth of bondage in the Russian North-East, the authority of the manorial courts was greatly extended, and the right to appeal dwindled. During the later Mongol period, the grandducal agents were not even allowed to interfere with the sentences and procedures of the manorial courts.

The fourth category of judiciary in the Grand Duchy, inherited from the time of the Kievan supremacy, were the Church courts, presided over by bishops, which extended their jurisdiction over the so-called church people: the priests, monks, nuns, townsfolk and peasants in the Church professions and the *miserable* people, such as widows, orphans, the blind, crippled or otherwise needy persons, including sinners. This class of people was exempt from regular princely or communal jurisdiction, hence there was no appeal to the prince's court from the sentences of the church or episcopal courts. In fact, at first the jurisdiction of the church courts was very broad, since it included all sinners as well. This included everybody who transgressed against church law. However, with the growth of princely authority, the extent of ecclesiastic jurisdiction also considerably dwindled. In general, within the competence of the church were divorces, separations, bigamy, heresy, apostasy, practicing magic, fortune-telling and inheritance questions.[10]

In the case of jurisdiction of the people's meeting courts, tradition, customs and prolonged practice were the bases for laws and administrative and procedural rules. In the princely courts, the will and the decision of the prince or Grand Duke established the laws and rules.

The famous *Rus'ka Pravda* or Ruthenian Truth, the old Kievan code of laws, a mixture of private, penalty and procedural legal regulations, presumably codified and given by prince Yaroslav the Wise to the people to live by, greatly contributed to the unification of the Ukrainian tribes and the formation of a Ukrainian nationality. It had little significance in the Russian North-East. Other legislation of the Kievan princes: the *uroky*, regulating financial matters, and *ustavy*, regulating the Church and other constitutional matters of a more fundamental nature, enacted by Volodymyr the Great and Yaroslav the Wise, and some later rulers, along with the Ruthenian Truth, had but little force and meaning in the Volga-Oka- and Klazma region.[11] Therefore, the will of the absolutist Grand Duke created laws in the Grand Duchy of Vladimir and through tradition they became a part of Russian social and political life.

Another and very significant branch of the country's administration in the Russian North-East was the organization of its defense by maintaining an armed force. The country's defense was originally based on two elements: the universal land militia, and the ancient Slavic retinue of Normanic origin. The universal land militia was mobilized for either major campaigns or an acute national emergency. Normally, every adult and able-bodied young male could be drafted, supplied with some weapon and horse and be expected to take part in the country's defense. Usually, however, the townsfolk were called to military duty, while horses and necessary supplies were requisitioned from the rural population. Only rarely did the free peasantry have to join the land militia, and when they did it was mostly to perform non-combat duties.

The princely retinue, *druzhina,* in the Kievan realm quickly became the center of the military organization and the core of its armed force. The power of individual princes was estimated according to the size, number and quality of their knightly retinue. Therefore, considerable sums from the public and princely-private revenues were used to increase and to maintain a high level of the retinue's military preparedness. The retinue always served in battle as a shock absorber of the enemy's primary charge. The outcome of the battles was dependent in most cases upon its tactical skills and maneuverability, as Vernadsky noted.

At first, the Varengian-Norse warriors were the retinuers of the prince. Later, the land's own *boyars* and other outstanding subjects, members of priestly families and the townsfolk, joined the retinues. Some foreigners also joined. The retinuers were personally dependent on the prince on a contractual basis. They pledged fidelity, obedience and service to the prince, while the prince had to provide them with protection and material subsistence (wages and board) if they remained in the court, or grant them landed estates and other privileges on a tenure of service basis. A number resided elsewhere and perhaps performed in addition some administrative, judicial or police functions. The outstanding retinuers, remaining in the princely court, constituted an inner council advising the prince or the Grand Duke.

Later, neither the retinue nor the universal land militia were of sufficient force to back up the political ambitions of the Vladimir Dukes. Therefore mercenary regiments were hired to increase the striking power of the Grand Duchy. When Yurii Dolgorukii struggled for the Kievan throne, he always personally led the mercenary and allied troops of the Cumans. Andrei Bogoliubskii also used mercenaries in his prolonged warfaring. The land militia participated not only in the dynastic wars and inter-city struggles in the years 1174-1176, but also in numerous other military encounters.

The cavalry was the main striking force in those days, while the infantry was only a subsidiary formation. Only later did it acquire a greater military signifiicance. A warrior's equipment included some defensive weapons, such as a helmet, a shield and a cuirass, and some offensive weapons, such as a sword, a spear and a bow and arrows. The army on the march was usually not followed by a large wagon-train of supplies, because the land it passed through had to maintain it, willingly or unwillingly. This was the unwritten law of war.[12]

Social Structure and Social Relations

Social differentiation in the Russian North-East, from the ninth to the thirteenth century, continued according to ancient Slavic and Finnic traditions. This meant the basic division of the human community into free and unfree people. The free stratum soon split into two: an upper and a lower class, according to wealth and family standards. Later, a half-free group of people evolved. This social stratification remained the very framework of social relations, which grew more elaborate and more complicated under the impact of Kievan liberalism, Christian charity and the developing absolutism of the Grand Dukes. However, the social structure of the Russian North-East, prior to the Mongol invasion, was not so rigidly locked in castes or classes as some other national communities were at that time, either in Europe or in Asia. Transitions from one class or stratum of the Rostov-Suzdal-Vladimir principality to another were not only possible but even frequent. The distinction between the upper classman and the slave was at tian charity softened rather harsh northern social relations and times blurred. At first, Kievan-Ukrainian liberalism and Christian charity softened rather harsh northern social relations and were responsible for the fluctuations among the upper and lower classes. Later, the indisputable despotic power of the Grand Dukes, who classified their subjects according to their usefulness to the state, disregarded social distinctions and differentiations. They elevated even the people from the lowest strata to high positions at court, in this way enabling them to join the upper class. Sometimes it took two or three generations to climb the social ladder, but this was not impossible.

The *boyars* were the upper, noble class of the Rostov-Suzdal-Vladimirian society. The origin of the *boyar* class was as highly diverse, as its composition was not homogeneous in respect to the social status of its membership at a later stage of evolution. Among the *boyar* aristocrats were the descendants of ancient Finnic upper classmen, and of ancient Slavic tribal chiefs and elders, clan chieftains and mercantile aristocrats, who through their wealth acquired prestige and higher social status. The princely Varengian-Norse retainers infiltrated the *boyar* class in large numbers. After they were assigned some high offices in the country's central and provincial administration, they were granted landed estates in service tenure and mingled with the old aristocratic stratum of the country's gentry. In addition, some able foreign adventurers, Ests, Karelians and Finns, Letts, Lithuanians and Germans, after having performed some outstanding military, administrative or mercantile service, were admitted to the *boyar* upper class. Able commoners could also rise to aristocratic status by the grace of the Grand Duke.

The *boyar* class was internally differentiated into several segments. The so-called *hearth-friends* of the prince, the members of his household and holders of the most elevated offices, were of the highest social rank. Oddly enough, however, the princely slaves, the *tivuni,* who also performed important administrative and judicial functions, were included among the *hearth-friends.* This circumstance helped to confuse and blur the social barriers between the nobles and the socially elevated slaves.

The rank of the *hearth-friends* was closely followed by the *grand boyars,* the wealthy, landed aristocracy, rather few in number. They were usually the main opponents of growing absolutist measures of the Grand Dukes and the representatives of *boyar* political interests and ambitions. The Vladimir princes did not hesitate to use violence and bloodshed to strengthen their own power at the expense of the rebellious *boyars*. The third noble stratum was the country *boyar* gentry, larger in number and less powerful than the grandees.

All members of the noble or upper class were endowed with personal freedom, full right to own property and inherit wealth. There was near equality among male and female beneficiaries. They also had freedom of economic pursuits and enjoyed an exemption from general direct taxation, such as the capitation tax and service obligations. They were protected by law against violence. Killing or injuring a nobleman was punished by fines or sentences twice as harsh as those for a commoner. The status of nobility was acquired either by birth or as a reward for faithful services to the prince or the Grand Duke and it was lost by conviction for a major crime, such as murder, manslaughter, robbery, desertion and treason.

The way of life and practical expediency created some social phenomena in the noble class, which had no legal bearing. For example, there was a distinction between the so-called senior *boyars*, who performed high-level administrative and judicial services for the prince, and the so-called junior *boyars* who were pages and servants at the court, and were traincd for more responsible duties later on. The *boyar* grandees resided in the countryside, accumulated fortunes, and even tried to imitate the princes of the Rurik house. They built castles and held their own retinues. Others were wealthier and more powerful than several junior and lesser princes of the ruling dynasty.[13]

The townspeople and the peasantry were, initially, the next two social strata, which constituted a sort of middle class of pre-Russian North-Eastern society. The towonspeople and the peasants, again, were internally differentiated into sub-groupings, the social barriers among which were unstable and fluctuating.

The European North-East was commercially and industrially rather poorly developed, with the exception of Novgorod and perhaps Pskov. The towns and cities were few in number, and small, hence the townspeople as a separate class was small and economically and politically weak. Even in Rostov and Suzdal, the townspeople were below the social status of those in Novgorod or Kiev. As a result, it was much easier for the Rostov-Suzdal-Vladimir and other North-Eastern princes to suppress the people's meetings, which essentially were the agencies of the townspeople. Moreover, large-scale urbanization efforts, the building of villages and towns and the bringing in of colonists from all over by the Suzdal-Vladimir Grand Dukes, Yurii, Andrei and Vsievolod, made the urban and rural populations in those new settlements dependent upon them for support and protection. This was another reason for the social and political weakness of the townspeople with respect to their princes or Grand Duke.

As a direct result of this colonization policy of the Grand Dukes, and because of the stormy historical past of the Volga-Oka-and Klazma watershed regions, the ethnic and racial composition of the townspeople was as heterogeneous as that of the nobility. The Ugro-Finns and their descendants, the Varengian-Norse elements, the Russian Slavs as the majority, the Ukrainians, Bulgars, Khazars and others populated the towns and cities of the Grand Duchy and the neighboring lands.

The townspeople comprised two major social groupings: a small segment of grand merchants, making up the stratum of the city aristocracy, and the majority of small merchants and artisans, making up the city lower class or proletariat. The city's mercantile grandees were actually the power behind the people's meeting institution in the larger cities, such as Rostov and Suzdal, which antagonized the Grand Dukes. In order to reduce their political influence, Yurii Dolgorukii transferred his capital from Rostov to Suzdal, and Andrei Bogoliubskii moved it from Suzdal to Vladimir and established his residence in Bogoliubovo. On the other hand, outstanding mercantile grandees could become the *hearth-friends* of the Grand Duke and then move up to the *boyar* nobility. Usually, the acquisition of large wealth enabled a city man to climb up the social ladder in medieval Russian society.

The townspeople at first enjoyed a great deal of communal autonomy, which included self-government by means of the *vieche* and some military and administrative duties, such as defense of the city or town, participation in the land militia, and collective responsibility in paying taxes and catching criminals. The towns and cities were divided into a number of boroughs according to local needs, and through these boroughs they fulfilled their responsibilities for defense and administration. However, with the growth of Vladimir absolutism, the autonomy of the urban communities quickly dwindled away and the *vieche* disappeared. Remaining duties were rigidly enforced by the princely officials.[14]

The rural population represented the vast majority of the entire population in the economically primitive Russian North-East. There were three social groups of the rural people: the free peasants, the half-free farm workers and the slaves. While the free peasants were something of a middle class, the half-free and the slaves were the lower classes. The "free" peasants were a traditional Slavic stratum under special protection of the prince. In remote Slavic pre-history, they probably enjoyed personal freedom and personal property rights, while farm land, forests and hunting and fishing rights were the possession of the clan. With the disintegration of the clan, the territorial community, the *mir*, assumed the collective ownership of lands, forests and rivers, while the male members of the commune might have had rights for their perpetual use. The possession and use of land was apparently related to fulfilling either the entire or partial military service obligation to defend the country. Since only males had military obligations in the land militia, only to them was the right to inherit given. The peasant, even by perpetual use of certain plots of communal land, was nevertheless restricted in gaining it, while females could never claim any right to land. Even among the *boyars* the right to own land was limited to the males.

In the course of time, the communal *mir's* ownership of lands, forests, pastures and rivers (having been anonymous to some extent) had been gradually taken over by the prince or Grand Duke, the only landlord according to the patrimonial doctrine of the Rurik clan. Therefore, Kluchevsky was correct when he stated, that there had been no full peasant property rights to land in the Kievan realm.[15] This was also the case in the Grand Duchy of Vladimir, where the Dukes had to mobilize all power at their disposal to fulfill their dream: a powerful state even under adverse conditions in the North-East.

Originally, as has been stated, peasants were politically full citizens, according to the old and liberal Kievan tradition, with rights and obligations for participation in the life of the village commune, with its self-governing and judicial functions. This included representation through the *vieche*, which engaged in collecting taxes, prosecuting criminals and rendering service obligations to the state and the prince.

The status of *peasant* was acquired by birth, by material and social elevation of the *half-free*, and by legal emancipation of a *slave*. The peasant could forfeit his social standing and become a slave as a consequence of a crime committed, indebtedness, bankruptcy, marriage with a slave or by way of a voluntary slavery contract. A contractual agreement could make a free peasant a half-free one.

However, these old "rights" of a peasant began to disappear very early among the northeastern Slavs. The princes of the Volga-Oka-Klazma watershed regions in particular, as "frontiers" rulers, had employed absolutist measures in strengthening the Northern Grand Duchy, and swiftly reduced the freedom of the peasantry, coercing it into building their state machine. By bringing in agricultural settlers and locating them in their possessions, the Grand Dukes made them their tenants. They tilled the soil, fished and hunted for the princes, soon becoming a soil-bound class, wholly dependent upon them and paying them rentals in produce and rendering other services. Similar colonization programs were sponsored by lesser princes of the ruling house, as well as by some grand *boyars*, who received latifundia estates in service tenure, and also by the Orthodox Church which was endowed with landed possessions by the princes and Grand Dukes. As a result, a class of soil-and-service-bound peasants gradually developed. The trend soon began to exercise an unbearable pressure upon the ancient stratum of the relatively free peasantry, since the princes, the nobles and the Church could not resist the temptation to reduce traditional peasant freedoms and to treat the peasants alike as fully soil-and-service bound, according to the new and more gainful precepts.

This over-all process toward general, peasant bondage was promoted to some extent by the old and well-known institution in the Kievan realm, of the half-free peasant or farm workers, the bought-ones, or *zakupi*. The half-free were the poor peasants, who had no land of their own on terms of perpetual-use, like the so-called free peasants did. They did not own even farm implements and tools. The bought-ones worked for others, on the soil of others, with supplied implements, as a sort of contractually hired or indentured farm laborers. This socially low class of landless people originated in the south of the Kievan state and was partially transplanted into the Volga-Oka regions. The half-free relationship was usually established on a contractual basis, with a distinct agreement of the peasant to remain personally free although materially dependent upon the masters, a free peasant, a *boyar*, a prince of the Church. The half-free did not participate in the self-government or the village commune, and were subject to the judicial authority of their masters. The master, on the other hand, also contractually accepted some obligations toward the half-free, such as furnishing them with working tools, food, some money and some personal property.

Since the Grand Dukes of Vladimir were interested in colonizing and cultivating all available land to support their political plans, they were probably inclined to turn the relatively small number of their half-free into the soil-tilling and soil-bound peasant tenants. The nobles and the Church followed their example. The trend helped, therefore, to gradually obliterate the institution of the half-free and to build up the soil-and-service-bound peasant class, which again, in its own way, was slowly absorbing the ancient stratum of the free peasantry. The process, which reduced the status of the free and the elevated to that of the half-free, moving the social position of the peasants toward the middle, was probably not completed until after the Mongol invasion.

The social status of the free peasant was not very high. A murder of a peasant was punished only by a fraction of the regular legal bloodmoney. It continuously decreased to the position of a soil-bound tenant-serf.

Already in the social-political framework of the Muscovite state, the conditions of peasant serfdom and bondage were growing ever more intolerable for the rural population until it hit the bottom of social degradation, turning most of the peasantry into near slaves.

The slaves, as a separate class of people with almost no rights and without any dignity, existed in the Russian-North-East during the Kievan era and later, although their number must have been relatively small, much smaller than in the Ukrainian South of the Kievan-Rus' realm. Prisoners of war were the oldest source of slaves; instead of being killed, they were made economically productive slave laborers, the social position of which at first was equal to that of draft animals. The master originally had complete authority over the life and death of his slave, while the common law took no interest in him at all; he had no legal personality and was not a member of the community. He could not own or possess anything. The slave had to work for his master, being fed, clothed and sheltered by him and treated like a piece of his property. Basically, the master was responsible for his slave's deeds, except in the case of murder. Later on, however, under the influence of Christianity, first as a result of moral teaching, and then, by reason of customs, and eventually by the evolution of legal concepts, the slave was treated more humanely. Although progressively new bases of slavery evolved, such as conviction for a crime, bankruptcy, indebtedness, marriage with a slave and being born a slave, Christianity had developed a number of new forms of slave emancipation or manumission. The master could be forced to free a slave on sufficient proof of cruelty; a prisoner of war could easily secure his freedom through ransom; a female slave received freedom if sexually abused by her master, or a non-free concubine and her children by her lord obtained freedom upon the latter's death.

The slaves, however, were also socially stratified. The stratum of the unfree princely *tivuni,* who served as administrators, tax collectors, manorial managers and other princely officials, was socially elevated. As princely or public officials, the *tivuni* were protected by a double bloodwite money against murder or manslaughter. Some of them were even *hearth-friends* of the prince, the instance which contributed to a permanent fluctuation of the social stratification, enabling a slave to become a *boyar*. Slave craftsmen and artisans who worked around the princely, noble or church manors, enjoyed better treatment than the common farm slave workers.[16]

Gradually, under the pressure of Christianity and agricultural needs, slavery disappeared in the Russian North East, but this was much later. The class of the soil-and service-bound peasantry absorbed the stratum of the slaves, having built a rather uniformly low social layer of rural population. The ethnic and racial composition of that rural population was highly diversified. The old stratum of the free peasants probably was prevailingly Slavic. Among the slaves, the conquered Finnic ethnic element probably prevailed at first. The imported farm settlers might have been Finnic, Bulgar, Ukrainian and other.

In the old Kievan-Rus' state a singular phenomenon of the church-people developed. This was a class of highly differentiated social elements, which for one reason or another, were exempt from the legal authority of the state and were fully subordinated to ecclesiastic administrative and judicial power. There were three subdivisions of the church-people: The clergy, both secular (white clergy) and manostic (black clergy), the people in the service of the Orthodox Church, and needy persons. The people in the service of the Church were of all social clements: *boyars,* townspeople, peasants and slaves. They either held church-owned landed estates in service tenure, or were tenants or soil-bound on these estates in the church-owned villages. They lived and traded in the church-owned towns, or were unfree laborers. The needy persons cared for by the church were the widows, the aged, the crippled and the orphans, as well as the *izgoii* – individuals who because of some unfavorable circumstance and extraordinary development had lost their previous social status. These included: the prince who lost his land, the priest's son who failed to become a priest himself, or a businessman who lost his business.

In the very liberal atmosphere of the Kievan realm, where the power of the state was progressively declining due to the continuous dynastic wars, the Church succeeded in acquiring a wide autonomy and an enormous authority. It developed into "a state within a state." Only the ecclesiastical courts of the Metropolitan and the bishops were competent to judge the church wards. However, in the Russian North-East, where the state was continuously growing in power, and instead of liberalism, the absolutism of the Grand Duke was taking over, the institution of the church-people and the autonomy of the Church itself never gained social and political significance as in the Ukrainian South. As a result, the class of the church-people soon disappeared.

Within the framework of the discussion of social relations in the Russian North-East and in the Volga-Oka-Klazma watershed, in particular, the position of foreigners residing there must be mentioned briefly. Even in Novgorod the Great, where foreign trading was well developed, foreigners were to some extent discriminated against and were forbidden to indulge in any domestic commercial activities.[17] On the other hand, in areas where the foreigners were less numerous and economically less significant, they were generally regarded with suspicion and were not trusted. Discrimination against them was intense. They were barred from engaging in domestic trading, settling permanently and owning landed estates. They were relegated to living in ghetto-like quarters if allowed to take temporary residence. If called upon to come as settlers to promote industrial and agricultural development of the northern lands, they were placed under the special care of the prince to protect them against possible hatred and excesses of the primitive native population, which never appreciated culturally superior foreigners. Chronicles relate the local antagonism of the Rostovians and the Suzdalians toward the Ukrainians brought to the Volga-Oka-Klazma regions by some princes.

The Varengian-Norse tradesmen and adventurers must have been considered in those remote times as rather "embarrassing" foreigners. Later on, they could scarcely be regarded as such. As part of the princely service they soon were Russianized and joined various social classes, in particular the *boyars* and the townspeople, of the North-Eastern national community.

The native and conquered Finnic populations were discriminated against. Extra tributes and contributions were required of the Finns. Their property was not respected; they were economically exploited, commercially cheated or exposed to direst robbery by the Slavic conqueror. Many of them were forced into slavery. Some Finnic tribes were exterminated and disappeared. Through a gradual assimilation process other tribes joined the Slavs and built the ethnic nucleus of the Russian nationality. The Lithuanians were also regarded as foreigners and treated accordingly. The tribe of the Goliads, whose settlements on the banks of the Ugra and Protva Rivers cut deeply into the regions dominated by the Russian Slavs, were forced to Russianize and assimilate, like most of the Finns.[18]

The Economic Process

The economic process in medieval society, based upon product specialization, was predetermined by its social structure and its social relations. After the social structure had been established, it began to deeply affect the economic process. According to the system of product specialization, the nobility defended and administered the country in the name of the ruler; the peasantry produced food and raw materials and the townspeople manufactured goods and provided for exchanging the food, the raw materials and the manufactured items between the areas of supply and demand, or of production and consumption.

The princes of the Rurik house, the nobility and the Church were economically important forces, since they owned most of the country's productive resources, the farm lands, forests, rivers and lakes, minerals, slaves and draft animals. At their initiative, all these were utilized in the economic process. These classes of people enjoyed the most freedom of action of all the population strata. They were thus able to promote production, exchange and distribution and to amass adequate capital funds for sponsoring, although slowly and gradually, the economic growth of the land. As wealthy "capitalists," the princes, *boyars,* the Church, and the grand merchants, supplied capital for all kinds of business ventures, and participated themselves, sometimes indirectly and secretly, and on other occasions directly and openly, on a partnership basis in various commercial propositions. These included the financing of the daring expeditions into distant Finnic territories for lucrative fur trading. They ran manorial farming and forestry, produced potash and tar, exploited iron pits and engaged in some foreign trading as well.

The peasants were the most important factor in the extractive economy of the Russian North-East. They were the main labor force. The peasants tilled the soil, raised some cattle, engaged in forestry, bee-raising, trapping and hunting small game, and fishing, thus being responsible for most of the production of national income. It was ironic that the economically most important and most productive peasant class during the age of extractive and farming pursuits was socially degraded and not appreciated.

The townspeople, on the other hand, performed a secondary

role in the underdeveloped economy of the Russian North-East, and contributed less to the growth of the nation than the nobility and peasantry. The town itself was commercially undeveloped and socially depressed, as well. The secondary position of the Russian town, with few exceptions, was no doubt one cause of the over-all economic retardation of the country.

Over-all, the national economy of the Russian North-East, in particular, of the Volga-Oka- and Klazma River basin, was poor, and far below the level of the economic development of other lands at that time, for example, of Ukraine, Greece or some West-European countries. In the virgin forests of the European Northern borderland, where organized human civilization was very much in its infancy, a rough struggle for survival was going on. From an economic standpoint, it was really a difficult fight, since those regions were poorly endowed by nature, with harsh climate, marshes, wild and inaccessible forests, with barely adequate arable land of only mediocre fertility for subsistence farming, and too vast and too distant an area for efficient trading.

A subsistence standard of living could barely be provided by those regions for the scanty population which settled there. Located great distances away from the cultural centers of Europe of that time and intermingling with the close-neighboring, backward Ugro-Finnic tribes, only made the way of life and the mode of production of the North-Eastern, pre-Russian tribes so much more primitive. This primitivism of simple business and economy only aggravated the problem of survival. This natural poverty of the country, combined with the backwardness of the population, resulted in a lack of any progress and perpetuated its primitivism.

For a very long time trapping, hunting, bee-raising and fishing in the more southern regions continued to be the leading pursuits, which supplied food and raw materials for survival. Their techniques, however, were inefficient and ineffective, due to the prevailing simplicity of the populace. Furs and hides were the chief commodities of the economy, and were used as trading articles or as materials for making clothing, for the winter in particular. Meat and fish were the basic diet, supplemented by some agricultural produce, such as grain, vegetables and fruit.

Setting traps and spreading nets and snares were traditional methods used by the common people for hunting. In time, they began to use knives, hatchets and spears with metallic ends, for a long time a scarce commodity in the North-East. Much later, the princes and *boyars,* using bows and arrows and swords, began to organize regular seasonal hunts, employing professional whips and falconers. This made hunting an economically gainful sport, a practice which originated in the Kievan South.

With the introduction of Christianity, fishing gained even a greater economic significance than before because of the severe Lenten and other abstinence regulations of the Orthodox Church. Fishermen, fishing in rivers, lakes and the sea to get food for themselves and their masters, (who owned the fishing rights,) and selling fish to others became, along with the hunters, respected tradesmen. The fishing tools were boats, nets, angling rods, and later, harpoons.

Hunting and fishing rights and privileges were protected by law and carefully guarded by the owners: the princes, nobles, the village collectives and the monasteries, a fact which proves the economic relevance of these two industries.

Farming was for a considerable time a secondary industry. Almost all work was done by unaided human hands because draft animals were used little. Implements were usually wooden and simple; fertilizing the soil by natural manure was completely unknown. Consequently, agricultural productivity was dependent solely upon land fertility, and this was very mediocre in the Volga-Oka- and Klazma basin. Due to the lack of roads and difficult access through forests and marshes, inefficient small farming, largely in the form of self-sufficing communal family house-holds prevailed. Crop rotation was unknown, and the two-or three-field system scarcely known or practiced, which considerably reduced soil productivity per plot of land. Production and consumption in the family households were carried out in a collecctive manner.

Furthermore, the agricultural poverty was greatly intensified by the patrimonial and semi-feudal forms of land ownership. The grand dukes, princes and nobles, as well as the Church, owned all the land and peasants were held in the position of tenants, either free or soil-bound ones. They were obliged to pay rental, to render various services and to bear the heaviest burden of public taxes. Three centuries or more later, this uncrystallized system finally developed into a general soil-bound, peasant serfdom, which contributed little to raising agricultural efficiency, while adding substantially to the rental and service burdens of the village population.[19]

Cattle raising was practiced on a very limited basis. The peasants did not breed horses, cows, hogs or goats to any extent. This was done, but on a small scale, if compared with the economically more progressive Ukrainian regions in the South, by the more efficiently managed farm economies, operated by the princes, nobles, and monastic houses or their officials. Horses were bred, but primarily for hunting and waging war, not for farm work. Manorial farming was a little more effectively and progressively run than peasant farming, since better methods were borrowed from the South. On the manors, iron implements, iron plows, hoes, harrows, shovels, forks, sickles and scythes were used much earlier as was the two-or three-field system applied sporadically to increase crop production. On the small peasant farms, as mentioned, wooden tools prevailed. Animal manure and animal draft labor came into practice sooner in the manorial economies, following the southern patterns. The Ukrainians, the princes, nobles, peasants and the religious, coming as immigrants or settlers from the Kievan South, brough with them updated farm techniques.

Rye, oats and barley were presumably among the leading crops. Vegetable and fruit rasing was literally unknown, except in some more southern regions of the North-East. However, some vegetables and fruits were consumed.

Handicrafts were backward as well, with little division of labor and specialization. In the countryside, clumsy jacks-of-all-trades, (farmers, fishermen, and trappers) also produced footwear, clothing, house utensils and primitive tools and implements, largely within the framework of the communal family household. A little industrial specialization existed in the town. But the towns and cities were few and small. Craftsmen were not organized and occupied a low social position. Therefore, the work efficiency of the craftsmen was low and could scarcely improve the low living standards of the people.[20] There were among the more or less specialized craftsmen: tanners, furriers, weavers, basket makers, wood-cutters, carpenters, fence-markers, blacksmiths, foundry workers, coppersmiths, tailors, hat makers and others. Some trades admitted women as well as men, although there was considerable discrimination between the sexes. Weaving, knitting and ceramics were the crafts for the females. The freemen as well as the half-free and slaves were engaged in crafts and trades.

The mining of iron, copper and silver, along with some metallurgy, and processing of metals, were primitive according to the standards of those times, and were conducted on a small scale and within the framework of small workshops. However, metallurgy was to some extent the foundation of the material culture of that era. The economy of the Russian North-East from the ninth to thirteenth century, where metallurgy was definitely inadequate, must be identified as an underdeveloped one, if compared with the Kievan Ukraine, Byzantinian Greece and Western Europe. However, since the political administration of the Grand Duchy of Vladimir was very much a militaristic one, it required a great deal of defensive and offensive arms and weapons and other heavy equipment, strong wagons and carts, the production of which could not go on without an ample supply of metals and efficient metallurgy. Hence, whatever could not be manufactured or obtained domestically had to be imported to support the war machines of the Grand Dukes.

Commerce was small in volume because of the lack of roads and poor transportation facilities which drastically hampered interregional and international exchange. Domestic trading was limited largely to the local town and surrounding country-side exchange of a few items only. The village supplied food and essential raw materials to the town, while the town gave the of that foreign trade was inadequate as a device toward increasvillage a few manufactured items. In many cases it was hard at that time to separate, in an economic sense, the village from the town, since in the village there were a few craftsmen of the jack-of-all-trades character, manufacturing various things, and in the town, the urban population, often along with its mercantile and handicraft activities, ran small farm operations to support its diet, as well. This instance reduced the need for commercial exchange even more. At a later period, however, the economic and social distinction between town and village became more pronounced.

The development of a substantial foreign trade to supplement shortages in the domestic market, although seriously attempted, did not reach desired levels for various reasons. First of all, lack of adequate roads and transportation facilities, as in the case of domestic trading, considerably hindered any growth of a large-scale foreign commerce and international exchange. Secondly, the princes and Grand Dukes favored imposing duties on imports and exports, as a convenient source of public revenue. They frequently applied even discriminatory duties and hurt what might have been of great economic importance to the emerging wealth of the nation. Thirdly, the primitive suspicion and dislike by the local population of the Russian North-East, of the more civilized foreign merchants and foreigners in general, did not favor prospects for international trade. Nevertheless, the peoples of Rostov, Suzdal and Vladimir and other Russian areas, engaged in foreign trade, and traditionally so, with the Finnic tribes, Volga Bulgars, Bashkirs, the tribes of southern Siberia, with Ukraine, and *via* Novgorod the Great, with Lithuania, Scandinavia and other lands. The principal articles exchanged in the limited foreign trade were furs, skins, some leather goods, lumber and other products of a forest economy, grain, salt, manufactured articles, products of the foreign metal-processing industries, fabrics and foodstuffs. Furthermore, transit trading was of considerable significance, involving grain shipments from Ukraine and lower Volga regions, and some luxuries. However, the volume

ing the wealth and the standards of living in the European North-East.

Moreover, the development of the Grand Duchy of Vladimir suffered because of the scanty population in relation to its vast territories. Consequently, there was a shortage of labor to cultivate virgin forest areas, and to develop crafts to any appreciable extent. The princes and Grand Dukes therefore, encouraged and supported colonization by the immigration of foreigners.

This colonization and settlement process, however, at times caused frictions which were harmful to economic development. Foreigners, disliked by the local population, were sometimes exposed to rough treatment and excesses. On the other hand, the immigrants, in order to protect themselves against the Slavic population, as well as against the Finns, who were not friendly either, preferred to rely fully upon the prince and gave him their complete fidelity and cooperation. By doing so, they became a stronghold of the growing absolutism of the Grand Dukes and other North-Eastern rulers. Thus, the early immigration and colonization in the Russian North-East contributed substantially to the development of the Russian absolutist constitution of later centuries, as mentioned above.

Moreover, the early absolutism of the Grand Dukes of Vladimir, having been of a militaristic nature, brought with it an increase in the financial burdens imposed upon the population due to war and defense expenditures. It also brought economic hardships due to the interruptions of regular business and farm processes. Both developments reduced the productivity of the national economy and impoverished the nation.

There were actually three ways available to overcome the poverty of the Russian North-East, in general, and of the Grand Duchy, in particular: internal rationalization of production technology of local industries, development of large-scale foreign trade to supplement the domestic economy, and eventually, conquest and plunder of wealthy neighbors. The inborn backwardness of the not yet ethnically crystallized Ugro-Finnic and Slavic elements did not favor rationalization at all, since rationalization required a certain degree of mental ingenuity and progressivism. Furthermore, as already noted, the discriminating social structure, exploitation of the soil-bound peasantry, unskilled craftsmanship, and great economic inequalities tended rather to perpetuate the backwardness and discouraged any initiative to rationalization. Therefore, little improvement of the economic situation could be expected from domestic progress in business. The limitations of foreign trading with respect to economic growth of the land have been briefly indicated.

As a result of the difficulties encountered in the peaceful development of their country because of meager natural resouces, the backwardness of the population and poor marketing, the absolutist rulers of Suzdal and Vladimir, backed by their huge (for that period) frontier armed forces, decided in favor of the third device for increasing their own and their subjects' wealth and prosperity, namely, the conquest and plunder of neighboring lands. The immediate objectives of the conquest and plunder were rather self-evident to the Grand Dukes: Kiev, Novgorod the Great, Volga Bulgars and distant Finnic territories, where either commercial wealth or natural resources were accumulated. These comprised the state of the economy and the economic policy of the Grand Duchy.[21]

At the end of this short analysis of the economic conditions of the Russian North-East, a final note on economic feudalism must be included. Earlier, Czarist historians paid little attention to the problem of feudalism in the Kievan realm and its individual lands, the Rostov-Suzdal- and Vladimir principality, in particular. This might have been caused by an inability to find convincing evidence of real traces of a true feudal order, Western style. Soviet historians, however, compelled to do all their historical research and interpretation in the light of the Marxist dialectical materialism, have been almost obsessed with the idea of a Russian feudalism. Having accepted a Marxist historical classification, they identified feudalism with any form of natural economy, and in that framework they have discussed the economy of the Russian North-East, and have designated its early era a feudal one.

Of course, the economy of the Rostov-Suzdal- and Vladimir principality was a natural one, *par excellence* with the extractive industries of trapping, hunting, fishing and farming, dominating the scene. In the Kievan-Ukrainian South, however, the peasants were largely free and there was no fusion of political and economic authority; the elements of feudalism could not be found. The situation seemed to be different in the Russian North-East, where the peasants were prevailingly soil-and-service bound. There was a socio-economic structural dependence of the lower social strata upon the upper ones, and of the latter-upon the suzerain, the Grand Duke. This had a distinctly political-constitutional flavor and so the elements of the feudal order had a strong expression there. This semi-feudal political and economic constitution became even more pronounced during the Mongol era and in the Muscovite state. Following Vernadsky's discussion of feudalism and the economic forces in the Kievan realm, it may be said, in conclusion, that in Kiev a kind of pre-capitalism prevailed, while in the Rostov-Suzdal an Vladimir principality, semi-feudalism was emerging.[22]

Cultural Life

The material civilization and the spiritual and intellectual culture of the Russian North-East was from the very beginning deeply permeated by the influences of the Ukrainian Kievan South, whose proximity to Greece and the Middle East and direct exposure to their Hellenistic cultural traditions, made the South much more civilized than the primitive North. As a matter of fact, Russia has been drawing from the rich Ukrainian culture for centuries, not only in the early Kievan era, when both Russia and Ukraine were living in the same political framework of the Kievan-Rus' realm of Ukrainian-Norse origin, but later on as well, when the political and national fortunes of both lands went separate historical ways, from the thirteenth to the eighteenth century. Of course, all segments of the cultural life of the Rostov-Suzdal- and Vladimir principality bore heavy imprints of Kievan civilization, in particular.

The whole culture of the North-East of that period, like that of Kiev, was deeply affected by Christianity and Christian thinking. Volodymyr the Great of Kiev introduced Christianity to his ethnically heterogeneous empire in 988, having received it by way of Greece and Bulgaria. This worthwhile undertaking, the Christianization of Rus' by Volodymyr, was by no means an easy task. Especially in the distant northern forest borderlands of his realm, where Russian Slavs and Finns lived a primitive, pagan life under the heavy influence of the *volkhvi*, the pagan priests of Finnic origin (of whom the Normans were afraid), Christianity made rather slow progress.[23] At times, force and violence were used by the princes to bring the people to the new religion and a faith in one God Almighty. At times the opposition of the pagan tribes was very intense and only destruction of old idols and places of worship, and bloodshed helped.

During the entire era of the Grand Duchy of Vladimir, in the Russian lands a kind of dual-belief, *dvoievieriie,* prevailed, which was a mixture of Christian and pagan religious, moral, and ritual elements. Meanwhile, in that early stage of religious development, Christianity was winning the contest, as a higher form of religion and also as an avenue for a superior civilization to penetrate the Russian lands.

The Christian religious cult, the Mass, the vespers and other devotions, holidays and sermons, together with the church law (canon law), greatly affected and regulated the way of life of the Russian Slavs, so much more, because Eastern Christianity did not use the Greek or Latin language, but utilized the old Slavonic tongue largely understood by the people. As a result, individual behavior and social customs and rules were "reformed" in a Christian sense. For instance, the treatment of slaves became more humane and several new forms of slave emancipation were developed. On the other hand, the psychological complex of the Slavic-Finnic ethnic alloy, evolving under the severe conditions of the North-Eastern frontiersland of Europe, became very formidable. It required a great deal of Christian effort to be modulated and moderated. In many instances, Christianization of the Rostovians, Suzdalians, Vladimirians, Riazanians and Kostromanians was highly superficial and shallow. They became Christians in form, rather than in substance.

Christian doctrine actually radiated from Kiev over the vast lands of the North-East. Since it was accepted from Constantinople rather than Rome, the entire East-European Christianity soon became decisively Orthodox. At first Catholicism there wasn't despised at all. The Catholics were in Novgorod, Smolensk and Pskov, and presumably in some other cities as well. From the Orient some manichaeist religious elements penetrated Eastern Orthodoxy at the early stage of the conversion process, but they were soon suppressed.[24]

Under the impact of Christianization, various segments of culture developed in the early Russian North-East: architecture, music, painting, writing, education, jurisprudence and others. Perhaps the development of architecture was the most striking and most impressive evidence of the cultural elevation that came with the introduction of Christianity. Early Russian architecture bore a heavy Byzantic imprint, alhough it also had considerable Romanesque, Georgian, Armenian and Oriental influences, the combination of which gave rise to a specific Russian architectural style. The churches were built with several onion-shaped cupolas, which made them different in this respect from the Byzantic and Ukrainian churches.

Probably the oldest church built in the Russian North was the Cathedral in Novgorod the Great (about 989). It had seven cupolas. In 1045, the Church of St. Sophia with six cupolas was also constructed in Novgorod. This followed Constantinople's and Kiev's example in which similar St. Sophia Churches were built as churches for a capital city. Architecture reached a very high level, and building was extremely energetic. During the last two centuries of Novgorod's independence some one hundred churches were built.

Numerous church constructions subsequently followed in various Russian cities and towns. The second half of the twelfth century and the early decades of the thirteenth century were the "Golden Age" of Suzdalian and Vladimirian architecture, promoted in particular by Andrei Bogoliubskii and Vsievolod III. Andrei, for example, invited builders from various lands: Germany, Greece, Ukraine, Georgia (Gruzia) and Armenia to build his beautiful churches. These included: the Cathedral of Mary's Assumption in Vladimir, 1158-1161, renovated by Vsievolod in 1194, and the Church of Mary's Intercession, near Bogoliubovo, 1165. Vsievolod built the St. Dimitrii Cathedral in Vladimir, in 1194-1197, and his son, – the St. George Cathedral in Yuriev-Polskii, in 1230-1234. It is a known, fact that the Roman Emperor Barbarossa sent his builders to Suzdal to assist Andrei in his architectural projects. Vsievolod also brought in architects from abroad. The peculiarly Suzdalian architectural style was later taken over by the Muscovite builders and became a Russian national style.

Andrei and Vsievolod and other princes to a lesser degree, constructed luxurious palaces, which gained the admiration of foreigners. Andrei's palace in Bogoliubovo consisted of a princely residence, cathedral, and several towers, all connected by arcades.[25]

There were no sculptures or statues, since they were considered a dangerous pagan tradition leading to idolatry. However, stone carvings and plastic ornamentation on the church and palace walls, picturing Christ, various saints, animals and birds, were quite common. *Icon* painting (pictures of saints) by Russian or immigrant painters was even encouraged by the Church authorities. The art of mosaics also began to develop at this time. However, only few examples survived from the old mural and *icon* paintings in pre-Invasion Russia. A complete evaluation of the extent of the development of art of that era has, therefore, not been possible. Later on, Novgorod in particular became famous for its *icon* painting.

The art of music developed again under various influences, being rather Eurasian than European in its character, as Trubetskoi stated, because of its many similarities with the Turkish, Bashkir, Tartar and other Asian music.[26] In this respect there is a striking difference from old Ukrainian music and singing, which was more European and less Asian in its nature. There was less Byzantic influence on old Russian music than on the other art forms such as architecture, painting or writing in the North. Of course, there were some Byzantic elements in old Russian Church music, which was originally most unisonal. The oldest Church song and hymn book from the eleventh century was produced in Novgorod the Great.

Old Russian music was closer to folklore, folk festivities and rituals. Reciting old sagas, *biliny,* about heroes and heroic events, accompanied by some instrumentation was a very popular form of folk art. Although it originated in Kiev, it actually survived only in the Russian North, where the environment was more favorable for that kind of folklore creativity. This was due to the slower pace of life and long winter evenings, as Spitsin noted, while in Ukraine the *biliny* were lost under the impact of subsequent and swift developments. Some sagas originated in the North-East, like those about "*Sadko, the Rich Merchant,*" and "*Vaska Buslaiev, the Adventurer,*" and were composed in Novgorod the Great. Cult and ritual songs about the seasons and the weather, economic cycles, social events — like weddings and funerals, religious songs and fairy tales — completed the range of this folk art. Theatrical creation did not develop separately as an art, because it was considered by the Church to be a pagan tradition, and was suppressed by church authority. Only along the lines of folklore festivities were some semi-stage performances occasionally produced.

Of course, the development of folklore was closely dependent upon the evolution of the language. The origin of the Russian language was Slavic and its separation from other Slavic tongues leading to its Great Russian identity has been placed in time by some linguists as early as the third century A.D. (still in its original Slavic settlements). M. Shakhmatov, and outstanding Russian linguist, in one of his celebrated works, *An Outline of the Ancient Period in the History of Russian Language,* admitted that the linguistic separation of the Eastern Slavs among the three language groups, the Russian, Ukrainian and Byeloruthenian, took place in the seventh and eighth centuries and was completed by the ninth century.[27] No doubt the distinct identity of the Russian language developed under the impact of Finnic and Norse language elements, since the Russian Slavic tribes were in contact with the Ugro-Finns and Norse warriors and adventurers very early in history and were influenced by them in various respects.

The Greek language also influenced the Russian to some degree, by way of Church teachings and Church books and the education of the upper class of the society, some of whom went to Constantinople for their schooling.

Books first came from Greece, Constantinople, and Bulgaria to the Kievan realm, and reached as far as Rostov and Suzdal. Under Greek influence, creative writing originated in the Russian North-East. The first books introduced there were from Kiev, brought by the princes, priests and nobles, and were written in the so-called Cyrillic alphabet. The books had originated in Bulgaria. They were Bibles, books of hymns and other works, largely translated from the Greek. Later on, some original creative writing developed in the culturally advanced Ukraine, such as life stories of various saints, journeys to the Holy Land, apocryphs or half-true and half-fictitious stories on biblical themes, early novels, poems, based on Byzantic and Oriental patterns, instructive legends and stories, chronicles and historical narratives, and also works on Christian faith and morals and human virtues. They were written partially in old Slavic and old Ukrainian, and were understood in the Volga-Oka-Klazma basin. They had been brought there from Kiev in various ways. A chronicler related, for instance, that Andrei's cohorts, after having pillaged Kiev in 1169, carried away books and other materials in order to launch a similar cultural development in the North.

In Novgorod the Great, the first original Russian literary works were created in the eleventh century. The city benefited greatly in this respect from its close contacts with Kiev and the West, drawing heavily from their cultural wealth. Early Novgorodian literature included the writings of the city's bishops and archbishops, such as Moisei and Vasilii, journeys and visits to the Hold Land, the *Novgorodian Chronicle* and Novgorodian *biliny* — sagas, manuscripts of the Holy Bible, like the *Ostromirovo Bible* of 1056-1057, and some other works. The writings which pertained to the city itself, like the chronicles, showed a great affection and attachment of the authors for the city. Novgorodian creative writing along with that coming from Ukraine provided the intellectual and cultural basis for the future Muscovite state and society in the Volga-Oka- and Klazma watershed region. These works were written in the Cyrillic alphabet on parchment, an intellectual luxury. The composition or copying of them required great effort, sometimes taking long years of tedious writing. Monasteries were largely the centers of book production and preservation, and only the clergy, members of the princely families, and upper classmen could enjoy the possession and use of the books.[28]

With the introduction of Christianity, education began to develop in the Russian lands. Yaroslav I, prince of Kiev, established a divinity school in about 1030 in Novgorod for 300 children. Prince Roman of Smolensk supposedly founded several schools in that city, on which he spent his entire fortune. Prince Constantine of Vladimir, Vsievolod's son, established a Greek and Slavic library collection and financed schools. In the late twelfth and thirteenth centuries, schools were already opened in many places, some on the elementary and others on higher levels. Religion, writing and reading, both in Slavonic and Greek, and mathematics were taught. Discipline in the schools was very strict. Some children, mostly boys, of the princely and noble families were sent to Greece for their education. Therefore, literacy among the upper classes was relatively high for that period. Most of the priests were literate, and the parish clergy was expected to assume the responsibility for running schools. The Russian North, which was considerably behind Kievan Rus', followed in her footsteps in advancing itself culturally. The small group of intellectuals of the pre-Invasion era read Homer, Plato, Aristotle and other Greek authors and philosophers.[29]

CHAPTER SIX

THE STRUGGLE FOR INDEPENDENCE

Ancient Ukraine

Having been of Slavic-Mongol, mixed ethnic origin, the Russian nationality was formed under the powerful impact of two political and cultural centers, the Kievan-Rus' realm and the Mongol-Tartar empire, which together predetermined the later development and growth of the Russian society and state. The Kievan-Rus' realm of Slavic-Ukrainian origin affected the early stage of the Russian national evolution giving it a Slavic imprint. Christianity and Christian civilization imparted European spiritual and intellectual trends and social structure. The Mongols subsequently taught the Russians tough discipline, the skill of empire building and the Oriental submision to authority. It is imperative, therefore, to learn of the historical past of the Kievan-Rus' realm and of the Mongol empire in order to understand historically, the spirit, character and the socio-political trends of the Russian nation and of its ingenious political creation — the Russian empire. Under the two foreign rules, Ukrainian Kiev and the Mongol Sarai, the Russians suffered much but learned a great deal as well.

The Kievan-Rus' realm, having politically dominated the Russian North-East, introduced the latter to the old European civilization. The prehistoric traces of human existence and life in the territory of Ukraine are much more ancient than those found and identified by archeological excavations in the Russian North-East. It follows, therefore, that organized forms of political life of ancient man inhabiting Ukraine were developed at a much earlier date than those in the North-Eastern borderlands of Europe, and in the Volga-Oka- and Klazma watershed regions in particular.

Near the end of the third millenium B.C., between the Neolithic and the Paleometallic ages, or during the Copper and Bronze Age, there existed in the Ukraine the so-called *Tripolian culture*. This culture reached a high level of development, as evidenced by ample archeological findings, such as tools, appliances, and especially their skillfully ornamented ceramics.

The ancient people who populated the southern Ukraine were politically organized. They were the Cimmerians of the Thracian ethnic group who came and settled there at the beginning of the first millenium B.C. The Thracian ethnic groups belonged to the Indo-European family of peoples. The first peoples of Ukraine to develop a higher civilization of transitional character in the Bronze and Iron stage, therefore, were of Indo-European origin. The Greek historian, Herodotus, wrote about the Cimmerians and their struggle against the invading Scythians around the year 700 B.C.[1]

The Scythians, probably of Iranian stock, retreated from their original settlements under the pressure of Eastern hordes from Asia, and dominated the Ukrainian areas for some 500 years. While the ruling Scythian horde was of Iranian extraction, other minor hordes, staying in Ukraine at that time, might well have been of Ugrian, Mongol and even Slavic origin. Vernadsky reinforces this in a discussion among scholars on the question of the ethnical character of the Scythians. He concludes that the names of the Scythian kings, mentioned by Herodotus and other authors, were definitely Iranian.

At the time the Scythians dominated the Ukrainian steppes the Greeks began to settle along the Northern shores of the Black Sea, and to develop their commercial centers of Tira at the mouth of the Dniester River, Olbia at the mouth of the Dnieper River and Kherson and Theodosia in the Crimean Peninsula. From there the Hellenic and Hellenistic cultures radiated powerfully over Ukraine and affected the psychology and the spiritual qualities of the future Ukrainian people.[2]

Around the year 200 B.C., the political and military power

of the Scythians declined and disintegrated. Another Iranian people, the Sarmatians, conquered and dominated most of the Ukrainian steppe regions and dwelt there until the first century A.D. They, in turn, were defeated by still another Iranian people, the Alans or Roxolanians, both similar to the Scythians and the Sarmatians in language and religious beliefs. They also dominated Ukraine. The Sarmatian way of life was characterized by the high family and social position of women. This, again, was a feature present in the later Ukrainians as opposed to the Russians. Both the Sarmatians and the Roxolanians were nomads who did not know any farming and lived by hunting, fishing, and raising cattle and horses. The influence of the Sarmatian and Roxolanian eras had considerable bearing on the history of Ukraine, which at times has been called *Sarmatia*. Its old name, *Rus'* had been deduced by some students of East Europe from the old Roxolanians and their land *Rox* or *Roxolania* in the vast Black Sea steppes.

During the first two centuries after Christ, numerous barbaric and nomadic tribes of the Besses, Kostrobes, Karpes and Bastarnes (Bastarnai) of Celtic, Germanic and other origins, invaded Ukraine but never stayed long. In the third century A.D. the Goths of Germanic origin came from the West and established a strong state on the banks of the Dnieper River with its capital of Danparstadt, perhaps the city of Kiev of the later date.

In the second century A.D., the Huns, mainly of Turkish and Mongolian extraction, started their pressure toward the West, having been forced out of their original settlements in Mongolia by a mighty Chinese offensive. In the fourth century, the Huns destroyed the Gothic state and dominated the Ukrainian territories, but also did not stay long before moving further West. In 453, with the death of the Hunnic leader Attila, the Hunnic menace dissipated.

According to more recent archeological and historical studies, the Slavs had firmly settled themselves in the sub-Carpathian regions and on the banks of the middle Dnieper River, by the first and second centuries after Christ. The bulk of the

Ukrainian population was of Indo-European and Arian stock, distantly related to the Tripolians, who at the end of the third millenium B.C. developed the famous *Tripolian culture* pastoral-agricultural in character in Ukraine. The Slavic tribes were also ethnically and linguistically related to the Cimmerians, Scythians, Sarmatians and Alans or Roxolanians, who in different eras populated the eastern and southern Ukrainian regions. According to archeological findings, therefore, from the third millenium on there had been some stability in the ethnical composition of Ukraine, predominantly of Indo-European stock, which was exposed to Hellenic and Iranian cultural influences. At the same time, the Russian North-East was predominantly Ugro-Finnic and more exposed to Siberian cultural influences. This established the most ancient differentiation in the ethnical and cultural background of the later Ukrainians and Russians.[3]

The rather short-lived Gothic or Hunnic rules left little imprint on the formation and ethnical composition of the population of the Ukraine. At the end of the fifth century, the Bulgars established their state on the banks of the Middle Volga River, while their other branch passed through Ukraine around 680, and then founded the state of Bulgaria in the Balkan Peninsula, the country which has been quickly and thoroughly Slavenized.

The end of the Hunnic period had a particular historical signifiicance: immediately thereafter the Slavs began their other migration and expanded their settlements over additional southern and eastern Ukrainian territories. By the sixth century the Slavic tribe or tribes, identified by the foreigners as the Antes, had organized a relatively strong political organization in the Ukraine. The legend of the three princely brothers, Kyi, Shchek and Khoryv, and their sister Lebed, having initiated the Kievan growth, might be reminiscent of the state of the Antes. In addition that political organization must have been the reason why the Bulgars only passed through Ukraine, and never stayed there, although her wealth and central location between the Orient and the Occident might have attracted them. The state organization of the Antes was rather advanced and strong, while territorially being strictly confined only to Ukraine and not including any "Russian" regions at all. The Hellenic cultural influences must have been rather considerable there.

In the eighth and ninth centuries some Ukrainian Slavs were under the rule of the Khazars, a people of mixed Finnic and Turkish origin. The Khazars were commercially motivated and their state on the banks of the lower Volga River fostered a commercial rather than a political imperialism. Economic motives caused the Khazar state to soon extend its boundaries as far as the Crimean Peninsula and the Dnieper River. However, Khazar rule over the dominated areas was a lenient one, since the Khazars were more interested in trading with the conquered peoples than in enslaving or exploiting them. Their capital was the city of Ityl at the mouth of the Volga.

In the ninth century there was still another invasion of Ukraine by the Avars or Obres. The Avars were related to the Huns and Bulgars, and their rule over the Slavs, although short, was very oppressive and left only bad memories among the forefathers of the Ukrainians.[4]

Two outstanding recent Russian scholars, Tretiakov, an historian, and Rybakov, an archeologist, disclosed in their studies of this period that from the fourth to the seventh centuries the ethnic character of East Europe might have been already established. The Ukrainian tribes settled the forest-steppe belt of East Europe from the Carpathian mountains to the middle run of the Dnieper River, on the banks of the Seim and Desna Rivers bordering on the Radimichians and Viatichians in the North-East, and on the banks of the Dniester and Boh Rivers in the South-West. The Russian and Byeloruthenian tribes dwelt in other parts of Eastern Europe.

The Kievan-Rus' Realm

In the course of the eighth and ninth centuries seven pre-Ukrainian Slavic tribes, the Polyanians, Dulebians, Derevlanians, Khorvatsians, Siverians, Tiverians and Ulichians finally merged and formed the Ukrainian people, the characteristics of which were even more clearly crystallized under later developments. These people subsequently built the Kievan state or realm, the political history of which goes back to the legendary dynasty of prince Kyi, who supposedly established the city of Kyiv or Kiev. Kiev became the capital of the land of the Polyanians, and Kyi and his brothers, Shchek and Khoryv, might have been Polyanian tribal princes as well. From the land of the Polyanians, who were so very commercially motivated and oriented, the growth of the Kievan state began. Already in the ninth century it was known among the Greek and Oriental peoples under the name Rus'. The name Rus' or Ruce of Rhos, in Greek, was derived either from the Ros River in the land of the Polyanians, or from the historical tribe of the Roxolanians who lived in the Ukraine, or from the Scandinavian Vikings, whose detachments roaming in East Europe were by some historical sources called the Verengians-Rois.[5] The interpretation of the source material has not been unanimous in this respect. The term Rus' was Latinized into Ruthenia and the adjective Ruthenian, which later was applied only to identify the old Ukrainians and never the Russians. On the other hand, the term Rus' was also Latinized into Russia, thereby provoking a great deal of confusion. Originally, the name Russia was used only when referring to the Ukrainian South, the real historical Rus', and not to the Suzdalians, Vladimirians or Muscovites. In the eighteenth century it was established by official decrees of the Russian emperors and through public usage to refer to the new Russian empire of Rossia by the Latinized term Russia.[6]

In the second half of the ninth century, two Kievan leaders or princes, Askold and Dir, ruled Rus' or Ruce. According to the Old Chronicle, Askold and Dir were two Scandinavian commoners who succeeded in seizing authority in already well and wealthy Kiev. Newer historical studies indicate, however, that both Askold and Dir might have been the last Slavic princes of the legendary Kyi dynasty.

In 860, Askold led a large-scale military expedition against Constantinople (Byzantium), which received much attention in the written historical materials of that time. This event has been regarded by some historians as the beginning of the historical era of Ukraine-Rus'. Askold's military expedition against Constantinople was no doubt associated with the close cultural and commercial ties between the Ukrainians and the Greeks. Soon, Askold and Dir were baptized and became Christian. This again strengthened the Greek influence upon Ukraine.

Around 880, Oleh or Oleg, doubtlessly a Norseman, came with a strong military force from Scandinavia via Novgorod the Great and occupied the Kievan princely throne, apparently in the name of prince Ihor or Igor, Rurik's son. Askold and Dir were killed, either because as the last Slavic rulers they were an obstacle in the path of the new Scandinavian dynasty or, because having been commoners, they dared to assume princely authority which was exclusively due to born princes or descendants of Rurik.

Oleh loved his new country, Ukraine-Rus'. Twice, in 907 and 911, he campaigned against the Byzantine empire to acquire better terms for the Ukrainian merchants in the well-developed Kievan-Byzantine trade. His Byzantine campaigning was very successful. It considerably improved the terms of trading in favor of the Ukrainian merchants, and confirmed the fact of the growing political power of Kiev.

In 913, Oleh invaded the shores of the Caspian Sea and fought against the Khazars. Three reasons were advanced for the invasion: (1) The Khazars continued to raise claims against Ukraine from earlier times and did not want to recognize her newly growing power; (2) Oleh and his warriors were attracted by the wealth of their capital of Ityl; (3) some difficulties had developed between the Kievan and Khazar merchants. Although the Caspian adventure was not successful, it attested to the growing political might of Kievan-Rus'. Oleh zealously tried to consolidate the country internally by forcing or persuading various Slavic tribes to submit to Kievan authority.

Building the Kievan realm, however, did not begin with the arrival of the Normans. There already existed several strong political organizations in the Ukrainian territory, the creations of Slavic organizational genius: the state of the Antes, the state of Valinana in the Volhinia, the political federation of the

Chervenski Horody, in Galicia, and the commercially developed state of the Polyanians. The Normans came to the Ukraine as military-adventurous detachments of various forces, not seeking to organize an empire. They pursued other ends: employment, or booty, and some of them were even commercially motivated. Having been hired by the princes, they were a welcome and a contributory factor in the process of building the Kievan-Rus' realm.

After Oleh's unfortunate death, caused by a snake bite (as the legend goes), leadership in Kiev was assumed by Ihor (Igor), who founded the princely Rurik dynasty. The Rurik dynasty ruled far beyond Kiev's decline in the thirteenth century, and continued to rule until the second half of the fourteenth century in the Ukrainian national, Galician-Volhinian realm, and also until the second half of the sixteenth century in the Russian national principalities, including the Grand Duchy of Muscovy.

Ihor campaigned widely to expand his empire of Kievan Rus'. He conquered the territories of various Ukrainian tribes, including the Derevlanians and Ulichians, who were reluctant to accept Kiev's supremacy. He subsequently fought the nomadic Pechengs in the Black Sea steppes, who at that time began to seriously threaten the Ukraine-Rus' and continued to do so for a number of decades.

The Pechengs, another barbarian tribe, had come from Asia during Oleh's rule in one of the never-ending waves of Asian invasions upon the European continent.

Meanwhile, peaceful and commercially motivated relations with Constantinople, based on the agreement with Oleh from 907 to 911, worsened. Finally, Ihor waged a war against the Greeks in 941, which was unfortunate for Kiev and disastrous for Ihor's naval detachments. His military expedition to the Caspian Sea shores and the Transcaucasian lands in 944-945 proved more successful than his Greek operation.

Prince Ihor developed a very effective administration of an already huge empire. In all larger towns and cities his viceroys were either the members of the Rurik family or other outstanding men, most of them Norsemen, as their names indicate. His zeal in consolidating the Kievan-Rus' realm brought death to him at the hands of the Derevlanians, who did not want to submit. His wife, Princess Olha or Olga (Helga) then ruled from 948 to 960 in the name off their minor son, prince Sviatoslav. She avenged Ihor's death, and subsequently searched for a new religion, becoming a Christian about 950.

On reaching maturity, prince Sviatoslav assumed the Kievan throne. From a military point of view his era was a glorious period in the history of old Ukraine. Sviatoslav was no doubt a military genius and his rule was characterized by number of large-scale war operations, most of which were very successful and helped strengthen and expand the Kievan-Rus' realm. Under his leadership the realm experienced the widest territorial expansion. Sviatoslav conquered additional lands of various Russian tribes and extended his domination in the North-East of Europe. He then undertook large-scale expeditions against the Volga-Bulgars and the Khazars. He defeated the Bulgars and conquered their capital city of Bulgar, a very important commercial center in the North-East; then moved against the Khazars. He took their important fortress of Sarkel and subsequently their rich capital of Ityl. Ityl was the most important commercial center on the borders of Eurasia. By capturing Bulgar and Ityl, Sviatoslav destroyed the political might of two significant East-European states and dominated the Volga-Caspian and Occident-Orient commercial routes and centers, increasing the power of the Kievan-Rus' realm. In the long run, however, the move was rather negative from a political point of view, since it opened wide the gateway from Asia to Europe, through which in later centuries the Asiatic hordes of the Torkmans, Cumans and Tartars invaded East Europe. Perhaps the states of the Bulgars and Khazars could have been political bulwarks that might have weakened the impact of these invasions upon Ukraine-Rus'. Actually, these invasions of Asiatic peoples put an end to the might of Kiev, other developments having only secondary and contributory importance.

On returning from military expeditions against the Volga Bulgars and Khazars, Sviatoslav defeated two aggressive

Caucasian tribes, the Osetens and the Chircasians, who had harrassed the southern borders of his empire. Having completed his Volga-Caspian project from 964-968, Sviatoslav turned his attention to the Balkan Peninsula and the Byzantine empire. He was attracted to the area by the wealth and commercial importance of Bulgaria, which he attacked with the initial tacit approval of Constantinople. Sviatoslav's splendid victories over the Bulgarians seriously frightened the Greeks, who were in a deadly struggle with the Arabs in Asia Minor. The powerful ally coming from the North, was a questionable ally, and too much of a threat for the future, for the Byzantine empire. An immediate outbreak of Rus'-Greek hostilities was, however, skillfully averted by Constantinople. Aided by the Greeks, the hostile Pechengs attacked Kiev, forcing Sviatoslav and his troops to leave the Balkans and hurry back to rescue Kiev from siege.

Following the Pechengian threat and overriding serious local opposition to his distant campaign, Sviatoslav resumed his Balkan project.[7] The Bulgarians rose against the invader, but Sviatoslav again defeated them in several battles and triumphantly marched through Bulgaria, taking one city after another. Prince Sviatoslav was already in control of three important trade routes, the rivers of Dnieper, Don and Volga, since his vast Rus' empire stretched throughout the whole of Eastern Europe. He also dreamed of dominating a fourth one, the Danube River. To make this possible, Sviatoslav attacked the Byzantine empire, but this proved unfortunate. He was beaten in a few important battles, and finally a compromise treaty was concluded between him and the Greek emperor in 971. On his way home Sviatoslav was attacked by the Pechengs on the Dnieper banks and was killed in action, and the Kievan army suffered a bad defeat.

Sviatoslav's sons were later involved in a bloody war of succession among themselves from which Volodymyr (Vladimir), later called the Great, emerged as a victor to become the sole ruler of the Kievan-Rus' realm for the next 35 years, from 980 to 1015.

Volodymyr first had to conquer the distant borderlands of his empire, which had reduced their dependence upon Kiev in the wake of the war of succession. He reunited Galicia in the West and the land of the Viatichians in the North-East with the Rus'. He was also involved in campaigning against the Pechengs, whom he defeated and pushed back to the Black and Azov Sea steppes by establishing a chain of fortresses and fortified towns along the empire's South-East border.

Volodymyr the Great had an alliance with two Greek emperors, Basil and Constantine, and helped them to overcome their difficulties in Asia Minor in exchange for their consent to Volodymyr's marrying their imperial sister Anna. The emperors later changed their minds and reneged on their promise to allow the marriage. A war came as a result. **Volodymyr invaded the Crimean Peninsula and took the city and fortress of Korsun.** The emperors then agreed to the marriage, which paved the way for the Christianization of Ukraine-Rus' in 988.

Historians have praised Volodymyr highly for his conversion to Christianity and introducing it to his vast realm. For this he has been designated the Great and a Saint. (The Orthodox Church subsequently included him in its pantheon of saints.) In this way Christianity reached the Russian North-East, which was the borderland of the Ukraine-Rus' realm at that time. Volodymyr sought to develop in this empire an efficient church organization and an education system. He initiated effective legislation to strenghen justice in his country and promulgated the so-called Volodymyr's *Ustavy* (decrees), which regulated the legal position of the Church and contributed to the consolidation of the nation. Furthermore, he improved the administrative scheme of the domestic governance of his territorially vast and multinational empire by the traditional means of viceroys, and initiated the development of diplomatic-foreing relations with other powers. His reign was the beginning of the Kievan "Golden Age."

Volodymyr's death provoked another war of succession. This one was among his sons, from which Yaroslav, later called the Wise, emerged as victor and supreme ruler of the Kievan-Rus' realm. The wars of succession among the chief contenders for the throne — Sviatopolk, the Sinner, Boris, and Yaroslav — were most serious. They involved Polish intervention in the internal matters of the Kievan-Rus' and also a temporary Polish occupation of the Kievan western borderland of Galicia. Galicia was reunited with the Rus' empire in 1030-31. Sviatopolk has been branded the "Sinner" for involving a foreigner, his father-in-law, Polish prince Boleslav, in Kiev's domestic affairs.[8]

After becoming the Kievan prince, Yaroslav had to fight against the Pechengs, who constantly harrased his realm. He defeated them once and for all, removing the Pecheng threat to his nation. But his military and political success was brief. Soon a new menace came from the steppes. New nomadic tribes came from Asia and occupied the Black and Azov Sea steppe area, and continued for many decades to disturb the peace on the southern borders of the Kievan-Rus state. In the 1030's the Torkmans came, but they did not present any serious menace to the Ukraine. After the Torkmans had been defeated and dispersed in the 1060's, a new threat from Cuman raids and invasions became ominous. The Cumans moved into the steppe regions and were continually hostile toward the Ukraine-Rus'. The Ukrainian princes had to wage many wars against the Cumans in order to protect their country from devastation. As a matter of fact, the Suzdal-Vladimirian Grand Dukes often allied themselves with the Cumans to reduce the power of Kiev.

Yaroslav developed extensive diplomatic relations with various West-European courts, the German empire, the Scandinavian countries, France, Hungary, and Poland, as well as with the Byzantine empire. As a result he succeeded in developing close dynastic ties with the various ruling houses of Europe of that time. Yaroslav's prestige was so great that foreigners eagerly sought such association with the Kievan court to enhance their own political authority and fame.

Having consolidated the nation and defeated foreign enemies, such as the Poles, Finns, Lithuanians, and Pechengs, in battle, Prince Yaroslav raised the prestige and might of his empire higher than any other Kievan ruler had done. He decided to undertake the greatest project of his life, that of conquering

Constantinople and making it the capital of his huge nation. The war began in the spring of 1043. The Ukrainian-Rus' armies, led by Prince Volodymyr, Yaroslav's son, were badly beaten in the decisive battles. As a result, Yaroslav's ambitious project failed. It was the last attempt on the part of Kiev to challenge Constantinople.

Yaroslav's reign was a continuation of the Kievan "Golden Age." The prince was greatly interested in the growth of the Church and its organization. He fostered and supported the development of the country's culture and education. He promulgated an important piece of legislation of medieval Ukraine, the code of *Rus'ka Pravda*, which contributed to the unification of the Ukrainian south, but apparently had little impact on the empire's North-Eastern borderlands, the Russian Volga-Oka-and Klazma regions. Yaroslav established new towns and built many churches and other buildings of outstanding architectural value. In spite of the few wars he waged, his reign was rather peaceful and characterized by Yaroslav's concern for his country's welfare. Historians therefore have called him "The Wise."

After experiencing the wars of succession and the difficulties of administering the huge and multinational empire, Yaroslav divided his country shortly before his death in 1054. The patrimonium of the Rurik house, established in Rus' the principle of seniorate, according to which the eldest prince of the Rurik dynasty was to rule in Kiev as a supreme authority over the entire Kievan empire, in part patrimonial and in part federative, from that time on. He gave Kiev to his oldest living son Iziaslav; Chernyhiv, Siversk, the lands of the Viatichians and Radimichians and Tmutorokan, to Sviatoslav; Pereyaslavl, Rostov and Suzdal, the Russian North-East, to Vsievolod; Volhinia to Ihor; Smolenski, to Viacheslav; and so on down the line, to each son a territorial share. Galicia was given to Rostyslav, Yaroslav's grandson.[9]

Yaroslav's division of the Kievan-Rus' empire was politically tragic. It immediately set two opposing trends into operation, which ruined and devastated the country and eventually made it an easy prey for the Mongol invasion. The ultimate downfall of Rus' followed in the thirteenth century.

Continuous wars were waged among the members of the Rurik

house for the seniority right and the Kievan throne, impoverishing the people and weakening the country. The chief contenders for the Kievan seniority seat were Yaroslav's three sons, Iziaslav, Sviatoslav and Vsievolod, who did not share the brotherly love their father wished them to have. They fought among themselves and with other brothers and relatives in dynastic wars. Iziaslav, for example, was forced to leave Kiev twice and three times he returned. An identical struggle continued among the grandsons of Yaroslav the Wise, as well.

With the progress of time, stronger decentralization tendencies dominated in the borderlands of the empire, aiming at the dismemberment of the commonwealth into a number of national states. The centrifugal and separatist tendency was very strong in the etnically varied Russian North-East, as has been pointed out in preceding chapters. Kievan difficulties in preserving political unity were gravely intensified by the Cuman raids upon the Ukrainian south, which were ably and energetically supported by the Suzdal-Vladimirian Grand Dukes.

In 1097, a princely convention took place in Lubech, as stated above, for the purpose of bringing peace to the war-torn commonwealth. The convention abolished to some extent the old seniority principle in order to end the senseless wars for the Kievan throne, but it introduced the patrimonium principle in the Rus' constitution. In this way it endorsed those centrifugal tendencies and the disintegration of the once powerful, multi-national empire. The patrimonium idea meant the right of each branch of the Rurik house to retain permanently its own (father's) land or principality, without seeking succession to the Kievan seniority seat. The significance of the Lubech convention for the separation process of the Russian North-East has been stressed before.

While these domestic and dynastic wars continued, foreign powers — Poland, Hungary, the Cumans, Lithuanians and others — desired to benefit from the Kievan calamities and were invading the borderlands or snatching away various territories of old Rus'.

The old splendor returned to Kiev under the rule of Volodymyr Monomakh, who reigned there for about twelve years. He succeeded in uniting nearly three-fourths of the old empire and increased the power and prestige of Ukraine-Rus' by pacifying the Cumans and raising the country's cultural and economic levels. After his death in 1125, his son Mstyslav succeeded in maintaining the greatness of Kiev. However, political chaos returned after his demise.

At that time the decentralization tendency of the Russian Volga-Oka-and Klazma watershed lands grew to full intensity and dramatic expression under Yurii Dolgorukii and Andrei Bogoliubskii, culminating in the fierce pillage of Kiev in 1169. The Ukrainian era in the history of Eastern Europe was over and the era of the Muscovite-Russian supremacy had begun.[10]

In the wake of Kievan disintegration, in the western corner of the empire, a Ukrainian national state, the Galician-Volhinian realm developed, which existed until 1349. Prince Roman I of Galicia and Volhinia actually united these two lands into one powerful principality and became the spokesman for the political interest of the Ukrainian South against the Russian North. He waged wars against the Cumans, who were constantly induced by Vsievolod III of Vladimir to harrass Ukraine. Roman was preparing himself for a major military encounter with Vsievolod in order to force him to stop his constant and harmful interference in Ukrainian domestic affairs. However, Prince Roman became involved in the German conflict among the Popes, Welfs, and the Hohenstaufens in a bid for the German imperial crown, and was killed in battle while attempting to cross the Polish territories, in 1205.

His son, Prince Danilo or Daniel, after several years of wars of succession, finally established himself in the principality. His reign was unsettled; he had to wage wars against other contenders for the Galician-Volhinian throne, as well as against foreign enemies, the Poles, the Hungarians, the Yatvingians, the Lithuanians and the Tartars. He subsequently had to pacify militarily the so-called "Tartarian people," the population in certain areas of the Ukrainian countryside, who under Mongol instigation, rebelled against the lawful princely authority.

In order to obtain active Western support in his struggle against the Mongols, Prince Danilo accepted a Church union with Rome and received a royal crown from the Pope. Nevertheless, his becoming a king did not save him from the Mongol menace and its supremacy. However, King Daniel at one time suceeded in uniting under his royal scepter almost all Ukrainian territories, including Kiev and Carpathian Ukraine.

The subsequent Galician-Volhinian rulers, all of the Roman family branch, the Princes Basil, Lev I, Volodymyr, Mstyslav, King George I, the princes Andrei, Lev II, and Boleslav-George II, with changing fortunes tried to maintain or increase the power of their realm, until in 1349 the Polish-Lithuanian interference ended the political existence of that Ukrainian state.[11]

The Kievan Impact Upon Russian Society

For over 300 years the Russian North-East remained under the cultural and political influence of Kievan Rus', which left an indelible imprint upon the later historical fortunes of the Russian nation. Above all, it was by the way of Kiev, that Christianity came to the Russian North-East.

No sector of the national life of the Russian Slavs has remained untouched by those 300 years of Kievan rule. The ethnic characteristics, the social structure, the government and administration system and the cultural processes of the Russian North-East have been predetermined by the era of the Kievan-Rus' domination. Without the Kievan impact the Russians probably would not have become and remained a prevailingly Slavic nationality. The originally Ugro-Finnic ethnic stock of the Volga-Oka- and Klazma regions and other areas of the European North-East, supported by its proximity to Asia and its political and cultural developments and influences, coming from the Turkish-Mongol Far East and Siberia in the course of the next few centuries after the Slavic colonization, could have made the Russians a nationality of Mongol extraction. The Slavs, colonizing these regions, were more civilized than the Ugro-Finns, but they could have been absorbed by the culturally inferior, numerically superior Mongolian stock. However, the powerful influence of Kiev and its civilization with Hellenic, Western and Iranian elements prevailed. Westernized civilization has proved in the later centuries to be stronger and much more progressive than the cultures on the Asiatic continent. On the other hand, the Ukrainian South was an Indo-European society *par excellence* and was prevailingly Slavic. These two forces, both cultural and ethnic, having dominated the Russian North-East, made it Slavic and European to a great extent. The Russian language, although incorporating many Finnic and German ingredients, became Slavic and belongs to the Slavonic family of languages.

The entire social structure of Novgorod the Great and the Rostov-Suzdal and Vladimir principality, with their stratification of the nobility, townspeople, peasants, slaves, and Church people, originated in Kiev. Of course, North-Eastern peculiarities affected specifically Russian social development. The social structure of Novgorod the Great was somewhat different from that in the Suzdal-Vladimir principality, while both Russian lands were different in social structure and stratification from the Ukrainian South in the Kievan empire as well. The Suzdal-Vladimir land featured a greater dependence of all classes upon the prince, less social impact of the Orthodox Church, less social and legal autonomy of the church people, stiffer class barriers and less class fluctuation. This was due to the greater power of the prince, and a more advanced evolution of semi-feudal institutions. By and large, the social structure in the entire Kievan-Rus' realm was fairly uniform, partially because of princely legislation and partially because of the interdependence of the social process in the framework of one political organization. In other aspects, that social structure was similar to the West-European patterns of social constitution.

The Russian North-East received its political constitution as a *patrimonium* of the Rurik dynasty. From Kiev came a dynasty which ruled there much longer than in Kiev itself or in other East-European lands. The Rurik house joined and interrelated the Russian North-East with the Byeloruthenian West and the Ukrainian South. The Rurik dynastic claims of the past have been used by the Muscotive Grand Dukes and the Russian Czars as justification for their aggressive and imperialistic moves against Byeloruthenia and Ukraine. Except for these unfounded dynastic pretenses, there were no objective reasons to justify Russian expansion over the Byeloruthenian and Ukrainian territories in the sixteenth and eighteenth centuries.

Through Kiev, the Russian North-East had been spiritually connected with Constantinople and influenced by Byzantine thinking in general, especially its political thought. In later centuries, after Moscow emerged as a strong state on the heels of Mongol supremacy, the Muscovite Grand Dukes turned for inspiration to Byzantine political ideas, and used them to substantiate their own monarchic theories and concepts toward strengthening their state and power.

The constitutional meetings of the princes of the Rurik house, in Lubech in 1097, which weakened or abolished the seniority principle as it instituted the patrimonial principle of succession of Kievan-Rus', decisively strengthened the centrifugal and separatist tendencies of the Grand Duchy of Suzdal-Vladimir and established this trend in the direction of full political independence from the Ukrainian South.

The entire governmental and administrative system of the Kievan state was at first imposed upon and then largely copied by Suzdal-Vladimir, as far as its central and territorial administrative agencies, judiciary and judicial system, and Church organization were concerned. Of course, with the progress of time, some local Russian organizational and administrative peculiarities developed. The ever growing despotic power of the Grand Dukes was in drastic contrast to Kievan conditions, and it progressively decreased the significance of the Council of Nobles and the people's meeting. The authority of princely officials was also becoming greater than that of the elected officials, some of whom completely disappeared, due to the growth of Vladimirian absolutism.

The legislation enacted by the Kievan princes, such as the decrees or *ustavy* of Volodymyr the Great, Yaroslav the Wise and Volodymyr Monomakh, including Yaroslav's code of *Rus' ka Pravda*, had a certain impact upon the formal and informal legislation of the Suzdal-Vladimir Grand Dukes and indirectly, upon the social life of Russian society in that century and later.[12] The Northern tax system and army organization developed on the Kievan basis as well, while the institution of the local village commune, the *mir*, was evolving in direct contrast to the Ukrainian individualism of later centuries.

The spiritual and intellectual impact of Kiev upon the Russian North-East cannot be over-emphasized. The "Cyrillic" alphabet, although originated in Bulgaria, was received by the Russians *via* Kievan-Rus'. They have been using that alphabet ever since, although it was modified and simplified later by Peter the Great and eventually by the Soviets as well.

The old heroic sagas, *biliny,* the spiritual songs, the ritual songs, the early folklore poems, fairy tales and apocryphic legends originated in the Ukrainian South, and from there were absorbed by the Russian North-East. Some originally Russian *biliny,* songs and poems came later.

From Kiev the translations of the Bible, literary collections of religious and secular works, historical chronicles, apocryphic collections, some translated from the Greek and others originated in the Ukraine, such as *Journeys of Virgin Mary,* novels, *About Varlarm and Josaphat, Trojan War, Aleksandria* about Alexander the Great, and *About the Indian Empire* went north to fertilize the intellectual life of the Russian Slavs.

Outstanding Ukrainian-Rus' writers, such as Metropolitan Ilarion with his "Word On Right and Blessing"; Bishop Ciril of Turiv with his writings on religion and morals; Metropolitan Clement Smolatych; Theodosius of Pechera, who greatly contributed with his writings to the perfection of monastic life; Nestor, the Chronicler, a monk from the famous Kievan Pechera monastery, with his *Primary Chronicle;* and Prince Volodymyr Monomakh with his "Instructions to My Children," were inspiring to later Russian writers. A great influence on Russian religious life was the "Pechera Paterik" about Pechera monks and their way of life. In the second half of the twelfth century, when the Vladimirian Grand Duchy was fully independent, an anonymous author wrote a work with broad appeal, entitled "The Petition of Danilo the Exiled," which was read in the North-East.

The most celebrated literary-poetic work from the end of the twelfth century, "The Song About Ihor's Host," which described and praised the struggle of the Ukrainian lands against the Cumans, more than any other work attested to the high level of intellectual and spiritual development in Kievan society. "The Song" greatly affected the cultural development of the Russian North-East. The later Russian poem "Beyond the Don River," describing the Russian struggle against the Tartars of the Kulikovo plain in 1380, was but an imitation and paraphrasing of an old Ukrainian "Song About Ihor's Host." Furthermore, Kievan musical and theatrical patterns were partially followed by the Russian North-East.[13]

Kievan influence on early Russian building and architecture was less intense. Kievan architecture developed in its own way, under the mighty impact of Byzantic architectural patterns, having added some style peculiarities of its own. This can easily be proved by comparing the construction of St. Sophia's Cathedral in Kiev with that of the same name in Constantinople. St. Sophia's Cathedral in Kiev, as Vernadsky noted, was an outstanding specimen of Byzantic style. It was built by prince Yaroslav the Wise and his successors, between 1037 and 1067. A number of tops or cupolas was its dominant characteristic.

Other examples of Kievan architecture included: the Church of the Tithe, constructed between 991 and 1039, the Church of St. Mary's Assumption, built around 1078, and the Church and Monastery of St. Michael, constructed around 1088. Beautiful and architecturally outstanding churches in Byzantic style were built also in other Ukrainian cities, in Chernihiv, Ovruch, Volodymyr-Volinsky, Peremyshl and Halych. All featured a number of cupolas of a rather gentle slope, richly ornamented with paintings and woodcuttings.

The influence of Ukrainian church and palace construction on Suzdal-Vladimir architecture was considerable, but the latter did not lose any identity of its own. The church cupolas in the Suzdal-Vladimir architectural style had a sharper, onion-like slope, and slightly different construction and ornamentation. All cathedrals and churches in large towns and cities of the Kievan-Rus' realm were of stone construction. Only later on, in smaller towns and the countryside were wooden churches built.[14]

The influence of the Kievan era upon Russian society was so much more intense, because it had come during the "infancy" and the "early formation years" of that society, having thus left an indelible imprint on the centuries that followed.

Chapter Seven

THE STRUGGLE FOR INDEPENDENCE

(Continuation)

The Mongols

The formation of the Russian nation was not, only deeply affected by the Slavonic character of Kievan Rus' at its early stage of development, but it was also greatly influenced by Mongol-Tartar rule, which prevailed in the European North-East for about 250 years, and in certain regions considerably longer. The Mongol era affected the evolution of the Russian nationality, before it was fully crystallized ethnically and rationally. Mongol culture intensely and deeply influenced Russian society in its entire historical perspective. It seems necessary, therefore, to learn something about the Mongols prior to their coming to the Russian North-East, and what influenced the social and political institutions of the Mongols, and predetermined their philosophy and policies before their conquest of Russia, Ukraine, Byeloruthenia and other lands of East Europe. This information permits a deeper comprehension of the cultural, social and political evolution of Russia and the spirit of Russian history.

The history of the Mongols began in the distant and dark centuries of the ancient world, about a millenium or so before the Christian era. At that time, the Huns emerged from the vast terrains of Mongolia, North of China. These were nomadic tribes, mainly of Turkish stock, but with substantial Mongol ethnical influx. The Chinese called them the Hsiung-Nu. The Hsiung-Nu were very aggressive and suceeded in forming strong political creations, threatening China for centuries. They attacked northern Chinese provinces, particularly when pressed by occasional shortages of food and threats of hunger in their Mongolian semi-arid steppes and deserts. During Chinese civil wars and periodical military weaknesses, the Hsiung-Nu intensely harrassed China. Around the fifth century, B.C., the Hsiung-Nu raids became especially annoying. About the third century B.C., the Huns had already organized a powerful empire from tribal federations, which extended from western Manchuria, across all of Mongolia, southern Siberia, into Chinese Turkestan, and south, as far as the Pamirs. The Hun military force was around 300,000 men at that time, and the government and administration of their empire was rather efficient.[1]

In order to stop the Huns and other Nomads from harrassing their Northern provinces, the Chinese constructed their famous "Great Wall" along the Mongolian border to protect their ancient nation and culture from nomadic destruction. Of course, the Huns also waged wars against other neighboring peoples. The Chinese attempted to organize various steppe tribes against the common enemy, the Huns, but with relatively little success. During most of that period the Mongols were under Hunnic domination or in alliance with the Huns. It may be concluded, therefore, that under Hunnic rule, the Mongols received first military and political training. Finally, in the second century A.D., the empire of the Huns began to crumble due to various reasons, primarily because of the mighty Chinese political and military offensives under the Han dynasty during its four centuries of rule, two centuries before and two centuries after Christ. And, by the middle of the fourth century, the attacks of the Sien-Pi and Juan-Juan tribes from the Asiatic North-East had administered such a blow to the empire of the Huns that they subsequently were forced to migrate westward.

With the gradual decline of the Huns as a power, new political formations developed in that part of Asia. The relatively strong state of Sien-Pi of Mongol origin and then the state of Juan-Juan, also with Mongol elements, dominated the political scene of Mongolia from the third to sixth century, A.D. In the tenth century, the state of Khitan or Khitai was organized by Mongol and Turkish tribes, at one time extending its power over Mongolia and parts of Manchuria and North China.

As a whole, however, until the thirteenth century, when Temudzhin, Genghis Khan, suceeded in building his vast empire, the various Mongol political formations had rather an ephemeral character. "Empires" were quickly organized by more outstanding tribal chieftains and then just as quickly dissolved on the death of those chieftains, whose personal abilities were the only foundation of power of these "empires." In fact, as Vernadsky said, at that time there was no common name "Mongols," generally applied to all those nomadic but related tribes of similar ancestry inhabiting Mongolia. The Mongols originally comprised a tribe along with the related Tartars, Merkits, Keraits, Naimans, and some others.

All these tribes pursued a nomadic life, which included steppe and steppe — semi-desert economy of cattle — raising, hunting, fishing, and limited trading. Tribal strife was common and continuous, resulting in conquests of neighboring territories, accompanied by ruthless exploitation of the conquered peoples, until the conquered freed themselves and succeeded in reversing positions. In this way the once conquered became the conquerors, exploiting their former oppressors. Many petty wars were waged, often instigated by the Chinese, who thought that in this way they would best serve their own interests and prevent any Mongol harrassment of their borders and border provinces.

In the eleventh century the chieftain of the Mongol tribe, Kabul Khan, became quite an important political figure among nomad tribal rulers in Mongolia. He raised the political prestige of his people and even dared to raid the lands of the Tartars and to attack the Chinese. Eventually he was badly beaten by the Tartars, and his Mongols were once again reduced to an insignificant tribal community among the nomads of the steppes and deserts of Mongolia. Esugay-Bagatur, Kabul's grandson, was only an unimportant tribal chieftain. However, because of the tradition of his clan and his own personal qualities, he was held in esteem by his people. Temudzhin, Esugay's son, elevated his tribe to the level of world-wide political and historical prominence. The impact of Temudzhin's mission was so great that the name of the Mongols has since been generally applied to identify all related nomadic tribes of Mongolia, including the Tartars.

After having surprised Europe with an invasion, the Mongols

rushed like a tornado through the eastern and central lands of the continent, spreading incredible terror. European historical sources compared them to demons, descending from hell, the legendary *Tartarus* of the Roman mythology; hence, they were given the name *Tartars* — the inhabitants of the *Tartarus*. This identification of the *Mongols* as *Tartars* has been retained in English, while in East Europe (Russia, Ukraine, Poland) the name *Tatars,* originally used in Mongolia for one specific tribe or one specific group of tribes, has been generally accepted to denote the Asiatic invader from the thirteenth century. "Tatars" is used interchangeably with the term *Mongols,* to identify Temudzhin's and his successors' cohorts for centuries to come. Following the Mongol invasion, forces under Batu's command in Eastern Europe were utilized in connection with some Turkish tribes. The term *Tatars* was extended in its usage to include those Turkish peoples who came with Batu or settled thereafter in the Kazan regions and the Crimean peninsula; the so-called Kazan *Tatars* and Crimean *Tatars.* Vernadsky has said that modern Orientalists, in order to become more scholarly and more precise, have coined a designation for these people — the *Turko-Tatars.*[2]

Temudzhin was probably born in 1167, although historians cannot agree as to the date. His father, Esugay, was poisoned by the Tartars when the boy was only nine years old. Great misfortunes befell Temudzhin's clan. Later, things began to improve. At eighteen years of age, Temudzhin already had proved himself a very able young man, and embarked upon his political career. Until 1206 he was involved in petty but bloody tribal struggles. In 1206 he finally succeeded in assuming leadership of the entire Mongol tribe and adopted the title of Genghis Khan, meaning Great Khan or Khan of Khans. From the very beginning of his political career, Temudzhin was obsessed with the idea of uniting all Mongols and their related tribes. He considered this to be his life mission, which he was realizing with stubborn consistency no matter what the price. His idea of "gathering all Mongols" was, no doubt, later reincarnated into Muscovy in the self-appointed mission of the Muscovite Grand Dukes of "gathering all Russian lands." This was also carried out by them with consistency and with no regard to the price to be paid for all their conquests. The Mongols learned from the Huns, and the Muscovite-Russians from the Mongols, how to conquer and to rule. The Muscovites are greatly indebted to Mongol political schooling.

Genghis Khan was doubtlessly a genius; he was an excellent organizer, an accomplished politician and diplomat, an outstanding military and political leader. He was to become a grand statesman who had to complete a great historical mission. Temudzhin believed deeply in his mission, which as he saw it, was entrusted to him by Heaven. His accomplishments he could explain only through Heavenly guidance. After having united all the Mongol tribes and having built his huge empire, he sought to extend the meaning of his mission beyond the interests of the Mongols. He dreamed of a commonwealth based upon the principles of justice and welfare. This idea again might have been reincarnated in later Russian messianism, at first permeated with Orthodoxy, and later with Communism.[3]

Having united all related tribes, the Tatars, the Merkits, the Keraits, the Naimans and others in 1211, Temudzhin invaded Northen China. Between 1212 and 1220, he conquered the Chinese provinces of Manchuria and Chinese Turkestan, and later the Moslem states of Central Asia. He soon reached and overran Transcaucasia. Through the passages of the Caucasian Mountains, his armies suddenly attacked the Cumans in the Black and Azov Sea steppes in 1222. The battle on the Kalka River was a major defeat of the Cuman and allied Ukrainian-Rus' armies by the Mongol Tartars in 1223.

Shortly before his death, Genghis Khan Temudzhin divided his huge empire among his four sons from his first marriage, Juchi, Jagatay, Ugedey and Tuluy, and established a seniorate of "Great Khan" to hold the empire together. Temudzhin died in 1227 and the authority of Great Khan was assumed by Ugedey with the unanimous consent of the electoral body, the *kuriltay,* after its first choice, Tuluy, refused the honor. It must be mentioned that Ugedey was actually preferred by his father, Temudzhin, as a future Great Khan because of his personal abilities.

Great Khan Ugedey and his successors, Guyuk, Mongka and Kubilay, and other members of the ruling clan continued the large scale Mongol conquests, and added to their commonwealth almost all of China, Manchuria, Korea, Asia Minor, Caucasia and Transcaucasia, the Volga Bulgars, Russia, Ukraine, and Byeloruthenia. For a time they penetrated militarily as far as Poland, East Germany, Hungary, and the Balkans. Karakorum in Mongolia was the capital of this vast empire.

Ugedey continued to rule successfully according to the Temudzhin's imperial master plan. Large conquests in China, Persia, Korea and Turkestan were made. Under his auspices as Great Khan, the assault on Europe was initiated and carried out by Khan Batu, Juchi's son. Ugedey's death in 1241 was "an important landmark in the history of both international relations and Mongol politics," to quote Vernadsky.[4] It terminated Mongol penetration of Central Europe and initiated serious internal dynastic and political strifes within the empire, which ultimately led to its disintegration.

Soon after Ugedey's death Jagatay also died and the succession became open. Ugedey's widow, Turakina, assumed regency in the name of her son Guyuk. However, the opposition to Guyuk's succession was very strong, particularly on the part of Batu, the mighty conqueror of East Europe, and soon to be the founder of the new Mongol vassal state, west of the Ural Mountains. The dynastic quarrels and *interegnum* lasted for four years. Batu subsequently boycotted Guyuk's election; he did not attend the electing *kuriltay* and refused to come to Mongolia to pay homage to the new Great Khan Guyuk.

Guyuk's reign was short and rather uneventful, although it must be said to his credit that he strengthened his authority among the Mongols and paved the way for future Mongol successes in the Near East. In 1248, Guyuk was apparently poisoned either by the agents of Batu or by Tuluy's widow. This was most likely a result of prolonged Guyuk-Batu rivalry.

Guyuk's death initiated an even greater political crisis in the commonwealth than that of Ugedey. A serious and bloody dynastic struggle ensued among the four branches of the ruling Temudzhin clan; the descendants of Juchi and Tuluy on one side, and the descendants of Ugedey and Jagatay on the other. Batu, Juchi's son, and Mongka, Tuluy's son, were the strongest candidates for the Great Khanate's office. Batu renounced his rights in exchange for Mongka's promise to give him a completely free hand in his newly established state of the Khanate of Kipchak, later, the Golden Horde. Mongka was elected Great Khan, but his enemies refused to acknowledge this fact. Mongka's first move was an introduction of a reign of terror and the bloody extermination of the opposition. Several members of Ugedey's and Jagatay's branches of the clan, together with their families and followers, were executed.

On the international scene, the Mongols continued their conquests during Mongka's reign. The Caliphate of Baghdad was taken, the conquest of Persia completed, and new inroads made in China. Mongka died in 1259.

The next year, in 1260, Kubilay, Mongka's brother, was elected Great Khan in a rather irregular way. A short civil war followed, ending in Kubilay's victory.

Great Khan Kubilay greatly increased the power and the territorial expansion of his empire. Theoretically, it extended from the borders of Poland and Wallachia in the West to the Pacific Ocean in the East, and from the Mesopotamian Valley, and along the borders of India, Tibet and Indochina in the South to the polar regions of Siberia and the Far East in the North. In the relatively short time of some fifty years the Mongols had built a tremendous empire, territorially more extensive than any other empire in history.

While limiting Mongol plans for conquest and political penetration in Europe and the Middle East, Great Khan Kubilay concentrated his interest on China. After his conquest of its southern provinces, China submitted completely to his authority and accepted him as its emperor of a new Mongol-Chinese Yuan dynasty, which was to rule China for several decades. Kubilay's consequent pro-Chinese policies antagonized the patriotic old Mongol party under the leadership of Kaidu,

Ugedey's grandson. This provoked a civil war. As a result of the war, however, Kubilay's authority was largely restored in Mongolia.

The Great Khan also sent his troops to Tibet, Burma and Indochina. After occupying some of its provinces, the autonomy of Tibet was recognized by Kubilay. The expeditions to Burma and Indochina actually ended in defeat for the Mongols, who could not stand the tropical climate, although some Indochinese states recognized Kubilay's political supremacy, being impressed with his power and anxious to avoid any further military involvement with the Mongols.

As mentioned, Kubilay paid little attention to European affairs. Later, in the period between Kubilay's death in 1294 and the downfall of the Yuan dynasty in 1368, the influence of the Great Khans and Emperors on developments in East Europe further declined to an all time low. It was an era of nine rulers who reigned in Mongolia and China rather briefly one after another, of whom only Timur, Kubilay's grandson, was an outstanding ruler. This was a period of political decay.[5]

As a result the Russian North-East was progressively less and less influenced politically by the Great Khans from distant Mongolia. Its fortunes were, however, gravely affected by the Golden Horde for decades to come.

The Invasion

The normal course of Russian history and Russian social, political, cultural and economic development from Finnic-Slavic elements, later under the influence of Kievan civilization, was gravely disturbed by the Mongol or Tartar invasion in the fourth decade of the thirteenth century. The Mongol armies launched their first attack on European soil in 1222-23, having invaded the Ukrainian Black and Azov Sea steppes and defeated the Cumans and some Ukrainian princes, who allied themselves with the Cumans, in a battle on the banks of the Kalka River, in 1223. Then, suddenly, the Mongols, apparently not ready to continue their European conquests and considering the penetration of the Ukrainian steppes as a strategic raid to get "the feeling of a European battleground," withdrew to Asia, making no attempt to invade any Russian principalities. Things quieted down for a while.

Meanwhile Juchi died. The territories north and west of the Aral Sea were given to him as his *ulus* or share in the empire by Genghis Khan. His job it seems, was to make conquests west of the Ural Mountains. Soon Genghis Khan also died. Apparently on the list of Ugedey's planned conquests there were priority projects ahead of the European ones. This could explain the lull before the storm. Between 1229 and 1232 rumors reached the Volga-Oka- and Klazma regions about Tartar raids on the Volga Bulgar lands, but all was generally quiet. Mongol forces were engaged mainly in the China, Korea and Persia encounters.

It was not until other conquests were to some extent completed that Great Khan Ugedey granted Butu, Juchi's son, the authority to raise new armies from the Turkish tribes, since in Juchi's *ulus* there were only 4,000 Mongol troops according to Genghis Khan's will. Nevertheless, after mobilizing the Turkish tribes, Batu's army was still inadequate for a Western campaign. Ugedey therefore ordered the other *uluses* of the empire to join Batu in his all-out, Pan-Mongol drive against Europe.

Although an immediate threat was apparent, as strong disquieting rumors indicated, the Russian principalities, and the Grand Duchy of Vladimir in particular, did not anticipate their danger and did nothing to prepare for their defense. The usual dynastic quarrels and strifes were going on among the princes of the Rurik house, concerning seniority rights and territorial claims. Finally, in 1236, Batu crossed the Ural Mountains with his armies of some 50,000 Mongols and 100,000 Turks and other auxiliary troops, followed by masses of people, old and young, women and children. He invaded the lands of the Volga Bulgars with the definite purpose of keeping them, and there were other territories he hoped to conquer permanently for his people to settle or to roam around in. Batu's invasion, therefore, resembled a migration of people looking for new homes, preceded by vast armies to annihilate any opposition by the native population of the conquered countries. In 1237, the capital of the Volga Bulgars was destroyed as a symbol of conquest.

Yurii II, Grand Duke of Vladimir, left the capital city to his sons and lieutenants to defend while he himself went to other Volga regions to raise new armies in order to resist the Mongol onslaught, the power of which seemed overwhelming. Meanwhile, in February 1238, the capital city of Vladimir was seized by Batu's army, pillaged, and destroyed. The Grand Duke's entire family perished during the seizure and burning of the city. The Mongols then followed Yurii. The main encounter between Yurii's and Batu's forces took place on the banks of the Sit River on March 4. The Vladimirian forces were outmaneuvered and beaten. The Mongols' victory was complete; Grand Duke Yurii was killed in the battle. The Grand Duchy of Vladimir was no more the example of Russian political power.

After the battle on the Sit River, the entire Russian North-East was open to the Mongols. There was no longer any serious military opposition to Batu's invasion.

The commercial state of Novgorod, always militarily weak, had scarcely any hope of stopping Batu's victorious march. But its wealth was certainly an attraction for him. His troops, having seized almost all regions of the Volga-Oka and Klazma watershed, proceeded quickly in the direction of Novgorod. However, some 65 miles east of the city, Batu brought his forces to a sudden halt and ordered them to march South. Novgorod was saved from destruction, but not from Mongol supremacy.

The master plan of European conquest was developed mainly by Subudey, Batu's chief of staff, an experienced military strategist well acquainted with the European scene, since he had taken a leading part in the Mongol invasion of the Pontic steppes in 1221-23. It was evidently his idea to attack the Russian North-East in the winter, since the Mongols were accustomed to the severe Mongolian winter climate. Furthermore, all successful maneuvers and operations of the Mongol-

Turk armies against the Russian princes, as well as later operations in Ukraine, Poland, and Hungary, must be largely credited to Subudey's strategic abilities. The Mongol halt 65 miles before reaching Novgorod and the turning of the route of invasion southwards were apparently dictated by weather conditions. The prolonged thaw in the North-East in spring could have greatly delayed Mongol plans, Subudey might have thought.

There could have been other reasons for Batu's sudden turn. When Batu and Subudey operated in the North, Mongka fought in the Caucasian and Pontic areas, slowly approaching Kiev, capital of Ukraine. Perhaps Mongka's progress was not sufficiently rapid, and perhaps his forces were inadequate to accomplish the job in the South. Batu therefore hurried to assist his cousin and political associate.

Batu's march southward was rather uneventful. In 1239 only minor military projects were accomplished, except the one against the Cumans who were forced to submit or to migrate. Some 40,000 Cumans, with Khan Kotian, left the Black and Azov Sea steppes and migrated to Hungary to avoid the Mongol oppression.

In the summer of 1240, Batu began the conquest of Ukraine. Mongka seized, pillaged and devastated Pereyaslav and Chernihiv and demanded the submission of Kiev. His envoys were killed. The Mongols were vengeful. They moved against the city, and took it in December 1241. The city's population was slaughtered mercilessly and it was looted, burned and ruined. The Ukrainian princes, following the Russian example, submitted to Batu's and Great Khan Ugedey's supremacy. Only a few resisted, but with no success. King Daniel of Galicia tried to outsmart Batu, but finally he also had to submit.

Hungary was the next object of Batu's conquest. As the land at the west end of the steppe zone, extending almost from Mongolia to Central Europe, it was an ideal home for the nomadic Mongols. The Hungarian King Bela, furthermore, antagonized Batu by giving shelter to Kotian's Cumans. Subudey, however, advised Batu to attack Poland first, for strategic purposes, possibly to ward off an attack upon the Mongols from the North-West.

Soon Poland, Silesia and Hungary were overrun by Batu's troops. The Polish-German forces were completely defeated by the Mongols in the Battle of Lignica, in Silesia; the Hungarian army was defeated in the battle on the banks of the Tisa and Solona Rivers, in April 1241.

The Mongol army, which had fought in Poland, then invaded Moravia and Bohemia, *en route* to Hungary, looting as it went. Hungary was pillaged and terrorized all summer long. Ukrainian, Polish, Bohemian, and Hugarian pleas for military assistance from the Western powers were ignored, while Sweden and the Teutonic Knights even sought to take advantage of the Russian calamity. However, they were beaten by Alexander Nevskii.

The death of Great Khan Ugedey on December 11, 1241, actually saved Central Europe. When the news about his death reached Batu in 1242, all military operations were ended and he marched back with his troops to his *ulus*, now west of the Ural Mountains.[6]

On his return from the Central European campaign, Batu established the Khanate of Kipchak or the state of the Golden or White Horde with its capital of the new city of Sarai on the banks of the lower Volga. Batu, as a good administrator, immediately introduced order and efficient government in his state, which stretched west of the Ural Mountains, over Russia, Ukraine, Byeloruthenia and the Don-Volga steppes, down to the shores of the Black and Azov Seas and the Caucasian Mountains.

Although it seemed at the beginning of Batu's invasion that all of Western civilization would perish under the overwhelming impact of the Asiatic hordes, this severe fate was, in fact, reserved for three East European nations: the Russians, the Ukrainians and the Byeloruthenians, whom the Mongols were to keep under their domination for centuries. Nevertheless, the consequences of the invasion proved to be of lasting significance in the development of the Russian people. The harsh lessons taught by the Tartars, and their techniques which were adopted by the Muscovites-Russians, made the latter capable of building an empire and successfully overrunning the Ukrainians and the Byeloruthenians, as Batu's hordes had done earlier.

First of all, the emerging Russian nation, prior to the Tartar conquest, was already an ethnic alloy with a very substantial Mongol content, i.e. the Ugro-Finnic tribes. Consequently, it was much easier for the Rostovians, Suzdalians, Vladimirians, Riazanians, Muscovites and other northern pre-Russian groups to adjust to "peaceful" coexistence with the Tartar suzerain, to accept his rule, and eventually to develop friendly relations with him. Secondly, the less developed culture of the northeastern community, with more Oriental elements than that of the Ukrainian and Byeloruthenian nationalities, made it more susceptible to Mongol social, political, legal, economic and other cultural influences than its western and southern, ethnically different neighbors. Thirdly, the prolonged Mongol rule over the Russians, some 250 years, together with Moscow's partial adoption of the culture of the Golden Horde, inevitably left a permanent impression upon Russian national psychology, as well as on Russian national institutions.

This was not the case in Ukraine and Byeloruthenia. Both countries had almost no Mongol tradition and were culturally more advanced, hence less susceptible to Mongol influences. They remained under Tartar rule for only 100 years. They did not, therefore, develop any far-reaching contacts or relations with Sarai and the Tartar suzerain. Being in the political framework of the Lithuanian-Ruthenian (Ukrainian) Grand Duchy and the Polish-Lithuanian Commonwealth, the Ukrainians and Byeloruthenians were more intensely drawn into the sphere of Western and Roman Catholic civilization. For these reasons, both nationalities successfully resisted the impact of Mongol institutions upon their national life, and became, therefore, even more alienated from the Russians as a result.[7]

Batu's intention was to keep a close check on East European, and especially Russian lands and their princes, in order to secure revenues by way of tribute collections, and a supply of auxiliary armed forces for Sarai's future military undertakings.

Therefore, immediately after having established the state of the Golden Horde (Khanate of Kipchak), Batu summoned the Russian princes to the lower Volga to receive from his hand the *yarlik*, the official Mongol confirmation of their rights to rule in their respective lands by the grace of the Khan, on paying homage to him as their suzerain. Initially, the Khanate of Kipchak was only a component territory of the Mongol commonwealth, therefore Batu's confirmation was not sufficient cause to establish a full-fledged *yarlik*. This was especially significant when Guyuk was Great Khan, and some Russian princes had to travel to Karakorum in Mongolia to get their *yarliks*. Prince Yaroslav of Vladimir, for instance, travelled to Mongolia to pay homage to Guyuk, and was poisoned there. Yaroslav's sons, Alexander Nevskii and Andrei, were instructed by Batu to undertake journeys to Karakorum, which they made in late 1247 or early 1248. Guyuk had been determined to exercise his supremacy over the Golden Horde and Russia, for which Batu could not stand. This was probably one of the leading causes of Guyuk's poisoning, apparently by Batu's or his accomplices' agents.

After Mongka became Great Khan, he delegated full authority in European affairs to Batu, his close political associate. Since that time, Russian princes in general were not required to see the Great Khan or to undertake the exhausting journey to Karakorum. The *yarlik* was granted by Sarai.

Initially, the Russian princes reacted to Mongol rule in different ways. Some resisted but in vain; others accepted it passively; still others cooperated. Eventually all had to recognize and honor their vassal relationship to Sarai, and Karakorum respectively, and to comply with Mongol demands. One by one, the Russian princes travelled to Sarai to pay homage to the Khan, to promise him assistance and tribute as signs of submission. Russia, as a whole, was regarded by Batu and his successors as a mere province of the Golden Horde. Some princes who directly refused to pay the tribute were punished by the Khans and had their autonomy reduced. For example,

Andrei of Vladimir (by Batu's *yarlik*) once refused to comply with his vassal obligation. Sartak, Batu's son, then led a punitive expedition against Andrei. He was ousted as prince of Vladimir, and his brother, Alexander, was enthroned as ruler by Khan's grace. Sometimes, princes who did not enjoy Sarai's confidence, were arrested or executed upon their arrival to pay homage, and never returned home. Their principalities were then given to others, more "trustworthy." Of course, there were those very submissive to foreign rule, who made numerous trips to Sarai with gifts and assurances of loyalty. Ivan I of Muscovy journeyed to the lower Volga nine times, his son, Simeon, five times, all to prove their allegiance to the Khan. Enthroning of princes was done in the name of the Khan and their authority was derived from the *yarlik*.

The Russian vassal lands had to pay heavy tribute and other taxes to Sarai. As long as they complied with these requirements, they were relatively autonomous. The Tartar suzerain interfered but little in the internal affairs of individual principalities. As a rule, only negligence, laxity or a great deal of intrigues among the princes themselves brought Mongol interference. At a later stage, some princes used the Khan's authority to get rid of their rivals.

The Fortunes of the Golden Horde

Batu died in 1255 and was succeeded by Sartak, who, in his father's time, was already a kind of co-ruler in handling the affairs of the Russian North-East. When Sartak died a year later in 1256, Ulagchi, Batu's other son, became the third Khan of the Golden Horde, but again for a short, two-year period. He died in 1258. Ulagchi summoned all the Russian princes to come to Sarai again in order to get renewals of the *yarliks*. Meanwhile, Great Khan Mongka, involved in his Chinese campaign, imposed new burdens on the Russian lands. He needed more troops and more money. As a result, permanent Mongol administration was introduced by dividing Russia into military districts. A new census for tax collection and recruiting soldiers was taken, and the tribute was collected most energetically. It was that time that Novgorod the Great had to submit to Mongol authority and financial administration, after its brief attempt to resist. Actually, Alexander Nevskii persuaded the Novgorodians not to continue their suicidal resistance. Vladimir and some other towns had experienced the heavy punitive hand of Sarai.

After Ulagchi's death in 1258, Berke, Batu's brother, assumed the authority of the Khan of the Golden Horde. Because Berke was preoccupied with conflicts in the Mongol empire and developments in the Near East, he paid less attention to the Russian North-East. He was already a Mohammedan, and that was a reason for his involvement in Islamic Asia Minor and for his misunderstanding with Hulagu, the Khan of Mongols in Persia. He became involved in the Mongol civil war between Kubilay and Arik-Buka, which strained his relations with Great Khan Kubilay. There has been historical speculation that Alexander Nevskii attempted to take advantage of the strained relations between Berke and the Great Khan, by planning an uprising against the Golden Horde to get more freedom for his principality.[8] This is, however, doubtful, in view of Nevskii's political realism and his policy of appeasement of the Mongols in general. It was to his surprise that the Suzdalians revolted against the Khan in 1262. Apparently no princes joined the revolt and Nevskii went to Sarai to ask Berke to spare the Suzdalians. This Khan did not have any other trouble with the Russian provinces, which were fairly submissive.

Khan Berke died in Tiflis in 1266 during one of his Near Eastern campaigns. He was succeeded by Batu's grandson, Mangu-Temir, elected by the regional *kuriltay* and confirmed by Great Khan Kubilay. Mangu-Temir pursued a benevolent policy toward the Russian lands. He eased tax collections and exempted the Russian Orthodox Church from census, taxation and military service, making the "church people" a privileged group by his special *yarlik*. In this manner he obtained the loyalty of most Russian princes. The princes of Rostov, on the other hand, were Sarai's special wards, who made pilgrimages to Mongolia to demonstrate their willingness to cooperate with the Mongols. The Rostov princes also initiated frenquent Russian Mongol intermarriages, which commenced a continuous mingling of Mongol and Russian blood. Prince Peter Ordinskii, "of the Horde," married a Mongol commoner, while Prince Gleb married a Mongol princess, while in Mongolia paying homage to the Great Khan in 1257.

Khan Mangu-Temir was also very benevolent toward Novgorod the Great because of its commercial importance. International trading was always extremely important for the economy and prosperity of the Golden Horde. Therefore the Khan valued Novgorod as an important northern trade center and outlet for Mongol foreign commerce.

Russian princes loyally joined Mangu-Temir's campaigns and distinguished themselves, militarily in particular, in the Caucasian exploits in 1278. In 1280, after Mangu-Temir's death, his brother, Tuda-Mangu became the Khan. However, Nogay, cousin of the two former Khans, an able warrior and statesman, previously an acting ruler of the lower Danube region, became so powerful that a dual authority of Tuda-Mangu and Nogay existed in the Golden Horde. Nogay's power was actually greater than that of the official Khan, Tuda-Mangu. Khan Nogay campaigned against Hungary, Slovakia and Poland, and succeeded in influencing Hungarian affairs.

Relations between Tuda-Mangu and Nogay were strained, and the Russian princes tried to play one against the other to their own advantage, either to broaden their freedom or to utilize the antagonism in their own dynastic or territorial quarrels.

Eventually, Tuda-Mangu was forced to abdicate in favor of Tele-Buga, his nephew, and Nogay's associate in the Hungarian campaign. But relations between Nogay and Tele-Buga rapidly deteriorated. Since Tele-Buga's wars in the Caucasian areas were not successful, his prestige declined. Nogay was only too glad to get rid of his embarrassing co-ruler. Tele-Buga was perfidiously arrested by Nogay and handed over to Tokhta, Mangu-Temir's son, another contender for the Khan's authority. Tokhta ordered the execution of Tele-Buga and his associates, and he became Khan of Kipchak, by Nogay's grace, in 1291.

Tokhta, however, did not intend to be a mere tool in Nogay's hands. He acted very independently in Russian affairs in order to make himself known as the suzerain over Russia. He enforced submission by large-scale punitive action against Vladimir, Tver, Moscow and other cities by looting them mercilessly in 1293, for their attempt to associate themselves with Nogay.

These Russian developments, in which two opposite camps were formed, some Russian princes supporting Nogay and others, Tokhta, (as well as rivalry in the foreign policies of each), resulted in a civil war in the Golden Horde which ended in Nogay's downfall and death, in 1300.

Tokhta, making himself the sole ruler of the Khanate of Kipchak, restored unity and reintroduced order. However, Russian princes continuously tried to take advantage of the unending intrigues and quarrels among various factions and political and dynastic orientations in the Golden Horde, intermingling their own Russian controversies and problems with those of the Mongols.

In 1313, Tokhta was followed by Uzbek, his nephew, as the Great Khan. Uzbek was a very aggressive ruler and involved himself and his Golden Horde in Byzantine-Bulgarian, Egyptian, and Lithuanian-Galician affairs. At the same time he tried to keep tight control over Russia by not allowing Russian princes to form any coalitions or federations to oppose the Khan's suzerainty. In this connection he had to undertake a few punitive raids on the territories and cities of the stubborn princes, who wanted to emancipate themselves from the Tartar protection. The pacification of Tver was especially severe, in which Uzbek utilized Muscovite and Suzdalian troops. By this time Moscow had already begun to acquire a prominent political position among the Russian principalities. Moscow was under the reign of Ivan Kalita, who maintained very friendly relations with the Khan.

Uzbek, who died in 1341, was succeeded by his son, Tinibeg, for a short while, and in 1342, Janibeg, the latter's brother, seized power and ruled until 1357. The gradual political decline of the

Golden Horde began during the second half of the fourteenth century. The decline started in 1357, when Khan Janibeg was murdered by his son Berdibeg, who wished to ascend the throne. The era of the "Great Trouble" in the Horde featured bloody struggles among Janibeg's three sons, Berdibeg, Kulpa and Nevruz, during which they killed each other. The prestige of the Juchi ruling clan slipped to an record low. Power in the Golden Horde was then captured by Mamai, who was not a member of the Juchi clan, therefore his authority was not generally recognized. The growing weakness of the Horde was revealed in the battle on the Kulikovo Plain on September 8, 1360, where Dimitrii, Grand Duke of Muscovy, badly defeated Mamai's cohorts. The battle is recognized as an indication of the rising power of the Muscovites, and as a vital part of their struggle for liberation against the Mongol oppressor.

Meanwhile, chaos in the Golden Horde continued. One Khan quickly replaced another while various regions of the Horde sought more autonomy. Some major landmarks in these developments were the victory of Khan Tokhmatish, from the Juchi clan, over Mamai, and then of Great Khan Tamerlane over Tokhmatish in 1395.

Tamerlane partially repeated the performance of Genghis Khan of two centuries earlier. Temudzhin was a pure Mongol and a heathen in his beliefs, while Tamerlane was a Turkicized Mongol and a Moslem.[9] Tamerlane began to build his empire in 1360 after he became the ruler of his native city of Kesh in Central Asia. He subsequently conquered Samarkand and became Khan. In his attempt to conquer Kazakhstan, he antagonized the Golden Horde, since Kazakhstan was considered a region of the traditional Juchi *ulus*. Tamerlane supported Tokhmatish in his quest for Sarai against Mamai and the other Khans of Kipchak, Urus-Khan and Timur-Melik.

After establishing himself in Sarai, Tokhmatish became one of the mightiest rulers of his time. He desired to restore the authority of Sarai over Russia and led one of the most devastating punitive actions of the Mongols against their disobedient vassals, the Russian princes. In 1382 Moscow, already the symbol of the Russian cause, was plundered and burned, along with other cities.

In 1386 an open conflict erupted between Tokhmatish and Tamerlane. It had been brewing for several years. For years the two Mongol Khans waged bloody wars against each other in Caucasia, the Volga-Caspian steppes and Central Asia. The Mongol trading centers were destroyed and the countryside ruined. Finally Tokhmatish was completely routed by Tamerlane in two decisive battles, one on the banks of the Kondurcha River, in the Middle Volga regions, in 1391, and the other in the Terek River valley, in Caucasia, in 1395. Tokhmatish gave only sporadic resistance. Tamerlane proceeded to plunder the lands of the Golden Horde. In July, 1395, he invaded the southern outkirts of Russia, the principality of Riazan, stormed the town of Elets and pillaged the countryside. But he apparently did not dare an all-out invasion of Russia, because the princes of the Russian North-East had carefully watched the deadly struggle between the Mongol leaders and had prepared for war just in case. For them, the strife among the Mongols meant either doom or emancipation. In August, Tamerlane ordered a retreat.

Tamerlane's wars against the Golden Horde dealt it a severe blow. Its political prestige was ruined and its foreign commerce, the basis of its economic prosperity, was gravely damaged. It soon became a vassal of Tamerlane's Khanate, and subjected to shattering civil wars and foreign interventions. Khan Edigey tried desperately to save the Horde, but in vain. Its days were over.

Already in the early part of the fifteenth century, the Golden Horde began to disintegrate. Some of its minor regions seceded and maintained their autonomy for a longer or shorter time. Toward the middle of that century, however, a major split came, which actually terminated the age of the "Tartar Yoke" of Russia. In 1445, the Khanate of Kazan on the Middle Volga separated itself from Sarai, and three years later, in 1449, the Crimean Tartars founded their own Khanate, independent of the crumbling Golden Horde. Thanks to the Polish King, Casimir IV, Akhmad was the last Khan of the Golden Horde to succeed in invading Russia. He was assassinated in 1481. The year 1480, when the Russians and the Tartars met on the banks of the Ugra River, and the Tartars retreated without daring a military encounter, marks the official date of the end of Mongol-Tartar supremacy over Muscovy-Russia and the beginning of Muscovite sovereignty. In 1502, the Crimean Tartars completely defeated the Golden Horde. Thereafter the Khanate of Astrakhan, established by 1466, attempted to continue Sarai's tradition in the lower Volga basin, but uneventfully.

The Tartar threat remained over the southern and southeastern borderlands of Muscovy in the form of raids for looting, plundering and slave-taking. The Grand Dukes of Muscovy had to build fortresses and foster colonization of the Azov Sea "wild fields" to stop the raids of the Crimean Tartars. Ivan the Terrible conquered and destroyed two Tartar states, the Khanate of Kazan in 1552 and the Khanate of Astrakhan in 1556, and annexed their territories to the Czardom of Muscovy, thus reducing the threat of harrassment by the Tartars. The Crimean Khanate continued to exist, although as a vassal of the Ottoman Empire, until 1787, when it was incorporated into Russia by Catherine the Great. Russia had come a long way since the European conquests of Khan Batu.[10]

The Mongol Impact Upon Russian Society

The impact of Mongol supremacy on early Russian society can be scarcely overestimated. Every aspect of national life of the Russians was deeply influenced by that prolonged rule, as was indicated in this author's introductory remarks. However, Russian historians have differed greatly in their evaluation of the role of the Mongols in the history of their nation. Soloviov preferred to deny any significance in the historical fortunes of the Russian people from the Mongol domination, while Grekov evaluated the role of the Mongols from a negative point of view, stating that the growth of Muscovy came only as a result of its prolonged struggle against the oppressor. Kluchevsky Diakonov and Vladimirskii-Budanov either paid little attention to or evaded the issue. On the other hand, Karamzin, Vernadsky,

Trubetskoi and others, including Kostomarov, a Ukrainian, have presented an opposite view: that of an enormous impact of the Mongols on the Russian society, without which the Russians would not have become what they are. Karamzin simply stated that "Moscow was indebted to the Khans for its greatness."[11] Trubetskoi, a half century ago, in his work *The Heritage of Genghis Khan*, elaborated on the details of the Mongol impact on the course of Russian history, indicating that the origins of Muscovy cannot be properly understood unless it is studied against the background of Mongol social and political institutions. These institutions shaped the initial fortunes of Muscovy, the precursor of the Russian empire.[12] Recently, Vernadsky has followed Trubetskoi's and Karamzin's way of reasoning. However, he made a fundamental error by attempting to prove the impact of Mongols on Russian society by comparing the Kievan society of the early thirteenth century with the Muscovite one of the late fifteenth century. This viewpoint can be argued against for several reasons.

First of all, the constitution of the Russian North-East in the pre-Mongol era was quite different from the Kievan-Ukrainian South. The ethnic composition of the population of the Volga-Oka basin was different. There the absolutist power of the Grand Duke already was on the rise and the subordination of all social strata to the interests of the state was quite apparent. Furthermore, the aggressive and imperialistic policy of the Grand Dukes of Vladimir was already evident. Most of these trends were absent in the Kievan South, where freedom of all social classes from any central state regimentation, economic individualism and the limitation of the princely authority by the aristocratic and democratic constitutional elements prevailed. It would be wrong, therefore, to imply that Mongol institutions initiated Muscovite absolutism, centralism and social regimentation. Mongol rule only strengthened and intensified trends already existing in the North-East, which otherwise would have never become quite so despotic.[13] Giles Fletcher, an Englishman who visited Muscovy at the end of the sixteenth century, stated that there "the state and form of their government is plainly tyrannical, as applying all to the behoofe of the prince, and in a most open and barbarous manner."[14] It was a direct reflection on the power of the Khans.

The intensity of the Mongol impact on Russian society grew with the passage of time; its nature did change as relations between the Mongol conqueror and the Russian vassal also changed from a hostile to a relatively friendly attitude. The deep penetration of Mongol influences into Russian society was a sort of "delayed action" through peaceful absorption in the sixteenth and seventeenth centuries, long after Russian emancipation from Mongol rule. This took place after the disintegration of the Golden Horde, when the Tartars were entering the services of the Grand Dukes of Muscovy in large numbers.

The Mongol impact on the Russians was a twofold one. On the one hand, the Tartars negatively affected social and political developments in the European North-East. The ruthless invasion, conquests, pillaging and burning of the cities and countryside, the repeated devastating punitive actions and atrocities, ruined the Russian lands and delayed their economic and social development. On the other hand, the hardships imposed by the Mongols on the Muscovite-Russians, only hardened the latter, strengthening their endurance and will to resist, making them more fit to cope with the demanding conditions of physical and political survival at that time. The endurance the Muscovites acquired and the discipline they learned, enabled them to become successful empire builders in the future.

The ruthlessness of the Mongol way of life, the Mongol thirst to conquer, the never-ending court intrigues in Karakorum and Sarai, assassinations of Khans and their top aides as an unwritten ingredient of the imperial constitution and as a means of aquiring power, and insecurity in court relations, certainly affected the formation of the constitution and the government machine of the Grand Duchy of Muscovy.

The Muscovite-Russian ruling circles not only learned from their Mongol masters, but later on, during the gradual disintegration of the Golden Horde, a great many Tartars entered the service of the Grand Dukes, bringing with them their psychology, approach and methods. Having been Russianized, they left upon the Russian soul their Oriental imprint.[15]

The Mongols affected the formation of the Muscovite society and state in important ways. The Mongol imperial idea of the divine right of the Khan was certainly reincarnated in the imperial thinking of Ivan III, Ivan IV, the Terrible, Peter I, the Great, and all other Grand Dukes and Czars of Muscovy and emperors of Russia of the earlier days. As a matter of fact, the title of "Czar" the Russians first applied to identify the Byzantine emperor, and later, the Mongol Khan, as supreme rulers. After the Byzantinian and Mongolian empires collapsed, the Muscovite Grand Dukes immediately considered themselves the heirs to the might and glory of both, having combined in their government Byzantine traditions and Mongol tactics. Furthermore, having added the dynastic claims of the Rurik clan on Ukraine and Byeloruthenia, the Muscovite Grand Dukes found full justification for their future imperial authority and unilaterally assumed the title of "Czar."

Symbolic in this respect is the so-called Monomakh Golden Crown (Hat), the jeweled and fur-trimmed crown of the Muscovite-Russian Czars, a masterpiece of Central Asian art from the thirteenth or fourteenth centuries. It was apparently given to Ivan of Moscow by Great Khan Uzbeg. A Muscovite imperial legend connects the crown with the Kievan Duke Volodymyr Monomakh, claiming that he received the crown and other insignia from Byzantium as recognition of his imperial status. Although there was no connection between Monomakh and the Crown, it was an ingenious legendary confusion of issues to establish the false but politically useful association of Moscow with Byzantium, Kiev and Sarai.

Genghis Khan compiled the Mongol customary law and furnished it with his own legal concepts. He gave his empire the code of the *Great Yasa*, of which several copies circulated until the sixteenth century. The code of *Great Yasa*, a sacred and magic book of laws, substantially affected the social and political life of the Mongols, and also indirectly influenced the medieval institutions of Muscovy-Russia, along with the indirect impact of the code of *Rus'ka Pravda* of the Kievan Rus'.

Although no complete authentic copy of the *Great Yasa* has been preserved, fragments of it have been communicated to posterity from several sources.[16] The *Great Yasa* contained moralistic precepts, as well as the imperialistic ideas of the Mongols, in regulating the government, administration and army of the empire. It was a mixture of Mongol international, commercial, civil and criminal law. On those *Yasa* principles, the ingenious Mongol state machine and army organization were introduced to their Moscovite counterparts. The Mongol elements in the constitution of the Grand Duchy of Moscow were largely responsible for its future greatness.[17]

The Mongol Khans preserved for themselves supreme authority over the Russian lands. Muscovite-Russian national life and national institutions developed rather autonomously, but were modified to some extent. However, the final result of that evolution was astounding.

In the old Grand Duchy of Suzdal-Vladimir there was a strong anti-democratic trend. The Dukes attempted to suppress the people's meeting and the Council of Nobles. The Mongol era only strengthened this trend. First of all, the Mongol invasions destroyed old cities, impoverished the townspeople and consequently abrogated the authority of the people's meeting. The office of the chiliarch, *tysiatskii,* which was considered a people's tribune, was abolished in the wake of these developments. The Russian princes in general, and the Grand Dukes of Vladimir and Moscow, were anti-democratic, and they quickly closed ranks behind the absolutist Khan and used his influence to further suppress the political influence of the populace.

Furthermore, princely authority was derived at that time exclusively from the *yarlik* mandate. The prince was completely free from traditional limitations within Russian society. His subjects had to submit fully by virtue of his Mongol mandate. The *boyar* nobility, being anti-populace, also supported the prince in his measures. Moreover, because the nobles lost their previous power, and only through princely protection could preserve their wealth and social prestige in view of Mongol supremacy, they became loyal to the khan and to the prince, the Khan's deputy. The princes and the *boyars* rarely opposed or rebelled against the Mongol suzerain, but the cities did so on many occasions. Therefore, the Khans favored the princes and nobles over the townspeople.

With the growth of the power of the Muscovite Grand Dukes, the *boyars* flocked to Muscovy to swear their allegiance to them, since they hoped to benefit most for themselves. In this way the nobles lost all remnants of their independence and became the servants of the Grand Duke and the state. At the same time, however, they acquired an even more elevated social position and more power over the lower classes. On the other hand, having associated themselves with the Grand Dukes of Moscow, they supported the growth of their absolutism and national unification measures.

The Grand Dukes of Moscow were more subservient to Sarai and the Khan than other princes of the Russian North-East. This gained them the complete confidence of Sarai. Soon the Khans entrusted the Dukes of Moscow with a mandate to collect tribute for the Golden Horde and to protect law and order in the Russian lands in the name of Sarai. This authority the Grand Dukes used skillfully to enhance their political power and prestige throughout Russia. Subsequently, having increased their absolutism and might under the protection of the Mongol Khans, they became foremost spokesmen for Russian political independence and national unification. Frequently under the guise of enforcing the authority of Sarai, they actually forced other Russian princes and principalities to recognize and to submit to Moscow's leadership and supremacy and to yield to their ruthless, Mongol-like unification measures.

The Mongol impact on the Muscovite way of life was perhaps most strikingly illustrated by the fact that Muscovite diplomatic protocol in the sixteenth and seventeenth centuries was entirely Mongol in character and completely alien to Westerners with whom Muscovy sought contracts. The differences in the protocols of Muscovy and the West produced a great deal of misunderstanding, confusion and aggravation among the Russian and Western courts and diplomats of the period.[18]

Meanwhile, the old Council of Nobles (*boyars*) disappeared as a central advisory body for the prince, as the social and political position of the *boyars* changed. The Council was replaced by the Grand Ducal cabinet, an inner council and executive agency composed of the chief officers of the new state and court administration. Other new offices developed under Mongol influence as well: the quartermasters; the *departmental boyars,* who headed various departments of princely domains; the great lieutenant of Moscow; the heads of the new administrative divisions and central functions; and some other *"great boyars."* Unlike the old Council of Nobles, the cabinet was fully dependent on the Grand Duke and remained in permanent session. The imprint of the Mongol impact was clearly visible in each individual branch of Muscovite jurisdiction and administration, as well.

Capital punishment, corporal punishment of free citizens, including the nobles and junior princes, use of torture as a procedural device to obtain confessions and information, also other minor elements of criminal law were introduced into the Russian legal system under Mongol influence, giving the Muscovite Grand Dukes very efficient tools to enforce their despotic power.

The Mongol administration system, called into play by the fiscal needs of Sarai and its attempts to assure an adequate supply of manpower for the Khan's military projects, was for a long time retained by the Muscovite Grand Dukes and used successfully for strengthening their own political authority.

The grandducal military organization was almost a copy of the Mongol system, reminiscent of the old Kievan military institutions. The core of the grandducal defense force was the so-called court or *dvor,* analogous to the Mongol *ordu.* It consisted of military retainers, junior *boyars,* who were wholly dependent on the Grand Duke and bound to military service to him and not allowed to terminate their allegiance at will. The member of the *dvor* was not a companion or associate of the prince, as was the case in the framework of the retinue or *druzhina* in the Kievan era. The retainer was a military servitor, sometimes for a term but usually for life. This relationship only enhanced the absolute power of the Grand Duke. The Mongol retainers in the Khan *ordu* were also fully dependent upon the Khan and constituted the core of his army organization.

In the fourteenth century the Grand Dukes, following the Mongol example, began to use general military conscription, which included the town and village populations, to carry out their large military operations. General conscription was much more comprehensive than the old country militia system, with the burden borne mostly by the townspeople. Dimitrii Donskoi, his son Vasilii I, and other Muscovite rulers later made ample use of general army conscription.

Obviously, the changed administrative and army system required a new approach to state revenues and expenditures. In this respect, the Grand Dukes also profited from the Mongol experience. Sarai taught Russian society a strict tax discipline. Collection of the Tartar tribute was an absolute must and and whenever a city or region failed to comply, it could expect a devastating punitive expedition from Sarai. Therefore, when the Moscow Grand Dukes assumed the commission of collecting tribute for the Khan, they had no trouble in getting general compliance. Along with the tribute, the basic unit of assessment still continued to be the wooden plow or *sokha*. The Grand Dukes collected a variety of other taxes, tolls and fees, like excises, customs duties, sales taxes on horses and cattle and market fees, to defray the costs of constructing their future empire. A host of new officials was established to cope with the fiscal problems.

The Mongol rule also deeply affected the social structure of the Russian North-East, as indicated above in connection with the analysis of the growth of the absolute grand-ducal authority. Russian society became a service-bound one. The junior princes gradually entered into service and vassal relationships with the Grand Dukes of Moscow, whose power was growing under the Khan's protection, and later on, as a result of Moscow's taking over the heritage of the Golden Horde. Minor principalities, such as Rostov, Nizhnii Novgorod, Suzdal and others, having been gradually absorbed by Muscovy in the process of Russian unification, lost their autonomy as their princes became grand-ducal servitors for life and were selected for government, administrative and military positions. Their service-bound relationship, along with the nobility, was more intense than that of any other class. Their allegiance to the Grand Duke could not be broken. Severing this relationship was considered a political crime which resulted in the loss of all property and social status, and might lead to imprisonment and even death. Later on, the rules of the game in this respect were the same for the princes and *boyars* as well. In the Kievan era things were quite different. The *boyar* could freely change his allegiance from one prince to another, and he could not be penalized for that through personal injury or loss of property.[19] Other classes the townspeople and the peasantry, except the slaves, were service-bound to the Grand Duke, although to a lesser degree, than the upper social strata. This was a direct result of Mongol patterns infiltrating Russian society.[20]

The Mongol invasion, and Sarai's prolonged supremacy also deeply affected the economic life of the Russian North-East. The initial looting, burning and ruining of the Russian cities and countryside resulted in destruction of wealth and property. Masses of people were killed or taken into slavery. This reduced the productive capacity of the country enormously. In addition, the Khans ordered the conscription of skilled craftsmen and artisans. Many blacksmiths, armorers, jewelers, saddlers, stone-cutters, masons, builders and other craftsmen left Russia and migrated to various parts of the vast Mongolian empire to serve the Great Khan's interests. This resulted in a further decline of Russian economic potentials. A prolonged, almost century-long, economic depression resulted from these developments, gravely impoverishing the land. Local demands for manufactured goods could not be met. The town and village population especially suffered in this respect, while in the princely, noble and Church manorial households a few craftsmen remained by the Khan's grace to satisfy the needs of the upper classes.

North-Eastern commerce suffered a severe blow through the

destruction of its centers. However, trading was a very important field in the Mongol economy, especially of the Golden Horde. It was the foundation of its prosperity and growth, as was pointed out before. Therefore, the Khans soon began to promote trade in the Russian lands as well, and Mangu-Temir's efforts in this regard were particularly significant. He encouraged Novgorodian commerce and granted immunity privileges to the clergy and church-related social groups. In other ways, also, he was benevolent to the Russians. This promoted a slow recovery which was largely achieved in the manorial economies.[21]

The spiritual and intellectual life of Russian society did not remain unaffected by the Mongols. During the course of the invasion, the spiritual and intellectual processes of the North-East were substantially impoverished: churches, parishes and monasteries, the centers of spiritual and cultural life, were destroyed, along with the decimation of bishops, monks and priests. The standard-bearers of that life perished in great numbers during the invasion. Recovery was begun by Khan Mangu-Temir, who granted immunity to the Church. In the middle of the fourteenth century, the old monasteries began to recover and new ones were built in the next century and a half. General hardship facilitated the growth of spiritual processes. New monasteries were largely organized in distant locations of the forest wilderness of the North-East.[22] New saints appeared in the Orthodox Church. The bishops kept busy in their attempts to re-establish an effective church administration.

On the other hand, the Russian national struggle for liberation against the Mongol oppressor inspired the old Muscovite artistic and literary creations. National heroes of that struggle were praised in folklore, songs and poems, old saga-*biliny* were paraphrased, legends created, chronicles written and stories composed to bear witness to the times. The close contacts with the Mongols and the Orient during that era introduced Mongol and Oriental influences into Russian folklore, also many Mongol, Persian and Arabic linguistic elements into the Russian language.[23]

Truly indelible was the Mongol impact on Russian society.

PART II

THE MUSCOVITE ERA

CHAPTER EIGHT

THE BEGINNINGS OF MUSCOVY

The Family of the North-Eastern Principalities.

After the first and terrible shock of the Mongol invasion, the social and political developments slowly began to return to a more normal, although new way of life. The new political environment of the Mongol supremacy made this "normal way" vastly different from that of the old, pre-invasion era. The Russian North-East was no more politically sovereign as it had been under the rule of the powerful Grand Dukes of Suzdal-Vladimir. A complete political dependence upon the Mongol Khans followed. From now on, the Russian princes could hold their lands and maintain their authority only with the Khan's grace. Hence, with the few exceptions of those proud ones who did not want to submit and lost their "appanages", *udieli,* or died on the battlefields, most Russian princes suppressed their personal pride and in a very servile manner tried to please the Mongol suzerain in order to retain their lands.

One by one, as it was pointed out before, frequently assisted by their families, *boyars* and retinues, the princes made their numerous journeys either to Sarai or to Karakorum, to please the Khans with their submissiveness and servility. For example, Grand Duke Yurii II of Vladimir lost his life when resisting the Mongol invasion in 1238, while his son, Grand Duke Andrei II, also of Vladimir, was forced to give up his throne and to leave the country, for attempting a revolt against the Mongol oppression. There were others like those two, but in most instances, due to the circumstances, the Russian princes went to the Mongol capitals, and even made frequent journeys there to secure and to keep in the good graces of the Khans, each time bringing rich gifts and making solemn promises of faithful and loyal services. All this was in order to receive the Khan's *yarlik* or mandate (or official confirmation of the rights) to rule in their respective lands in the name and by the pleasure of the Mongol suzerain.

Alexander Nevskii made several trips either to Sarai or to Mongolia; Ivan I Kalita was in Sarai nine times and his son, Simeon the Proud, five times; the princes of Rostov, Tver, Riazan and other Russian lands were frequent visitors of the Khan. The princes had to accept and to live by the idea that their authority was not given to them by God, or derived from their hereditary and agnatic rights, or entrusted to them by their people, but that it was granted to them by the Khan, and that they could keep it only through their absolute submission and loyalty to the Mongol suzerain.

This servility to the Khans, and the traditional autocratic attitude of the North-Eastern princes toward their subjects, strengthened by the patterns of the Mongol despotism, formed a curious dual character feature of the Muscovite-Russian political constitution. Servilism toward those placed above and autocracy toward the subordinates, was a feature of Oriental origin. That dualism produced, of course, the political atmosphere of insincerity, and then projected itself into the whole social life of the Muscovite-Russian society.[1] *

Because the Khan's *yarlik* was the sole source of the princely authority, the contenders for certain lands and principalities had to involve the Khans in their dynastic quarrels to convince them about their respective agnatic rights and pretenses. Hence, Sarai soon became the center of the Russian political intrigues among the princes of the Rurik house which sometimes lacked any regal quality and thus exposed the true characters of those princely contenders. He who could lie, slander and bribe the best and was more servile and could promise better guarantees of loyalty than the other, frequently succeeded in getting the *yarlik*. Any other reasons and motives in deciding the dynastic quarrels were ignored by the Khans.

The faithfulness in submission to the Khan was proven best by the Russian princes by their compliance with the tribute obligation, the tax which was paid regularly by the Mongol dominated lands and peoples to the Khan as an evidence of their allegiance to his suzerain authority. At first only Mongol agents, usually with the full support and necessary assistance of the Russian princes, collected the tribute, while later on Sarai gradually authorized certain more trustworthy and servile princes to be tax collectors. The dukes of Moscow, who proved their allegiance to Sarai and gained the confidence of the Khans more than any other Russian princes, were particularly efficient in this respect.

They soon learned how to use their new authority to their own advantage. It does not mean that other princes of Rostov, Tver or Riazan, did not try that too, but they were not as successful. Under the guise of tax collection or attending other interests of the Khans, the Grand Dukes of Muscovy interfered with the internal matters of other North-Eastern principalities, strengthened their own political position and even extended their territorial possessions through the absorption of some new lands, originally under their tax jurisdiction. In most cases of those aggressive acts, the Grand Dukes acquired Mongol approval.

They also proceeded with skillful cheating of the Khans of their legitimate tax revenues and kept part for themselves in order to increase Moscow's wealth. They even, at times, falsely accused rival princes of treason toward the Khans to justify punitive actions in the name of the Khan, with substantial Mongol military assistance, like that one organized by Ivan I, Kalita against Tver in 1327. These expeditions were either to expand territorially, to gain more confidence of the Mongols in pursuing their own long-range plans, or simply for booty. Other princes, in particular those of the leading political centers of the Russian North-East during the Mongol supremacy, like Rostov, Vladimir and Tver, also tried similar political maneuvers to enhance their political positions, but without the same degree of success, until they were ultimately forced to pass over all the leadership of the Russian lands into the hands of the Grand Dukes of Muscovy.

Actually, the political prominence of Rostov, Vladimir, Tver and Moscow came one after another different time periods during the Mongol era of the Russian history, all four struggling against each other for the supremacy in the North-East of Europe. Minor principalities and border territories were, however, by no means only passive spectators or objects of dynastic and territorial warfares. Novgorod, Pskov, Riazan, Pereyaslavl, Yaroslavl, Kostroma, Mozhaisk, Kolomna, Bielooziero, Nizhnii Novgorod and other principalities actively participated in those struggles, either willingly — to protect their interests, or unwillingly — drawn in by the leading contenders for supremacy in the Russian North-East.

The Mongol domination, especially its imposition of tribute, at times provoked rebellions. Also, the insincere and subservient attitude of the Grand Dukes and princes of Vladimir, Moscow, Rostov or Tver, claiming Khan's mandates not always in accord with the local Russian interests, induced bloody insurrections, like those of Vladimir in 1252 and of the Suzdalian cities in 1262, and that of Tver in 1327. As it was pointed out before, the princes rarely took part in those anti-Mongol rebellions and uprisings. The Mongol masters nearly always answered such hostility with punitive military actions, accompanied by burning and looting the Russian cities, towns and countryside and wholesale taking of slaves.

At times, simply rapacious booty raids were undertaken by the Tartars or by some of their subservient Russian princes, which laid waste certain regions of the Russian North-East. Soloviov estimated that between 1228 and 1462, the Russian North-East suffered over forty such Mongol expeditions, which, along with some eighty other foreign interventions and invasions by the Lithuanians, Poles, German Knights and Swedes, and ninety dynastic wars among the princes of the Rurik house, impoverished the land. Life was difficult in those days. Of course, the entire North-East did not suffer equally from those bloody struggles. The borderlands in the East and South-East suffered the same from those foreign and domestic wars, while the western borderlands were exposed to different troubles. The eastern and south-eastern borderlands were hurt mostly by the Tartars, including the invasion by Tamerlane, while the western provinces were harassed most by the Lithuanians, German Knights and Swedes, who had no compassion for the ill fortunes of the Russians under the Mongol yoke, but tried to take advantage of their political difficulties.[2]

Immediately after the invasion, which brought the pillage and destruction of the power of Vladimir, the city of Rostov assumed a leading position among the north-eastern communities. Naturally, the princes of Rostov gained prestige. Rostov even dared, in 1262, along with some other important urban communities of the Suzdal region, to initiate an anti-Mongol revolt to resist the tough terms of the Mongol financial and tax policies. The revolt did not succeed, and harsh Mongol revenge was prevented by Alexander Nevskii's intercession. Later on, however, during the rule of Great Khan Mangu-Temir, who otherwise was more friendly to the Russians, Rostov became a favorite of Sarai, while the Rostov princes, the descendants of Constantine, Grand Duke Vsievolod's III eldest son, wholeheartedly cooperated with the Khan to suppress any possible revolts of the Russian populace and otherwise were subservient to the Golden Horde, making frequent journeys to Sarai.[3] Meanwhile, Vladimir restored itself to a dominant political position in the Russian North-East, and then gradually lost its power after the reign of Grand Duke Alexander Nevskii. This came about for two reasons. First, there were no outstanding personalities among his successors on the Vladimirian throne, second, the Khans apparently did not like the Vladimirian leadership among the Russian lands, fearing a potential threat to their continued supremacy in the North-East. The Khans preferred to be arbiters among the numerous and quarreling Russian princes as a security against any possible unification of all Russian lands in the name of a national liberation movement against the Mongol rule.

After Yurii was killed in action in 1238, resisting Batu's invasion, his brother, Yaroslav, assumed the grandducal throne, which he held for some eight years (1238-46). He was succeeded in short intervals by his brother, Prince Sviatoslav, who reigned only for two years (1246-48), and his sons, the Princes

Mikhail, Andrei, Alexander, Yaroslav and Vasilii. Mikhail ruled only in 1248, while Andrei — for some four years (1248-52), Alexander Nevskii — eleven (1252-63), Yaroslav — seven (1264-72) and Vasilii — only for a short four years again. In 1277, Alexander's son, Prince Dimitrii ascended the grandducal throne and ruled in Vladimir until 1294, succeeded by his brother, Andrei, from 1294-1304. The third brother, Prince Daniel, resided in the tiny principality of Moscow. Upon the latter's death in 1303, his son, Yurii, succeeded him. During Yurii's reign, the center of political power in the Russian North-East began to shift to Moscow. For three decades, the principality of Tver challenged Moscow's ambition.

In the wake of Russian allegiance to the Mongol Khans, the Russians not only had to pay tribute, but also had to render military services and participate in various Mongol conquests. Hence, the Russian military detachments, sent by various princes as evidence of their loyal submission to the Mongol suzerain, fought in various wars all over the vast empire. In the latter part of the thirteenth century, for example, the Russian troops fought in South China. Also, Khan Mangu-Temir ordered the Russian princes and their military detachments to join him in his expedition against the Alans in the north Caucasus. A number of princes joined the Khan and were praised by him and richly rewarded for services rendered.[4] On the other hand, the Mongols considered themselves the protectors and allies of the Russians, and helped them in the defense of their western frontiers against the Lithuanians, Poles and German Knights. Therefore, although the Mongol invasion and founding the Golden Horde checked and substantially delayed Russian colonization and ethnic expansion in the East, they certainly helped the Russian princes to resist foreign pressure in the West and preserved the provinces of Novgorod and Pskov as forever Russian.

After Yurii's II death, Prince Yaroslav, his brother, assumed the grand-ducal throne, upon which he was confirmed by Khan's *yarlink* in 1242. In 1246 he undertook his fateful voyage to Karakorum to prove his allegiance to the Great Khan. His assumption of the throne, initially without the Tartar mandate, was evidence of the fact that at first the Khans did not interfere with the question of succession among the princes of the Rurik house, and that subsequently they became involved in the problem by the political developments in the Russian North-East. They were drawn into internal matters of princely successions either by the lack of loyalty of some princes, or at the request of other princes.

Yaroslav continued to maintain the seniority right among the Russian princes and of Vladimir among the Russian lands, and represented common Russian political interests toward the outside world. He repulsed the invading Lithuanians in 1239, who were just in the process of building their powerful Grand Duchy and were soon to dominate entire Byeloruthenia and most of Ukraine. Yaroslav's son and deputy in Novgorod the Great, Alexander, following his father's advice, defeated the approaching Swedes in the battle on the Neva River in 1240. Then he defeated the invading German Knights, who succeeded in the short-lasting conquest of Pskov, in the battle on Lake Peipus, the famous encounter on the ice where the Germans were literally massacred in 1242. Three years later, in 1245, commanding a large Russian army drawn from all parts of Russia, Alexander defeated the aggressive Lithuanians on his father's authorization. The Russians in the European North-East proved to the Lithuanians to be unbeatable, hence the latter directed their conquering zeal to the South, where the Byeloruthenians and Ukrainians gladly accepted the Lithuanian military assistance in their opposition to the Mongols, and soon joined them politically and culturally in the creation of the Grand Duchy of Lithuania or the Lithuanian-Ruthenian Commonwealth.

Yaroslav's death resulted in a lengthy struggle for succession among his sons and other relatives. At first, his brother Prince Sviatoslav, who did not distinguish himself in any way, and shortly, Yaroslav's sons, Prince Mikhail and Prince Andrei, called the Second, succeeded each other for very brief intervals. Grand Duke Andrei II was an ambitious and patriotic ruler, who, after initial submission to Sarai, planned an all-out revolt against the Tartars and a liberation of the Russian North-East from the hated foreign oppressors. However, he lacked political realism. At that time the Mongol power was too overwhelming. The revolt failed and Andrei lost his throne and had to flee from the country in 1252. Andrei was succeeded by his already famous brother, Grand Duke Alexander Nevskii, who distinguished himself as the prince of Novgorod the Great, there acting as his father's viceroy. Andrei had been supported by the *boyar* aristocracy and the town population, and admired for his staunch opposition to the Tartars, while Alexander was generally hated for his submissiveness to Sarai.[5] However, history reserved for Alexander and not for Andrei its praise and distinction, because the first had more of a conception of political pragmatism in his time and was, therefore, more successful. Alexander's political opportunism was more advantageous for the Russian North-East than Andrei's patriotic stand in that era of Russian history.

Alexander Nevskii and the Subsequent Decline of Vladimir

Grand Duke Alexander Nevskii was, no doubt, an outstanding personality and an outstanding ruler. A Russian patriot, to be sure, but a very perceptive politician as well, who was rightly convinced that at that stage of the powerful Mongol supremacy, firmly settled over the entire East European area, any attempt to challenge it was simple madness, and would be Russian political suicide. The tragic examples of other Russian princes and principalities which tried to rid themselves of the bothersome Mongol yoke and ended in disaster, only reassured Alexander in his conviction. Hence, he decided to live in allegiance, peace and even friendship with the Mongol oppressor, in order only to get all possible advantages for the Russian cause from that submission to Sarai. In the long run, a twofold gain was derived in this way. First of all, further devastations of the Russian lands were considerably curtailed, and secondly, Russia secured herself an ally, who assisted her in her offensive and defensive military encounters with the western adversaries, Lithuania, Sweden and the German Knights.

The reality of the Mongol supremacy drove Alexander to an opportunistic political dualism. While deeply hating the Mongols, he cooperated with them to the fullest extent, making a bad impression on his contemporaries. They held him to be a traitor to the Russian cause who sold out his country to the Tartars.[6] On the other hand, he defended the Russian North-East most resolutely and devotedly against any other foreign aggression, strengthening his autocratic rule as a guarantee of the future unity and security of his country. In this respect too, he exploited the Mongol friendship to his advantage. Alexander properly appraised the power of the Khans, while at the same time he completely distrusted the Christian West. He never believed that the West would assist the Orthodox East in its political calamities of the Mongol supremacy. This he was taught on two accounts. First, King Daniel of Galicia and Volhinia (West Ukraine), who was in a similar predicament as Alexander, looked for Western assistance, and became fully disillusioned. Except for moral support, he got nothing from the West, no military help at all. Secondly, the Swedish, German and Lithuanian aggressions at that time against Novgorod the Great and Pskov indicated the true intentions of the Western neighbors with regard to the Russian political difficulties most convincingly, as mentioned before.

Alexander proved his submissiveness to the Khans by his frequent visits to Sarai and his journey to Mongolia in 1247. When his brother conspired against Sarai, Alexander denounced him, took the Tartar side, and then, with Khan's approval, assumed his brother's grand-ducal throne. Otherwise, he assisted the Mongols in any possible way, helped them to suppress local Russian anti-Mongol revolts and assisted Mongol agents in conscription of the population and collection of taxes. This way, however, he did succeed in diverting a few Mongol punitive raids on various Russian regions which might have suffered the slaughter of their population and devastation of the country.

When Sartak assumed Khan's authority, Alexander immediately went to Sarai to get his *yarlik* confirmed, while Andrei refused to do so, nursing his plans of resistance. Sartak sent a punitive expedition against Vladimir, which resulted in the expulsion of Andrei from the throne and the devastation of Vladimir and other cities in the Suzdalia in 1252. When, however, Ulagchi became the Khan, Andrei was pardoned and made the prince of Suzdal in 1256, through the intercession of Alexander.

In 1256-57, Great Khan Mongka and his Mongols were getting ready for their Chinese campaign. They needed more troops and more money. Hence, new hardships were imposed upon the subjugated peoples, including the Russians. A census of the population for soldier conscription and tax collection was held. Having well remembered the terrors of Sartak's punitive expedition of 1252, Vladimir and other cities and principalities, such as Riazan and Murom, did not hesitate to cooperate with the new Mongol demands. But Novgorod the Great, which so far did not experience the heavy Mongol hand, did not want to submit and refused to accept the Mongol agents. The situation was menacing. Alexander intervened to divert a disaster. Together with Andrei and Prince Boris of Rostov, and a large army, he forced Novgorod to cooperate, accept the Mongol officials and administrative scheme and pay the tribute taxation. Or course, Alexander's popularity was not enhanced by that action, but the city was spared from any devastating Mongol revenge.

In 1262 another major Russian revolt erupted. The cities of Rostov, Vladimir, Suzdal and Yaroslavl gave the initiative, being provoked by heavy Mongol taxation. The people's meetings were called and decided in favor of a general uprising against the oppression. At the beginning of the revolt, several Mongol agents were killed. Whether any princes were involved in the rebellion has not been ascertained. Nasonov's hypothesis of Alexander's direct involvement in the revolt is wrong. The fact is that after the outbreak of the revolt, Alexander hastened to Sarai and asked Khan Berke not to send any punitive expedition, promising him that the cities would submit and pay taxes and damages. Vernadsky was correct in saying that Alexander "hardly would have dared to face Berke had he himself been implicated in the riot."[7] During his stay in the Horde and negotiations with Berke, Alexander fell sick; he died on his way home.

In defending his country, Alexander fought with great persistency against the Western enemies. It was his obsession since he was prince of Novgorod the Great out of his father's will. In 1253, he supported his brother Prince Vasilii of Novgorod, in a campaign against the Lithuanians when they tried to invade the territories of that city. In 1256, Alexander led a large army against the Swedes, and in 1262, he sent his troops in support of Novgorod the Great, which at that time was in alliance with the Lithuanians who fought against the rapacious German imperialsm, disguised under the so-called missionary work of the Teutonic Knights to Christianize the European East, including the Orthodox Byeloruthenians and Russians. In the defense of the western frontiers, Alexander Nevskii was champion of the all-Russian cause. For his untiring efforts to protect his country against the revengeful punitive actions of the Mongols, he was canonized and made a saint by the Russian Orthodox Church. The Church showed a great and long-range political understanding and perception of the developments. However, Alexander's submissiveness to the Khans certainly had another effect; it hurt the prestige of Vladimir among the other Russian lands and principalities.

With Alexander's death, his brother, Prince Yaroslav II, assumed the grand-ducal throne, of course, with subsequent confirmation in Vladimir by the Mongol *yarlik*. His rule was marked by a progressive decline of the grand-ducal authority and Vladimir's prestige. The Russian North-East was gradually disintegrating. Individual principalities were assuming more and more autonomy and paying less attention to Vladimir. Soon the princes who acquired the grand-ducal throne began to care more for their own hereditary appanages or *udieli* where they resided permanently, than for Vladimir, to which they made only occasional trips. The diminution of Vladimir's authority was clearly indicated by the resolute disassociation of Novgorod the Great and Pskov from the Grand Duchy.

These two commercial centers were never great military powers. They were always looking for some strong political protectors. At first, Novgorod accepted its allegiance to Kiev, and then with the latter's decline, that of Vladimir. With the growth of the Mongol influences over the Russian North-East, Vladimir could scarcely function any more as a political and military protector of the social and commercial interests of Novgorod and Pskov. Moreover, Alexander's servility to the Khan and some of his actions along that line angered those two commercial communities. They progressively loosened their ties with the Grand Duchy, dependence upon which could not offer them anything more except a bothersome interference with their internal affairs.

In 1269-70 Novgorod refused to go along with the wishes of Grand Duke Yaroslav which were beyond the stipulations of a previous agreement. Yaroslav appealed to the Golden Horde, but Khan Mangu-Temir took Novgorod's side in the dispute. That greatly reduced the prestige and the authority of the Grand Duke. The Khan ordered him to negotiate new terms with the city and told him to respect its ancient liberties and commercial interests of free trading with the other Baltic ports. Of course, Mangu-Temir was interested in bringing Novgorod closer to the trade patterns of the Golden Horde which was *nota bene* economically trade oriented. The Mongol commercial considerations were decisive in the Khan's position in the conflict between Novgorod and Vladimir. On the other side, Novgorod must have used the powerful tool of persuasion in the form of rich briberies of the Khan himself and his officials which shortly became an indispensable ingredient in the Russian court intrigues in Sarai. Things got worse as the problem of princely successions and its solutions shifted more and more to the road of Sarai's court intrigues.

The case of Novgorod the Great induced other lands to

pay gradually less attention to Vladimir and become more independent of the senior princes in their domestic affairs in exchange for a rather loose allegiance to the Khans. Yaroslav's successor, his brother, Prince Vasilii, tried to restore Vladimir's seniority over Novgorod with a bloody war, this time assisted by Mongol troops. But the attempt did not reverse the long-run declining trend in the political fortunes of Vladimir's grand-ducal authority. The victory of the centrifugal appanage system over the old principle of seniority of Vladimir in the Russian North-East seemed to be inevitable. The history and the fate of the Grand Duchy after the reign of Yaroslav II was chaotic and troublesome, especially under Alexander's two sons, the Princes Dimitrii and Andrei III, who alternately ruled in Vladimir in the period from 1276-1304. The era was filled with dynastic and personal warfares and bloody struggles. Princes, *boyars,* and various cities were involved in the turmoil, ably instigated, supported and intensified by the intrigues manufactured in Novgorod, which was constantly using all possible means to reduce Vladimir's power to prevent it from regaining control over the ancient free city. During this period princes and cities often appealed to the Khan for arbitration or assistance. The Mongol troops frequently invaded the Russian lands, called by one prince or another to overrun the territories and cities of one principality or another. The princely feuds with *boyars* and the people's meetings were revived, after at first having been suppressed by the princely authority, supported by the Khans.

As a practical result of those developments, the Grand Duchy of Vladimir ceased to be a senior political entity, although its leadership traditions were not completely forgotten. Nevertheless, it was unable to discharge its old responsibilities for the common Russian cause any longer. Hence, the defense of the western frontiers against the Lithuanian, Swedish or German aggressions, so ably and courageously championed by Alexander Nevskii scarcely two decades ago, became the exclusive task of Novgorod and Pskov, who by this time, acquired their cherished and almost full political sovereignty in their relations with the western neighbors and in their relations to the Mongols.

Of course, since the senior and grand-ducal traditions were not entirely forgotten in Vladimir, its Grand Dukes even during that dim era attempted to act as the senior rulers, whenever an opportunity rendered itself. Thus, Grand Duke Andrei III continued along the tradition as the chief representative of all Russian lands in their relations to the Golden Horde. He also tried to assume the leadership in the wars against the Swedes in 1293 and 1301. The Swedes harassed the interests of Novgorod the Great. Andrei helped Novgorod despite his own grievances with the ancient city. This exemplified his all-Russian thinking, but he was too weak to enforce his seniority to the full extent.

Meanwhile a new era of Russian history had been started. Prince Daniel, Alexander's third son, became the ruler of the small principality of Moscow, to which he paid exceeding care, since he apparently had no chance to succeed to the grand-ducal throne. Perhaps he did not even want that position. Daniel died in 1303, before his brother, Grand Duke Andrei III. In this period of complete disintegration of Vladimir's political seniority and before Moscow succeeded in assuming its unquestionable leadership, the entire Russian North-East was divided into a great number of small princely appanages or appanage principalities, still being split into ever smaller appanage lands among the grandsons and the great grandsons of Grand Duke Vsievolod III, the Great Nest, of Vladimir and some other descendants of the Rurik house. As a consequence of such constitutional practice, at the beginning of the fourteenth century, the Russian country was a mosaic of a very large number of principalities with centrifugal tendencies, diminishing in power, wealth and authority of their princes and the rising power of the *boyars*, and at times, of the people's meetings as well. In many instances, the princes in their small appanage lands almost ceased to be sovereigns, and were rather latifundium landowners with semi-feudal rights, having rather, as Kluchevsky said, ownership authority over the population living in their possessions. Hence, in those instances not the sovereignty but the property rights of the prince gave him authority over the free and unfree strata of the people. In other instances, whenever the prince had a strong personality, he usually knew how to insist upon his traditional supreme rights.[8] It was Moscow's historical mission to combine those numerous principalities and lands again into one powerful and united state, while the mission of Vladimir in its time was to connect the pre-Mongolian and the Mongolian periods of Russian history, and to give it the necessary feature of continuity.[9]

The Ascendancy of Moscow: From Daniel of Moscow to Ivan I, Kalita

Moscow was first mentioned by a chronicle as a meeting place of Prince Yurii I, Dolgorukii of Suzdal and Prince Sviatoslav of Novgorod Siversky, having been, perhaps, one of Yurii's summer residences. As a village, it must have existed long before 1147. In 1147, the prince of Suzdal must have had a palace or a summer house there, while a few years later, apparently in 1156, Yurii ordered the construction of defensive walls around the settlement and "laid the foundations of the future town of Moscow." In 1177, the prince of Riazan conquered the town and burned it along with the surrounding villages. At the time of the invasion, Moscow was already the seat of a junior prince.

Located in Suzdalia, close to the borders of the Riazan principality, Moscow was for a long time politically unimportant, though participating equally with other north-eastern cities and towns in the eventful and at times tragic developments of the thirteenth century. It endured burning, looting and devastation by the Tartars or by the Russian princes themselves, involved in their petty feuds. Actually, the path of political prominence was first trod by Moscow with Prince Daniel's death and his son's, Prince Yurii's, ascent to the Muscovite throne and his acquisition of grand-ducal authority. Yurii was using his Muscovite principality as a military and political basis for the realization of his ambitions and plans as the Grand Duke of Vladimir, however, not relying solely upon Vladimir's traditions. This was also the beginning of a prolonged and bloody political rivalry between Moscow and Tver in their contest for leadership and supremacy among the Russian lands and toward their final all-Russian unification. Moscow emerged as the victorious power from that contest over old Vladimir and competitive Tver.

Various historians have attempted to explain why that small and obscure town of Moscow succeeded, in the relatively short time of some 150 years, to ascend to a first class position among the Russian lands, overcoming the rivalries of numerous contenders for "seniority" to become the capital of the Czardom of Muscovy, the immediate predecessor of modern imperial Russia. There have been many reasons given to account for that historical fact. In reality, the rise of Moscow was the result of a concurrence of many forces, which formed that new power in Russian history. First of all, Moscow's geographical location was mentioned by such historians as Platonov, Presniakov and Kluchevsky, as the factor which enabled it to remain in the political background or to appear actively on the political scene at the right time. It was an unimportant frontier outpost during Vladimir's political supremacy; unimportant enough as not to antagonize the powerful dukes. During the latter's decline, because of its convenient central location, Moscow was not immediately exposed to the fierce impact of the Mongol raids and expeditions, as for instance, the border principalities of Riazan or Nizhnii Novgorod were. Nor was it victim to the aggressive moves of the Grand Duchy of Lithuania, like Pksov, Novgorod the Great and Tver, who were absorbed by their relations with their western neighbors, the Swedes, the German Knights, the Poles, and the Lithuanians.

Secondly, Moscow being more centrally located among the Russian lands, could afford a more Russian "universal" look upon the affairs of the North-East of Europe, without being primarily concerned with the relations with the Mongols or with the western powers, but equally with both aspects of Russian foreign affairs, by having an all-Russian approach to those national problems. This gave Moscow an upper hand in the matters of the national struggle for consolidation and unification of all Russian lands.

Nevertheless, these two factors alone would not have decided the victorious political fortunes of Moscow without its exceptional luck of having, in a relatively short time, very able, skillful, canny and ruthless rulers, such as Ivan I, Kalita, Dimitrii Donskoi, Vasilii II and Ivan III. They followed each other at short intervals, and built Moscow's greatness. Other princes in the Russian North-East, judging from their political effectiveness, could scarcely measure up to the stature and personalities of the Muscovite princes and Grand Dukes.[10]

While the Khans looked rather with disfavor upon the Grand Dukes of Vladimir and their ambition to lead and to unite the community of the Russian lands, they agreed to the Muscovite aspirations in this respect. It seemed that the diplomatic skill of the Muscovite Grand Dukes was so outstanding, that it lulled down Mongol suspicion and obtained Sarai's consent and even cooperation in building and affirming the Muscovite leadership. On the other hand, timing was in favor of Moscow. The Mucovite Grand Dukes had to deal with the Mongols not at the very peak of their power, as the Grand Dukes of Vladimir had to do, but at the time when their might had already passed that point and had begun to decline, dissipate and disintegrate.

Moscow also defeated Tver in the contest for Russian leadership again because of the more skillful and successful policies of the Muscovite rulers. Tver tried to play politics. It meekly associated itself with Lithuania and also submitted insincerely to the authority of the Khans. The Tver pattern of foreign policy did not succeed. Mocow was more pragmatic; it more faithfully associated itself with the Golden Horde and was almost always hostile toward Lithuania and other Western nations; it always preferred an alliance with the Golden Horde until the very time came when it was strong enough to break with the Mongol suzerain altogether. Then also the Grand Duchy of Lithuania was no longer a threat to the Muscovites, since it was gradually being subjugated by Poland under the pretext of the Polish-Lithuanian Union.

The Muscovite policy did succeed since it secured for the princes and then for the Grand Dukes of Moscow a more continuous and more loyal Mongol assistance. The political foresight of Moscow's princes was outstanding. Nevertheless, still another instance should not be forgotten, when attempting to explain the phenomenon of Moscow's rise to political prominence and that is the role of the Russian Orthodox Church. The Church was no doubt a unifying force among the politically differentiated Russian lands. The Muscovite dukes had immediately grasped the availability of a great potential advantage from a possible association of their political ambitions with the religious mission of the Church. They soon managed to identify the interests of the Church with the interests of Muscovy and to present them to all Russians as one great cause. Subsequently, the Orthodox Church became the willing tool of the Muscovite-Russian imperial maneuvers.[11] Of course, Moscow's success in this respect also must be attributed to the outstanding political abilities of its rulers.

The political ascendancy of Moscow to national prominence began with tragic pains of an extremely bloody and prolonged dynastic feud between prince Yurii, Daniel's son, the surviving direct male descendant of Grand Duke Alexander Nevskii, and prince Mikhail of Tver, Nevskii's nephew. While the prestige of Vladimir was declining, so was Tver's power gradually rising, indicating a trend in the Russian North-East to move its political center toward the West, farther away from the Golden Horde and closer to Europe. Also Moscow was west of troubled Vladimir.

Having based his dynastic claims on his direct descendance from Alexander Nevskii, being his grandson, prince Yurii of Moscow made an immediate bid for the grand-ducal throne, following Grand Duke Andrei's death. Yurii's claim was so much more well founded, because already at Daniel's time, in 1302, Moscow had acquired supremacy over the old principality of Pereyslavl, the princely seat of early Kievan time, which prior to 1302 was under Vladimir's control. Historically, the instance could be considererd as a link in Moscow's gradual process of at first allying itself with and then extending its authority over Vladimir. Prince Mikhail of Tver, pretending to the leadership in the North-East, vigorously opposed Yurii's bid, raising his own pretenses to Vladimir's grand-ducal throne. The dynastic warfare flared up and lasted for years.

Yurii meanwhile attempted to expand his control over Novgorod the Great, Nizhnii-Novgorod, Kostroma and other neighbor lands, in particular, the principality of Mozhaisk. As a result of annexation of Mozhaisk into the principality of Moscow, Yurii established the Muscovite domination over the entire upper flow of the Moscow River which gave him some economic control over more extensive territory than Muscovy itself. Meanwhile, Prince Mikhail invaded the regions of Pereyaslavl to undermine Yurii's political position.

Both contenders tried by various means to increase their political powers and support of their grand-ducal bids. The *boyars* and townspeople of various north eastern lands were intensely involved in the intrigues and struggles in support of either contender for the grand-ducal throne and all-Russian leadership. Of course, Yurii and Mikhail had to submit their cases to the Khan's ultimate decision. The Khan bargained for the highest price while both Yurii and Mikhail played a very low and shady game, exposing each other. Finally Prince Mikhail succeeded in receiving the Khan's mandate for the Vladimir Grand Duchy in 1304 in exchange for a high price of financial obligations toward the Horde which he could hardly meet. This soon brought him at odds with Sarai. Yurii never actually accepted the fact of Mikhail's grand-ducal authority and intrigued continuously against his rival. Conflicts erupted intermittently, making the political and social situation in the Russian North-East utterly confusing, while the Grand Duchy disintegrated and the all-Russian national interest was seriously hurt. Mikhail called himself the Grand Duke of all-Russia. However, his prestige was never great among other Russian lands.

Mikhail, following the old Vladimir's tradition, wanted to impose his supremacy over Novgorod. The city did not wish to give up its recently acquired independence from the weakening Grand Duchy and asked Yurii of Moscow and the Khan for assistance. At first, in 1312, Mikhail prevailed by subjugating the city with the Tartar help and reduced the city's ancient liberties. Yurii, who meanwhile became the prince of Novgorod, had to leave the city, went to Sarai, married the Khan's daughter, stayed there for a long time conspiring against his deadly foe. In 1316, Novgorod rebelled against the Grand Duke Mikhail again, expelled his agents and defended itself successfully against his armed intervention. At this time, Yurii, now Khan's son-in-law, who worked on Mikhail's doom and actually instigated the city's rebellion, returned to Muscovy with a large Mongol military force and Khan's blessings and defeated Mikhail. Mikhail made a mistake. He captured Yurii's wife, the Mongol princess, who died in captivity. Yurii immediately accused his arch enemy of poisoning his wife. The incidents irritated the Khan and he summoned both Mikhail and Yurii to Sarai where the first was imprisoned, tried and excuted for his lack of loyalty.

Although Yurii got rid of his enemy and acquired the *yarlik* on the Grand Duchy of Vladimir, his political troubles did not end. First, the heavy financial obligations toward the Horde in exchange for the grand-ducal throne, to be borne by the Russian population, were intolerable and he could scarcely meet them, as Mikhail could not before. And then, Mikhail's son, Prince Dimitrii, challenged Yurii's authority and continued to intrigue and plot against him in Sarai as well, raising the point of his not meeting his financial responsibilities, thus putting his loyalty toward the Golden Horde in doubt. Yurii could not get his country's support in his troubles, and finally, when he went to Sarai in 1324, he was assassinated by Dimitrii and his hirelings. In turn, the Khan punished Dimitrii for the crime by executing him. Prince Alexander of Tver, Dimitrii's brother, became the Grand Duke, but not for long. In 1327, anti-Mongol rebellion erupted in Tver; the Khan's agents were beaten and killed.[12]

Meanwhile Prince Ivan, Yurii's brother, settled in Moscow with the Mongol blessing. The Tver rebellion was immediately used by Ivan to advance himself politically. He went to Sarai and declared his loyal submissiveness and readiness to assist the Khan in the suppression of Tver. Heading a large Mongol punitive expedition force, in 1327 Prince Ivan crushed the revolt of Moscow's rival city and became the Grand Duke a few months later in 1328. Alexander left the country temporarily and went to Lithuania for shelter.

Ivan I, Kalita or Moneybag, of Moscow, as Grand Duke of Vladimir, actually initiated the permanent unification of these two important cities into the one state of Muscovy. Although in the later period some interruptions in this association did occur, eventually the Grand Duchy of Muscovy prevailed and became the Czardom of Muscovy of which Vladimir was only one of the cities. Then, for the next half century, four Muscovite rulers put forth all their efforts to establish the new center of political power in the European North-East. At first, they made it the leader among various principalities and lands, subsequently, they united all Russian ethnical territories under one scepter. Ivan I, Kalita, ruled from 1328 to 1341; his eldest son, Simeon I, from 1341 to 1353; his other son, Ivan II, from 1353 to 1359; and Ivan's son, Dimitrii Donskoi, from 1359 to 1389. During these sixty years, there were three major political issues the Muscovite Grand Dukes had to undertake: to keep good relations with the Horde, to champion the cause of the Muscovite-Russian unity, and to deal with the growing power of Lithuania.

In the best traditions of Alexander Nevskii, Ivan Kalita submitted to the Khan. He considered that policy to be his best assurance of a free hand in his dealings with the many problems he faced. Of course, like Alexander Nevskii, he antagonized many Russians by his servile attitude toward Sarai. He ignored that and cunningly used his friendship with the Khan to his advantage. Meanwhile Tver, Novgorod the Great, and Pskov exhibited a growing friendship with the Grand Duchy of Lithuania to rid themselves of the Khan's bothersome interference. Lithuania's growing political and military power was gradually absorbing various Byeloruthenian and Ukrainian territories and extending her influence over the western Russian regions. She seemed to Ivan Kalita as the single and most serious threat to the ideal of Russian unification. He knew from his own experience the traditional Mongol loyalty to all faithful vassals of the Khan. Hence, he leaned so heavily on the Mongol protection in his unification measures. Otherwise, Ivan used intrigue, lies, denunciation, cheating, blackmail and assassination techniques in order to overcome any centrifugal tendencies of the western regions, as exemplified by the Alexander of Tver instance.

Alexander returned in 1335 and assumed his reign with Khan's consent but still keeping up good relations with Lithuania. Ivan immediately seized the opportunity to increase his influence over Tver and to make it dependent upon Moscow. However, this did not terminate the Moscow-Tver antagonism. The Lithuanians continued their attempts to interfere with the western Russian provinces and intensified their animosities toward Moscow. Ivan paid in kind by plotting against Lithuania and her Russian friends, drafting Sarai in his maneuvers.

In order to advance the all-Russian cause, Ivan successfully used his church policy, in this respect actually following the pattern outlined by Yurii, his predecessor. The Orthodox Church was a big landowner in Russia and was looking for a powerful protector of its material wealth. Yurii and Ivan hurried to establish themselves in the eyes of the Church as the worthy champions of its secular interests and religious ideals. In 1300 the Metropolitan seat was established in Vladimir to raise its declining prestige. In 1304 Metropolitan Maxim died. Grand Duke Mikhail wanted to seat his own candidate as the Metropolitan, but the Patriarch of Constantinople, the theoretical head of the entire Orthodox Church, appointed Peter for the seat. The Grand Duke opposed and denounced the new Metropolitan while Yurii of Moscow supported him ardently. Eventually, Metropolitan Peter was duly installed in 1310.

As a result of that prolonged ecclesiastic and political conflict, Mikhail lost and Yurii gained a mighty support of the Church, which soon proved to be of tremendous value to the cause of unification. Peter allied himself wholeheartedly with Moscow and favored Yurii's protection over any other Russian prince. He lived in Moscow most of the time and from there he directed the affairs of the Russian Church. He died in Moscow in 1325. Peter's successor, Metropolitan Theognost, officially transferred his seat to Moscow, making it the capital of the Russian Orthodox Church. The political and religious impact of the move has been paramount. First of all, the Church aspired to the ecclesiastic universality of the Orthodoxy in general, and that of the Russian one in particular, and this automatically strengthened Moscow's centralist position and centripetal tendency of other lands toward Moscow in the religious aspect.

This religious aspect soon radiated over the political scene in accordance with the traditions of the Eastern Church to lean heavily upon the secular power, as was the case in the Byzantic empire. Secondly, the Church, having received protection from Moscow's dukes, showed them loyalty and support, which in turn enhanced their political position and strengthened their all-Russian prestige. And thirdly, the instance had a lasting religious and dogmatic aspect, since it initiated the future Muscovite-Russian *Ceasaropapism,* the complete subordination of the Russian Church to the Russian political power and its willful use for political imperial ends with no regard to its religious mission.[13] Grand Duke Ivan did not foresee the long-range consequences of his alliance with the Church, but he well understood its immediate political gains for the Muscovite state. He did everything possible to make Moscow the spiritual center of all the North-East.

Ivan was also an excellent manager of the economic, and especially the financial affairs of his state. Because of that he got the surname of *Kalita or Moneybag.* He was very thrifty, but he also shrewdly cheated the Khan by taking from the tribute collection, and did so without producing any suspicion. From the money he saved and accumulated, he purchased land whenever and wherever possible. He bought principalities from minor princes who lost their "sovereign" rights *de facto* or were not capable of managing their landed estates. These new acquisitions Ivan added to his state domains to enrich himself and his Muscovy. Furthermore, he spent substantial money on ransoming Christian people from the Mongol captivity and settled them on the purchased land and in the acquired villages in order to increase the economic productivity of those Muscovite domains. Ivan's business and financial talents, together with his growing political power, made him popular among the *boyars*, who were increasingly associating themselves with the Muscovite duke and getting from him the protection of their properties and social status. In this way, the nobles, along with the Church, became another force which in the long run contributed to the advancement of Muscovite centralism. They expected to gain more from associating themselves with Ivan and his successors, than from any other Russian prince; hence, they were in favor of the centripetal tendency around Moscow and somehow induced other princes willingly or unwillingly to acknowledge Moscow's "seniority" and leadership.

Ivan I, Kalita died in 1341. He had realized the presence of the centrifugal and decentralist tendencies on the part of various princes, even among his close relatives, and so he left a testament to his sons in order to prevent the Muscovite Grand Duchy from breaking up into smaller appanages. Preventing that possibility was the only guarantee of its future greatness and its ultimate fulfillment of the mission of the Russian unification. Ivan's testament made his eldest son the over-all trustee of the joint family ownership, the Muscovite state. Although the other sons received their territorial shares, they could no longer freely dispose of them. All shares were unalienable and component parts of the family-owned entity, the Muscovite principality. Ivan did not use the term "appanage" to make his intention clear, while the reapportionment and redistribution of the territorial shares was dealt with as a family affair.[14]

The material security of the junior or minor princes was then arranged by the additional interprincely agreements, like that among Ivan Kalita's sons. The agreements also safeguarded the rights of the *boyar* nobles to own land and to move freely throughout entire Muscovy. For the sake of safety of their landed estates and their use, the nobles preferred to preserve the unity of the Grand Duchy and sided with the Grand Duke to prevent political particularism, dynastic quarrels and loss of political stability, in general. The later interprincely agreements and practical developments in the Grand Duchy under the rule of Ivan's successors strengthened that trend of the Muscovite centralism and progressively weakened the position of the junior princes, and subsequently blurred the distinction between them and the *boyars* in service-tenure relationship to the Grand Duke, as pointed out before.

The Years of Upheavals:
From Simeon, the Proud to Dimitrii Donskoi

The political development under Ivan's successors, Grand Dukes Simeon, the Proud, Ivan II, the Meek, and Dimitrii Donskoi were going into two centripetal directions, occasionally disturbed by the returning centrifugal tendencies, provoked by some ambitious princely opponents to Moscow's leadership. But it seemed historically clear, that Moscow had already captured the leadership in the European North-East and would keep it for some time. The first trend expressed itself in the continuous effort of those three rulers to unify the Muscovite principality internally by stressing the authority of the Grand Duke by gradually diminishing the powers of the junior or minor princes who had progressively been reduced to the upper aristocratic status in the grand-ducal service. The second materialized itself in the stubborn attempt of the Grand Dukes to bring other Russian lands, from outside the Muscovite principality, under their undisputed and sovereign authority. The Muscovite Grand Dukes ruthlessly destroyed constitutional, personal and real property rights of other princes, lands and peoples in the North-East. They were not always successful in this respect, as Dimitrii Donskoi's example illustrated. He could not marshal unanimous support of other Russian lands in his warfare against the Mongols in 1380.

The era of those three rulers of Muscovy was a very stormy one. The princes of Nizhnii Novgorod and Riazan assumed the grand-ducal titles to oppose Moscow's claim on seniority and wanted to disassociate themselves from it. The separatism of Novgorod the Great, Pskov and Tver, who allied themselves with Lithuania, along with the centrifugal tendencies of Nizhnii Novgorod, Riazan and other lands, plagued the reign of the Grand Dukes Simeon, Ivan II, and Dimitrii Donskoi, at times causing a temporary decline of Moscow's authority and prestige. The Lithuanian interference with the western Russian regions was considerable. These regions played their political game between the Grand Duchy of Lithuania and the Golden Horde and against the Muscovite ambitions. Eventually those lands had to recognize the leadership of and accept allegiance to Moscow. As Platonov said by quoting the chronicle: "Simeon the Proud had all Russian princes under his hand."[15] It might have been the chronicler's literary exaggeration of the political situation, but it well illustrated the over-all tendency.

Simeon assumed the throne in 1341 and was confirmed by the Khan. The Khan theoretically affirmed Simeon's authority over all Russian principalities, the fact to which the mentioned chronicler might have referred. In reality that "authority" meant the grand-ducal jurisdiction over the entire process of the Mongol tribute collection and Simeon's position as intermediary between Sarai and the other Russian principalities in the Russian-Mongol relations. It was this jurisdiction which all Muscovite Grand Dukes, starting with Ivan Kalita, used so ingeniously toward advancing the cause of the all-Russian political unification. Nevertheless, the privilege was received by Simeon at the very high price of heavy financial commitments to the Horde, and he, when trying to collect the tribute at that rate, ran into the above difficulties with various Russian lands. The instance intensified the centrifugal trend, repulsed these lands from Moscow and drew them, especially the western provinces, more closely to Lithuania.

Otherwise, Simeon succeeded in cementing Muscovy internally by the agreement with his brothers, who in accordance with their father's testament, fully recognized his seniority rights. But, when Grand Duke Simeon died in 1353, during a great plague which decimated the population of East Europe, the political upheavals, following his death, delivered ample proof of the still shaky status of Moscow among the North-Eastern principalities and lands. In particular, Prince Constantine of Nizhnii-Novgorod made a bold attempt to seize the grand-ducal authority. His bid was not popular, and Simeon's brother, Prince Ivan, the Meek or Red, was confirmed by Sarai as the Grand Duke to follow in the family tradition.

Ivan's short reign of six years was continuously tormented by the growing power of Lithuania. At that time additional Byeloruthenian and Ukrainian lands joined the Lithuanian-Ruthenian Commonwealth, and its Grand Dukes made a resolute effort definitely to dominate some Russian western regions, as well. The Lithuanian-Ruthenian threat continued and intensified during the reign of Grand Duke Dimitrii until the death of the able Lithuanian-Ruthenian ruler, Grand Duke Olgierd, in 1377. Otherwise, a growing unrest in the Golden Horde slightly relieved Ivan's difficulties. His death released another outburst of dynastic warfares among the Russian princes and Moscow's leadership was contested again.

This time two Dimitriis fought for the grand-ducal throne: Prince Dimitrii of Moscow, Ivan's son, to whom history later on gave the surname of "Donskoi" because of his celebrated victory over the Mongols in 1380 in the Don region, and Prince Dimitrii of Suzdal, son of Constantine of Nizhnii-Novgorod. Dimitrii of Suzdal was tempted to repeat his father's bid for the grand-ducal title.

Since, however, the Golden Horde experienced at that time its great political trouble due to the succession wars among Khan Janibeg's three sons, complicated by subsequent intervention of other candidates, both Dimitriis could now rely more on their own forces while playing one Mongol candidate for the Khan title against the other. In fact, however, it only increased the intensity of the struggle in Muscovy. Soon both Dimitriis received the grand-ducal *yarliks* from two different Mongol rulers, rapidly succeeding each other in the course of the general chaos in the Horde. Finally, in 1365, the bloody dynastic conflict in Russia was ended with the victory of Prince

Dimitrii of Moscow, who retained the grand-ducal authority. But his authority did not remain unchallenged for long.

Already in 1366, he had to wage a war against Tver, where leadership ambition was reviving. Then, the *yarlik* on the Grand Duchy was repeatedly granted by Sarai to Prince Mikhail of Tver, and the old Moscow-Tver rivalry was, perhaps, purposely intensified by the Mongols. Dimitrii did not intend to submit to Sarai's decision and give up his seniority. The war between Dimitrii and Mikhail lasted for years, but eventually the latter had to recognize Moscow's political supremacy, for several reasons. First of all, he could not meet his financial responsibility toward the Khan, and consequently lost his support. Secondly, the Lithuanians, who supported him all the way, changed their minds and deserted him, causing his and their own political defeat in the anti-Moscow struggle. And third, Dimitrii was certainly a more able and much shrewder statesman. In conclusion, Tver promised to refrain from any direct negotiations with the Lithuanian-Ruthenian Commonwealth and the Golden Horde, although it still retained a considerable degree of autonomy.

In the Dimitrii-Mikhail contest again the paramount role of the Russian Orthodox Church in strengthening Moscow's position was shown. Metropolitan Aleksei, like his predecessors, Metropolitans Peter and Thegonost, exhibited a most aggressive loyalty toward the Muscovite throne. He himself ruled Moscow as a regent during Dimitrii's minority, and thereafter considered him the God-appointed bearer of the Orthodox universality and future Russian unification. Aleksei planned to extend his ecclesiastic authority, with the help of powerful Muscovy, over all Eastern Europe. The existence of a separate Metropolitan seat in the Ukraine for the Ukrainian Orthodox Church in the Lithuanian-Ruthenian Commonwealth, in particular, antagonized him very much. This annoyance was intensified because the jurisdiction of both Metropolises was, from the very beginning not clearly defined, but rather gravely confused through the political interferences of Muscovy, Lithuania and Poland.[16] On the other hand, Aleksei's ambition to become the Metropolitan for Russia, Ukraine and Byeloruthenia fit well into the grand imperial plans of Moscow as a stepping stone in first gaining at least some ecclesiastic influence upon these three countries before any political control would become possible. Maybe Aleksei thought in terms of politics and religion when he aspired to the jurisdiction over all East Europe?

With these ideas in mind, Metropolitan Aleksei in a blasphemous and sacrilegious way supported Dimitrii, abusing his ecclesiastic authority in the feud between Moscow and Tver and in Moscow's anti-Lithuanian policy. He used the devices of Church blessings for Dimitrii and his allies, and those of interdicts and excommunications against Dimitrii's enemies. A breach of allegiance to Dimitrii was usually declared by Aleksei as a crime against the Church, the universality of which was, in his mind, identified with the political success of Moscow. The Lithuanians and the Russians who allied themselves with Lithuanians, were branded as "enemies of the cross" or "godless fire worshippers" and excluded from the Church. Although Aleksei was canonized by the Orthodox Church, in reality his abuses of the ecclesiastic authority for the sake of political expediency scarcely justified the move. In the long run, Aleksei deeply hurt the moral and religious "sanctity and purity" of the Russian Orthodoxy by initiating the trend of its complete subordination to the secular power of the Grand Dukes and Czars of Muscovy-Russia. The Czars in the best traditions of the Greek-Byzantine empire, badly abused it for the sake of advancement of their political plans. Of course, the Russian Church in the future secured many political successes from Moscow. Aleksei's action initiated the making of the myth of "Moscow being the third Rome," which later on became a lasting cornerstone of the Russian imperialism in the Ukraine, Byeloruthenia, the Balkans and the Middle East.[17]

No doubt, Aleksei's condemnation of all Moscow's enemies helped Dimtirii to marshal many believing Russians behind the cause of the Muscovite mission to unite all Russian lands. Many who abhorred Dimitrii and Moscow and later on, also

Dimitrii's successors because of their ruthlessness, joined them only in order not to endanger the salvation of their souls. Although, after Metropolitan Aleksei's death in 1378 the alliance of the Orthodox Church with Moscow's political scheme weakened for some time, the old trend was then restored. Aleksei's successor, Metropolitan Cyprian, was not a Moscow enthusiast and preferred the independence of his Church from any secular power. He inclined toward a Church union with Rome, to which Moscow's rulers were opposed. Hence, Dimitrii lost at that time, at least partially, the unconditional support of the Church in his political projects.

Dimitrii's *yarlik* upon the Grand Duchy dated back to the 1360-ties, but his confirmation on that throne and reduction of the tribute by the new Khan Mamai followed in 1371. However, the earlier double dealings of the Mongols with Dimitrii of Suzdal and with Mikhail of Tver, deeply antagonized him and produced serious frictions between Moscow and Sarai. Dimitrii did not hurry with tribute payments. On the contrary, he fought against the Volga Bulgars, a loyal vassal of the Horde, defeated Riazan, and invaded the Mordovian lands, where the Mongol detachments were stationed. Also, together with Nizhnii-Novgorod and Riazan, Dimitrii defeated the Tartars in a few small encounters. Khan Mamai was aroused and sent his troops to punish the Muscovites and their allies. Grand Duke Dimitrii routed those troops in the battle on the Vozh River, Oka' River tributary in 1378.

Meanwhile, having some domestic difficulties, the Khan decided to teach Dimitrii a good lesson. He concluded an alliance with the Lithuanian-Ruthenian Grand Duke Yagailo (Jagiello) for a joint action against Muscovy, which seemed to develop into a serious threat by that time for both, the Golden Horde and the Lithuanian-Ruthenian Commonwealth. In Muscovy, on the other hand, there was intense anti-Tartar feeling. Dimitrii was preparing an all-out and all-Russian, anti-Mongol crusade, although he could not succeed in mobilizing all Russian lands under the banner of the liberation from the Mongol yoke. Novgorod the Great, Pskov, Nizhnii-Novgorod, Tver and some other principalities did not join the crusade, in this way challenging Dimitrii's "seniority" as well.

They had serious reservations. At first, they were afraid of antagonizing the Khan, being uncertain about the outcome of Dimitrii's anti-Mongol adventure. And second, they were suspicious of Muscovy. It could be a treacherous deal for them to exchange a relatively mild tyranny of distant Sarai for a rather intense Russian "unity" under Moscow's control, the rapaciousness of which was well known to them. Meanwhile Riazan tried to play against both ends, maneuvering between Moscow and Sarai, and as a result of its duplicity, the city and the land were pillaged and devastated by both, at first by the Mongols, marching against Dimitrii, and then by the Muscovites, taking revenge for Riazan's infidelity. Dimitrii's own people and his vassal princes constituted a considerable military force of 150,000 men to resist Mamai's invasion.[18] Negotiations with Sarai's envoys did not bring any positive results.

Grand Duke Yagailo was supposed to join his forces with those of Khan Mamai in September 1380 to knock out Dimitrii. Dimitrii did not wait for that at all. His armies, blessed by Abbot Sergei of the Trinity Monastery for the crusade, intercepted the Mongol force of some 200,000 men on the Kulikovo plain, where the Nepriadva River joins the Upper Don. The fierce battle took place on September 8. Dimitrii himself was knocked unconscious for a few hours, but the Muscovite armies won a splendid victory by completely routing Mamai's troops. The Tartars were taken by surprise, completely disorganized and were forced to flee from the battlefield. Although the Muscovites captured a rich booty, the encounter was otherwise a very costly one, in terms of lives lost. Yagailo missed the battle by only two days of march.

On the eve of the battle on the Kulikovo plain, there was in Muscovy a general feeling of apprehension and an anticipation of an approaching disaster of a merciless Mongol revenge for Dimitrii's arrogance But the battle was a sign of the declining Mongol power, which for over 150 years seemed to be invincible. It was also a sign of growing Muscovite power. The Kulikovo incident made an impression upon the contemporaries, the Russians themselves, the Lithuanians, Ukrainians, Byeloruthenians and West-Europeans. Historically speaking, it marked a dawn of a new era.[19] It was not the termination of the Mongol supremacy, but it was the beginning of the end. This was the first successful attempt in some one hundred years of political struggle that concluded in a complete liberation of Muscovy from the Mongol-Tartar rule. In this battle, Grand Duke Dimitrii earned his heroic surname "Donskoi."

Of course, the immediate development of events brought a grave disappointment upon the Muscovites. Meanwhile, Khan Mamai was defeated by new Khan Tokhmatish, and the latter led in 1382 a revenge expedition against Dimitrii, his Muscovites and his allies. He invaded extensive Russian territories, tricked Moscow to open its gates to the Mongol detachments, when Dimitrii was raising more troops in the north, and pillaged and burned the city. Also other Muscovite cities and towns were sacked and devastated by the Mongols. Then Tokhmatish retreated with rich booty without affording an open encounter with Dimitrii's forces.

Once again, Russian princes, one after another, including Dimitrii himself, hurried to Sarai to offer and swear their allegiance to the Khan. Grand Duke Dimitrii remained a vassal of the Golden Horde until his death in 1389, but since the Kulikovo incident the Mongol grip over Russia loosened the previous firmness. Tired of fighting lonesome battles against the Mongols, Dimitrii put all his energy during the last years of his reign into strengthening Muscovy. He successfully ended his long conflict with Riazan who recognized his seniority. He also strengthened the political ties of Moscow with Novgorod the Great, Nizhnii-Novgorod and other autonomous principalities. There was an unquenchable desire to rid themselves of the embarrassing Muscovite protection. The trend of getting away from Moscow manifested itself among the Russian lands immediately after Dimitrii's death.

Within Muscovy itself, the position of the Grand Duke toward the junior princes was decisively affirmed in the direction of his absolutism. The old seniority principle had gradually been replaced by the idea of grand-ducal sovereignty. The political rights of the junior princes continued to fade away and gradually were replaced by their new elevated social standing as the upper aristocrats, holding possessions assigned to them by, and bound to loyalty to, the Grand Duke. However, Dimitrii's testament held to the traditional patrimonial principle and harbored the danger of subsequent splitting of Muscovy into numerous principalities and making his life work void.[20]

Chapter Nine

THE GREAT DUCHY OF MUSCOVY

The Struggle for Consolidation: Vasilii I and Vasilii II

There is no clear-cut demarcation line to separate the previous period of the political beginnings of Moscow from that of the Muscovite Grand Duchy under the four able rulers, Vasilii I (1389-1425), Vasilii II (1425-1462), Ivan III, the Great (1462-1505), and Vasilii III (1505-1533). Kluchevsky said the following to identify the age: "... pale phantoms succeeding one another on the suzerain throne under the names of Ivan I, Simon, Ivan II, Dimitrii, Vasilii I and Vasilii II.... All the Muscovite princes, down to Ivan III, are as like one another as a string of peas, so that the observer is often puzzled to decide which of them is, say, Ivan, and which Vasilii."[1] However, Kluchevsky is not correct either in minimizing the personalities of those Muscovite rulers, who in fact were outstanding, and who energetically enlarged and strengthened their Muscovy. Nor is he correct in painting a rather romantic picture of those turbulent times, or in failing to paint out the essential changes, which were gradually creeping in and separating the two periods.

Two or three important developments may be taken into consideration as the marking stones of the changing times between the evolving Muscovite power and the Muscovite grand-ducal status. First of all, the battle of the Kulikovo plain marked the initiation of Moscow's emancipation from the Mongol suzerainty and the beginning of a new social-political twist of a gradual Mongol influx into the service of and dependence upon the Muscovite Grand Dukes. The creation of the Tartar princedom of Kasimov by Vasilii II is the outstanding example of this. Secondly, although since Ivan I, Kalita, Moscow was practically the residence of the Grand Duke of Vladimir and the Metropolitan of the Russian Orthodox Church, it finally became the real capital of the Muscovite Grand Duchy. Prince Dimitrii Shemiaka, Vasilii II's adversary, fought for the dominance of Muscovy and not for the acquisition of the title of the Grand Duke of Vladimir, like the two Dimitriis did a few decades before. And thirdly, since the Vasiliis, Moscow, and not any other city of the North-East, was the center of the political events of the all-Russian scope. Of course, serious troubles for Moscow were not yet over.

With Dimitrii Donskoi's death, centrifugal and decentralization trends immediately recovered in the Russian North-East. Novgorod the Great, Nizhnii-Novgorod, Pskov, Riazan and Tver attempted to overthrow any shadow of their previous dependence upon Moscow. Mikhail of Tver tried anew to capture the grand-ducal authority. However, Prince Vasilii, Donskoi's son, inherited the throne in 1389 and was duly confirmed by Sarai. The entire period of the two Vasiliis was characterized by very close cooperation with the Tartars in the true tradition of Ivan Kalita, although without that earlier submissiveness. Of course, the continuous chaos in the Golden Horde substantially helped both rulers to maintain their independence of political action.

As a result of the generally favorable attitude of the Horde toward Moscow, to which there were serious historical exceptions, Vasilii I managed to purchase the *yarliks* on Nizhnii-Novgorod, Gorodets and some other minor principalities on the eastern and southeastern frontiers of Muscovy and in this way extended the territory and authority of the Grand Duchy. But otherwise, Vasilii's control over Riazan was rather weak. Novgorod the Great, despising the Muscovites and their despotic rulers, continuously kept close relations with the Lithuanian-Ruthenian Commonwealth, and even negotiated with Sweden and the German Knights, while Tver during the first quarter of the fifteenth century made itself virtually independent from Moscow.

The Orthodox Church did not give Vasilii the same loyal support as it had given his father. Metropolitan Cyprian and his successor, Metropolitan Photius, had a more "universal" outlook on church matters and wanted to unite and protect all Orthodox peoples without singling out any particular one. Hence they showed more friendliness toward the Lithuanian-Ruthenian Commonwealth and its Orthodox population and rejected Moscow's self-styled religious mission.

In Muscovy itself the internal political difficulties were mounting. The conflict between the *seniority* and the *patrimonium* principles of succession continued to mar the dynastic relations and to weaken the authority of the Grand Duke. The occasional Tartar raids impoverished certain Muscovite regions. Such instances provoked the process of territorial redistributions among the members of the Muscovite house in order to give each and every one an equitable share to live up to the princely status. The redistribution device was applied largely according to Donskoi's testament, who dreamed of the liberation from the Tartar yoke and at the same time realized fully its dangers.[2] The frictions between Grand Duke Vasilii and his two princely brothers, Yurii and Constantine, did not add to Vasilii's peace of mind and to the grand-ducal authority or Moscow's power, either.

Vasilii was, however, a very shrewd politician and diplomat. When the Tartar alliance appeared to be of little advantage because of Sarai's internal trouble, and the opportunity for more independence from the Khan was offered, he moved closer to the Lithuanian-Ruthenian Commonwealth. At that time, the Commonwealth was ruled by the able Grand Duke Vitovt (1392-1430), and achieved its greatest territorial extension. This induced Vasilii to ally himself with him. Out of political expediency he married Vitovt's daughter to strengthen Moscow's dynastic ties. It did not stop him, however, in waging war against his father-in-law, if it seemed to him politically worthwhile.

The Lithuanian-Ruthenian Commonwealth was a serious threat to Moscow for several reasons and had been for decades, as it was pointed out above. Able Lithuanian rulers, Mendog, Gedymin, Olgierd and others, extended their domination over Byeloruthenia and Ukraine by defeating the Tartars. The Ukrainian and Byeloruthenian territories willingly accepted the authority of the Lithuanian Grand Dukes. The Orthodox Ukrainians and Byeloruthenians were of a higher cultural level and introduced the pagan Lithuanians to Christianity. The Lithuanians never treated the Ukrainians and Byeloruthenians as second-ranked citizens or grand-ducal subjects but as full-fledged and equal partners in the Commonwealth. The old Ruthenian or Ukrainian was the official language of the Grand Duchy. Already in the second half of the fourteenth and at the beginning of the fifteenth centuries, three nationalities lived in friendship and union within the framework of one political organization.

The Lithuanian-Ruthenian Grand Dukes then assumed the mission to include under their authority all Byeloruthenian and Ukrainian lands, and desired to extend their rule over the aristocratic-democratic Commonwealth of Novgorod the Great and the territory of Pskov, which were extremely hostile toward the presumptuous Muscovites and also showed leanings toward the West. Hence, in the normal course of political developments, the interests of Muscovy clashed with those of the Lithuanian-Ruthenian Commonwealth and continued to clash intensely for more than two centuries. These conflicts were then inherited by Poland, which, under the disguise of a federation with Lithuania, incorporated the Lithuanian-Ruthenian Commonwealth, and definitely crushed the liberties of the Lithuanians, Ukrainians and Byeloruthenians after the so-called Union of Lublin in 1569.[3]

The Muscovite and Lithuanian-Ruthenian political conflicts were motivated by the assumptions of the Muscovite rulers who referred to their imaginary claims to Ukraine and Byeloruthenia, these skillfully manufactured from the historical tradition of the old Kievan authority of the Rurik house. The Muscovite Grand Dukes unilaterally declared themselves to be the heirs of the Kievan Rus' Commonwealth, while the existence of the Lithuanian-Ruthenian state claimed the same on a more factual base, since Ukraine, the cradle of the Kievan Rus', was an integral part of the latter. The Lithuanian-Ruthenian Commonwealth denied the Muscovite pretenses. Furthermore, Moscow, as it was shown before, also assumed a self-styled mission of being the leader of the Orthodox Christianity, and could not tolerate a separate Metropolitan seat in Ukraine. Moreover, the Ukrainian Metropolis had heavy Western leanings, while the Muscovite one was ardently anti-West and anti-Catholic. These developments helped to deepen the controversies.

The extension of territory and prestige of the Lithuanian-Ruthenian Commonwealth was a real challenge to Muscovy. Vasilii's alliance with Vitovt did not last long. Once Vitovt failed in his attempt to organize an anti-Tartar crusade and was defeated by the Tartar forces in the battle of the Vorskla River in 1399, Vasilii deserted his father-in-law and returned to the traditional Muscovite alliance with the Horde. In 1406, Muscovy engaged in a war against Lithuanian-Ruthenia, supported by a large Tartar military force.

The friendly relations with the Horde were not permanent, as twice Vasilii faced a very serious Tartar threat. First, Khan Tamerlane, one of the greatest military geniuses in the world's history, overran Riazan and other south-eastern regions of Russia producing a deadly threat for Moscow in 1395. Vasilii decided to resist Tamerlane militarily, while the latter, having realized the possibility of heavy losses to be encountered in an open war with Vasilii, withdrew. The religious Russians thought they were delivered through a direct intercession of the Virgin Mary.[4] Then, Prince Edigay, insulted by Vasilii's exploits in the North-East, invaded Muscovy in a surprise attack. In 1400, Vasilii waged a war against the Volga Bulgars, captured their capital and devastated their land, which was allied with the Golden Horde. Edigay decided to punish Moscow for disobedience and the default in tribute payment. Secretly, in order not to let Vasilii know about his impending plans, and under the disguise of preparing for a war against Lithuania,

Edigay suddenly attacked Muscovy. Vasilii had been informed by his Tartar friends about Edigay's real intentions. Prince Edigay appeared at Moscow's gates on December 1, 1408, but failed to take the city, and retreated, after receiving 3,000 rubles indemnity. Nevertheless, his Tartars devastated the countryside and restored the autonomy of Nizhnii-Novgorod, which had been acquired by Vasilii as part of his patrimonial possessions. Egiday did not encounter Vasilii's main forces, therefore, the very purpose of his expedition — to break Moscow's growing power — did not materialize. As a result of this and other unfortunate Tartar operations, Vasilii, at the latter part of his reign befriended the Lithuanian-Ruthenian Commonwealth and was less cordial to the Golden Horde, upon which his political dependence was largely nominal. At his death, Grand Duke Vasilii I made Vitovt the guardian of his widow and his son.

Grand Duke Vasilii's death in 1425 released one of the most prolonged, bloody and savage, succession wars in Moscow's history. The heroes of that 20-year-long dynastic warfare were Grand Duke Vasilii II, Prince Yurii, his uncle, Vasilii and Dimitrii Shemiaka, Yurii's sons. The warfare lasted intermittently until 1453, when Dimtrii Shemiaka was poisoned, leaving Grand Duke Vasilii II in uncontested control. Meanwhile, amid the struggle Prince Yurii died, his son Vasilii and the Grand Duke Vasilii II were blinded. The whole dynastic warfare resulted from the ancient conflict between the above mentioned principles of *seniority* and *patrimonium* succession. Prince Yurii, Vasilii's I brother, was the senior in the family, and claimed the Muscovite throne, while Vasilii II claimed it too as his father's *patrimonium* (*otchina* or *udiel*, before).

Vasilii II ascended the throne as a boy and he remained under the guardianship or regency of Metropolitan Photius and the Muscovite *boyars*, who were generally very loyal to their sovereign and faithfully championed his rights to the grand-ducal throne for the reason indicated above. The loyalty of the Church, the servitor princes, the nobility, the people of Muscovy and the hired Tartars, plus his own cruelty, enabled Vasilii II to overcome all obstacles. He did it, in particular with the help and assitance of his loyal followers, like princes V. Serpukhov, S. Obolenskii, I. Striga-Obolenskii, nobleman F. Basenok, Metropolitan Iona and some others.

Vasilii was certainly the most ruthless and cruel of all the Muscovite rulers prior to Ivan IV, the Dread or Terrible, of whom he was a worthy predecessor. Poisoning, blinding, imprisoning and murdering were among his political weapons, which he administered equally to his enemies, such as princes Vasilii and Dimitrii, his rivals to the Muscovite throne, and to his friends and supporters, such as Prince Vasilii Serpukhov, whenever he deemed such action to be politically expedient. The *Chronicles* were horrified and terrified by Vasilii's savage cruelty, although the historical past of the Russian North-East has never been exactly drenched in loving care.[5]

It is astonishing that such a cruel ruler could have enlisted such loyal support of his people in general. On the other hand, Vasilii's ability to pick the right lieutenants was certainly an outstanding quality of his personality. His statesmanship cannot be denied, so much more, because during the last fifteen years of his reign he was blind. Furthermore, Vasilii's political ability could be proven by the use of the hired Tartars for the growth of Moscow. They were not exactly loved by the Russians, but it did not bother Vasilii at all. At that time the Golden Horde progressively distintegrated and new Tartar Khanates were formed in various parts of East Europe. Numerous Tartars were migrating and looking to enlist the service of new lords. Vasilii accepted them wholeheartedly and used them extensively in strengthening his rule. Of course, not all Russians liked it and even accused him of selling out Russia to the Tartars.

At first, the dynastic warfares reduced Moscow's prestige, but during the last two decades of his ruthless rule, Vasilii managed to restore that prestige fully, having contributed to the consolidation of the Grand Duchy and extension of its political influence over other territories. It was the real conception of the future Czardom of Muscovy.

During the reign of Vasilii II, the relations with the Lithuanian-Ruthenian Commonwealth and the Tartar Hordes were the main issue of the Muscovite foreign policies, also determining the course of the domestic developments to a great extent. Grand Duke Vitovt, originally entrusted with the guardianship of young Vasilii II, did not hesitate to interfere in the Muscovite-Russian affairs. In 1426 and 1428 he intervened in Novgorod the Great and Pskov, during the Muscovite succession war, when Moscow changed hands. Tver and Riazan, relying on Vitovt's interference in Muscovite affairs and on Moscow's internal weakness, recovered their independence from the Grand Duke almost fully. Finally an agreement was reached between the Lithuanian-Ruthenian Commonwealth and the Grand Duchy of Muscovy to accept the Ugra River as a demarcation line of their political influences and territorial claims.

Meanwhile, the Tartars began to present an acute threat. The Golden Horde was falling apart. In 1445, Kazan, in 1449, the Crimean, and in 1466, the Astrakhan Khanates were established. The internal struggles in the Horde continued among the warring factions, while the pretenders for leadership tried several times to enforce the Tartar rule over the Muscovite-Russian North-East. Mongol prince Ulu Mahmed who once sought Vasilii's support, invaded and settled in the region of Nizhnii-Novgorod, and from there repeatedly raided various Russian provinces, and besieged Moscow itself. Riazan was raided several times; other regions also suffered from the Tartar exploits. Muscovy was invaded twice, in 1455 and 1461.

In July 1445, Grand Duke Vasilii attacked Ulu Mahmed's detachment, was defeated and taken prisoner. This created a chance for Prince Dmitrii Shemiaka, Vasilii's cousin, and his followers, who hoped to remain the rulers of Moscow. They urged Ulu Mahmed not to release Vasilii. But Vasilii had friends, in particular Ulu Mahmed's sons, Kasim and Yakub. He was released from prison after paying 25,000 rubles ransom and returned to Moscow, bringing many Tartars with him who became his most trusted lieutenants and servants. In 1446, Prince Dimitrii and his associate, Prince Ivan Mozhaiskii, seized Moscow, and subsequently captured and blinded Grand Duke Vasilii for his real and alleged crimes.[6] Though blinded, Vasilii finally managed to return to the grand-ducal throne with the help of his loyal and trusted supporters. Dimitrii Shemiaka fled to Novgorod, where he was poisoned by Vasilii's agents in 1453.

Blinded but not subdued, the Grand Duke began to restore his authority. Following his earlier commitment toward his loyal Tartar friends, princes Kasim and Yakub, he established the princedom of Kasimov under Kasim's rule and Moscow's protectorate. Its capital of Gorodets on Volga was later renamed Kasimov. The new princedom was supposed to be a bulwark in Moscow's defense against the Kazan and Sarai raids. Historically, the creation of that princedom may be considered the practical termination of the Mongol supremacy over Muscovy-Russia. It meant that since that time and during the last decade of his reign, Vasilii was fully independent from any Tartar suzerainty.

In 1456, Vasilii invaded and incorporated Novgorod the Great, to stop the Lithuanian interference and to punish the city for its pro-Shemiaka sentiments and acts of the earlier date. The ancient city became an integral part of Muscovy, although for a time it retained some of its traditional liberties. Similarly, the Muscovite control over Pskov was also strengthened. Riazan accepted Moscow's protection by the decision of its dying prince, placing his son under Vasilii's guardianship. Although Tver retained its autonomy, it had to acknowledge Novgorod's incorporation and its being an integral part of Vasilii's patrimonium, a part of Muscovy. The city also pledged its support for Vasilii against the Tartars, the Lithuanian-Ruthenian Commonwealth, and the German Knights.

The rising power of the Muscovite autocracy was best reflected by its attitude toward the important Church event of the time. In 1439, the Council of Florence convened, and attempted to restore Church unity between the Catholic West, with its capital in Rome, and the Orthodox East, with its capital in Constantinople. The Greeks, threatened by the invading Turks, hoped for some assistance from the Catholic world, and were ready to end the prolonged Church disunity. However, the Muscovites did not want any part of the union. The idea of Western influence upon Muscovite politics was highly antagonistic to the chauvinistic Muscovite-Russian mind, which was very suspicious of foreigners. Metropolitan Isidore, who was in Florence and championed the cause of the Church union, was imprisoned upon his arrival in Moscow. The council of the Russian bishops, under the influence of the rising Muscovite *caesaropapism,* condemned the Florence Union in 1443.[7] The idea of Moscow's mission of becoming the third Rome of a true Christianity was subconsciously growing in the Muscovite minds. In 1453, Constantinople fell into the hands of the Turks; this encouraged the Muscovite leaders to consider Moscow the capital of the Orthodoxy.

During the latter part of his reign, Grand Duke Vasilii made his son Ivan his co-ruler, following the Byzantine tradition, which Moscow was about to take over, although unilaterally. In his testament Vasilii followed the patrimonial principle, while entrusting his widow and his sons to the protection of the Polish King, Kazimierz or Casimir. The strong political foundations of Muscovy, including Vladimir, Novgorod the Great, Nizhnii-Novgorod and other lands as its integral parts, prevented any disintegration, on his death in 1462. He was followed on the throne by his son and co-ruler, one of the greatest statesmen of Muscovy-Russia, Ivan III, the Great.

Political Consolidation: Ivan III, the Great

The era of the two Vasiliis, I and II, could be considered an historical unit of the Muscovite struggle for consolidation. The era of Ivan III (1462-1505), and Vasilii III (1505-1533), should be treated as the unit during which the actual consolidation and structure of the Muscovite autocratic state was concluded. Ivan I, Kalita, subservient to the Mongol suzerain, received his share of some 6,000 square mile territory, which had increased by the end of the reign of Vasilii II to some 15,000 square miles, a domain practically free from the Mongol interference. Ivan III and Vasilii III then produced an aggrandizement of the Muscovite state, which became absolutely sovereign after the Ugra River incident in 1480 and entered the high waters of international politics of the European continent.

During Ivan's III time, before all the Russian ethnical territories were consolidated under the Muscovite scepter, the Muscovite-Russian imperialism was born, developing its plans to absorb Byeloruthenia and Ukraine, Muscovy's immediate Slavic neighbor lands. When the opportunity presented itself, Ivan III declared himself, though unilaterally and arbitrarily, the heir of the Kievan-Rus' state, of which the Russian North-East was once only a colonial borderland. The birth of the Muscovite-Russian imperial drive under Ivan III was strengthened by the doctrine of Moscow as the Third Rome and the heir of the Byzantine empire. The idea was also activated by Ivan in the consequence of his marriage to the Princess Sophia Paleologue, a niece of the last Byzantine emperor. Of course, these developments have started a new era of Russian history, very different in many respects from the Russian past.

Ivan III ascended the Muscovite throne as a twenty-two-year-old man, who was already familiar with state affairs, having been the co-ruler with his blinded father, Grand Duke Vasilii II. The blindness of his father actually enabled him to get a better grasp of Muscovite politics. On the other hand, he was also an outstanding personality, a great, though a ruthless statesman. His ambition was his own limitless power, and also the glory of a consolidated Muscovy. He approached his ideals from various angles; by extension of the authority of the Grand Duke over all Muscovy and other Russian lands; by strengthening Muscovy's international position; by raising certain historical and political claims to other, non-Russian lands; and by using the Orthodox Church as a political tool of his aggressive moves. In doing all these things, Grand Duke Ivan III simply followed in the footsteps of his predecessors; he improved the techniques and was more successful, because he started from a stronger and wider political base.[8]

First, Ivan put all his effort into the issue of Muscovy's consolidation. Vasilii's II testament gave Ivan the largest territorial share of the *patrimonium* and the grand-ducal authority, but did not exclude the possibility of a future dismemberment;

as previously stated, his four brothers, princes Andrei Senior, Yurii, Boris and Andrei Junior were also given each a princely share or domain. Ivan initially honored his father's will, though he absolutely insisted on his grand-ducal seniority and sovereignty, and did not intend to allow any breaking up of the Muscovite *patrimonium*. His brothers did not like Ivan's autocratic impositions, and prolonged frictions developed. In 1472, Prince Yurii died, and Ivan immediately appropriated Yurii's entire domain to his own grand-ducal possessions over the opposition of his other three brothers. Using pressure, duress, compulsion and even extortion techniques, Ivan induced his brothers to officially accept his seniority position by the inter-princely agreement of 1473. On his part, however, Ivan did not commit himself to anything. He convinced his brothers to join him in his campaign against Novgorod the Great, but refused to share the proceeds of the victorious exploit. The city and its lands were incorporated in his grand-ducal domain. The embitterment of his brothers was deep.

When Ivan entered into serious conflict with the Golden Horde, his brothers tried to exploit the situation to their own advantage. They opposed Ivan and plotted against him by negotiating the support of the Polish King Casimir for their case. Casimir was seriously annoyed by and afraid of the rapidly growing Muscovite power and was organizing an anti-Moscow crusade, negotiating the project with the Golden Horde, the German or Livonian Knights and Sweden. Princes Andrei Senior, Boris and Andrei Junior were drawn into the project. King Casimir's undertaking did not materialize; a war resulted among Ivan and his brothers as a consequence. Pskov suffered mostly, and was considerably destroyed. At the critical moment of Khan Akhmad's invasion in 1480, Ivan succeeded in negotiating a truce with his brothers and inducing them to join their forces with his to face the Mongol menace in a united way in exchange for a promise to meet their demands. Immediately after the Mongol threat was over, Ivan again mendaciously forgot his word given to his brothers. The conflict between brothers continued.

Another agreement between Ivan and his brothers similar to

that of 1473, asserted Ivan's grand-ducal sovereignty and his supreme authority in the military and matters of foreign relations and limited the junior princes in this respect. The relations among the brothers remained highly strained to the very end, because of Ivan's iron determination to proceed with the consolidation project. With the subsequent death of his two brothers, Andrei Junior and Boris, Ivan incorporated their domains, although with some delay until Boris' two sons died. From the very beginning, Prince Andrei Senior exhibited more independence from Ivan than the other brothers. In consequence of his insubordination, he was imprisoned by Ivan and there he died. Andrei's sons had to live and die in exile, while the Grand Duke appropriated all these territorial domains to enlarge his authority and Moscow's power. By his insistence on the sovereignity of the Grand Duke in all matters, Ivan in fact abolished the old concept of the hereditary and patrimonial rights of the junior princes and established a new principle of the temporary grand-ducal grants, which could be enjoyed by those princes as long as they remained loyal to the throne and lived up to their commitments toward their suzerain, the Grand Duke of Muscovy.[9]

Secondly, Grand Duke Ivan III, the Great, did not wait with the other political undertakings until the internal consolidation of Muscovy was completed. He tangled with many problems at once. From the very begining he assumed the famous project of "gathering all Russian lands," referring to the Kievan tradition of one "Rus'." Pressure, force, war, exortion and blackmail were used also in this area of Ivan's politics. In order to dress his imperialistic zeal in more acceptable forms, Ivan applied interprincely agreements and even tolerated some sovereign rulers in various parts of the Russian North-East, until the proper time would come for him to crush any such autonomous or semi-independent communities or principalities. "Gathering all Russian lands" proceeded as described below.

Under pressure, Prince Mikhail of Vereia was gradually transferring various parts of his principality to Ivan, and with his death, the latter acquired Mikhail's entire *patrimonium* on the basis of a testament, which was carefully prepared in the Muscovite chancery on Ivan's order. Also the princes of Yaroslavl, under similar conditions, transferred their domains to Ivan and entered into his service. Later, the princes of Rostov did the same. In 1472-1473, the city and region of Perm, once a vassal of Novgorod, was dominated by Moscow. In 1478, the final annexation of Novgorod the Great followed, under the conditions as described in an earlier chapter.

After its unfortunate experience with Vasilii II, Novgorod continued to exhibit independent tendencies and negotiated with the Lithuanians to rid itself of Moscow's rule. This was against the earlier commitments taken on by the city. Hence, Ivan invaded it in 1470. The leaders of the pro-Lithuanian party were either executed or escaped abroad. The city paid an indemnity, but it was still allowed to retain some ancient liberties. Ivan was not known to keep his promises, and continuously interfered in the city's matters. The dissentions in Novgorod were growing. Taking advantage of the turmoil, Ivan increased his interference even more, which indirectly indicated his intention to suppress the city's ancient liberties once and for all. The pro-Lithuanian party recovered in Novgorod and anti-Muscovite feelings were clearly expressed. In response to these developments, Ivan invaded its territory, besieged the city, and after some negotiating, the Novgorodians had to accept Ivan's dictation. Novgorod's ancient constitution was abolished and a complete incorporation of the city in the Muscovite state structure followed. The leaders of free Novgorod were imprisoned, deported or executed, its foreign trade suppressed.[10]

The principality of Tver soon followed the other Russian lands in its political fortune. At first, in order to save its independence, the princes of Tver joined Ivan's anti-Novgorod campaign with the latter's promise to respect Tver's autonomy. But Ivan failed to respect his earlier commitment. Hence, Prince Mikhail of Tver negotiated for Polish support for his case. Under the pretext of Tver's Polish conspiracy, Ivan invaded the principality in 1485 and incorporated it into the Grand Duchy of Muscovy without any hesitation. It was the end of the one and a half century long rivalry between once powerful Tver and Moscow, for which the bells tolled. Four years later, in 1489, Ivan forced Viatka into submission. Riazan was a satellite of Moscow and at least half of the principality was Ivan's domain by way of a bequest since 1503. As a result of the untiring consolidation effort of Ivan's Muscovy, the end of his rule should find that only Pskov and another half of the principality of Riazan remained semi-independent states out of the great number only a few decades before.

The third sector of Ivan's policies was the export of Muscovite imperialism beyond the Russian North-East, which was already manifest in the early period of his reign. In 1501, in a conversation with a Hungarian envoy, Ivan raised his claims upon Ukraine and Byeloruthenia, once territorial parts of Kievan Rus', whose heir he considered himself. His dynastic pretenses as a member of the Rurik house might have been fantastic and presumptuous, but historically they have represented the birth of the Muscovite-Russian imperialism, at first directed against the two immediate neighboring countries only, but in the future becoming limitless and insatiable. In the twentieth century it reached all six continents of our globe.

The developments in the Polish-Lithuanian federative state helped Ivan III considerably to put his foot in the door. The Poles were driving a hard Catholic, pro-Uniat line, in accord with the ideas of the Florence Union. The anti-Orthodox and Polonization policies gravely antagonized and deeply hurt the patriotic and Orthodox Ukrainians and Byeloruthenians. Some of those Ukrainian and Byeloruthenian princes thought about a secession from the Federation and a restoration of the old Lithuanian-Ruthenian Commonwealth, completely independent of Poland. An unsuccessful plot was even organized on the life of King Casimir. After the plan to secede from the Polish-Lithuanian federation failed to materialize, some Ukrainian and Byeloruthenian princes began to transfer their allegiance to the Orthodox Muscovite Grand Duke, hoping that by the move they would be able to preserve their Orthodox faith, their respective nationality and political autonomy. Although it was not customary according to the standards of that time to consider a transfer of allegiance to mean that the landed estates of the transferee came under a new territorial sovereignty, Ivan assumed that, and immediately raised his sovereign claims upon such areas. The Polish-Lithuanian government objected, since Ivan's action was contrary to the previous agreements between Lithuania, on the one hand, and Moscow, Riazan and other Russian principalities, on the other. Under Ivan's unceasing pressure, the Polish Lithuanian government had to yield, and by the treaty of 1494, Muscovy acquired some Byeloruthenian territories, along with Lithuania's relinquishing some of its old claims to some Russian areas and its recognition of Ivan's new title of the Grand Duke "of all Rus'."[11] The assumption of that new title by Ivan, originally only a Grand Duke of Muscovy, clearly indicated his intention of activating his aggressive claim upon the Ukrainian and Byeloruthenian territories south and west of Russia.

In order to ease the strained Lithuanian-Muscovite relations, which had become an historical tradition, Alexander, Grand Duke of Lithuania who a few years later was crowned king of Poland, married Ivan's daughter, Princess Helene. However, things turned out differently. The religious element was introduced by Ivan to keep the issue acute. Ivan maintained that Helene was forced to become Catholic against a previous agreement on this point, although she denied that. Relations were strained again. Meanwhile some other Byeloruthenian princes and nobles, resisting the Polish inspired religious and national discrimination, went over to Moscow and were warmly accepted by Ivan. All these developments led to an open war, desired by the aggressive Ivan. In 1500, the Muscovite troops invaded the borderlands of Lithuania. For two years the war was waged, until 1503 when a truce was concluded, which gave Muscovy additional Byeloruthenian and Ukrainian areas with nineteen towns, including the city of Chernihiv, the ancient residence of the Ukrainian princes from the Kievan times.[12] Ivan's military pressure to dominate additional Byeloruthenian and Ukrainian territories was soon resumed by his son and successor, Grand Duke Vasilii, to materialize the objectives of the Muscovite-Russian imperialism in that area.

The fourth leading aspect of Ivan's policies was the ultimate conclusion of the lasting issue of the Mongol-Tartar suzerainty over the Russian North-East, which in the time of Vasilii II, was mostly nominal. Tribute had not been paid for some time. However, the Mongols had not yet given up their claims upon Russia. Khan Akhmad of the Golden Horde invaded the Russian territories in 1472, burned, pillaged and devastated the countryside and towns. Four years later, in 1476, Akhmad demanded that Ivan come in person to Sarai, but Ivan failed to do so. Although he deeply angered the Khan, negotiations were dragging between the two parties without any satisfactory conclusion in sight. Finally, Akhmad negotiated an anti-Moscow alliance with Poland-Lithuania, and moved his armies against Muscovy. Ivan carefully avoided any open military encounter, because first of all he feared the Tartar-Lithuanian alliance, and secondly, he did not trust his own brothers who were waiting for an opportunity to punish him for his unfaithfulness. He continued negotiations with Akhmad about his possible withdrawal, while the latter delayed his action, waiting for the Lithuanian ally to arrive, who failed to do so.

Two armies, the Tartar and the Muscovite, were facing each other from the opposite banks of the Ugra River for the entire summer of 1480, each not daring to attack the other. In November, without any major military encounter, Khan Akhmad ordered a retreat of his troops, because of trouble in his own camp. Shortly thereafter, on his march home, the Khan was assassinated. This was the last attempt of Sarai to restore its supremacy over Muscovy-Russia, and thus, the year 1480 may be taken as a definite end of the Mongol "yoke" over the Russian North-East. In 1502, the Crimean Horde of the Tartars exterminated the Golden Horde.[13]

Ivan left Muscovy unified, territorially enlarged, politically strengthened and free of any bothersome foreign interference. His succession, however, was marred by a complication. His son from his first marriage with Princess Maria of Tver, died early but left Ivan a grandson, Prince Dimitrii. From his second marriage with Byzantine Princess Sophia Paleologue, Ivan had several children; Vasilii, the oldest son, was pretender to the crown. There were two parties at the Muscovite court and among the *boyars*, concerning the succession, one favoring Dimitrii and another — Vasilii — as the heir to the throne. Ivan, who believed that only he was entitled to decide the issue, at first made Dimitrii the co-ruler and his possible successor. Nevertheless, court intrigues, sponsored by his second wife, Vasilii's mother, induced Ivan to change his mind. Prince Dimitrii was arrested and died in prison four years after his father's death. Vasilii received the right of succession and assumed the throne in 1505.

"... Ivan impressed upon the contemporaries the idea that the grand prince [duke] was an autocratic monarch to whom princes, as well as commoners, were equally subject."[14] In order to elevate the prestige of the throne and the dignity of the sovereign grand-ducal authority, Ivan introduced to the court an elaborate ceremonial and protocol of great pomp, and adopted symbols and emblems of the grand-ducal authority for its external manifestation. Of course, those changes in the formalities at the court had a heavy Oriental influence, unappreciated by the European diplomats, who, by that time had become frequent visitors to Moscow. Having brought Sophia Paleologue from Rome to marry, Ivan then invited to Muscovy many Greek and Italian educated people, craftsmen, artisans, architects, and other skilled men, who helped to advance the Muscovite civilization. With their assistance, Ivan constructed new churches, fortresses and castles, cast cannons, coined coins, and developed his foreign diplomatic relations. It was, therefore, a beginning of the "Westernization" of Muscovy-Russia.

Further Growth: Vasilii III

Ivan, following tradition, divided his country among his sons, yet he introduced a very essential modification into his testament. He definitely affirmed by his last will the undivided authority of the Grand Duke. Vasilii III, the Grand Duke, received an immeasurably larger territorial share with the largest cities, like Moscow and Novgorod, 66 in all, while the other four brothers got some 30 small towns. For him alone the coinage of money, control of all foreign relations, judicial power over serious crimes, and the right of inheriting the domains of the deceased relatives without male descendants, were exclusively reserved. Vasilii alone was to be sovereign with the grand-ducal title, to whom all other brothers and relatives were subject. The younger brothers and junior princes, whose sovereign rights were erased, had to submit to Vasilii's grand-ducal seniority without any reservation. It was, as all historians agree in their evaluation, an unquestionable triumph of the Muscovite absolutism, the roots of which could already be detected in the political formation of the Russian North-East in the late Kievan era. Yurii Dolgorukii, Andrei Bogoliubskii and Vsievolod III initiated the trend in the Rostov-Suzdal-Vladimir principality, as it was indicated in the proper chapters above.

Grand Duke Vasilii III lacked the statesmanship qualities of his great father, but he tried not to fall behind Ivan III in any sector of Muscovite policies of that time. He continued the Muscovite consolidation project, the unification process of the Russian North-East, and did everything in his power to raise the authority and prestige of the Grand Duchy in the international arena by promoting the idea of the Muscovite-Russian imperialist growth.

Vasilii, having insisted on his grand-ducal absolute authority, did not hesitate to drive a hard political line against his brothers. The relationship was not a loving one at all. In 1511, he accused one of his brothers, Prince Simeon of Kaluga, of treason, who then planned to escape to Lithuania. Only by the intercession undertaken by the Church and other family members, were harsh measures prevented on Vasilii's part. Another brother, Prince Dimitrii, was severely reprimanded for disobedience. Prince Yurii, a third of Vasilii's brothers, was continuously spied upon by the grand-ducal agents, and even accused of treacherous plotting with Lithuania. The Grand Duke controlled his brothers to the fullest extent and always showed them his suzerain authority. Their domains were simply relegated to the position of the landed estates of the civil-law character within the Grand Duchy and without any sovereign political nature of their own. In fact, the Muscovite Grand Duchy was by now one sovereign and undivided entity, rapidly losing its traditional family-patrimonial character.

This internal situation of Muscovy made it easier for Vasilii to proceed with the continuation of Ivan's project of "gathering all Rus' lands" toward a complete unification of Russia. The annexation of Pskov and the rest of the Riazan principality were the prime issues in this respect. Pskov's subservient participation in the Muscovite anti-Novgorod expedition in 1470 was in vain. Vasilii forced his representatives on the free city which antagonized the Pskovians and caused anti-Muscovite feelings to increase. Then, using those hostile feelings as an excuse, he ordered Pskov's leaders to come to Novgorod to discuss the situation and mendaciously imprisoned them upon their arrival. Subsequently, the Pskovian *"vieche"* accepted Vasilii's demands. The city's ancient aristocratic-democratic institutions, including the *"vieche,"* were abolished, the bell to summon the people for meetings was carried away, and the whole territory was fully incorporated into the Muscovite state, while the grand-ducal administration was introduced. The Pskovian leading merchants and *boyars* were deported to distant parts of Muscovy, while their landed estates were given to the incoming Muscovites to prevent any possibility of a new disobedience or revolt. Ivan's Novgorodian imperialist experiment was literally repeated by Vasilii.[15] In 1513, Vasilii incorporated the province of Volok, and in 1517, he imprisoned the last prince of Riazan and annexed his domain.

In all instances, in Novgorod, Pskov, Viatka, Yaroslavl, and other regions, deportation of the local leaders, confiscation of their landed estates, resettling their reliable elements, bloody liquidation of any opposition, bordering on the genocide practice, were recurringly applied as early forerunners of the Soviet-Russian mass genocide of the twentieth century, as the political devices of lasting domination of the conquered lands. It has served as historical proof of the undeniable fact, that genocide was not a Communist invention but a traditional Muscovite-Russian imperialist technique so frequently applied in the past toward conquered countries and peoples.

Curiously enough, the Russian Orthodox Church has in almost all cases endorsed these political cruelties of the Grand Dukes and Czars by advising the defeated to submit obediently to the authority of the Muscovite rulers, no matter how harsh a fate might be in store for them.[16] The Russian Orthodox Church was becoming more and more a subservient tool of the Muscovite secular politics in line with its *caesaropapism,* and rapidly abdicating any ecclesiastic independence.

The issue of the Muscovite pressure upon Ukraine and Byeloruthenia was also kept alive by Grand Duke Vasilii III. In 1512, he was already at war with Poland-Lithuania, and the military operations lasted until 1522, ending with a provisional truce agreement. In 1514 the Muscovite troops occupied the city of Smolensk in Byeloruthenia, and remained there despite the battle of Orsha in which Vasilii's regiments were defeated and in spite of the fact that the city was only temporarily left in Muscovite hands according to the truce provision. In 1523, Vasilii completed the occupation of the Ukrainian province of Novgorod Siversky and incorporated it into the Muscovite state, while its last prince was thrown into prison, being accused of plotting with Poland. Usual Muscovite measures were applied there to prevent any new separatist movement. At approximately that time, the Muscovite-Ukrainian struggle of the modern era began, and was to last for centuries. Ukrainian Prince Constantine Ostrozhsky actively fought against the Muscovites on the Polish-Lithuanian side as a subject of that Federation. The leader of the Ukrainian Cossacks, Ostap Dashkevych, after some unfortunate experience with Vasilii, fought against Muscovy in 1515 and again in 1521, having allied himself with the Crimean Tartars. In 1515, he attempted to recover Novgorod Siversky and Chernihiv, two Ukrainian provinces, from under the Muscovite sphere of influence, but it ended in failure.[17]

During the reigns of Ivan III and Vasilii III, some 40,000

square miles of land were added to the Muscovite state, making it a dominant political power in East Europe, a serious competition to the Polish-Lithuanian Federation. Vasilii III left Muscovy to his son, Czar Ivan IV, the Terrible or Dread, as a first-rate political power. Ivan was Vasilii's son from the latter's second marriage with the Ukrainian princess Helen Hlinsky (Glinskii). Helen gave him two sons, Ivan and Yurii. Vasilii divided his empire between the two, with Ivan's grand-ducal seniority provision. However, Yurii's early death enabled his brother to preserve and to enlarge an undivided Czardom of Muscovy under one scepter. Vasilii's first marriage with Solmea Saburov was childless and ended unhappily. Vasilii divorced her and sent her to a distant monastery to take the veil, and then married Helen Hlinsky over the Church and *boyar* opposition.

Platonov gave the following brief appraisal of Grand Duke Vasilii III: "The last 'Assembler of Russia' was domineering and vain, and lacked many of the fair traits of his father, Ivan III. Vasilii loved power and praise, and his associates were people who favored and flattered him."[18] But he was certainly motivated by the state interest of his Muscovy. Vasilii's advisers flattered him, while some of his political successes must be credited to them, from whom monk Vassian, Metropolitan Daniel, Prince Vasilii Kholmskii, Prince Mikhail Hlinsky, a Ukrainian, and Vasilii Tretiak-Dalmatov, were probably the most influential ones at one time or another.

Moscow — The Third Rome and its International Position

Soloviov, a great Russian historian, once remarked that Europe "discovered" Muscovy-Russia approximately at the same time as it discovered America. It was not incidental. Muscovy was becoming at the dawn of the modern centuries a high-ranking power, pretending for leadership of all Orthodox peoples and involving itself in international relations, after its internal consolidation and unification were completed. This brought Muscovy into direct contact with various foreign countries, with which it had previously no common boundaries and no immediate contacts. Europe could not fail to take notice of the new political might, the Grand Duchy or Czardom of Muscovy, which began at that time to exhibit its imperialistic drives beyond the Russian ethnic territories. Various developments brought about the change in the international position of Muscovy-Russia.

Constantinople, the traditional metropolis of all Orthodox Christianity, was declining, and in 1453 it fell into the hands of the "unfaithful" Turks. The event terminated, for the time, Constantinople's free and independent exercise of the Orthodox leadership. At first, the southern Slavs, especially the Bulgarians or rather the Bulgarian monks, to be specific, developed the hypothesis of Bulgaria with its capital of Tirnovo to take over the heritage of Constantinople. But their hopes soon failed. Some of those monks came to Muscovy and there helped to build up Moscow's political and ecclesiastic *"ego."* They saw the growing Muscovite power and hoped to establish there the leadership and protection of the Orthodox Slavs, menaced by the acute aggressiveness of the Ottoman Turks who had proceeded with the conquests of the Balkans and the Near East. The Bulgarian ideas flattered the vanity of the Muscovite Grand Dukes, and fitted into their political aspirations and plans. It also fertilized the thought of the Muscovite theologians, who were chauvinistically Orthodox and patriotically Muscovite at the same time.

The idea of the Catholic-Orthodox Church union, initiated by the Florence-Ferrara council of 1439 progressively antagonized the Muscovites, who began to aspire to the Orthodox leadership. They were generally suspicious of the foreigners, and the papal supremacy from abroad was both antagonistic to the Muscovite psychology and unacceptable for the *caesaropapistically* thinking Grand Dukes and Muscovite Church hierarchy. The Greeks, who initially conceived and accepted the Union, were looked upon with contempt and considered traitors of the true faith. The Muscovite-Russian Church elected its own Metropolitan independent of Constantinople's formal consent and assumed the role of a leader of the Orthodox Churches. The Eastern Churches were traditionally looking to Constantinople as the metropolis of the united Orthodoxy under a Greek Orthodox Emperor with the strong *caesaropapist* feature of its ecclesiastic organization. From 1453 there no longer existed an independent and sovereign Constantinople or supreme ruler and Church protector, the Emperor. It produced a missing link in the organizational structure of the Eastern Orthodoxy. All eyes then turned toward Moscow and its powerful Orthodox rulers, the Grand Dukes, who were occasionally using the title of the Czars, the sovereign supremes. The Golden Horde was disintegrating and soon the Muscovite sovereignty became an established fact, while the ambitions of the Grand Dukes were running high.

At the very height of Sarai's supremacy, the Russian Church was subservient to the Mongol Khans as sovereign secular rulers and were addressed at times as the Czars. From them the Orthodox Church received protection and even favors. There the element of the *caesaropapism* was evident too. With Sarai's disintegrating power, Moscow naturally appeared an automatic heir and political successor inheriting the responsibility of protecting the Orthodox Church. Fate seemed to favor Moscow, and Moscow was ready to take advantage of it.

The Muscovite-Russian Orthodox thinkers then searched for historical, theological and political facts to justify the elevation of Moscow. Monk Spiridon, an unrecognized Metropolitan, who allegedly was ordinated by bribing Turkish authorities and who had been interned in a northern monastery on his arrival in Muscovy, wrote epistles and treatises on the religious mission of Moscow and its sovereigns. Being acquainted with old legends, Spiridon asserted in an epistle that Rurik, the ancestor of the "Muscovite" dynasty, was a descendant of Prussus, brother of Caesar Augustus of ancient Rome, and that Prince Volodymyr (Vladimir) Monomakh, received his crown, called Monomakh's cap, from the Greek Emperor, Monomakh, to indicate his royal elevation. In this way, Spiridon hoped to elevate the position of Moscow and its rulers, connecting legendary speculations with Rome and Constantinople, and suggesting Moscow as an heir to both. Spiridon's historical fictions were given wide circulation and publicity under the tittle "Tales of the Prince of Vladimir." The interest of the Muscovite state required that, in general, acceptance of this fiction be achieved.[19]

Orthodox thinker, Abbot Yosif (Joseph) Sanin, uncompromising glorifyer of Muscovite absolutism, uncritically paraphrased the thought of a Greek from the sixth century, Deacon Agapetos, by saying that: "although the Czar was like other men in his physical characteristics, in his power he was similar to God in Heaven."[20] Monk Spiridon, Abbot Yosif, Metropolitan Daniel and many other Russian Orthodox leaders of the ultraconservative school did everything possible to build the grandducal prestige as a guaranty of the safety and future growth of the Orthodoxy, which was being threatened by the Moslems, Catholics and Uniates. The Orthodox Church needed political support, and the Grand Duke, an ardent Orthodox, had the power to provide that support. This was the major trend of thinking of those *caesaropapist* "theologians and philosophers" of the Russian Church.

The Grand Dukes readily accepted these fictitious, "theological" arguments of their supremacy and "traditionally" established elevation in the secular and ecclesiastic matters. Such acceptance was dictated by the political expediency at the dawn of the Muscovite-Russian imperialist drive. The persistence of the ecclesiastic and political circles in this matter soon brought forth ample fruit. The people of the Russian North-East were thoroughly brainwashed by their teaching, that they were quoted to answer the foreign visitors by saying: "We do not know it, only God and the Sovereign know." There is no doubt that the old Mongol state doctrine of the Great Khan having been a Son of Heaven, influenced the Muscovite conception of the divine authority of the Grand Dukes or Czars, in support of the *caesaropapist* Byzantinian tradition in the North-East, since Moscow had succeeded Sarai politically.

Still another legend was fabricated to substantiate the theory of Moscow's mission. It had been declared that the Apostle Saint Andrew blessed the area of Kiev and prophesied that there the growth of the true Christianity would take place. Since the Muscovite rulers considered themselves the heirs of Kievan Rus' and Moscow the heir of Kiev, the Russian theologians concluded that the Russian Church derived its origins directly from the Apostle, and not from Constantinople. The emotional appeal of the legend was great.

Subsequent writings of Filotei (Philoteos), a Pskovian monk, gave a final touch to the growing myth of Moscow's being the "Third Rome," and the leader of the Eastern Churches. He wrote that the "First Rome" had fallen because it had betrayed the true Christian faith by becoming Catholic. The "Second Rome," Constantinople, had fallen because of a similar reason; it had indulged itself in the papal union and then was taken by the Turks. Now Moscow, the "Third Rome," has taken over and has remained faithful to the true Christianity, and because of its faithfulness it will stand forever, and there will be no fourth Rome. Filotei's declaration put Moscow on top of the world, as far as the mentality of the Muscovite-Russian, secular and ecclesiastic, leaders was concerned. Moscow in this way got a blanket endorsement to champion the cause of Eastern Christianity.[21]

The Muscovite Grand Dukes had first used the slogan of "gathering all Russian lands" to promote and to justify their aggressive moves against the various Russian principalities and independent communities. After the unification of Russia under one Muscovite scepter had been accomplished with considerable assistance from the Russian Church, the doctrine of Moscow's being the third Rome became a skillful device of the Muscovite-Russian imperialism in Ukraine, Byeloruthenia, Lithuania, the Balkans, the Near East and the Caucasian lands for centuries to come, disguised under the pretext of Moscow's defense of the Orthodox Christians against the menace of the Catholic and Moslem pressures.

In order to give external support to those hypothetical assertions of Moscow's elevated position, Ivan III married Princess

Sophia Paleologue, the niece of the last Greek Emperor. It revitalized the idea of Moscow's connection with the Byzantinian traditions. For the same reason, he adopted the Byzantinian coat of arms to become the Muscovite-Russian imperial emblem as a visible sign of the continuation of the past Byzantinian glory. The Orthodox Church here again hastened in its subservient manner to assist the absolute monarchs. The miraculous passages of the holy *icons* from Greece to Muscovy-Russia were held as evidence of that insoluble connection between Constantinople and Moscow and as a proof of the Muscovite Orthodoxy to rank first among all other Eastern Orthodox Churches.

The Grand Duchy of Muscovy rose to the status of a power and its image was held high. This, of course, necessitated on its part a development of wide international relations, since it assumed an international mission of championing the cause of Orthodox Christianity. The broad international relations were helpful in Moscow's political growth, too. The wide international fame of Muscovy flattered the vanity of its rulers. Grand Duke Ivan III initiated, and Grand Duke Vasilii III continued to widen the foreign relations of Muscovy with other powers. These foreign relations could be classified in the three currents: the relations with Moscow's recent master, the Tartars; the relations with its immediate neighbor countries, Poland-Lithuania, Sweden, and the German Knights; and the international contacts with distant nations, such as the Holy Empire of the German Nation, the Ottoman Turks, France and Egypt.

Originally it was one Golden Horde of the Mongols to deal with, but Ivan and Vasilii had to deal with two and then with three different Hordes of the Kazan, Crimean and Astrakhan Tartars and other smaller tribes roaming the border areas of Eastern Europe. With the Kazan Horde Muscovy was sometimes friendly; at times Moscow imposed its own proteges as Khans; and at times waged wars. Lithuania and the Crimean Tartars constantly attempted to undermine either the good relations existing between Moscow and Kazan or to loosen the political grip of the former over the latter. A much more serious problem was presented by the relations with the powerful Crimean Horde. Ivan III was on relatively good terms with the Crimean Khan, Mengli-Girey. He allied himself with Mengli-Girey in his struggle against Poland-Lithuania. Rich gifts and even monetary payments were going from Moscow to Crimea to persuade Mengli-Girey to stay friendly with Ivan. However, Vasilii did not manage the problem as well. Crimea and Poland-Lithuania allied themselves against Muscovy, trying to weaken the Muscovite control over the Kazan Khanate, as it has previously been stated.

The Hordes fought against each other, while Ivan and Vasilii attempted to turn these conflicts to Moscow's political advantage. This still did not save the Russian North-East from periodical Tartar raids, devastation of the country and decimation of the population, which was either killed or taken captive to be sold in the slave markets of the Crimea or the Near East. The fate of those Christian slaves in the Mohammedan lands was tragic. In 1521, the Crimean Khan, Mohammed-Girey, aided by Lithuania and actively supported by the Ukrainian Cossack detachments, reached the gates of Moscow, and demanded the resumption of the annual tribute payment by Vasilii to the Crimean Khanate as the successor of the Golden Horde. He did not retreat until Vasilii had promised to do so. The promise was never fulfilled by the Grand Duke and the devastating Tartar raids continued on the south-eastern borderlands of Muscovy.[22] Because of these raids by the Crimean Tartars for booty, Ivan, Vasilii and their successors were forced to build fortresses and watchtowers and to keep guards in the "wild fields" in order to bar or at least to delay the impact of those Tartar raids. Meanwhile, vital and continuous mercantile trading activities were going on between Muscovy and Crimea.

Moscow's relations with the immediate neighbors were not too friendly. Prolonged warfare had marked the relations with the Polish-Lithuanian Federation, involving the Muscovite pretenses to the Ukrainian and Byeloruthenian territories. The

Ukrainians, in particular their Cossack formations, whose center was in the Sich, were largely anti-Muscovite. Bloody encounters were also featured in Muscovite relations with the German Knights, who pressed for more territory in the Baltic area, while the Muscovites wanted a "window" to Europe through a wide access to the Baltic Sea, which the Knights and the Swedish tried to shut by dominating its entire eastern littorals. Then, the German Knights allied themselves with the Muscovites against the Polish-Lithuanian Federation, which proved to be disastrous for them. Poland-Lithuania defeated them completely, and from the blow they actually never recovered.

The relations with Sweden were unevenly strained. The Baltic Sea littoral was largely the issue. Historically, Sweden was waging wars with the Vladimir principality and the Commonwealth of Novgorod the Great. The political conflicts were then inherited by the Muscovite Grand Dukes. To bar the advances of the Swedish and the German Knights, Ivan built the fortress of Ivangorod on the eastern bank of the Neva River, and in 1496, he concluded an alliance with Denmark directed against Sweden. In 1508, conflicts with Sweden were temporarily settled by an armistice agreement. Relations with the Hanseatic League were very strained, caused by Ivan's harsh treatment of Novgorod the Great, a member of the League. Ivan tried to break the League's monopoly of foreign trade. Vasilii, however, changed the Muscovite attitude toward that commercial association of cities and resumed contacts with it in 1517.

Muscovy's contacts with Ottoman Turkey were directly related to its attempts to establish some diplomatic relations with distant nations. Ivan first contacted Constantinople in 1492, and in 1497 a Muscovite envoy was sent there without, however, producing any appreciable effect. The relations were somewhat strained, because of the Turkish aggressiveness in the Black and Azov Sea area. Grand Dukes Ivan and Vasilii, however, constantly rejected any plan to join an anti-Turk crusade, that the popes tried to organize for the protection of Western Christianity. On the other hand, the Sultan was not in a hurry to develop close relations with Moscow and remained cool to Vasilii's suggestion of assisting him in his struggle against Lithuania and the Crimean Tartars or in persuading the latter to leave Moscow in peace. Meanwhile Moscow's fame of being the "Third Rome" of the Eastern Orthodoxy spread. In 1482, and again in 1492, Georgian (Kakhetian) envoys visited Moscow and asked in the name of their sovereign, King Alexander, for Ivan's protection for the Caucasian Christians, menaced by the Mohammedan imperialism.[23] Approximately at the same time, Grand Duke Ivan tried to contact Egypt.

Both Ivan III and Vasilii III understood the importance of the international recognition of Moscow as a device of advancing its political position, and sought to make contact with the West-European courts. The exchange of messages between Moscow and Rome were frequent. The popes attempted to persuade Ivan and Vasilii to join an anti-Turk crusade, as mentioned above, and eventually to accept the Church union with Rome. Neither project materialized. Moscow was definitely anti-Catholic and anti-union, and did not want to get involved in any crusade. The contacts between Moscow and Rome were actually lacking any substance. The Muscovite attempts to start diplomatic relations with the Holy Roman Empire did not bring any visible results. The German-Muscovite, anti-Polish alliance was of negligible practical value; Moscow's attempt in 1518 to draw France into a similar international arrangement proved unsuccessful. The several visits of Muscovite envoys to the court of the Holy Roman Empire aimed at finding a husband for Ivan's daughter, also proved to be unsuccessful. An important dynastic tie of Moscow with a West-European ruling house would have certainly enhanced Moscow's international prestige.

In 1482, Moscow diplomatically contacted Hungary, and during the visit of the Hungarian ambassador to Moscow in 1501, Ivan publicly expounded his territorial claims upon Ukraine and Byeloruthenia. This was the official initiation of Muscovite imperialism extending beyond the Russian ethnic lands. Ivan and Vasilii maintained contacts with Venice and other Italian city-states, from where they got foreign architects, craftsmen, artisans and other specialists. Those West-Europeans brought to Moscow their skills, which were utilized to advance the country's civilization.

Although those first attempts to contact foreign nations produced little in immediate gains for Moscow, in the long run they represented a significant step forward by involving the new political power of Muscovy in the civilized European community of nations.

CHAPTER TEN

THE MUSCOVITE SOCIETY IN THE FOURTEENTH AND FIFTEENTH CENTURIES

The Government

In previous chapters, when the Kievan and Mongol impacts upon Muscovite society were analyzed, several essential aspects of various social institutions of the principality, and then of the Grand Duchy of Moscow, were mentioned.[1] Now a more detailed account of the formation of the Muscovite society in the fourteenth and fifteenth centuries will be presented. In the course of time, these institutions decisively affected the entire Russian North-East, as the Muscovite power spread and gradually absorbed other Russian lands and territories.

Right from the very beginning, there were influences of the Mongol suzerain upon the formation and development of the upper strata of Muscovite social and political life, which lived in their deepest inner "self" alone, and evolved according to its essentially national roots and patterns. With the dissipation of the Mongol power, two trends were put in motion which eventually crystallized these essentially Muscovite-Russian institutions. First of all, along with the disintegration of the Mongol empire, Mongol influences thoroughly penetrated the entire social structure of Muscovy by a kind of delayed and indirect action. There was a mass influx of Mongol ethnic elements into Muscovite-Russian society in the fifteenth and sixteenth centuries, bringing with them Mongol mentality, Mongol organizational and administrative concepts and skills, Mongol legal and social criteria and Mongol perception of reality. Hence, Muscovy became a kind of an heir of the Golden Horde, particularly with respect to social and political traditions. Secondly, during the entire era of Mongol domination and under the Mongol political superstructure, essentially Russian dynamic social forces were constantly developing and working, which were freed along with the Mongol disintegration and proceeded to dominate the social evolution of the North-East. Hence, Muscovy became a social blend of Russian institutions with substantial Mongol elements in all sectors of national life, the government, the social and economic process, and the spiritual and cultural sphere.

At first, the Muscovite state was not sovereign, but subordinate to the Mongol suzerain, like all other lands of the European North-East. Then, after the battle of the Kulikovo plain, the Muscovite grand-ducal government became more and more independent, as Mongol power diminished and disintegrated. And, in the second half of the fifteenth century, the Grand Duke of Moscow emerged as an absolutist sovereign, a monocratic suzerain, the *samoderzhavets* and *gosudar,* with greater royal power and authority than any European ruler of that time.[2] Here it would be worthwhile to remember that the absolutist trends in the princely authority were already present in Suzdal and Vladimir, long before the Mongol invasion. Then, those trends were substantially strengthened by the Mongol pattern of the absolute and unlimited power of the Khan, the son of Heaven.

The despotic and unlimited authority of the Muscovite Grand Dukes was crystallized in the fifteenth century, having been clearly reflected in the changed official terminology of the time. Until the fifteenth century, the Grand Duke was called "lord", *gospodin,* in most of the North-East, and since that time, he was addressed exclusively as the "suzerain", *gosudar,* Of course, the absolutist trend in the princely power was present also in other Russian lands and principalities. However, with the complete victory of Moscow and the consolidation of all the North-East under its leadership, the trend had remained permanent and only the Grand Duke of Moscow succeeded in carrying on the absolute authority as the suzerain of "all Russia." Already Ivan III and Vasilii III at times called themselves "Czars," the nomenclature once reserved only to the Khans to indicate their sovereign and supreme authority of divine origin. After the Russian liberation and the Mongol disintegration, the Grand Dukes were believed to have inherited the absolute authority of the Khans, having received it through the grace of God and not from the people's original sovereignty; hence, not indebted for it to anybody on earth. Furthermore, the elaborate crowning ceremony, resembling the installation of the Byzantine emperors, and the elaborate court protocol, after the fall of Constantinople, indicates the Muscovite inheritance of Byzantine political and ecclesiastic traditions. All these factors contributed to the establishment of grand-ducal absolutism, combined with strong Oriental elements. The writings of Spiridon, Filotei and others only affirmed the exaggerated concept of the Muscovite-Russian suzerainty and Czarism.

The formation, and then the crystallization, of the undivided authority of the Grand Dukes of Muscovy began with Prince Daniel's acquisition of Moscow as his hereditary territorial share *(patrimonium* or *votchina)*. There the private law ownership concept and the princely power over the subjects progressively merged, in order to culminate 150 years later in the grand-ducal suzerainty, after the authority of the Mongol Khan lost its practical meaning. Grand Duke Ivan III did not bother any more to officially acquire the once indispensable Mongol *yarlik*, the Khan's approval of his rule and dignity. The all-embracing and absolute authority of the Grand Duke received its clear-cut and final shape under Vasilii III.

The unprecedented comprehensiveness of the grand-ducal authority meant, of course, a complete abolition of the ancient governing institution of the people's meeting or *vieche*. For a long time the Northern princes, with the exception of the Novgorod and Pskov lands and some other tiny communities, had attempted to suppress the *vieche*. In Moscow, it was most apparent. There the last shade of the *vieche* power disappeared in 1374. At that time the office of the *chiliarch* or *tysiatskii* was abolished, which for some time had represented the voice and the interest of the common people. It was incompatible with the all-comprehensive, undivided and unlimited authority of the absolute Grand Duke. The *boyar* nobility substantially helped the Grand Duke, as it was indicated before, in suppressing the sovereignty of the people and the power of the people's meeting, since the *boyardom* was hostile to "mob rule" and rather associated itself with the despotic ruler of noble blood. In the grand-ducal service, the nobles and the gentry acquired material wealth and social prestige. Hence, the *boyars* became one of the pillars of the rising grand-ducal power.

The Muscovite Grand Dukes consequently built their absolutist power throughout the generations. They usually gave their sons or grandsons, who were intended to inherit Moscow's throne, the largest territorial shares with wealthy estates and important cities in order to secure for them the economic basis for their undivided and unlimited grand-ducal authority, and in this way be assured that the junior princes remain subordinate. Also the interprincely agreements, enforced by the Grand Duke by way of pressure, invoked duress, or even violence, furthered the affirmation of the grand-ducal power. The Grand Duke became the collector of the Mongol tribute, the intermediary between Sarai and Muscovite society as a whole, including the junior princes, nobles and the common people. He was the supreme justice in all serious crimes, the commander-in-chief of all armed forces, almost the lord of life and death of his subjects, and *de facto* the supreme head of the Muscovite-Russian Orthodox Church due to the prevailing *caesaropapist* philosophy of the time.

The Grand Dukes recognized the state council as having only advisory power. It consisted in fact of two bodies, the inner council and the plenary *duma*. The small and permanent advisory body in constant session was a kind of a grand-ducal cabinet, said Vernadsky. It consisted of top officials of the grand-ducal court and administration: the *majordomo*, the quartermaster-general, the master-general of stables, the treasurer-general, the great lieutenant of Moscow, other chiefs of departaments or *puti* (ways), the so-called departmental *boyars*, the great *bolshoie boyars*, who were admitted to the grand-ducal court because, perhaps, of their personal dignity or social status, and the *chiliarch*, the representative of the people's interests, until the office was abolished in 1374, Ivan III began to admit commoners into the council, in the faculty of state secretaries, *diaki,* to perform various state functions. These were the full-fledged members of the inner council. Usually they were outstanding men in their fields. Unlike the *boyars,* however, they could be freely appointed and dismissed by the Grand Duke at his pleasure. It was the highest body, and was consulted in all important domestic and foreign affairs. Usually its meetings were presided over by the Grand Duke himself or by the so-called first councilman. This function for the great part of the reign of Ivan III was performed by Ivan Patrikiev.

The plenary body of the *boyar duma* or advisory council was called to session only in very important or extraordinary cases, as decided by the Grand Duke, such as dangerous foreign invasions or large-scale political projects to be undertaken, such as incorporation of Novgorod the Great. The body consisted of all members of the inner cabinet or council and all leading nobles of the land. No doubt, the plenary *boyar duma* lost a great deal of its significance and influence on state affairs in Muscovy, as compared with the pre-Mongol era in the North-East, because of the growth of absolutism.[3]

The grand-ducal administration consisted of central and provincial or regional offices, some being prevailingly state and public and others of more princely and private character. There was, however, no clear-cut differentiation between the central and regional or the public and princely private competence of those offices and officers. This is indicative of the fact that the Muscovite state administration of that time was not yet fully developed, and the state machine was still in constant flux; it matured much later. There were substantial reasons for that. During the building process of the Muscovite power, new lands and territories, with different legal systems, customs, traditions and socio-economic arrangements, were incorporated, producing administrative confusion. State and princely manorial affairs were conducted differently in different regions. There were no common standards. In general, state administration was responsible for the collection of tribute, army conscription and judiciary procedures, while the princely manorial or court administration oversaw matters of court maintenance, maintenance of the standing army troops, the *dvor*, management of the grand-ducal estates, stables, falconries, hunting grounds and other manorial economic affairs, and the supply of food. All those affairs were attended by the so-called departmental or *putnii boyars*, members of the inner council of the prince. With the growth of Moscow, the manorial administration acquired even greater national significance, while the twofold system continued with constantly shifting responsibilities.

The majordomo, *dvorskii*, was apparently the highest officer of the court and central administration. He managed all court personnel, the courtiers and servitors at the palace, and they all were subordinate to him. He was the chief administrator of all grand-ducal estates and the judge of all peasants in those estates. All grand-ducal economic affairs in general, were attended by the majordomo. With the progress of time, some old offices, originating from the pre-Mongol era, slowly disappeared and some new ones evolved, partially under the Mongol influence. Some offices existed only for a short while. In general, however, the following central agencies of departments with their chiefs, the *putnii boyars*, assisted the Grand Duke. The quartermaster-general, definitely of Mongol origin, administered military affairs. The master of stables took care of the horse breeding in the grand-ducal estates, a very important function from the military point of view. These horses were an essential ingredient in the constant aggressive military moves of Muscovy. The treasurer-general administered the financial affairs of the Grand Duchy. He managed and supervised the public collections (taxes, fees and other receipts) and expenditures. The grand-ducal "private" finances were managed by the *dvorskii*. Among the functions of the court at the time, along with its maintenance, defense of the country, the country's general administration and judiciary, also some police function must have been included. The *Chronicles* mentioned, for example, that Grand Duke Ivan Kalita wiped out robbers in his lands.

The state regional administration was headed by the lieutenants, residing in all major cities, to whom the regional chiefs for rural districts were subordinate. Their main function was judiciary, along with some administrative responsibilities in their districts. The minor judicial officials, the *tivuns* and *yarigas*, assisted the lieutenants and the regional chiefs in their state functions. The regional division of the Grand Duchy into districts, called *t'my*, were of Mongol origin as regional tax collection and army conscription territorial units. The Grand Dukes, after achieving full independence, decided to retain the old Mongol territorial administration system, although the nature and character of those districts in the framework of the Muscovite state had changed. The chiefs of the court departments, *puti*, of the central government had, of course, their agents, operating in various districts of the land. The ducal domains throughout the Grand Duchy were managed by proper managers of the manorial system.

However, the state administration did not extend over the Church and *boyar* domains, which were ruled by their own patrimonial, administrative and judicial authority of the Church dignitaries and nobles. The common people (peasants and townspeople) in the ecclesiastic and noble estates were only indirectly subject to the grand-ducal jurisdiction.

The state officials of the higher and lower ranks were appointed for a rather short time and on a rotating basis in order to give a chance to many and to prevent possible abuses of power. Compensation for services was either in the form of the real estate grants in service tenure, or of the privilege given to the respective officials to keep a share of their tax and non-tax collections, for which they were responsible to the state. Furthermore, to most offices the principle of the so-called *kormlenie*, the feeding, was attached. It meant that the district's population, had to supply food and other living necessities, to feed and to maintain those officers of the government. In most cases, when the officials abused their authority and collected too much in taxes or fees or acted too harshly, the people's complaints usually led to the ouster of the guilty and the appointment of other eligible noble candidates in their places. Greed and the abuses of authority were also the cause of those short-lived tenures and frequent appointments of new officers in place of the old ones. The complaint procedure was, however, a costly and a prolonged one.

Initially, the Grand Duchy was not ruled by a uniform law. Various provinces and newly acquired lands ruled themselves in their traditional and customary ways, all similar in their general outlines and highly different in their particular details. Then, the Grand Dukes, Ivan III and Vasilii III, began to issue the charters for various lands. Since those charters followed certain basic rules, they were the first step in the unification of the law and government of Muscovy. Especially the administrative and judiciary procedures were slow to become standardized throughout. The main step in this direction was undertaken by Ivan III in 1497. A Code of Law, the so-called *Sudebnik*, was promulgated in that year by the Grand Duke, being prepared by a committee headed by Prince Ivan Patrikiev. It was a collection of regulations to be a guide for the judges of the higher and lower courts, enumerating various crimes and their foreseen punishments, describing in an affirmative way the relations between the employers and the employees, the owners of the landed states and the money lenders, and the owners of the landed estates and their peasants. The *Sudebnik* generally affirmed the freedom of the peasants to move from one place to another under certain conditions and at certain times. The time customarily and legally foreseen for the peasant moving from one state or district to another, came once a year, two weeks in the fall, around the St. George's Day. The peasant was allowed to move after he met all his financial obligations toward the landowner, after he paid for the house and paid all his debts.[4]

The Judiciary, Finances, and Military Affairs

The judicial system in Muscovy experienced a considerable evolutionary change, along with the other government branches. At first, the Khan was the supreme justice over all Russian princes, as well as all Russians who were in the Mongol army or in any Mongol service, or lived in any immediate Mongol region, all were subject to the Mongol jurisdiction. Furthermore, all cases between the Mongol and Russian parties were also tried and sentenced by Mongol judges and according to Mongol law. However, for the most part, the princes and later on the Grand Dukes were the supreme judges over their subjects in the Russian North-East, with no Mongol interference.

Then, with the decline of the Mongol power and the elevation of the grand-ducal authority, the Grand Dukes became the supreme justices throughout the country. They had also the clemency privilege. From the Grand Duke, and not the people, the top officers of the court, the regional lieutenants and the minor district judges and their appointees derived their judicial power and faculty. The majordomo, *dvorskii* and other central officers, the departmental or *putnii boyars,* like the master-general of stables and the quartermaster-general, had and exercised their judicial authority over the personnel in their respective departments and field divisions. The minor local judges, the *yarigas,* the origin of which was Mongol, also functioned in the name of the Grand Dukes, although their predecessors from the pre-Mongol era derived their ancient judicial authority from the people and the people's meetings.

The *Sudebnik* differentiated three kinds of courts. The supreme court, headed by the chairman of the *boyar duma* and in which the *boyars* and the courtiers took part. There was no appeal from the decisions of that court. The *boyar* court had to report its findings to the Grand Duke, who made the final decisions. The special case courts, presided over by a *boyar* or a secretary, *diak,* were specially set up for specific cases. The findings and decisions of those courts were to be submitted to the supreme court for final approval of those findings and decisions. In the provinces and districts the judiciary was left, as pointed out, in the hands of the lieutenants, district chiefs and *yarigas.*

The Muscovite criminal judiciary adopted many Mongol legal concepts and elements of justice. The death penalty, corporal punishment and the use of torture as the device to obtain confession or information in the Muscovite judicial system and legal procedure, were definitely of Mongol origin. Only in Novgorod the Great and Pskov, corporal punishment was introduced under Western influence, where it was a well known legal practice. Ivan III enumerated in his *Sudebnik* various crimes, for which the death penalty was foreseen, such as sedition, theft of Church property, homicide, arson, mendacious framing of others, murder, brigandage and crimes against the state.[5] Death penalty could be administered by hanging or decapitation, while in Novgorod the Great drowning in the Volkhov River was applied.

However, the Church, its clergy, its possessions and the population under its jurisdiction, were exempt from the regular grand-ducal administrative and judicial scheme. It meant that all clergy, black and white or monastic and secular, religious and needy persons, and the urban and rural population in the Church's towns and villages were subject to the judicial power of the Metropolitan and the bishops. Until 1443, the Patriarch of Constantinople might have claimed the supreme ecclesiastic judicial authority over the top echelon of the Church dignitaries, but not thereafter. Also, the possessions, and the towns and peasant population in the princely and noble domains were exempt from the grand-ducal judiciary and administration. There the patrimonial judiciary of the lord of the landed estates prevailed. Nevertheless, with the progressive transition of the originally autonomous junior princes into the status of the dependent servitors of the Muscovite throne, although of the highest social level, the grand-ducal judiciary began to penetrate slowly their previously independent patrimonial authority. The people of the towns and villages of the servitor princes, the *boyars* and the petty country gentry were at times exposed to the grand-ducal judiciary as well as the supreme authority of the Czar. This became the indisputable socio-political philosophy of the Muscovite state. The absolute authority of the Grand Duke also began to substantially limit the autonomy of the Church.

The growing Muscovite Grand Duchy was steadily developing its finances to sustain its political growth by means of constant warfare. The original state domains and the state domains acquired, either as a result of the confiscation of the landed estate of the hostile princes and *boyars* or in the consequence of the secularization of Church properties, constituted a very important source of the public revenues. New acquisitions of originally privately owned estates came about during the constant conquests and annexations by the Grand Dukes. The project of the secularization of the ecclesiastic domains was considerably eased up for the state by the "schismatic" and "heretic" religious movements of the time. The so-called Trans-Volga hermits and the sect of the Judaizers questioned the right of the Church to possess wealth. Hence, the Grand Dukes used this as an excuse to appropriate monastic estates, while officially opposing and suppressing the unorthodox "heretics." The state domains were managed by appointed managers, the rural population of which was directly subject to the grand-ducal administration and judiciary.

From among the taxes, the Mongol tribute was the most important Muscovite source of revenue, at first only partially and later totally converted for the use of the Muscovite state. At the very beginning of their acting as the Mongol agents for collecting the tribute, the princes of Moscow embezzled a part of the tribute in order to use it for strengthening their principality. At the later phase of the Mongol supremacy, the Grand Dukes received the privilege to collect the tribute through their own financial agents, who replaced the early Tartar officials, the *baski*. The population of the North-East was so well disciplined by the Mongol tax system that the Muscovite Grand Dukes had no trouble and did not run into any opposition when collecting the tax as sovereigns for their own revenue. The so-called "plough" was the basic unit of assessment of that direct form of taxation, referring to one farm unit as the levy's basis, the rates of which were changing with the time. The basic assumption was that one peasant farm possessed and used only one plough to cultivate the land.

A very important levy was the so-called *kormlenie* or feeding tax, paid in kind, in the form of the district's products like food, fuel, and fur and textile for clothing, to support the district's public officials. The levy was mentioned above, in passing. The local population had to feed and maintain the grand-ducal appointees in various higher and lower offices. The *kormlenie* included first of all the so-called "entrance fee," to be delivered to the newly appointed official when starting his duties, and then it comprised regular supplies, normally at Christmas time, Easter and Sts. Peter and Paul Day. The quantity and composition of each delivery by one household were normally regulated by custom and tradition. However, the abuses of the appointees in this respect were great. Hence, Vasilii II and Ivan III began to regulate statutorily the kind, amount, composition and manner of the *kormlenie* levy, intending to ease the plight of the helpless population. Special charters were usually issued to various regions, old or newly annexed, generally regulating the problem. Finally, Ivan's Code of Law, the *Sudebnik*, gave some finishing touches to the solution.[6]

Then, there were scores of other, mostly indirect business taxes, such as district and local tolls, the *myta*, the road and bridge tolls, levied against the carload, and various fees, charged at various stages of shipping and trading. There were taxes upon cattle, such as roping tax, horn tax, and branding tax. The weight tax was a strictly marketing levy. Certain state fees were collected upon rendering public services, such as marriage license fees and court fees. Customs duties were raised from imports and exports of goods, when crossing the grand-ducal boundaries. They were discriminatory in their nature, reflecting the traditional suspicion of the Muscovites toward the foreigners.[7]

Later on, in order to clarify the tax situation, some direct tax levies, such as the tribute and the *kormlenie*, were consolidated into an over-all tax, called *obrok*, collected according to the custom and law from the peasant tenants by the owners of the landed estates, and delivered to the proper government officials. It was a considerable simplification of the taxation procedure. Then, along with the direct levies in kind, the rural and urban population had to render some services to the state, like labor around the castles, public roads and bridges and public domains. Labor service obligation was then imposed upon the village population by the *boyar* and gentry landlords, called *barshchina,* leading directly to serfdom and bondage.[8]

The Russian North-East was for a long time divided into numerous small and semi-sovereign territorial units (principalities) with their own taxes and especially numerous tolls, fees and tariffs. These hampered commercial activities. Therefore, at first the Khans, who were greatly interested in trade, and then the Grand Dukes continued to grant privileges of tax exemptions to the Church, and in particular, to the monasteries, largely involved in commercial operations, to various cities and commercial communities and groups, to ease up the unbearable situation and to promote trade. Trading was an indispensable component of the economic process of Muscovy, which otherwise was poorly endowed with necessary production resources.

Princely lieutenants, district chiefs and the minor officials and assistants to the lieutenants, such as the *tivuns* and *donoshchiks* (collectors and reporters), were engaged in collecting the tax and non-tax receipts, from which respective shares they were entitled to retain as their compensation for the public services rendered.

With the territorial and political growth of Muscovy, its economy was also constantly expanding. In particular, territorial specialization of various regions came into prominence, causing ever greater volume of exchange transactions among those economically different regions, among the towns and the villages, and inducing more foreign exchange. Hence, the need of a more efficient medium of exchange was becoming apparent. But there was a pressing shortage of money in old Muscovy, largely because of its economic primitivism. In the thirteenth and fourteenth centuries, fur and livestock were still used as simple media of exchange, the so-called soft commodity monies. Then ingots, pieces of metal and Mongol coins came into circulation. Since the era of Tokhmatish in the Golden Horde, the Muscovites coined their own money, some 200 *diengis* from one *ruble,* or approximately half a pound of silver. Credit was not yet developed; only mercantile credit in merchandising, and some business credit among friends. A little consumer credit was in limited use. The princes, *boyars*, country gentry, monasteries and wealthy merchants supplied production capital, but interest bearing credit operations were generally considered to be sinful, although it was rather widely practiced. The interest charges ran as high as 33 per cent per annum or considerably higher in the cases of a fully illicit lending business.

The maintenance of the grand-ducal court, the maintenance of the justiciary and administration and the country's defense were the main area of the grand-ducal and state money disbursements.[9]

The Muscovite-Russian political history was more aggressive, imperialist and military than that of many other lands. Hence, the problem of keeping a large-scale military force was, for the Grand Duchy and its Grand Dukes, of utmost importance. The revenues from the ducal domains, tax receipts and other public incomes were used for that purpose. The Muscovites had acquired a thorough knowledge of army organization patterns. The old Suzdalians and Vladimirians participated in many Mongol military ventures in China, Central Asia and Caucasia. Then, the Muscovites either served in Sarai or in other places throughout the Golden Horde or used Mongol services in the army or administration of the Grand Duchy.

The core of the Muscovite army was the grand-ducal "court" armed force, the so-called *dvor*, the imitation of the Mongol *ordu*, vastly different from the old princely retinue of the pre-Mongol era, at that time shaped-up according to the Kievan patterns. The *dvor's* armed force consisted of the grand ducal court servitors, the princes, *boyars* and the country gentry, bound to service either for a certain period of time or for life, and fully dependent upon and subordinated to the Grand Duke. The members of the "court" armed force were not the companions or friends of the sovereign, like the members of the old princely retinue of the Kievan era were, but his servants. The supreme administrative power over the *dvor* rested with the quartermaster-general.

The Muscovite army of the fifteenth century was divided, according to the original Mongol pattern, into five large military units or divisions, called the center, the left wing, the right wing, the advance guard, and the rear guard. Also some Mongol arms, such as the *arkan* (lasso), were used by the Muscovite warriors, along with the traditional bows and arrows, swords, axes, spears and shields. Firearms were introduced in the Muscovite army at the end of the fourteenth century. Cannons came first into use, probably imported from Bohemia, while hand guns became known in Muscovy much later.

The *dvor* or the court armed force was a standing army of the Grand Duchy, while in the case of a national emergency (a foreign invasion or a large-scale military venture, like Dimitrii Donskoi's anti-Mongol crusade or the anti-Kazan expedition of Ivan IV), general conscription mobilized the whole country's militia. The country's militia consisted of the gentry warriors and the townspeople's troops. Peasants were not generally mobilized. The gentry troops, under the command of a warrior-leader or *voyevoda* were in most part cavalry units, while the townspeople militia, also led by a separate *voyevoda*, were exclusively infantry detachments. In addition, since Ivan III, the third category of the military formation, the Cossacks, exclusively infantry units, were used in defense of the borderlands and in the foreign wars as well. The Cossacks were a para-military class, spontaneously organized in the steppes borderlands of the European continent to withstand the Mongol threat. In the southeastern frontiers of the Muscovite state, the Cossack formations emerged, initially a class of socially heterogeneous people and mixed ethnical origin. A little later, they gave rise to the development of the important socio-political phenomenon of the Don-Cossacks, who subsequently began to strive for political autonomy and even political independence. However, the most famous at that time became the Ukrainian Zaporozhe Cossacks, a distinctly Ukrainian socio-political group. The Zaporozhe Cossacks soon became the standard bearers of the Ukrainian national aspirations to full political independence from Polish rule and the untiring champions of the cause of the Ukrainian nation and the Orthodox Church.[10] Other Cossack formations evolved later in other parts of East Europe and were used regularly by the Muscovite-Russian rulers to defend their frontiers. When assisting the Muscovites in their campaigns, the Cossack detachments were usually under the command of their own chieftains, called *atamans*.

The Social Structure

The social structure of Muscovite-Russian society of the fourteenth and fifteenth centuries resembled, of course, the social order of the North-East from the pre-Mongol era, as well as that of European lands of the time. It had, however, many peculiarities of its own. There were essentially three classes of the Muscovite people, the nobles, the townspeople and the peasants, with the clergy having its own social status, as before, but with various social novelties. Slavery was practically non-existent. Each class was again internally differentiated, while their over-all social status considerably worsened under the impact of the Muscovite absolutism, which reduced their class rights and privileges.

The nobility was at the top of the social structure. Since the middle of the fifteenth century, the class of the nobility was headed by the servitor princes of the Rurik, Gedymin or Mongol descent, all claiming some distant relationship with the ruling houses in Muscovy, Lithuania or in the Horde. Either those princes or their predecessors might have once been sovereign rulers in their patrimonial principalities or at least members of the ruling families. With the growth of the Muscovite power, those princes were forced to give up their political independence, and entered either willingly or unwillingly into the services of the Grand Duke as his servitors, usually for life. Essentially, they were not even free but at first closely dependent upon the Muscovite Grand Duke to a much greater extent than the *boyars*. Along with their close social and political dependence upon the Grand Duke, the servitor princes enjoyed an elevated social position. They filled the top offices at the court and in the country, in the administration and the army. At the end of the fifteenth century, a system of office filling was already developed in Muscovy according to the importance of the state or court position and the social status of various noble families, the so-called *miestnichestvo*. In the sixteenth century, the whole *miestnichestvo* system was based on two official or semi-official registers of the noble families and the respective government and army positions. The whole system worked in a highly complicated way, and not always to full satisfaction of all concerned, because the court, the servitor princes and the *boyars* were very particular in this respect.[11]

The servitor princes usually signed a pledge of allegiance and service, not to be broken in any way, otherwise, they could lose their tenure service estates. Furthermore, the interprincely agreements among the Grand Dukes and the semi-sovereign princes in most cases provided not to condone or tolerate any disloyalties or service changes of the servitor princes. Hence, they were very much service-bound, while for some time the *boyars* continued to enjoy their traditional freedoms. Nevertheless the service-bondage of the princes soon enabled the Grand Duke to establish a firm grip over the other higher social strata, the *boyars* and the country gentry. His control over the servitor princes gave him an excuse to curb the freedoms of the *boyardom*, who originally could transfer their allegiance and services to other sovereigns without losing their hereditary property rights on their patrimonial estates. In the sixteenth century, the *boyardom* and gentry were already in the same servitor position as the princes, upon which the possession and use of their landed estates were fully dependent. Grand-ducal Muscovy actually put all social classes either in direct bondage, like the servitor princes, the *boyars*, the country gentry and the Church, or in indirect bondage, like the townspeople and the peasants.

The grand *boyars* and the minor boyars or country gentry made up two other segments of the noble class. They all could have been initially classified into two groups, the free *boyars* and the service-bound *boyars* or gentry. The free gentry possessed private patrimonial estates, *votchina*, as was pointed out before, which they owned and could initially retain independently upon their term or for-life service allegiances. They could own the estates in the territory of one prince, and render services to another. They were usually petty army officers or minor officials in the state or grand-ducal administration. Soon, however, under the impact of the growing all-comprehensiveness of the grand-ducal authority, the free *boyar* gentry was progressively losing its traditional freedoms or liberties, in particular, the unconditional property right on the patrimonial lands, and became practically equal to the service-bound *boyardom*, the land holding of whom had a service-tenure, *pomestie*, character.

The service-bound *boyars* or gentry (courtiers or *dvorianie*) were originally under the jurisdiction (administrative and judicial) of the majordomo or *dvorskii*. Some of them were raised to the noble level from their original slavery position. The service-bound gentry, having enjoyed a greater degree of confidence of the Grand Duke, usually staffed the higher level posts of the state, court, judicial and administrative machine of the Grand Duchy, including the top management of the grand-ducal manorial domains. While in service, those service-bound boyars received maintenance from the Grand Duke or were compensated by service-tenure holding of landed estates for use and enjoyment. They actually became the nucleus of the Russian nobility of the later centuries, then commonly called the *dvorianie*. The nobility of all social levels was bound to render military services, when called by the Grand Duke to do so. The whole idea of the traditional noble, with hereditary and patrimonial, land holding was definitely crushed by Ivan III and Vasilii III as incompatible with the absolute power of the Czar.

The second social stratum were the various classes of the townspeople. Stratification of the urban class prevailed in the North-East prior to the Mongol invasion. Their upper echelon was made up of the rich wholesale merchants, exempt from most tax burdens and compulsory labor services. As the city aristocracy, they assisted the Grand Duke in the financial matters of the state and court and even sometimes advised him on domestic affairs. The lower segments of the townspeople consisted of retail merchants, master craftsmen, artisans and all kinds of unskilled workers. They all paid taxes, and supplied labor for municipal and state projects. Ivan's Code of Law, the *Sudebnik,* defined the different scale of compensation for offenses against the members of those various groups of the townspeople, testifying to considerable and significant social stratification. Out of economic and military considerations, the townspeople were forced into a permanent community-bound class in the later stage of their social evolution.

The peasants were the third and the lowest class in the old Muscovite society, since slavery was practically non-existent. The peasants paid most taxes and rendered most of the labor services to the state and the Grand Duke, but had practically no military obligation. The free peasantry largely disappeared as a social institution in the second half of the fifteenth century in the state of Muscovy. Hence, all peasants were service bound to their landlords and bore collective responsibility for the financial and labor duties of the village community. Only a few peasants managed to rise to the status of the courtiers, *dvorianie,* or to maintain themselves relatively free in some parts of the Russian North-East. They were, however, the exception to the rule. The peasants at the end of the fourteenth century were generally called the "christians" or *khristianie,* regardless if they were bound to the Church, the state, grand-ducal, princely, boyar or gentry landed estates.

Their social position considerably worsened under the Muscovite rule. For example, during the Mongol period the peasants in Church service were free from the tribute payments and other state burdens (taxes and labor services). Also, the so-called "black soil peasants" in the state-owned domains were at first much freer. They could not be removed from the lands they were settled upon as long as they paid the taxes and tilled the land. The "black soil peasant" lived and worked in the previously princely, *boyar* and Church estates, which were confiscated by the Muscovite state under one pretext or another, mainly to support its growing military machine and its imperialist projects. But then, under the complete authority of the Muscovite Grand Dukes, a slow enserfment process bound them to the soil. Also, during the continuous, internal peasant settlement program in Muscovy and its borderlands with a view toward increasing the economic value of the land, the tenant peasants were at first freer. Soon, however, due to the labor shortage, soil bondage arose there. Also the financial indebtedness of the peasants toward the ecclesiastic and secular landlords sped up their enserfment and soil-bondage, which were definitely established in the sixteenth century throughout Muscovy.[12] Of course, the Muscovite social structure had a decisive bearing upon the economic process of the European North-East in general.

The Economic Process

The economic system of the Muscovite-Russian North-East of the fourteenth and fifteenth centuries in a broad sense resembled medieval European feudalism. It was essentially a primitive agricultural economy, still substantially dependent upon trapping, hunting and fishing, and inadequately supplemented by cattle raising, and slowly emerging crafts and mercantile activities. The sovereign Grand Duke was the landlord of the quasi-vassal, servitor princes and *boyars,* while they exercised, to some extent, the power of landlordship upon the enserfed peasantry. The economic foundation of social stratification and status was not, however, so clearly established as in West Europe. The institutions of the service tenure, *pomestie,* land holding of the princes, *boyars* and gentry and of the tenant land holding by the peasantry, resembled feudalism to some extent. Nevertheless, the simultaneous existence of small and insignificant servitor princes of small fortunes and of the influential and rich *boyars,* and relatively independent "black soil peasantry" along with the peasant serfs, was peculiarly Muscovite.

Only the Marxist historians and economists, out of their

ideological expedience, have insisted upon defining the era as feudalistic to build it into the Marxian pattern of the socio-economic evolution and the Marxian materialist interpretation of history. However, that Marxian assumption of the social evolution of mankind from the primitive, to the feudal, to the capitalist, to the socialist, and finally, to the communist economy cannot be scientifically demonstrated by the Muscovite-Russian case. Unless a slightly advanced natural economy would be simply termed a feudal one, without regard to particular "feudal" features present in the medieval West European societies.[13] As long as there was the hereditary land possession of the princes and nobles, and since the peasantry in Muscovy were relatively free, the socio-economic system was not even close to true feudalism.

Agriculture was, in the second half of the fifteenth century, the leading sector of the Muscovite economy. There were essentially two farming institutions: the princely, *boyar* and monastic manorial economies, and their pillar, the tenant peasant, soil-bound and service-bound farms. Farming in the princely and monastic domains was usually more advanced. The three-field system prevailed, animal manure was at times applied, and draft animals and some iron implements were used in many cases. The peasant-operated small-scale farms were much more backward. The simple two-field approach prevailed, no draft animals were used to till and no animal manure was applied to fertilize the rather poor soil. Mostly wooden tools and implements were available to the primitive peasant farmer.

There was practically no horse breeding among the peasants. The historical sources refer only to princely and, perhaps, *boyar* horse breeding. This was done mainly out of military considerations for the cavalry troops. The *chronicles* refer to the office of the master of stables of the grand-ducal court, who took general care of the herds of stallions and mares of the grand-ducal domains. Goats, hogs and cows were raised to a rather modest degree, and more so in the southern parts of Muscovy.

Of course, the tenant holding and tilling of the soil of the grand landlords by the peasant farmers against certain payments, crop shares and labor services to the manors, completed the organizational structure of Muscovite agriculture. Clearing the woods by farm settlers continued to conquer new land soil for farming. In order to attract the peasant colonists, at first the cleared land was given almost as a property to the peasants, either by the state, the Grand Duke, the monasteries or the nobles in an attempt to cope with a chronic labor shortage. And the peasant payments and responsibilities were few. Soon, however, serfdom and soil bondage were extended over those newly settled regions.

In general, it was a typically subsistence economy, producing largely for its own consumption. Grain, fruit, milk and milk products, vegetables, flax, meat and other goods were produced to be consumed in the framework of the hereditary *patrimonium* or the landed estates in service tenure. Very little was produced for sale outside the given territorial community. So much more, because in the suburbs of the towns farming was also extensively practiced to supplement the diet of the urban population.

Primitivism of farm technology was unfortunately associated with the exploitation of the peasants, who actually supplied most of the food and raw materials from their farm units, and who also rendered most of the labor for their own farming and for the manorial economy as well. The peasants paid their rentals and taxes, mostly in kind, but in money too. Some of those payments were then accumulated, as mentioned, in the so-called *"obrok"* levy. Along with the tenant obligations, including the labor services, at Christmas, Easter and Sts. Peter and Paul's Day, the peasant had to bring to the landlord additional gifts, which burdened him substantially.

Three kinds of ploughs were used in Muscovy. A regular iron plough was mostly used in the more advanced princely and monastic manorial farming in the central Muscovite regions; a wooden plough with only an iron share was to be found in the more progressive and wealthier farms; while the peasants largely worked with a light wooden plough or *sokha*. Primitive harrows, hoes, scythes, sicles and other farm implements were slowly coming into use, at first in the manorial economies, and then in the peasant small-scale farming. Oats, rye, millet, peas, flax and other products were raised in various parts of Muscovy. Collective use of meadows and forests by the village communities prevailed.

Of course, extensive animal trapping, hunting and fishing supplemented Muscovy's natural economy in supplying food and raw material. Trapping and hunting continued to be exceptionally important, since big game and furbearing animals were plentiful in the enormous forest areas of the North East. All classes of the population were involved in hunting or trapping. The princes and *boyars* hunted for the love of it as well as to get meat and fur. The peasants trapped and hunted to supplement their meager diet. Fishing was, for the most part, peasant work or done by the village or manorial fishers. Lakes and rivers, where fishing was done, were mostly owned by the princes, monasteries or *boyars*. Hence, their fishing rights were legally protected.[14]

Manufacturing took place within the framework of the small-scale establishments of the town, village and manor craftsmen and artisans. Town artisans were largely the free urban proletariat, while village and manor artisans were largely the serfs. Carpenters, joiners, wheelers, turners, saddlers, coopers, potters, weavers, tanners, furriers, shoemakers, smithies, masons, bridge-builders, dwelling builders, tailors, hatmakers were the various tradesmen, resulting from the growing specialization and division of labor. Tools and implements were mostly wooden; iron utensils and tools were rather rare, although iron ore was mined and some iron produced in the regions of Novgorod the Great, the White Sea, the Lake Ladoga, Yamskii, Ustiuzhina Zhelezopolskaia and Kapor. The scarcity of iron things and implements was largely because of primitive production technology. Silver was mined near Novgorod, but silver and gold articles were largely import items, along with copper or bronze candlesticks, knives, frying pans. Their possession and use was limited to the wealthy princely and *boyar* households.

Salt production was an important aspect of the old Muscovite economy. It was obtained on the shores of the Northern Sea, on the banks of the North Dvina River, in the Vologda region and other places. The evaporation process was applied to produce salt, and it was done primarily in the princely and monastic domains, such as the Troitskii and Simionovskii monasteries. It was a costly way to obtain salt, however. Throughout Muscovy the processing of agricultural and hunting and fishing products took place. The village and manorial distilling, the manorial and urban brewing, baking, weaving and other industries were slowly developing. It has been pointed out before that the first impact of the invasion upon the crafts and trades of the Russian North-East was highly unfavorable. The Khans at first drafted most of the craftsmen for their services, and forced a great many of them to leave the European North-East and go to various parts of their vast empire. This tremendously retarded the industrial development of the North-East for many a decade. Only the monastic domains were in a little better situation, since the Khans left there a certain percentage of the artisans upon the request of the Church authorities. Things began to improve in this respect around the middle of the fourteenth century.[15]

Commerce, both domestic and foreign, was developing on a small scale, because all production and consumption was narrowly confined to relatively self-sufficient territorial economic units, either the hereditary patrimonium, *votchina*, or the in-service tenure possession, *pomestie*, village or manor, consisting mostly of the usual village-town exchange. Hence, domestic trading developed as an exchange between the rural economy, producing wood and wooden products, products of hunting and fishing, wax, livestock, grain, flour, some fruits and vegetables, and the manufacturing urban economy, producing clothing, footwear, pots, implements, arms, coffins and other things of everyday usage. Only the large towns were real commercial centers, while small towns and townships also participated in the farm and forestry economy.

Trading centered along the bulky produce, shipped mostly by water routes. Otherwise, it was largely handicapped by poor and inadequate transportation facilities and bad commercial policies of numerous small and semi-independent principalities and territories in the North-East as late as the second half of the fourteenth century. These tended to collect various duties and tolls whenever possible. Their demands were at times almost impossible to meet. Things improved a little with Moscow's annexation of new territories, since some local taxes and tolls were abolished, but not much. Only food and salt were transported over really great distances, since they were necessities. Food and salt were even important items of Muscovite foreign trade. Exchange among Novgorod the Great, Tver, Suzdal, Moscow and a few other real metropolises of the Russian North-East reached a more appreciable volume.

In order to reduce or abolish those obstacles to mercantile trade due to the internal duties and tolls, at first the Khan as the suzerain, and then the Grand Duke, granted privileges of exemption from those burdensome and unjustifiable and often arbitrary charges. The monasteries were first to acquire such privileges, and the leading cities and some princes and wealthy *boyars* followed. Later in the fourteenth century, several cities negotiated commercial agreements to trade "without the frontiers." Such treaties were concluded for example, between Novgorod and Tver, Novgorod and Suzdal, Moscow and Riazan, and Moscow and Tver.

Local trading was done at the bazaars, marketplaces, and fairs. The bazaar and marketplace trade was almost a continuous affair, while the fairs, which were larger in scale, were held only on some specific days of the year, usually associated with some religious holydays. The fairs, as in the rest of Europe, represented not only an important economic institution, but they also were significant social affairs as well. The monasteries, having a more advanced farming system and also practicing progressive trade, organized their own fairs and even operated their own boats on the rivers for shipping their own and other merchandise for mercantile purposes.

Thriving monastic trade was enhanced also by those exemption privileges, so lavishly granted to the monasteries by the Khans or the Grand Dukes. The Troitse-Sergeievskii, the Cyril-Bielooziero, and the Cherepovetskii monasteries had the greatest commercial importance in the old Muscovy, along with a few minor ones, having included in their mercantile operations also some foreign trading as well. Trading was done by merchants and monasteries for their own consumption as well as for profit. The princes and the *boyar* nobles participated in it rather indirectly through their agents and by lending money. In 1382, the Muscovites were already in control of the trade and shipping on the Volga River. Foreigners were excluded from the Muscovite domestic trade by custom and law, in order to reserve for the Muscovites-Russians all the benefits from it.[16] In the domestic and foreign commerce the Muscovites were quite discriminatory, being traditionally suspicious and hostile toward the foreigners, to whom they always denied an equal chance.

Physically, foreign trade was limited to a few items and a few places. Novgorod and Pskov excelled other cities of the North-East in this respect, the first was even a member of the Hanseatic League of the West-European cities. But, the Muscovite conquest of those democratic communities put an end to their thriving foreign commerce. Pares said the following to the point: "In 1487 fifty of the leading merchant families were transported to Vladimir; the next year, on the report of a plot against John's (Ivan's) governor, 7000 of the gentry were moved to the environs of Moscow; Moscow families, in the same wholesale way, were moved into the territory of Novgorod.... To please his ally, the King of Denmark, who was a bitter enemy of the Hanseatic League, John (Ivan) seized all the German merchants at Novgorod with their goods, their warehouses and their chapel, and from this blow the trade of Novgorod never recovered."[17] The actions of the Muscovites in Novgorod might have summarized their over-all approach to the foreigners and to foreign trade.

The Russian North-East exported timber, furs, and a few other items, such as locks from Tver; it imported luxuries, grain, salt, and some other foodstuffs. Foreign trade did not develop substantially in Muscovy, because of numerous controls, restrictions, discriminatory practices, and the suspicion of any foreigner or any native having contacts with the foreigners. This policy intensified with increasing Muscovite absolutism. Free trade seemed somehow irreconcilable with the doctrine of the Muscovite absolutism.

Nevertheless, economic considerations were immeasurably essential in the Muscovite political projects. Inspired by the idea of Russian unification and consolidation, the Muscovite Grand Dukes were in constant need of new economic resources to feed their war machine. At first, the retainment of the tribute surplus, when acting as agents of Sarai, collected in other lands and principalities of the Russian North-East, helped the Grand Dukes from Ivan Kalita to Vasilii II to materialize their political dreams. Subsequently, direct conquests and annexations were applied toward those lands and principalities to enrich Muscovy and to enable her to continue with her consolidation plans. In later centuries, economic considerations motivated Moscow to adopt the identical policy of conquest toward foreign lands and non-Russian peoples. The continuance of unrestrained imperialist growth, the conquests and contiguous colonization of Ukraine, Byeloruthenia, Central Asia, Siberia, and Caucasia, are only a few examples of that policy.

The Church

The Orthodox Church in the Russian North-East, a religious institution, very soon became an arm of the grand-ducal government in accordance with the prevailing *caesaropapist* doctrine of Byzantine origin. Previously, it was subservient to the Mongol Khans. Hence, it could be discussed as a semi-government institution closely related to the Muscovite government and administration.

The first impact of the Mongol invasion damaged the organizational structure of the Church. Many church buildings were burned and destroyed; a few bishops and many priests perished; the faithful were left without spiritual guidance and without places of worship. Nevertheless, the Church recuperated in a relatively short time. First of all, the Mongols were religiously very tolerant and had respect for any religion. Secondly, the ecclesiastic domains were more efficiently managed and were relatively more productive, and the Mongols badly needed that productive Church farming and trade to boost their own war machine and commercial process.

In order to take full advantage of the efficient monastic economies, the Khans granted the Church privileges and immunities from various tolls and taxes, with respect of the Church organizational units, religious activities and business operations in exchange for the church loyalty and its prayers for the Mongol suzerain. *Yarliks* were granted to safeguard the religious places of worship, the clergy and the church domains. The population in the church domains were exempt from state jurisdiction and subordinated exclusively to the ecclesiastic authorities in most civil and criminal cases. Infringement upon the Church immunities and privileges were punishable by law.

The Khans intended by the privileged treatment of the Church to make it a loyal arm of their rule over the Russian North-East and to keep the people in subordination to the Khan as the protector of their Church. Once the Muscovite-Russian Grand Dukes became the Mongol agents, they began to assume some influence upon ecclesiastic matters, and as such agents, they also acquired the Church's cooperation as well. The Eastern Churches in general, and the Muscovite in particular, were always looking for a mighty protector, who was either Emperor, Khan or Grand Duke.

The Khan originally installed the Metropolitan and the bishops. Practice, however, left very much to the decision of the Muscovites and Constantinople. Then, the Grand Dukes assumed all the authority of confirming the newly appointed or chosen ecclesiastical dignitaries. At first the bishops traveled around their respective dioceses, rebuilding the Church organization, which suffered so much during the invasion. They created new parishes, established new monastic communities, encouraged the building of new churches and new monasteries. Independently, numerous hermits, living apart from society deep in the woods or distant and inaccessible places, sincerely tried to raise the religious life of Vladimir-Muscovite society.

In 1300, the Vladimir Grand Dukes succeeded in making the city of Vladimir the seat of the Metropolitan. Then shortly thereafter, the seat was transferred to Moscow, as the latter began to assume the political leadership in the North-East. At first, the Metropolitans visited Sarai as the center of the secular power, but soon most of them willingly submitted to the authority of the Grand Duke. Along this line was the strange alliance between Grand Duke Dimitrii and Metropolitan Aleksei. Whoever fought against Dimitrii was declared "an enemy of the cross" by Aleksei. The anti-Catholic and anti-Church union feelings of the Muscovite Church and the Grand Duke considerably strengthened the bond between the Muscovite Orthodoxy and the Muscovite autocracy. The break with Constantinople over the issue of the Church union in 1443, was another step toward the full submission of the Muscovite Church to the Muscovite state and its Grand Duke. Shortly, any crime against the state was considered a sin against God and the Church. Servility of the clergy toward the throne was common. With Constantinople under the Turk domination, there was no other loyalty to be shown by the Muscovite Orthodox Church, but toward the Grand Duke.

From now on, all political and conquest plans and projects of the Muscovite rulers were in most cases justified and obediently sanctioned, and the conquered (Novgorod, Pskov, or Viatka) were admonished by the Church to accept the Muscovite rule and to be loyal to the Grand Duke, the true head of that Church. The writings and doings of Sanin, Spiridon, Filotei and Metropolitan Daniel are enough to prove the point.[18]

There was, however, one issue in old Muscovy on which the state and the Church could easily clash. It was the question of the ecclesiastic land possessions. Ivan III and Vasilii III desired to secularize those estates and to use them in support of their political plans. The secularized land was given to the gentry in service tenure and settled by the peasants to strengthen the economy and the war machine of the state. Ivan III proceeded resolutely with the secularization of the ecclesiastic estates, in particular in the newly conquered or annexed lands. The hierarchy of the Church strongly opposed the move and the clash might have been imminent, but for its internal frictions.

In the first place, the religious dissenters, called falsely the Judaizers, along with opposing monastic life, rejecting the veneration of *icons* and the prayer for the dead, rejected altogether the institutionalized Church with its hierarchy, services, buildings, and in particular, with its wealthy possessions. Hence, they advocated the secularization of the Church domains, as one of the ways of returning to the true faith. Furthermore, the Judaizers proclaimed the reason to be supreme to faith. Therefore, the Judaizers actually put in doubt all basic principles of the official Church and undermined the material basis of its existence. The official Church, in order to make the Judaizers repulsive to the Muscovite-Russian people in general, accused them of pro-Semite feelings and of distorting the true faith with elements of Judaism. The accusation might have been only partially correct. However, the Grand Dukes were lenient toward the sect, because of its support for the secularization project. It frightened the hierarchy of the Orthodox Church.

On the other hand, the so-called Volga hermits, organized by Nil Sorskii, highly venerated by the people, preached poverty for the clergy, condemned the rich life of the monastic communities, advocated hermitage and complete rejection of worldly possessions, stressed spiritual perfection over the religious formalism and came forcefully in support of the secularization of the eclesiastic domains. Ivan III and Vasilii III were strongly attracted to the "heretic" idea of secularization of the Church estates, as expressed by the hermits and the Judaizers, but they were not so keen about Sorskii's insistence upon the secular nonintervention in the Church's spiritual and religious matters and the Church's full religious independence. Hence, the official Church did not dare to oppose too aggressively the grand-ducal secularization of some ecclesiastic possessions for the state's economy and war reasons. It was definitely in favor of the *caesaropapist* views and hoped eventually to gain the Grand Dukes for its official cause.

At first, the Church suffered a few setbacks from the dissenters, but finally it prevailed with the help of the Grand Dukes, having accepted an even greater dependence upon their secular authority in ecclesiastic matters. While Nil Sorskii was allowed to die in peace, other "heretics," such as Maxim and Vassian, were severely punished for their opposition to the Church and its official *caesaropapist* philosophy. The Muscovite autocrats could not tolerate any diminution of their authority over the Church and in this way sacrifice its use as a powerful government arm in building the Muscovite-Russian empire.

The official Muscovite Orthodox Church evolved in a way particularly convenient for the state policies. It put faith, the blind and uncritical obedience to the Church precepts and the ritual and external observance of religion, ahead of reason. It simply refused to debate the "heretics" and was ready to exterminate them by execution, burning or hanging for the sake of faith and salvation. Reasoning in religious matters was considered sinful. The primitive Muscovite people were thrown into the Orthodox "spiritual bondage," which subsequently radiated into the areas of their social and political life and forced them to be blindly and subserviently obedient to the authority of the Grand Dukes, who indirectly, headed their Church.[19]

The Culture

Muscovite society of the fourteenth and fifteenth centuries was primitive, when judged by contemporary European standards. Schools and libraries were practically non-existent, with the very few exceptions of the major political centers, such as Novgorod, Pskov, Tver and Moscow. And when they existed nobody really read those meager Greek, Latin or Old-Slavic collections. Primarily, the Church sponsored some informal schooling and preserved liturgical books but rarely any literary works. The princes and the nobles were, as a rule, not interested in those things.

The early Mongol era of the Russian North-East was a definite cultural regression in comparison with the pre-Mongol Suzdal-Vladimir principality, which was under the powerful spiritual influence of the Kievan Rus'.

The slow cultural revival of the North-East came in the wake of the rise in the spiritual and religious life, inspired by the unfortunate experiences of the Mongol invasion. The troubled Russian Slavs looked to God and religion in the hour of their trial. On the other hand, since the East-European Orthodoxy was connected with Constantinople, the Byzantine influences were at work in this cultural revival, although the West-European (Italian and Scandinavian) and Oriental elements were also felt.

The reconstruction of the old and damaged church buildings and the construction of new ones seemed to be the most important aspect of that religious renewal. The houses of prayer were indispensable. Hence, in later decades many new churches and monasteries, and then palaces and public buildings, were constructed in all major cities and towns of the North-East. The Romanesque style of West Europe, the Scandinavian, Byzantine, Armenian and Georgian styles of architecture could easily be detected there, while, of course, the old Suzdal-Vladimir construction patterns were dominant throughout the country.

The fusion of the Suzdal-Vladimir style with those foreign structural forms from Europe and Asia, ultimately resulted in the development of the national Muscovite architectural style, which then at the end of the fifteenth century was accepted throughout the all Russian North-East. It was a harmonious and a richly decorated construction pattern. Italian architects and builders were at that time brought to Moscow to beautify the new capital of the emerging empire. Their task was in reproducing the old Suzdal and Vladimir cathedrals in the city of Moscow in order to continue the tradition. Obviously, those Italians could not help but introduce some Italian construction elements in their works. Also in the fifteenth century, the thoroughly Muscovite construction style of wooden churches widely spread throughout the countryside and small towns. Being Muscovite in their character, they differed from the old churches with much stronger Byzantine architectural influences. The arch-conservative Church circles opposed the new architecture for a while. [20]

Along with the architecture, early Muscovite-Russian painting also developed. Having been under the prolonged Byzantine influence, it showed, according to the art historians, less refinement, more spontaneity and sincerity, and more motion. The colors were brighter. The style was formed somehow in the second half of the fourteenth century. *Icon* (pictures of saints) painting developed largely due to the prolonged cultural isolation of the North-East from the European centers during the Mongol domination. It was the leading form of artistic painting, since the *icons* were in large demand to decorate the churches, and in particular, the wooden ones, the palaces and the dwelling premises of the common people as well. Soon the primitive people began to develop a superstitious belief in the supernatural powers of those pictures, especially in emergencies. This neatly increased their demand and popularity, and gave rise to a large scale reproduction of the old *icons*, and even some reproductions had a high artistic value; others had none. At one time a movement even began to spread in the North-East, having been a distant renaissance of Byzantine events, toward suppressing the adoration of those *icons* as being a form of revival of pagan idolatry.

In the fourteenth century the Italian influence also affected Muscovite painting, the revival of which was impressive. Andrei Rublev, who was compared with Fra Angelico in the West, and Dionisii of the Ferapont monastery marked the era of the painting of grace and great beauty. Also in this area of artistic painting an opposition of the arch-conservative Church circles developed to condemn new ideas and, to a great extent, retarded the evolution original and inspired Russian painting, although it could not suppress it entirely. Frescoes and mosaics, used to decorate the stone churches, did not develop, and remained rather confined to the Byzantine patterns, although the elements of national originality in the application of colors could be found even there. Novgorod and Moscow were the centers of painting and other decorative arts.[21]

Church singing did show some progress and change from the old diatonic chant, *znamienii*, which was rooted in the ancient Byzantine basis. It came slightly closer to the Muscovite folk singing in the course of the fifteenth century. At that time also a new chant was originated, the so-called *diemiestviennii*.

The revival and the growth of the literary life of the North-East also rooted in the spiritual process of the Orthodox Church. The sermons, the lives of saints, the stories and legends with moral overtones, and the biographies of famous princes, such as Aleksander Nevskii and Yaroslav of Vladimir, initiated the literary revival after the invasion blow. The usual theme in those writings stressed the tragedies of the Mongol invasion to be sustained by the people of the North-East as a punishment for their sins. Then, Bishop Serapion of Vladimir related the punishment to the persistence of the dual faith of *dvoievierie*, a confusion of the Christian and pagan religious elements among the people.

Along with the growing Muscovite-Russian patriotism, centered at first around the ruling dynasty of the Rurikovich and the Orthodox Church, the chronicle writing and compiling was developing in the fourteenth century, such as the *Rostov Chronicle*, the *Tver Chronicle* an the *Laurentian Chronicle*. They were followed in the fifteenth century by the *Trinity Chronicle* and the chronicle compilation edited by Metropolitan Fotii. Fotii's compilation then served as the source in the sixteenth century for significant chronicle digests, such as the *Voskresensk and Nikon Chronicles*, which registered the facts of the Muscovite political growth.[22]

In the literary fiction of that time two trends could be detected. On the one hand, it exhibited the patriotic and anti-Mongol feelings of the Russian Slavs in the way of new versions of sagas and stories. The heroic struggle against the steppe nomads was pictured there, as in the stories about the battle on the Kulikovo Plain and in the story called "Beyond the Don River," the *Zadonshchina*. The *Zadonschchina* was clearly a rather poor Muscovite version of the old Kievan masterpiece, "The Song about Ihor's Host," from which the *Zadonshchina* plagiarized a great deal. On the other hand, the beauty and attraction of the adventurous life in the steppes was pictured in much of the fiction of that time as well. *The Lay of the Destruction of Riazan* related the horrors of the Mongol revenge.

The Mongol influence upon the early Muscovite literary works has been considerable, evident also in many Tartar and Turkish expressions used and found there. However, since illiteracy, even among the princes and nobles, was common in old Muscovy, numerous literary creations were developing and communicated by the oral tradition more succesfully than by the written word. In fact, the stories and sagas were usually written down in later periods.[23] Some translations of foreign literature, such as *The Tale of Troy*, sermons, translated and written originally, a great deal of writing on the lives of saints, like that of Metropolitan Peter, full of fiction and lacking facts, secular biographies, like that of Prince Mikhail, and tales, often inherited from the Kievan era, completed a rather modest picture of the literary creations of the Muscovite society of the fourteenth and fifteenth centuries.[23]

CHAPTER ELEVEN

THE MUSCOVITE CZARATE

Ivan IV, The Terrible or Dread as a Ruler

Two periods of Muscovite-Russian history, the era of Ivan the Terrible (1533-1584) and the era of the "Time of Troubles" (1584-1613), were of utmost importance for the over-all development of the Russian nation. The era of Ivan IV represented a complete crystallization of the Muscovite-styled absolutism. The "Time of Troubles" of the *smutnoie vriemia*, which followed almost immediately was a cry for socio-political changes and reforms and for more freedom. Czars were meanwhile elected by the country's landed council or *ziemskii sobor*, the new government agency which came into existence under Ivan IV. The constitutional status of the landed council was not certain, however, during the entire era of the "Time of Troubles". It was honored to some extent, although partially silenced, perhaps as inconsistent with the spirit of the Muscovite absolutism.

Both periods were accompanied by some highly unfavorable developments, resulting from the unhappy fusion of Slavic and Mongol elements in the national Muscovite-Russian psychology, by the contrasting Oriental and Occidental spiritual and intellectual undercurrents. This unhappy biological, psychological and spiritual union gave birth to cruel monstrosities during the reign of Ivan the Terrible, for which not only Ivan himself but all his cruel accomplices were responsible as well, and to the anarchistic upheavals during the "Time of Troubles."[1] In fact, it is surprising that Muscovy was able to survive those socio-political convulsions, and quickly re-emerge in the course of the seventeenth century as an empire under the new dynasty of the

Romanovs, the dynasty which was supposedly related to the ancient house of Rurik.

In the time of Ivan IV, Muscovy grew territorially and politically. During the "Time of Troubles," especially after Godunov's reign, it decayed and disintegrated. The "Time of Troubles" was also characterized by a prolonged constitutional illness of the country at the early stages of its rise. It was an unbalanced time, full of social-political contradictions and inconsistencies. Eventually, after the "Time of Troubles" passed away, because of the preponderance of the healthier national undercurrent tendencies, building the empire along the paces and patterns set up by Vasilii II, Ivan III, Vasilii III and Ivan IV in particular, was resumed. Their imperial patterns were then preserved over the centuries, and were taken over by the Soviet regime of the so-called Union of the Soviet Socialist Republics in the twentieth century, to indicate the continuity of the political philosophy and practice of the Russian people. This six-century continuity of imperial and imperialist Muscovite-Russian policies cannot be explained by the ruthlessness of the government alone. It must have been deeply rooted in the psychological predispositions of the people, of which the government was only a socio-organical representative.[2]

The cruel and ruthless system of the Soviet secret security police, the name of which was frequently changed, the Cheka, G.P.U., N.K.V.D., or M.V.D., reminds one only too well of Ivan's *oprichnina*. The Soviet policy of genocide, mass deportation, forced migration of peoples to quell opposition resembles too closely the practices of Vasilii II, Ivan III and Ivan IV, and of other Muscovite rulers, only to mention the cases of Novgorod the Great, Viatka or Kazan. Shuiskii's denunciation of Godunov was a prototype of Khrushchev's denunciation of Stalin, or Brezhnev's of Khrushchev. Elaborate tortures, confiscation of properties, complete disregard for human dignity, political pragmatism, contempt of international agreements, and other similar devices of "politics," once employed by Vasiliis, Ivans, Peters and other Czars and Czaritsas, have also been favored methods of the Soviet rulers. The Soviet state machine operated by means of a small and exclusive group of the communist party membership, closely dependent upon the state, resembles the Czarist system of rule, based upon nobility of blood. The state machinery was created mainly by the reforms of Ivan IV and Peter, and it has continued since.[3]

Ivan IV acquired the surname of "The Terrible" or "The Dread" during his fifty-year reign, which left a deep and indelible imprint upon the over-all development of the Muscovite-Russian empire, marked by cruel and perverted ways of rule. Although on the surface Ivan's cruelties could hardly be explained from the point of view of political expediency, in historical perspective, they can be, perhaps, evaluated as the subconscious and instinctive measures undertaken by the Russian political genius to cope with the problems of building and maintaining the huge multinational empire-to-be. Hence, during Ivan's time, Muscovy was already a multinational state. Otherwise, the plurality of the racial and ethnical groups on the Muscovite political territory in East Europe and Asia would never have allowed the Russians to become the empire builders. This may also explain why the Russians and Russian history always so readily forgot and excused the cruelties and atrocities committed by their rulers against humanity for the sake of Russia's political greatness. Instead of condemning Vasilii III, Ivan III and Ivan IV, Peter I, Catherine II, Nicholas I and Josef Stalin for their political crimes, Russian history glorifies them and calls them "great" for what they did to make "Mother Russia" a grand empire. These rulers substantiated the Muscovite-Russian messianism by identifying it at times with the all-Russian cause, Orthodoxy, Panslavism or international Communism.[4]

Ivan IV was doubtlessly an outstanding personality, a genius, perhaps, but a twisted one. When Grand Duke Vasilii III lay on his deathbed, Ivan was only a three-year-old child. His mother, Grand Duchess Helen, assumed the regency, assisted in state affairs by her lover, Prince Ivan Ovchina-Telepniev-Obolenskii, who headed a group of noble *boyars* close to the throne at that time. Ivan's childhood was a most unhappy one, surrounded by court intrigues, continuous bloody strifes among the rival families of the servitor princes and the ancient *boyars*. These strifes, feuds and conflicts between those two upper social strata, the servitor princes and *boyars*, were brewing during Vasilii's reign, but the Grand Duke knew how to control them, at least in part.

Now, after the stern man was gone, the strifes flared up anew with a great force since the social-political antagonism between these two groups was intense. The *boyars* intended to cherish their old relative freedom and influence upon the throne when the opportunity rendered itself, while the servitor princes, being fully dependent upon the throne by the nature of their service, wanted to become the top layer of society, an ambition which endangered the social status of the boyardom. Conspiracies among the *boyars* and the princes, representing various groups of interests and political parties, often involved even foreign (Polish, Lithuanian and Turkish) intrigues. Most of the time it was directed against Helen and her advisors, and at times against Ivan himself, as well. Warring parties did not hesitate to use any devices in their struggle, including assassination, murder, tortures, imprisonments, deportation, intrigues, and humiliation of the young Czar. The authority and prestige of the throne were bloodstained and at their record low. The acts of violence were at times carried out in the presence of the Czar, literally at the foot of the throne, ignoring the dignity of the high office and the elevated place, as Florinsky pointed out.

In 1538, Grand Duchess Helen, Ivan's mother, was apparently poisoned in the course of the prolonged palace strife, while her lieutenant, Ivan Obolenskii, was imprisoned by the victorious faction, and was left there to die of starvation. However, the action did not change the Muscovite political scene; only the "actors" were different. This time, the violent years were promoted by Shuiskiis, Bielskiis and Glinskiis. The atmosphere of mendacity, cruelty and hate at the court was even strengthened. The prestige of the Orthodox Church suffered a great humiliation from the hands of the rival cliques as well. Metropolitan Daniel, a faithful champion of the *caesaropapist* doctrine, was ousted. His successor, Metropolitan Yoasaf, was imprisoned in a distant monastery. The Muscovite court was in a state of upheaval.

Ivan's young and formative years were completely ruined by those cruel and bloody developments; his inborn good qualities of character were largely distorted and the bad reinforced. Consequently, his unhappy youth preconditioned, to a great extent, the ways and patterns of his reign in the years to come. Throughout his life, Ivan harbored a deep resentment toward the *boyars*, whose insincerity, duplicity and disrespect for the throne hurt him gravely and provoked in him some subconscious hate toward the nobles and a complete lack of confidence in them. In his own literary heritage, Ivan wrote with anger about the indignities inflicted upon him by unfaithful nobles in his young years. As a powerful Czar, he revenged those indignities by torturing, deporting, imprisoning and executing the *boyars* upon mere suspicion.

If Ivan were sick, then he suffered schizophrenia (disintegrating or splitting personality, losing contact with the real environment), which projected itself in Ivan's psychology in the way of paranoia and mania of persecution, also associating itself with a substantial degree of sadism. The sickness was certainly provoked by the environment of his childhood and adolescence, which awakened and then activated his inborn and dormant but sickly psychic predispositions. Although his sickly predispositions manifested themselves in his early age, the year 1553 seemed to be the turning point toward the worse. Most of his cruelties and acts of violence resulted, of course, from his sick mind, for which he cannot be held fully responsible, judging objectively from the psychiatric point of view. However, it is surprising that the Muscovite people submitted themselves to the terror filled rule of a sick man for so long. It is indicative of the mass psychology of the people concerned. The unbalanced character of Ivan manifested itself in whatever he did.

Thus, after having killed his son in an angry passion in 1581, Ivan did not experience any peace of mind at all, but was haunted by a guilty conscience until his death in 1584. There were actually two Ivans. One, a good one, a conscientious sovereign and a Muscovite patriot, wanted to enlarge the empire and to improve its conditions, and was a religious and God-fearing man. There was also another Ivan, a cruel sadist who took pleasure in torturing other human beings, a savage tyrant and a sexual maniac, for whom nothing was sacred. The fusion of those two "personalities" resulted in a monster. Ivan the Terrible or Dread was an unbalanced man, a philosopher and a merciless sadist who tortured people amidst their untold pains and agonies, a sexual pervert and a pious man, a common murderer and a reformer of religious life, a Christian of a most rigid attachment to the Orthodox dogmas and their external observance, culminating with a complete disregard for their inner and spiritual meaning.[5]

As a young boy, Ivan associated himself with a group of equally wild and at times irresponsible youngsters like himself, roaming on horseback in the spacious fields of the countryside or galloping aimlessly through the streets of Moscow, scaring, whipping or at times even hurting the peaceful subjects of his, who fled from the streets, whenever they saw their "beloved" monarch approaching, who supposedly represented their God on earth. The cruelty of the Czar was apparent on many occasions. The Pskovian instance was indicative, no doubt. The city of Pskov sent its delegates to Moscow in 1547 in order to present its complaint about Ivan's appointed lieutenants, who apparently had badly abused their authority. Ivan became furious. Without paying careful attention to the words of the delegates, he ordered boiling wine poured over their naked bodies, their long hair and beards burned with candles, and left them lying on the floor in expectation of even worse tortures. The envoys were saved from being mercilessly and senselessly murdered by the Czar by an apparently harmless occurrence of a falling bell from a church tower, to which an ominous meaning was given by the superstitious Muscovites. And Ivan allowed himself that cruelty at the time, when he actually was still a benevolent monarch and not yet the sadist, obsessed by the mania of persecution of his later years, Florinsky remarked.

The Novgorodian instance was another illustration of Ivan's sick irresponsibility. The city of Novgorod the Great was suspected by the Czar of plotting to rid itself of the Muscovite supremacy and to accept the allegiance to the Polish-Lithuanian Crown. Novgorod was then immediately invaded by the Muscovite troops in 1570 and mercilessly devastated. An orgy of blood, murder and plunder was arranged there. Churches were burned, desecrated and robbed, the priests were flogged, tortured, murdered and otherwise mistreated. The common people suffered as well. This was done, to be sure, by Ivan on a rather mere suspicion of a Russian city in his own realm, and not of a foreign city on enemy territory. Perhaps the semi-democratic traditions of Novgorod made it the target of the Czar's ferocious assault; he believed in absolutism and abhorred any shadow of democracy, but certainly his sick psyche was there at work. Similar experiments, like that in Novgorod, were performed by Ivan in Torzok and Klin, on a smaller scale but with equal cruelty.

The schizophrenic nature of the Czar showed itself most dramatically in his attitude to the Orthodox Church, as mentioned before. Ivan IV, the Dread, was apparently one of the best educated men on the Vladimir-Muscovite throne before the age of Catherine II. He read a great deal, and so he was a great scholar for his time. In his letters and other writings, one can find numerous quotations from the Holy Bible, chronicles and historical narrations, usually, however, given in a distorted version. His education was largely acquired under the influence of Metropolitan Makarii (1542-1563) who was probably his only devout friend and associate until the latter's death. Makarii, a disciple of Abbot Joseph Sanin believed firmly in the Czar's authority in church matters, provided, however, that the Church's ancient rights and privileges would be fully honored. After Makarii's death, Ivan quickly forgot the teachings of his friend and mentor on that point, and submitted the Church to most humiliating experiences; he disregarded its "holy" nature to the fullest extent.

After Makarii's death, Ivan changed the Metropolitans like gloves, having no regard for their office. Metropolitan Anastasii was soon induced to retire; his successor, Metropolitan Herman, was ousted from his seat immediately; Metropolitan Philip was soon sent to a remote monastery for displeasing the Czar and there he was strangled by one of Ivan's chief *"oprichniki"* or officers. Bishops, abbots, priests, monks and other religious men were very rudely treated either by the Czar himself or by his agents; they were frequently exposed to indignities, humiliations, imprisonments, deportations, or even death penalties by strangulation or drowning, as in the case of Metropolitan Philip or Archbishop Leonid of Novgorod. Priests were at times killed in the churches, when they said masses or devotions. The Chuch in many cases was singled out by Ivan as the object of his sadistic practices, culminating usually with most elaborate tortures over which he sometimes presided. At the same time, the Czar rarely missed a mass and frequently received Holy Communion. He worked on the rules for monastic life and on the ceremonial of installing the Metropolitan.

During his long rule, Ivan liquidated thousands of fully innocent people. Peculiarly, the salvation of their souls was his big worry. Hence, he ordered lists of his victims to be compiled, and sent those lists, which included over four thousand names, to various churches and monasteries with strict orders to pray and say masses for the peace of their souls. Obviously, the number of four thousand victims of Ivan's terror rule was a dramatic underestimation. Here again is a picture of the confused and cruel piety of the Czar.

Ivan, as pointed out, suffered a mania of persecution, and most historians have agreed, this was largely responsible for his bloody works. He thought of himself as being hated to the extent that everybody, including his closest associates and lieutenants, were conspiring and plotting against him. His mistrust and suspicion were illustrated in his alleged writings. There he denounced the real and imaginary enemies he suspected or saw everywhere around his court and throne. Hence, Ivan did not trust anybody except, perhaps, his first wife, Anastasia, during the early era of his reign, and the previously mentioned Metropolitan Makarii. In general, his friends and associates did not last long, and most of them perished sooner or later during various spells of the Czar's insane thirst for revenge and the blood of his foes. He suspected plots among even his closest lieutenants. At one time, in the latter part of his rule, Ivan contemplated the necessity of leaving Muscovy as an escape from his enemies. He negotiated the possibility of political asylum in England.

The rule of terror in the land and the frequent changes in the sets of advisors and chief lieutenants certainly did not contribute to the social and political stability of the Muscovite state. Those lieutenants who lost Ivan's grace were usually exterminated through horrible tortures, often attended by the Czar himself. Especially during the second part of Ivan's reign, all segments of the Muscovite and non-Muscovite population suffered under the bloody terror, be they servitor princes, the descendants of the Rurik and Gedymin houses, *boyars,* ecclesiastic hierarchy, townspeople or peasants. Nobody was safe from the Czar's untempered anger. To make things even worse, Ivan normally did not limit his thirst for revenge to those he suspected. He extended punishment over a wide circle of their families, including their wives, children, and relatives, their friends and associates, and even their servants and serfs. Then, after the wave of executions was completed to Ivan's satisfaction, the executioners were executed to blot out the traces of the cruel deeds. After all, the Czar did not trust those executioners at all; those people were bad and ready to do any dirty job, including conspiring against Ivan.

In this way, the Czar's former closest advisors and associates, such as the priests Sylvester and Aleksei Adashev, were removed from the court after 1560. Sylvester was imprisoned in a remote monastery, while Adashev either committed suicide by poison or was poisoned in the Dorpat prison. Then, Ivan's one-time favorite henchmen, the two Basmanovs, Prince Viazamskii and others, were disposed of amidst the intolerable tortures. Maliuta-Skuratov, Ivan's most trusted executioner, then met sudden death at the hands of his comrade-executioners, the *oprichniki.*[6]

Ivan's family life bore the same stigma of abnormality, due to his sexual excessiveness. He was married some seven times.

Three of his wives were apparently poisoned, either by Ivan's order or by his enemies; the former is more probable. Two others were imprisoned in distant monasteries or forced to take the vows. One was drowned by Ivan's order. He also decided to get rid of his seventh wife, Maria Nagoi, to permit a new marriage with Maria Hastings of England. Only the refusal of the British court to cooperate with Ivan's plan, as well as his own death, saved Maria Nagoi from a sudden and cruel end. At the same time, he had many mistresses and regularly indulged himself with his close associates in wild sexual orgies. In 1581, Ivan killed his son and heir to the throne, Ivan Ivanovich, by a blow of his staff, when the latter attempted to protect his wife from his father's obscene brutality.

Ivan's Reign

Ivan the Terrible or Dread had an exalted view of the Muscovite Czardom and hinself as its ruler, and he gave a clear-cut expression of that view. An example is his correspondence with Prince Andrei Kurbskii, once his loyal associate, and then a refugee in Lithuania to avoid persecution after the ouster of priests Sylvester and Aleksei Adashev. In those four letters Ivan developed most of his political philosophy of the Muscovite absolutist Czardom, which had, in his words, a divine origin. The Czar was God's representative on earth, while Moscow, his seat, was not only the "Third Rome," but the "Second Jerusalem," the capital of the true Orthodox Christianity, as well. Moscow's dynasty, having been related to Roman Caesar Augustus by the way of his brother, Prussus, had been the most illustrious of all European ruling houses. This insane hypothesis Ivan expounded in his conversations with foreign envoys and visitors. Consequently, he had little respect for other European sovereigns, in particular, the electoral ones, like the Polish King. Heredity established the indisputable legitimacy of the Czar's absolute power.[7]

Ivan stated that the divine authority of the Czar was comprehensive, that no earthly institution, like the Council of Nobles, might ever limit the will of the sovereign in any way. The Church must be fully subordinated to the Czar, God's representative. Hence, he severely and cruelly punished the ecclesiastic hierarchy and priests whenever they happened to displease him. He probably held this not only for a disobedience against the sovereign but also for a sin against his divinity.

Ivan's views were not novel, but they were clearly expressed and supported by the Czarist authority, and from now on they substantiated Russian political philosophy, and built the foundation for the Muscovite-Russian system of the Czarist absolutism for many centuries to come. Ivan on his part tried by many quotations from the Holy Bible, chronicles, historical narrations and political writings and not always logical parables, to support his philosophy. He certainly tried hard to live up to its principles. His exalted views of the Muscovite state and himself, as its sovereign, were greatly promoted by his paranoic state of mind and an over-all love of grandeur.

Upon his reaching the age of seventeen in 1547, Ivan the Terrible decided to assume the rule and insisted on being solemnly crowned the Czar of all Russia. Previously, as was pointed out above, the title "Czar" was only loosely and occasionally used by his two predecessors, Ivan III and Vasilii III. Earlier, during the Mongol supremacy, the title of "Czar" was submissively handed over to the Khans by the chronicles and other old documents to indicate their supreme sovereignty. Also prior to Ivan there was only one known historical instance of a solemn coronation of a Muscovite ruler or ruler-to-be. Prince Dimitrii, son of Ivan III, was crowned as a co-ruler because of his father's will. He was soon ousted by the intrigues at the court. Hence, the idea of a coronation was Ivan's IV constitutional novelty as was the permanent use of the Czarist title.

The idea of coronation was presumably impressed upon Ivan by Metropolitan Makarii, who apparently wanted in this way to symbolize the unification of all Russian territories under one sovereign, in the secular as well as the ecclesiastic sphere. It was performed by the Metropolitan, but Ivan was not happy.

The act did not carry enough prestige, the Czar thought initially. In 1557, Ivan asked the Patriarch of Constantinople to confirm his new dignity. The Patriarch was willing to perform another coronation ceremony on the ground that the previous one was not fully valid since carried out by a Metropolitan only. With that exchange of views, the case had rested. Ivan did not pursue the matter further, apparently later being satisfied with his unchallenged authority as a Czar.

The reign of Ivan the Terrible or Dread can roughly be divided into two periods. The first one, a more positive and constructive one, lasted approximately up to 1560, when his first wife, Anastasia, died. She had a wholesome influence upon the ill-tempered Czar. The period was filled with positive reforms and "benevolent" measures. It should not be forgotten, however, that during that good period the Pskovian instance of torturing the envoys took place. Hence, Ivan's cruel inclinations were gradually developing during his early years to culminate later on in the *oprichnina* institution. There wasn't, however, any clear-cut demarcation line between the two said periods of Ivan's rule.

The change in the Czar's mood began to manifest itself in 1553. He became ill and at his bedside he insisted that his advisors and associates take an oath of allegiance to his infant son, Prince Dimitrii, as their new ruler. The advisors hesitated, and by so doing, they antagonized Ivan gravely. As long as Anastasia was living, however, the political matters continued about the same. Metropolitan Makarii, priest Sylvester, Aleksei Adashev, Prince Kurbskii and others of the group close to the Czar, continued to advise him as before. Nevertheless, Ivan's suspicions and dislikes were already brewing intensely, finally to erupt with fatal consequences for the entire Muscovite state and society. Meanwhile, Metropolitan Makarii, along with Anastasia, had a considerable and tempering influence on the Czar.

After the military successes in Kazan and Astrakhan, Ivan turned his attention to the West. He planned to open a "window to Europe" by conquering Livonia and Curland and in this way gaining access to the Baltic Sea. His advisors, Sylvester, Adashev and others, had a different idea in mind. Why not, after the conquest of the Tartar kingdoms of Kazan and Astrakhan, defeat the third Tartar state, the Khanate of Crimea. In so doing, they would rid Muscovy once and for all of its traditional enemy, the Tartars, who continued to seriously threaten its eastern and south-eastern borderlands. For them the Baltic project seemed to be less urgent. The Czar and his so-far trusted advisors were hopelessly split, and soon the final breach between them came.

The second period of Ivan's reign was a negative one, full of terror and bloodshed, and accompanied by serious setbacks in foreign affairs. Soon, priest Sylvester and Aleksei Adashev and others were dismissed. Some of Ivan's former advisors, like Prince Kurbskii, left the country to live in exile to save their lives. Ivan accused them of using him as a figurehead to promote their own plans and ambitions. In 1564, the Czar established his ill-famed *oprichnina* or separate political domain, which resulted in the most ruthless security police rule for years to come. The unbearable terror was in full swing, while Ivan was leading a life not only below the dignity of a monarch, but of any decent man. In spring 1584, Ivan the Terrible or Dread died, having taken monastic vows on his deathbed to complete his twisted life by a twisted piety in his last hour.[8]

Domestic Affairs and the Oprichnina Institution

During the long reign of Ivan IV, many things changed in the Muscovite state. At first, the Czar relied heavily on his advisors, who changed frequently. Then he assumed full despotic rule. Immediately after the death of Grand Duke Vasilii III, his wife and Ivan's mother, Grand Duchess Helen and her lover and trusted advisor, Ivan Ovchina-Telepniev-Obolenskii ruled the country. After Helen died, apparently poisoned in 1538, and Ivan Obolenskii starved to death as a result of a palace revolution, the Princes Shuiskii, Glinskii and Bielskii assumed, for the time being, the leading political role at the court. In 1543, Shuiskii's group was removed from any influence and its leaders executed. For four years, until the summer of 1547, the Princes Glinskii, Yurii and Mikhail, were influential. The Moscow fire in which some seventeen hundred people perished, was used by some *boyars,* under Shuiskii's and Zakharin's leadership, to rid the Muscovite court of the Glinskiis. So far, the *boyars* were the dominant factor in Muscovite politics.

Since 1547, a new era began in the political scene of the Muscovite state. Ivan was solemnly crowned the Czar of all Russia and a new breed of advisors came to the Kremlin, not necessarily drafted from the circles of the landed *boyar* nobility. Priest Sylvester and Aleksei Adashev were the leaders of the so-called "select council," while Metropolitan Makarii was the power behind the throne. At that time several important reforms were undertaken. The ancient and outdated taxation system of *kormlenie* or feeding themselves to maintain materially the government appointees, was gradually abolished and replaced by new district electoral officials, while the districts or regions were collectively responsible for the maintenance and activities of those elected officials. The new approach, which bore the incorrect impression of a landed self-government, was called *zemstvo* or landed administration.

In 1550, a new Code of Law or *Sudebnik* was prepared, largely based on the old legislation. In 1556, a decree was issued to regulate the complex of rights and duties of holders of landed estates in service tenure, including the matter of military service. In 1550 or 1556, the first *zemskii sobor* or landed council was called to convene by Ivan's order, to advise him in important state matters. The members of the *zemskii sobor* were appointed by the Czar, however, and not elected by the people. Also an attempt was undertaken to improve the organization of the Muscovite Orthodox Church. Ivan himself was deeply involved in the reorganization process. The results of the reform remained rather a dead letter without any visible improvement of the ecclesiastic state of affairs.

Things were, however, changing rapidly from bad to worse

since Ivan's illness in 1553, and then, Anastasia's death in 1560. The open breach came as the mania of persecution and sadism of the Czar progressed and became more intense, and there was no more Anastasia to calm Ivan's badly unbalanced mind. The opposition of the select council to Ivan's plan for Livonia in 1557-58, worsened the situation. Priest Sylvester, Aleksei Adashev and others from the group were dismissed. Revengeful Ivan exterminated many former advisors, their families, friends and associates; their properties were confiscated Some of them escaped their doom by admitting their guilt and giving a guaranty of loyalty. Others escaped to foreign lands, like Prince Kurbskii, with whom Ivan carried on his alleged correspondence for a period of fifteen years. There was no longer room in Ivan's sick mind for any constructive measures.

Suddenly in the early days of December 1564, Ivan IV left Moscow, with all his family, court, treasury, and retinue, and settled down in Aleksandrovskaia Sloboda, near the famous Muscovite Troitse-Sergieivskii monastery. An entirely new style of Ivan's rule in domestic matters was initiated. He actually remained there for the rest of his life. Moscow was then the official capital of the state, while Aleksandrovskaia Sloboda was the unofficial one.

In January 1565, the Czar sent two epistles to Moscow. In the first he bitterly attacked and accused the *boyars* and the clergy, including the Metropolitan, as traitors, thieves and embezzlers or accomplices of those, and he wrote, they discouraged him so much that he decided to give up his realm and to settle somewhere else, according to the will of God. He threatened his subjects with abdication. In the other letter, directed to the lower social classes, the merchants, artisans and commoners, Ivan said that the common people were not responsible for the bad conditions in the realm and the Czar's distress.

The two letters plunged the Muscovites into a state of shock. Soon, a delegation was sent to the Czar in Aleksandrovskaia Sloboda to ask him to reconsider his decision and not to desert his subjects. The delegates had no difficulty in persuading Ivan to change his mind, and to continue as the Muscovite sovereign. In fact, the whole spectacle was only Ivan's maneuver to get what he wanted from the very beginning. He agreed to grant the request of his people, but on his terms only. He demanded the establishment of a monarch's separate domain in the country, the so-called *oprichnina*, exempt from the general administration scheme of the state, where he, Ivan IV, would have full freedom of action to deal with traitors and other unreliable elements. Such was the prime condition upon which he was ready to resume his rule. In addition, Ivan requested an indemnity of 100,000 rubles to cover the costs of his moving to Aleksandrovskaia Sloboda. Upon his return to the capital, immediately several *boyars*, suspected by Ivan, were executed. More executions followed. The idea of a monarch's separate domain might have been in Ivan's mind for a long time. Already in 1550, he removed hundreds of original, mostly aristocratic, owners of landed properties from around the capital by compulsion, and settled one thousand carefully selected men there. These were the lesser *boyars*, whom he gave the best land. They were organized into a special regiment of the "Moscow Nobles" to increase the security of the capital.

The original document establishing the *oprichnina* has been lost, but the institution was well described by various written source materials of that time. Initially the monarch's special domain comprised some twenty selected towns with their countryside, scattered in various parts of the country.[9] However, gradually it extended well over one-third of Muscovy, represented by a separate administrative apparatus, at times only paralleling and at times even abolishing or superseding the regular landed or *zemshchina* system. In general, the *oprichnina* was represented by the Czar's agents, while the *zemshchina*, by the *boyar* elected officials.

Kluchevsky suggested two aspects of the *oprichnina* institution, a territorial one and a purposive one. As to the first, the Czar wanted a territorial sanctuary of his own, where he would take refuge from his "rebellious" *boyars*. As to the purpose, he wanted to create within his special domain a superior security system, safeguarding the Czar and his Czardom by dealing resolutely and strongly with all kinds of treacherous elements which might have endangered the safety and security of both. At a later time, Ivan renamed his special domain and his agents "the court" or the *dvor*. Something similar to the notorious *oprichnina,* without all of its negative features, however, and in the territorial aspect only, was tried some 250 years later by Czar Paul I. Paul I set aside "from among the possessions of the state" certain "immovable properties" or estates, and called them "cantonal properties." Paul's cantonal properties were, however, territorially a very negligible portion of the empire; they were never extended over any additional sections of the country, like the *oprichnina* did, and never had any security or police aspect.[10]

Ivan's separate domain soon extended even over the ancient patrimonial estates, while the descendants of the formerly appanage princes either of the Rurik or Gedymin houses and the ancient *boyar* families were forced to settle in other parts of the country, in numerous instances, in the Muscovite borderlands. Their landed properties were then given to the Czar's trusted *oprichniki* or agents of the separate domain, the *oprichnina,* to strengthen the indisputable absolute power of the monarch throughout Muscovy. The resettlement process in the regions of the separate domain, not a compact territory but districts scattered in various parts of the realm, was carried out on a large scale, and was called by Ivan "sorting out the folks." In this way Ivan intended to destroy the ancient and influential families and to replace them with a new upper class without any ties to the lands and people, and completely dependent upon the Czar. The *oprichniki* were hated in their new environment, which made them so much more loyal to the sovereign.

The entire resettlement process was done rudely and under the pretext of suppressing the treacherous, disloyal or suspected elements. The *oprichnina* sectors were established, for example, along the trade routes and in the strategically important regions to increase their safety. Deportations, imprisonments and executions were applied in a wholesale manner in order to attain the intended objective. The whole system of the *oprichnina* rule was very cruel. On mere suspicion of disloyalty, people of all classes were severely dealt with by Ivan's special agents, who enjoyed their cruelty, since they usually received the properties and estates of their victims in return for services rendered. When Metropolitan Philip opposed the Czar on this point, he was strangled by Ivan's special agents. Nobody felt safe under the *oprichnina* regime, not even the *oprichniki* themselves who were also exposed to the police terror whenever they failed to please the sovereign, like the two Basmanovs, father and son, Prince Viazemskii and some others, who were put to cruel tortures and death. Hence, streams of emigrants moved away from the central Muscovite regions toward the distant borderlands of Kazan, southeast of the Oka River and further, to the Don-Volga regions, which were fairly well colonized by the end of the sixteenth century.

The *oprichniki* or special agents of the Czar developed into a powerful security police force, at one time under the leadership of Maliuta Skuratov-Bielskii, directly responsible to Ivan. They were dressed in black, rode black horses, with a broom and a dog's head fastened to their saddles, symbolizing their office. The broom and the dog's head were supposed to manifest the work the special agents had to do, to sweep away the traitors and kill them like dogs. The *oprichniki* were referred to as "the blackness of hell" or "the darkness of night," feared and dreaded by all. At first, there were one thousand of them, but later on the number of the special agents was increased to six thousand. Although they were supposed to be a new breed of the Czar's trusted guardsmen, there were among the *oprichniki* the representatives of the old and noble families, such as Shuiskii, Skopin, Trubetskoi, or Sitskii.

Prince Andrei Kurbskii, Ivan's foe, had the worst opinion of the Czar's special agents. He said: "that the Czar hath gathered unto himself from all Russian lands men vile and filled with every sort of cruelty."[11] They plundered the *zemshchina* districts, which were actually outside their authority, and under the pretext of exterminating treason, invaded private homes and dragged people directly to the torture chambers and abused their victims beyond any human imagination. Even new kinds and methods of torturing people were devised by the special agents, who feared no one and were responsible to no one but the Czar himself. He, however, encouraged and rewarded cruelty, and frequently assisted his *oprichniki* in the torture chambers to quell their victims with their common sadism.

Having been Ivan's special domain, the *oprichniki* were fully exempt from the competence and jurisdiction of the country's regular administration, hence no agency and no official could call them to account for their criminal deeds. This was the worst thing that could happen to the Muscovite people. There was nobody to turn to for protection. The special domain was a separate "state within a state." The G.P.U. or M.V.D. of the Soviet era vividly resembled the *oprichnina* institution, their predecessor. They too were exempt from the regular administrative and military Soviet scheme and were given a free hand in dealing with the so-called counterrevolutionary elements. From their action, there was also no appeal. Millions of human beings perished as a result of the G.P.U. - M.V.D. terror. All opposition to the Czar was suppressed by the *oprichnina* rule. Likewise, the terror of the Soviet security police quelled almost all opposition to the Soviet-Russian regime of the Bolsheviks under Lenin and Stalin. The historical comparison only proves the fact of the traditional Muscovite-Russian ruthlessness in quelling and liquidating all resistance against the Muscovite-Russian thirst for ruling in an absolute and unrestrained way. Mere Communist ideology could not be held wholly responsible for the Soviet terror regime in the twentieth century. It has been in the Russian blood and psyche for centuries. The *oprichnina* alone is evidence of this fact.[12]

The *oprichnina* had a short-run and a long-run objective. In the short-run, Ivan planned to quell all opposition and to maximize his safety. He suffered, to be sure, a mania of persecution. In the long-run, however, the objectives of the special domain of the Czar were of a fundamental and constitutional or structural nature for the whole country and society. Through the deportations, confiscations of properties, resettlement process and colonization of the Muscovite borderlands, Ivan intended to destroy once and for all the remnants of the previous power of the old princely and *boyar* families and to uproot altogether the traditional social structure of his Muscovy, which otherwise could have recovered and could have threatened the Czarist absolute rule at any later time. He intended to uproot completely the traditional hereditary patrimonial or *votchina* rights and to replace them fully and unquestionably by the service-tenure or *promestie* approach to the land property, which was duty-bound and over which the Czar had complete control. Moreover, the *pomestie* landed properties were entrusted mostly to the trustworthy men.

As a consequence of the continuous social flux and uncertainty due to terror, no doubt, the economic basis of the central Muscovite regions was substantially weakened for a while. It might have been the cause of the Muscovite military defeats in the Livonian war, waged mainly against Poland-Lithuania and Sweden.[13] On the other hand, the colonization of the borderlands as a result of compulsory resettlement and voluntary flight, especially of the peasant population looking for safer and better living conditions, had a tremendously beneficial impact upon the Muscovite state in its economic and political aspects. The no man's land east and southeast of the Oka River, some Kazan regions and even the Don-Volga area, became ethnically Muscovite-Russian and were soon economically included in the construction of the Russian empire. This might be considered as a very long-run achievement of the *oprichnina* terror, the gains of which by far outran the wildest speculations of Ivan IV, the Dread.[14]

Czar Ivan IV looked upon the *oprichnina* as his private property, said Kluchevsky. Then, Ivan decided to divide his realm between his two sons. He planned to give the landed regions, the *zemshchina*, to his eldest son as his heritage, and his special domain, the *oprichnina*, to the younger one, as his mere appanage.

Later, the Czar got a curious and half-insane idea. He placed at first the *zemshchina* under the rule of a Christianized Tartar prince, Ediger Simeon, taken prisoner in Kazan. In 1574, Ivan even arranged a form of a coronation of another Tartar prince, Simeon Bekbulatovich, and made him the "Czar of all Russia," while for himself he retained only the title of the "Lord and Prince of Moscow." Whenever meeting Bekbulatovich, Ivan paid him homage, as to his sovereign. After two years, Ivan got tired of the insane masquerade. He banished "Czar" Simeon Bekbulatovich to Tver and himself again assumed all absolute authority. In the latter part of the 1570's, the *oprichnina* institution died a sort of natural death.

Foreign Relations and the Dynastic Plans

The reign of Ivan IV was by no means a peaceful one. It was full of domestic and foreign upheavals and successes. Ivan was very active in foreign affairs, by which he thought to raise the international prestige of his realm. Involved were the Muscovite relations with the Crimean Tartars, who were believed to be the heirs of the Golden Horde and continuously harassed Muscovy. The Khans of the Crimean Horde dreamed of restoring the previous Tartar supremacy over Moscow, which was scarcely possible because of the growing power of the Czar. But meanwhile they either undertook themselves or sent their *beys* on periodic but never-ceasing raids for booty and slaves, devastating the land and decimating the population of Muscovy. The Khans could scarcely hope for any territorial conquests. The Mongol age in East Europe was over once and for all, but the threat of the Tartar raids was imminent still for centuries to come. The slaves carried away by the Tartars from Muscovy, Ukraine and Byeloruthenia were sold in all major slave markets in the Crimea and Asia Minor to Turkey, the Middle East, Africa, and even Europe. The raids were undertaken annually by several detachments, invading and plundering various parts of East Europe. The human and material costs of those Tartar expeditions were intolerably heavy.

Furthermore, the Crimean Tartars were always ready to make any gainful anti-Muscovite deals with Poland, Lithuania or any other land, as long as they promised booty and slaves. Obviously, the Muscovites were seriously annoyed. Forts were built, outposts established, and semi-military settlements organized in the eastern and southeastern borderland in order to reduce the danger of those Tartar raids and expeditions and in this way to bring peace and tranquility into the life of those border regions and the central districts as well. This did not help much. Hence in 1571, a special commission was set up, headed by Prince Vorotynskii, to develop a comprehensive plan for the defense of the eastern and southeastern borderlands of the Czardom against the Tartar threat.

After the successful completion of the Kazan and Astrakhan campaigns in 1553 and 1556, there was, as was mentioned before, a strong sentiment among some of Ivan's advisers to attack the Crimean Horde, the third Tartar state, and knock it out of existence, and so to free Muscovy from the Tartar threat forever. However, Ivan preferred his Baltic plan at that time and the said campaign was not undertaken.

In 1571, suddenly a large-scale Tartar army, under Khan Davlet-Girey himself, invaded the southeastern provinces of Muscovy and soon reached Moscow and besieged the city, meanwhile burning the suburbs, devastating the countryside and carrying some 150.000 slaves from among the peaceful population. The Muscovite troops could not prevent the disaster because a large portion of it was engaged in Ivan's Livonian adventure. A year later, in 1572, the Tartars tried to repeat their performance, invading the Muscovite territories again with an army of about 120,000 men. This time, however, the Tartars were stopped by Prince Vorotynskii before they reached the gates of Moscow, thus preventing the repetition of the tragedy of 1571. However, the whole situation was not changed much. Muscovy continued to live under continuous tension, expecting a devastating Tartar raid at any time on any part of its vast territory. The prolonged Livonian war continued to weaken considerably the Muscovite military power to resist the Crimean Tartars. Perhaps the idea of priests Sylvester and Adashev, and the other advisors to knock out the Crimean Horde first, before any other military project would be undertaken, was a better strategy than Ivan's own obsession with a "window" to Europe, which tied up a great deal of the Muscovite military and economic potentials for some twenty-five years. On the other hand, Ivan may have appraised the situation correctly and realized that his forces were still too weak to undertake the task of defeating the Crimean Horde.

At any rate, during Ivan's reign a long chain of about fifteen forts and towns were built, from Alatir and Temnikov to Rylsk and Putivl, and additional outposts established to protect the southeastern borderlands against the Tartar raids. Additional towns and forts were later built during the "Time of Troubles," such as Voronezh, Kursk, Bielgorod, Oskol and Valuiki, as well as a few others. Also, in order to defend those borderlands, the Muscovite government began to employ the Cossack formations.

Ivan's attention was absorbed in and considerable economic and military effort of the Muscovite state was therefore invested in Moscow's relations with its Western neighbors. The Livonian war, which lasted some twenty-five years, was the highlight of the Muscovite Western policy. Ivan, as pointed out above, wanted to open a route or a "window" to Europe. The project was mostly economic in its nature. The route would make possible more trade with the Western countries and would bring industrial know-how to Muscovy. Ivan constantly invited many Western artisans, craftsmen and artists to come to Muscovy and to make their skills available to its economy. They came in waves, looking for money and opportunities.

Before the Livonian war was started, some success had already been achieved by Muscovy to get closer to the West, especially to England, of which Ivan was apparently an admirer. English political and economic power in those days considerably impressed Ivan, the ruler of a still primitive country. The said success was not scored by the Muscovites, but by the English, it could have been, however, of a great significance for Moscow. Commercial ties had existed between Muscovy and England long before. Only it was very difficult to travel from London or any other English harbor to any Muscovite port. It was particularly difficult to reach Moscow from there. Shipping goods was often hindered by foreign powers, such as Denmark, or the goods were simply intercepted and confiscated. Muscovite protests were mostly ignored.

Hence, the discovery of new route from England to Muscovy in 1553, going from London around the Scandinavian Peninsula and by way of the White Sea to Archangelsk, almost in the polar region of Muscovy, and from there overland to Moscow, was hailed by Ivan. The discovery was made by Richard Chancellor, the head of a maritime expedition of three ships sent by the Fellowship of English Merchants for Discovery of New Trades. Richard Chancellor was received with honors by Czar Ivan, who thereby granted monopolistic trade privileges to the Muscovite Trading Company in London. However, it did not stop the moody and unpredictable monarch from withdrawing all the privileges, imprisoning the English merchants in Moscow and seizing all their goods later on, after the English refusal to enter an Anglo-Muscovite treaty alliance — something very much desired by Ivan. Later relations improved, because of vital interests in London and Moscow alike in the Anglo-Muscovite trade.[15]

Although the discovery of the new trading route via the White Sea was a progress in the commercial relations between Muscovy and West Europe, the route was still too long and too cumbersome. During the winter months it was scarcely usable. Hence, Ivan dreamed of acquiring an access to the Baltic Sea via the Livonian land. The opportunity to interfere in the Livonian internal matters suggested itself to Ivan during the reformation process there. A quarrel developed between the Archbishop of Riga and the Grand Master of the Teutonic Knights, concerning the secularization of their Order. There was also a lasting conflict between the Knights and the local Livonian and Estonian population which was constantly exposed to German abuses and exploitation practices. Taking advantage of those conflicts, Ivan came up with the demand of Muscovite protection over Livonia, for which he also insisted on a tribute payment from the Livonian people. At first, having seen its weakness, Livonia complied with the demand of the tribute payment, but failed to do so a little later. In response to the Livonian default, Ivan invaded the land in 1558, and the prolonged Livonian war began.

At first the whole land was overrun by the Muscovite troops and badly devastated. An immediate reaction set in. The German Knights sought the protection and assistance of their other neighbors, who seemed to be the lesser evil to the half-savage Muscovites. Soon, Livonia accepted the Lithuanian, Courland — the Polish, Estonia — the Swedish, and the Island of Oesel — the Danish protection. This, in fact, involved all these powers in the war, in which Muscovy, Poland-Lithuania and Sweden were the main contenders.

The first stage of the war was rather successful for Ivan, but neither of his rivals wanted to yield, and finally in 1572 a dramatic turning point in the conflict came. Ivan suffered a major defeat from the Polish, after Stephen Batory of Transylvania, an able military leader, was elected the new King of Poland. Stephen Batory defeated Ivan's troops in several battles, having taken Polotsk and Velikii Luki, and having immediately threatened Pskov in 1581. Pskov and Novgorod would probably have been taken by the Polish-Lithuanian armies but for the intervention of the Holy See of Rome. Possevinus, a Jesuit priest, was sent as a papal envoy to Batory to mediate peace and to save Ivan's throne. Ivan used political trickery to win Rome on his side. He vaguely indicated to Rome his willingness to explore the possibility of a union of the Muscovite Orthodox Church with the Holy See. Rome, eager to spread Catholicism throughout the world, naively believed in Ivan's hints, fell into the trap, and threw all its prestige behind the idea of inducing King Stephen Batory, a Catholic monarch, to spare Ivan and in this way to promote the expansion of Catholicism in East Europe. Meanwhile, in 1578, the Swedes badly defeated Ivan's troops. Hence, Muscovy was ready to negotiate peace.

Nevertheless, by the peace treaty of 1582 with Poland-Lithuania, Muscovy was forced to give up all its previous acquisitions in Livonia. In the following year, in 1583, the treaty with Sweden was even more disadvantageous for Ivan. Sweden acquired Estonia and previously Muscovite territories along the shores of the Gulf of Finland, from the town of Narva to the Lake Ladoga. The "window to the West" was shut for the Muscovites tighter than ever before and the Muscovite project of a westward expansion proved to be total failure, partially compensated, however, by considerable eastern acquisitions accomplished meanwhile.

The Muscovite defeat in the prolonged Livonian war came about largely because of the economic and military superiority of the Western powers. Moscow was hopelessly primitive, according to European standards. Ivan could hope only to defeat barbaric East-European and Siberian Tartars and other natives of Eurasia, but he could scarcely check the Crimean Tartars, and he and his Muscovites were by no means any match for their Western neighbors. It took later Russian Czars to open that "window to Europe."[16]

Ivan's relations with the outside world were not exactly friendly; things developed in this way rather than as he had intended. The relations with Sweden were tense for most of the time, except for a brief interval during the reign of King Eric. For Poland and its electoral kings, Ivan had only contempt. He considered himself an absolute and hereditary monarch, the authority of whom was of divine origin, by far superior to the Polish-Lithuanian rulers, whose authority was greatly limited. But at one time, when the Polish throne was vacant, Ivan was ready to trade his exalted views about his office for the electoral Polish crown. He promised the Polish noblemen to respect their traditional liberties, and he was even willing to extend those liberties for the price of the Polish throne. Nevertheless, the Poles were afraid to gamble and get such a despot for their king.

He was not very fortunate in his relations with England, of which he was an admirer as was pointed out before. He pressed for an alliance with London, but the English showed no enthusiasm for the idea. Finally, Ivan was so insulted by the English attitude toward his "friendly" proposal that, in one of his letters to Queen Elizabeth, he called her a "common wench."

Ivan IV, practically the head of the Muscovite Orthodox Church, had no use for Rome, which represented rather the principle of the superiority of ecclesiastic authority over the secular monarchs, a principle contrary to Ivan's political philosophy. Roman Catholicism was, in Ivan's eyes, an unforgivable heresy. He was convinced that the Byzantine Empire fell in 1453 as the victim of the Ottoman aggression because of the Patriarch's sinful attempt at times to super-impose himself over state matters, which was definitely the Roman pattern of things. He did not like the thought of this happening to his state. Hence, Moscow's attitude toward Rome and the Papacy was traditionally cool and even hostile. Only once, in the grave political situation during the latter part of the Livonian war, as mentioned, he pretended an agreeable relationship to the Holy See and sought papal assistance in mediating a peace treaty with Poland-Lithuania. He hinted at that time even a possibility of a Muscovite Church union with Rome and pretended his willingness to join an all-out anti-Turk crusade of the Christian world, the idea sponsored by the Pope. Ivan was insincere in this matter, however, and as soon as the Polish danger passed away through Rome's mediation, he discarded the previous signs of an apparent or imaginary rapprochment with the Holy See completely, as if they had never existed. Any arrangement with Rome, or the Holy See of the Catholic world, seemed at directly at odds with Ivan's own doctrine of *caesaropapism*.

In order to give to his exalted office of Czardom even more splendor and prestige, Ivan IV tried, along with his attempted ties of foreign relations, to develop dynastic links with the Western royal courts. At first, he sent his envoys to Warsaw, asking for the hand of Princess Catherine, sister of the Polish King, Sigismund August, and promising Poland the land of Estonia for the marital deal. He was not accepted, and shortly Catherine married Prince John, the future King of Sweden instead. Ivan was deeply insulted and for a long time he nursed plans of revenge. He tried to make a deal with Eric, King of Sweden, in some way to lay his hands on Catherine, to get her to Moscow and to make her his concubine. Only a revolt in Sweden against the half-insane Eric making John the King, freed Catherine from the embarrassment and terminated the whole unpleasant case.[17]

After the failure of his matrimonial plans in Poland, Ivan turned his attention to the London court. At first he wanted to marry Elizabeth, the Queen of England. But the plan was completely unrealistic. Then, Ivan dispatched two envoys to London to look for a proper match among the relatives of the Queen. Mary Hasting was the Muscovite choice, which, however, was never taken seriously by the London court. The East-European barbarian with a bad name all over Europe could not be seriously considered for a husband for a relative of Elizabeth, according to English standards. Hence, Ivan was forced to temper his dynastic ambitions, and to take wives from among his Muscovite subjects.

Eastern Expansion

According to the tradition of his royal predecessors, Ivan IV, the Terrible or Dread, scarcely ever missed an opportunity to expand territorially the Muscovite state or to add to its splendor by way of war, diplomacy or otherwise. Ivan's attention, politically speaking, encompassed all directions, while the western and eastern segments of his foreign policy seemed to be most important to him. He could not be persuaded by his advisors, for example, to concentrate on the campaign against the Crimean Tartars in the south, while close relations with the European courts and the European economies attracted him very much. Ivan learned the hard way that he could not accomplish a great deal nor add to the splendor of his Czardom there.

Ivan's era was a time of almost continuous warfare with the Tartars, Poles, Lithuanians, Swedes and other peoples of minor political stature on the borders of his already vast state. Nevertheless, the political destiny of Muscovy-Russia was in the East and the eastern imperialist expansion so far. Ivan III had already conquered Perm and opened the avenues for the Muscovite drive toward the Ob river. Otherwise, the interest of Vladimir, Novgorod the Great and Moscow in the eastern lands, toward and beyond the Ural mountains had been an ancient one. The Tartar Khanates of Kazan and Astrakan, established on the ruins of the Golden Horde, certainly barred the Muscovite eastward expansion, while the political frictions with Kazan dated back to Ivan's predecessors, and continued during his own rule as well. Hence, in 1551 the conquest of the Khanate of Kazan was a decided project.

Ivan raised two large armies. One was supposed to protect Muscovy from the possible assault of the Crimean Tartars, who continuously harassed its south-eastern borderlands, while the other one was readied against Kazan. The fortress of Sviazhsk was built to check the Kazan Tartars. In 1552, the strategic maneuver of two army flanks — one stationed against the Crimean Tartars and the other against Kazan — was repeated. Then, the anti-Kazan army invaded the Tartar territory and besieged the city. In October, the Muscovites took Kazan, using gunpower in the campaign for the first time in their history. The Kazan fortifications were blown up, enabling the Muscovites to defeat the Tartars completely, since they were not yet acquainted with the new weapon.

The Muscovites plundered and then burned the city, murdered its inhabitants and annihilated the Kazan army in the most ferocious way. The Kazan Khan was captured and baptized by force. The Khanate was overthrown and the territory annexed to the Muscovite Czardom. A new city of Kazan was then built, where the Tartars were allowed to live only in the suburbs. It took, however, a few years until the new territorial acquisition was really pacified and made into a Muscovite province. Fortresses were built throughout the land of Kazan, such as Chebaksari, Tsivilsk, Yaransk and Ufa, in order to make the Muscovite rule there really effective.

Ivan then continued his plan of a complete domination of the entire Volga basin. Four years later, in 1556, the Astrakhan campaign was undertaken, and the Kazan performance repeated. The city of Astrakhan was taken by the Muscovite troops, the Khanate overthrown, and the territory of the so-called Nogai Tartars incorporated into Ivan's emerging empire. With the annexation of the Kazan and Astrakhan lands, Ivan really brought the entire Volga basin under Muscovite domination. In this way large stretches of land were acquired for Muscovite political and economic expansion, the opening of the avenues to the Ural Mountains and the Caspian Sea and beyond was accomplished, the traditional trading routes to the Orient were made Muscovite and opened for Muscovite merchants and traders. The harassment of the Muscovites in these areas, by the natives, was soon reduced to a minimum. Ivan became a national hero. And soon large-scale colonization of those regions was under way, provoked by the intolerable living conditions in the central Muscovite districts due to the *oprichnina* measures. "The banished prince-*boyars*," as Platonov said, "were followed by their serfs, and, in many cases, by the free peasants who did not take kindly to the new proprietors. . . . The fields of Kazan and the black earth south of Oka were more fertile than the soil which they were giving up; and last, but not least, there was no reign of terror in those borderlands."[18]

The conquest of Kazan and Astrakhan included under the Muscovite rule a score of different minor ethnic groups. This actually initiated the process of making Muscovy a multinational state, held together only by the ruthless political terror of the Muscovite-Russian imperialist Czars from that time on. The Mordovians, Cheremisians, Chuvashi, Votiaks and soon also Bashkirs or Bashkirians were forced into submission. The ethnical absorption of the Cheremisians, who inhabited the territory along the Viatka river and middle Volga, was accomplished in the sixteenth century. At that time, they actually adopted the settled way of life. Also the Chuvashi, who lived south of the Cheremisians, were absorbed into the Muscovite national society of the sixteenth century. Obviously, the Muscovite conquest of Kazan advanced that ethnical absorption process.

The Mordovians, settled off to the right of the upper – middle Volga run, were under the rule of the Suzdal-Vladimir principality before the Mongol invasion. In 1329, they were conquered by the Mongols, and subsequently, with the establishment of the Kazan Khanate they became subjected to that rule. In 1552, with Ivan's conquest of Kazan, the Mordovians were annexed by the Muscovite state. Then, the intense Muscovization of the people and forceful introduction of Muscovite stern rule provoked a Mordovian uprising against the Czarist oppression in 1580. Although partially suppressed, the Mordovians continued to exhibit anti-Muscovite feelings during the "Time of Troubles."[19] Some time before, by the conquest of Novgorod the Great, Muscovy incorporated vast lands in the North, also inhabited by numerous ethnic groups and included them in its political orbit, from the Baltic shores on to the slopes of the Ural Mountains, such as the Chud, Vod, Yam, Karelians, Saomi, Komi, Voguls, Ostiaks and the Samoyeds, to anticipate its future multination characteristics.[20]

Of course, as long as the Khanate of Kazan was in political existence, any effective penetration of the Muscovites toward and beyond the Ural mountains was greatly hampered. With the fall of Kazan all this ended. Muscovite adventurers, merchants, industrialists, hunters and trappers immediately followed the ancient Novgorodian routes toward the East, looking for fur, skins, timber and other products of the forest and forest-steppe regions of the Eurasian borderlands. Hunting, trapping, trading and exploiting the natives offered considerable profits. Before long, using overland routes and by the tributaries of the Perchora and Ob rivers, the Muscovites reached the frigid mouth of the very Ob river, following the ancient trading escapades of the Novgorodians, the grand mercantile people.

The penetration of Bashkiria actually began as early as 1468, but it crystallized after the fall of Kazan. In 1557, Bashkiria was forced to pay a regular tribute to Moscow. In 1586, the town of Ufa was built as a stronghold of the Muscovite rule. However, the final subjugation of the country followed later on, after many uprisings and revolts of the Bashkirians were suppressed by the Muscovite troops. The native Bashkirians could not come to terms with the abusive and rapacious Muscovite officials who wanted to become rich fast by exploiting the Bashkirian people and Bashkirian land very badly.

All this opened the gate to Siberia. The rich raw materials of fur-bearing animals, inexhaustible fish reserves, abundant timber reserves, and above all enormous lands, were irresistibly attractive to the Muscovites.[21] So much more because Siberia was sparsely populated. By 1660, the population of Russian-dominated Siberia totaled some 288,000 people. Some eighty years earlier its numbers could not have been much different. Furthermore, the Tartar and other Siberian tribes of that time were very primitive, no match for the more advanced Muscovites. Hence, the conquest of West Siberia was not supposed to present Moscow any problem.

The West-Siberian population was mostly Tartar, settled along the Ob, Irtysh and Ingul Rivers. It was still partially nomadic, engaged mostly in trapping, hunting, fishing and deer raising, and very little farming. In 1563, the West-Siberian tribes were united in a Siberian kingdom, under their leader, Kutchum. The town Isker on the Tobol River was its capital. The kingdom was not at all powerful, and above all the Siberian Tartars were not yet acquainted with firearms. Further eastward, the banks of the Yenisey River were populated by numerous tribes of heterogeneous ethnic origin. The Tunguses were most numerous of them all, living in the clan system and engaged, like their western and eastern neighbors, in trapping, hunting and fishing. Along the Lena and, partially, the Yenisey Rivers, the Yakutes, the nomadic herdsmen, trappers and hunters, lived. The Muscovites contacted those tribes during the latter part of the sixteenth century.

The Muscovite-Russian penetration of West Siberia proceeded from the north, along the Tobol, Ob, Irtysh, and Yenisey Rivers. In 1574, several expeditions were sent there by the outstanding Muscovite merchant-industrialists, the Stroganovs. The explorers were ordered by the Stroganovs to investigate the routes to the new "sable areas." A few years later, the Muscovites reached Mangazeia, on the Taz River, and by the end of the sixteenth century, after having penetrated the whole area, they reached the Yenisey river.

The most important of all exploration expeditions was the one outfitted by the Stroganovs and led by Cossack Yermak in 1580, which actually dominated Western Siberia. Yermak's "army," consisted of some 580 Cossacks and several hundred of Stroganov's men, and was dispatched in 1581. Soon, the Kingdom of Kutchum was conquered by this small military force, whose superiority over the Tartars lay in its firearms.

The land of West Siberia became Muscovite-Russian in 1583. Yermak's expedition, like many others of the sort, penetrating Siberia and later on the Far East, was a semi-private and commercially motivated venture, which in its conclusion advanced Muscovite rule there. At the bottom of the whole project was Stroganovs' annoyance with the harassment of their commercial interests in the Ustiung region by the local tribes. The natives there, who supposedly recognized the authority of the Kingdom of Kutchum, interfered with Stroganovs' salt and fish procurements. Hence, the Stroganovs sent Yermak, actually against the will of Czar Ivan who feared some political complications as a result of such a far-fetched venture. Ivan threatened the Cossacks with hanging and the Stroganovs with the confiscation of their wealth, if they dared proceed with the project. The expedition was sent anyway. However, after Yermak's raid into Western Siberia proved to be a success and the new land was annexed, Ivan disregarded his initial threats and approved the move wholeheartedly, while Yermak and his Cossacks became national heroes.[22]

This means that Muscovite rule there was secure from the beginning. As in the cases of Kazan, Astrakhan, the entire Volga-Don basin, Bashkiria and other newly annexed lands, it took years of Muscovite-Russian military effort to subdue the resistance of the native nationalities, who opposed the oppressive Muscovite rule and strove for freedom from foreign supremacy. Repeated uprisings and revolts took place in West Siberia. Yermak himself perished there during one of those bloody skirmishes in 1585. With the iron fist of a determined imperialist who built an empire and forced others to join in the construction project, the Czardom of Muscovy-Russia eventually obliterated the opposition. In West Siberia, towns and strongholds were built by the new lords, Tiumen in 1586, Tobols in 1587, and others, such as Berezov and Narim, later on, when things became a little uncertain there during the "Time of Troubles." These towns became important centers of Russian administration in Siberia.

CHAPTER TWELVE

THE TIME OF TROUBLES

The Brewing Volcano; Czar Fiodor I, and Czar Boris Godunov

The "Time of Troubles" or *"Smutnoie vremia"* in the Muscovite state actually began with the death of Ivan IV, the Terrible or Dread. Ivan tailored his Czardom to fit his personality, a twisted but great one of a ruler of stature. At his death, the country was badly exhausted because of the many and prolonged wars, and still in a state of shock from the regime of blood-curdling terror. With Ivan's death a sudden relaxation came. Such changes, from tensions to relaxations and vice versa, do not promote a social balance; things can easily get out of control under pressures. Furthermore, the country was economically impoverished. Heavy war taxes made the people suffer. Warfare never allows a normal economic process to evolve. Wars and *oprichnina* terror dislodged many people and released a continuous movement of the population from the central to the border regions of the Czardom, disturbing the normal flow of business as well.

Socially, the land was disorganized, too. Ivan by his *oprichnina* institution disloged the old *boyar* class and created a new upper class which, from the very beginning, were set against each other. Only Ivan's firm hand kept a relative calm and did not permit any open and bloody social encounter to erupt. On the one hand the new breed wanted to preserve and also to expand their class privileges at the expense of the lower-stratum of population, while, on the other hand, the peasant-serf population longed for freedom and land ownership attainable only by way of reducing the elevated social status of the *boyars* and the royalty. The periodic misfortunes of droughts and floods caused local famines, contributing substantially to the stress of living in an ailing society and to the menacing consequences of starvation and economic depletion.

From the steppe borderlands in south Ukraine on, throughout the Don and Volga basin, the new breed of adventurous and freedom-loving men, the Cossacks, sought to establish for themselves a new way of life, which did not fit into the framework of the Muscovite autocracy at all.[1] The Cossacks were a special phenomenon brought about by the clash between the Arian and the Mongol ethnic masses in East Europe. The East-European Slavic communities developed the Cossack breed as their defense against the never-ceasing assaults of the Tartars upon the territories long under their authority. The Cossacks served also as the vanguard and a military protection of the Slavic colonization of the East-European steppes, extending deep into Eurasia, toward Siberia and Central Asia. Having assumed the defense of the borderlands, the Cossacks desired freedom and landownership, which were largely denied to them by the central government in Moscow. Their antagonism toward the central government was so much more intensified because they were ethnically heterogeneous and hardly Muscovite in their feelings and convictions. Hence, a clash developed between the aristocratic Muscovite autocracy and the ethnically and socially different community of the Cossacks.

Moscovy needed a ruler of strong personality to cope with the difficult situation and the numerous and mounting problems of a people torn with conflicts. But Czar Fiodor, Ivan's son, was not that kind of leader. Consequently, the volcano seethed more dangerously than ever. During the "Time of Troubles," from Ivan's death in 1584 to the election of Mikhail Romanov as a new Czar in 1613, Muscovy passed through various social and national upheavals of different characteristics. At first, during Godunov's and the first Pretender's time, the *boyar* nobility struggled for the recognition of their social status and political power. In turn, this provoked an antagonistic struggle of the lower classes for their social recognition under Bolotnikov and the second

Pretender. Finally, the national crisis aggravated by the foregoing intervention of the Poles (who were of a different religion), promoted a patriotic counter-reaction of the Muscovites to defend the country and their Orthodoxy during the nominal reign of Wladyslaw of Poland and the *de facto* state of *interregnum*.

Czar Fiodor I has been described by his contemporaries as a feeble-minded and sickly religious man who liked to ring the church bells and to attend masses and devotions. Unlike his father, Ivan the Terrible, in almost every way, Fiodor was completely unable to cope with his responsibilities. He was actually *yurodivii*, a human being of a semi-idiotic state of mind, always grinning stupidly and talking incoherently, but enjoying the respect only of the overly superstitious. The *yurodivii* were believed to be under the special protection of God and so no harm should be done to them under the penalty of mortal sin.[2] Hence, during his entire reign from 1584 to 1598, Czar Fiodor relied upon advisors, who, in his name managed the state machine, because he could not do it himself. Luckily, his advisors and subordinates were able men serving the Czar and the country rather honorably.

Ivan the Dread, who had killed his other son a few years before his own death, realized too well Fiodor's limitations, and therefore appointed Nikita Romanov as the chief advisor and tutor to his feeble-minded younger son. Nikita Romanov died shortly after Fiodor had assumed the throne and Boris Godunov, the new Czar's brother-in-law, soon managed to become the real power behind the throne. Boris Godunov came from a junior *boyar* family of Tartar extraction, which had recently emerged into social prominence as a direct result of the *oprichnina* upheavals. Boris himself was not an *oprichnik* (Czar's special agent), though he was among the favorites of Ivan the Dread. His immediate influence upon Czar Fiodor was through his sister, Irene Godunov, whom he had managed to marry off to the *yurodivii* Czar. This influence through his sister, the Czaritsa, and his background as "newbreed" nobility made Boris rather unwelcome among such ancient families as the Shuiskiis. Golovins or Vorotinskiis. The grand old nobles conspired against Godunov by promoting the idea of Fiodor's divorcing Irene and in this way of getting rid of Boris as well as ousting the Czaritsa from his court.

The quarrels, open hatred, and hostilities between the old aristocratic families and the new breed of courtiers, *dvorianie*, such as the Godunovs and Romanovs as well as the opposition to Boris Goudnov in particular, merely set the stage for greater troubles. While the new breed was reaching for more influence under Ivan, the old guard wanted to regain its previous importance in shaping political and social affairs. Open warfare between the two noble wings was held in check only, as mentioned, by Ivan's firm hand. It blew up, however, in full force during the first years of Fiodor's reign, causing in part the serious complications of the "Time of Troubles." With the progress of time, the differences between the two segments of the nobility were smoothed over and the cleavage mended by way of intermarriages. Common interests with respect to the lower social strata eventually produced a new and consolidated yet heterogeneous ruling class by the end of the seventeenth century. Meanwhile, however, as the sixteenth century merged into the seventeenth, the turmoil within the upper crust of Muscovite society encouraged the lower classes to break the bounds of the ancient social structure and to overcome the restrictions of serfdom and of landlessness especially.

As long as Czar Fiodor was alive, though feeble-minded and unable to rule autocratically himself, he still represented the prestige of the throne and the certainty of the ancient dynasty of Rurik. The conflicting social and political interests of rival segments in the kingdom were but undercurrents in the state, though strong and sharp. After Fiodor's death, when no direct descendant could legally claim the throne of the Rurik in Moscow and the succession became dubious, matters got out of hand. The class conflicts led to bold and mighty attempts to overpower the state and government machine.

In the first years of Fiodor's reign it had already become apparent that Boris Godunov was the actual ruler of Muscovy exercising all autocratic powers in the name of the Czar. Using the confidence of the Czar as his power base, Godunov gradually began to dissolve the opposition against him. Some of his enemies were sent into exile or forced into out-of-the-way monasteries or were liquidated. Prominent among those Boris had removed from power were such leaders as the Golovins, Prince Mstislavskii, Prince Shuiskii, the Metropolitan Dionisii and the majority of their relatives, friends, and followers.

In carrying out these reigns of terror, Boris was immune because he had a domineering influence upon his sister, Czaritsa Irene, who in her own turn greatly influenced the feeble-minded but trusting Czar Fiodor. Godunov became, during Fiodor's reign, the actual regent of Muscovy. This situation was very well known abroad. The British referred to him as "the Lord-Protector of Muscovy." Furthermore, the private wealth of the Godunovs helped Boris significantly in establishing his political position at the court. Fiodor's limitations and Godunov's caution, not to make any mistakes or blunders, made the era a relatively peaceful one. Quite likely, Boris Godunov had already begun to nurse the idea of gaining the crown for himself in the event of Fiodor's death. The Czar's sickly disposition did not promise a long rule. Godunov could not be sure of the time to make his move and the vague possibility of his future ascent to the throne made him, in all probability, a cautious "Lord-Protector."

Boris Godunov took all possibilities into account: Fiodor was sickly; there was no male descendant from the marriage with Irene Godunov; his half-brother, Prince Dimitrii born of Ivan the Dread's seventh marriage with Maria Nagoi, was canonically excluded from the succession since only two divorces and three marriages were validly recognized by the Orthodox Church. Nevertheless, Boris could not be sure. The mysterious death of the eleven-year-old Prince Dimitrii in 1591 might be traced to Godunov's plans, although Platonov and other historians have denied the possibility.[3] After Ivan's death, Prince Dimitrii and his mother, Maria, and some other members of the Nagoi family were exiled to the city of Uglich, in order to prevent any attempts to upset Fiodor's reign and the peace of the land. Godunov, no doubt, was behind the scheme. In Uglich, the exiles were guarded by a certain Bitiagovskii, an agent of Moscow. The life in Uglich was uncomfortable for all concerned because unpleasant occurrences were to be expected at any time. On May 15, 1591, Prince Dimitrii was mortally wounded and died shortly thereafter. Maria Nagoi and some of her relatives, having witnessed Dimitrii's death, accused Bitiagovskii and his agents of plottoing the murder of the young prince and aroused the Uglich mob against them. The anti-Moscow rioting continued for several days, during which Bitiagovskii, his son and some of his men were killed.

As soon as the news of the Uglich riot reached the capital, the central government sent an investigating commission, headed by Prince Vasilii Shuiskii and Metropolitan Gelasii, to ascertain the facts of Dimitrii's death. The comission, having investigated the matter, prepared a report in which Prince Dimitrii was said to have died from a knife wound, inflicted accidentally during an epileptic attack. The Moscow government accepted the report at its face value, and then proceeded sternly to restore order. Maria Nagoi was punished by having been put in a convent. Her relatives were largely exiled to the distant region of the North for exciting the crowd and having caused the bloody rioting. The people of Uglich were punished for their unruliness. The town was decimated: some townspeople were immediately executed, others were imprisoned or sent into exile. Even the bell, which usually announced the people's meetings and, on that fateful day, had called the people to revenge Dimitrii's death, was carried away to blot out memory of the incident.[4] Public opinion, however, did not accept the credibility of the official report, prepared by government agents, and openly blamed Bitiagovskii and his men for murdering the probable successor to the throne. Boris Godunov was generally believed to be the mastermind behind the whole plot. The matter has remained largely unsolved, like so many other dramatic political mysteries of the past. As a matter of record, the chief investigator of Dimitrii's death, Prince Vasilii Shuskii actually reversed himself twice in giving the account of the developments.[5] This will be explored further later on.

Soon after the unhappy Uglich incident, a daughter was born to Czar Fiodor and Irene Godunov, but she died a year and a half later. Fiodor's health had begun to deteriorate rapidly and the Czar died in January 1598, leaving no male heir to the throne, and "all his estates to his wife," Czaritsa Irene. She could easily have become the sovereign, but she declined the crown and entered a monastery. In this way, the ancient dynasty of the Ruriks, which had ruled in East Europe for almost seven and a half and in Moscow for almost three centuries, passed into history. Muscovy was left without any direct succession to the throne save for Boris Godunov, the strongman behind the throne for a number of years, who had long harbored the thought of becoming the Czar.

Immediately after Fiodor's death, Patriarch Yov (Job) offered the crown to Boris Godunov in the name of the Orthodox Church, the *boyars*, and the entire population. Boris refused. He requested a more legal and official coronation through the convention of the landed council, *zemskii sobor*. He anticipated strong opposition to his reign and apparently wanted an unchallengeable mandate. He had much in his favor. As the actual ruler of Muscovy in Fiodor's time, Godunov had promoted the establishment of the Orthodox Patriarchate in Moscow, the victorious war with Sweden, the final domination of West Siberia and the repulsion of the Tartars from the gates of Moscow. But he had several liabilities as well. Contenders to the vacant throne could be found among the leading personalities of contemporary Muscovy, such as Fiodor Romanov, son of Nikita, the first regent, appointed by Ivan the Dread to protect the young and feeble-minded monarch only to be succeeded by Godunov, Bogdan Bielskii, the trusted lieutenant of Ivan the Dread, and Simeon Bekbulatovich, the hero in the short-lived farce of two rulers in Muscovy during the years 1574-1576. Furthermore, Boris Godunov was still a controversial figure to the old *boyar* families.

The period was one of crisis: no direct descendant to the crown, several contenders for the throne, and general unrest throughout the land. The election of a new Czar was urgent. Accordingly, the landed council was summoned to convene by Patriarch Yov. Meanwhile, Boris Godunov, the Lord-Protector of Muscovy and not at all sure about the outcome, ordered all frontiers closed and suspended all diplomatic relations. By intrigues, promises and briberies he tried to insure his election, relying chiefly on his unique court position. Yet, and this must be strongly affirmed, the landed council that finally elected Boris Godunov the new Czar of Muscovy was perfectly constitutional, though consisting of only court-appointed representatives from various territories and classes. Although the convention was not yet electoral, it could neither be considered a hand-picked body of Godunov's followers despite his efforts to influence the selection of membership. It was on Boris's part a perfectly legitimate political game, largely managed by Patriarch Yov, his ardent supporter because Godunov had done so much for the Muscovite Church by elevating it to the dignity of the Eastern Patriachate.

Once elected, Boris was offered the crown but duly refused it, as the custom was then deemed proper. At last, after being asked a second time by the council, Godunov agreed to submit to the "people's choice and will." Godunov's election by the landed council in 1598 did not terminate the opposition and the court intrigues. The old aristocracy was determined somehow to get rid of Godunov. Their hatred for him led to anti-Godunov agitation among the people. This was to change the cource of events substantially. Although at first, in Czar Fiodor's lifetime, Godunov's rule had been a rather benevolent one, it now became a regime of terror. The suspicious, newly crowned Czar ruthlessly executed, deported and confiscated properties to suppress the opposition. A spy's or informer's charge of opposition was enough to doom a person.

The *boyar* class particular lived under continuous danger, for the *oprichnina* era seemed to have returned. Bogdan Bielskii, one of Godunov's adversaries, was tortured and subsequently imprisoned in a distant place of the Volga region. Fiodor Romanov, another outspoken adversary, was forced to hide as a monk under the name of Philaret in a remote monastery. Other members of the influential and popular family of the Romanovs were tried, imprisoned or exiled. Even the old and blind Prince Simeon Bekbulatovich, a most unlikely threat to Godunov's rule, was given no peace. The people of Moscow were specifically required to repudiate Bekbulatovich as a candidate for the throne. The *boyar* class was purged to rid it of disloyal elements. The reign of terror prevailed. The aristocratic grandees as well as the common people were frightened and intimidated. This provoked even more intense attempts by the old *boyar* families, threatened by Godunov's terror regime, to intrigue and plot against the new Czar.

Meanwhile, things took a more unfavorable turn against Boris Godunov. The widespread famine of 1601 and 1602 produced more trouble and dissatisfaction and lasted until the middle of 1603. Chaos was everywhere. Some 400,000 human beings perished because of the famine; cannibalism broke out sporadically, hordes of dislodged marauders roamed the countryside, robbing, plundering and burning. Godunov's measures terrorized runaway peasant serfs without a place to hide and simply aggravated the general turmoil.[6] These social problems in turn seriously complicated Godunov's political situation. The *boyar* grandees were determined to exploit every opportunity to rid the country of this most horrendous Czar to save themselves from the frenzied inhumanities of the new *"oprichnina."* Gossip spread by the nobles among the people blamed Godunov's crimes and sins for the catastrophic famine and misfortunes of Muscovy. Indeed, he must be sacrificed for the good of the country. Thus, the *boyars* masterminded the plot of the Pseudo-Dimitrii (the Pretender) to even the score with Godunov once and for all.[7]

The fate of the Pretender might have been quite different had Czar Boris Godunov not died during the turmoil of April 1605. Actually a great ruler, Boris had had the odds stacked against him. At home, his autocratic rule had advanced the state. Internationally, he preserved peace, while fighting Fiodor's war with Sweden victoriously. He had sponsored the reconquest of Western Siberia, negotiated the profitable trade agreements with England and the Hanseatic League, and in his relations with the Holy Roman Empire, insisted on full recognition and parity of the Muscovite sovereign with the Holy Roman Emperor (the German Kaiser). Godunov was behind the establishment of the Orthodox Patriarchate in Moscow, as was pointed out previously. He invited and brought to his land foreign craftsmen and artisans, builders, architects and military experts from Europe to modernize the Muscovite way of life. He planned to establish a university in Moscow and sent young Muscovites to study abroad in order to enrich the culture of his land.[8] He promoted trade, reduced taxes, improved the state revenue collection, suppressed usury, and cared for the poor and destitute by promoting welfare of all kinds.

During the famine of 1601-1603, Godunov distributed grain among the needy and initiated what today would be called a public works program to relieve the merciless miseries of the unemployed poor. But these welfare and public-works measures proved to be quite inadequate, and were unable to avert the disastrous plight of the state brought about by the famine and accompanied by widespread social disintegration. The Czar was also a great constructor of fortresses, towns and churches. He surrounded the suburbs of Moscow with whitewashed bricks, fortified Astrakhan, strengthened the walls of Smolensk, rebuilt with bricks the Moscow trading center (Kitaigorod) and erected towns in the Muscovite borderlands to strengthen Moscow rule. Many of these construction projects resulted from Godunov's public works program to relieve the difficulties of a highly disrupted economic and social situation as Clarkson pointed out correctly. In spite of all these remarkable deeds toward the end of his reign, Boris actually plunged into a sea of storms. "The Time of Troubles" was at hand, brought on largely by Boris Godunov himself.[9]

The Social Struggle; the First Pretender and Czar Vasilii Shuiskii

Boris Godunov had been suspected all along by many, as Fletcher testified, as the chief conspirator to murder Prince Dimitrii of Uglich, the younger half-brother of Czar Fiodor I, though the official report of the events, prepared by Prince Vasilii Shuiskii suggested the contrary. Especially after 1601, rumors were persistent that Prince Dimitrii had miraculously escaped the assassin's knife and was now living in hiding awaiting the proper time to claim the throne. The *boyar* nobles popularized rumors in an underhanded attempt at getting rid of Godunov in retaliation for his abuses and efforts against them. The years of famine, social discontent and political turmoil were a fitting background for the Pseudo-Dimitrii intrigue.

Dimitrii, the Pretender, first appeared at the court of a Polish nobleman, Jerzy Mniszek, in Sambor in Galicia, where he obtained the privately sponsored support of the Polish gentry, including the help of Mniszek himself. Mniszek at that time was in some financial straits and apparently considered the whole adventure a good way to better his material position. Nevertheless, Pseudo-Dimitrii received no official backing from the Polish royal government, but was allowed to tacitly use Polish territory for his scheme. The identity of the first Pretender has never been fully established on the basis of historical records. It is generally believed, however, that he was Gregorii Otrepiev, once a serf of Prince Cherkasskii, Romanov's relative, a runaway monk, who was subsequently used both by the Muscovite *boyars*, probably at Fiodor Romanov's behest, and the adventurous Polish gentry for separate and semipolitical ends. In 1604, Pseudo-Dimitrii became a Catholic and at once gained the support of some Catholic circles in Poland, who hoped to use him to Catholicize the people of Muscovy. The Pretender was soon engaged to Marina Mniszek, the daughter of his Polish mentor, to consolidate his political position, from his view, and from the view of the Poles to increase the Polish influence upon him.

In October of the same year, Pseudo-Dimitrii, with some 400 Polish nobles, 1200 Ukrainian Cossacks, Muscovite adventurers of the noble stock, and a considerable number of fugitive peasant serfs, crossed the Muscovite border from the Polish-Lithuanian side to advance toward Moscow. Southern Muscovite provinces, believing the Pretender was the true Dimitrii, moved into his camp. The nobles were happy that the Godunov era was nearing an end, while the lower classes, seeing the Cossacks and the fugitive serfs with Pseudo-Dimitrii, hailed him as the liberator from noble oppression. The misunderstanding and conflicts of interests among the classes soon proved fateful. The Pretender's march on Moscow at first identified itself with a Muscovite national movement, a cause for which the 400 Polish gentry and 1200 Ukrainian Cossacks had no genuine sympathy.

In the first military encounter between Godunov and the Pretender at Novgorod Siversk, in the northern Ukraine, nominally under the Muscovite rule, Pseudo-Dimitrii's army was badly mauled and completely routed in the late fall of 1604. The Pretender had to retreat to Putivl to organize a new army against the Czar's armed forces. Meanwhile the Don-Cossacks began to join Pseudo-Dimitrii's cause, hoping in this way to lessen the tyrannical Muscovite rule in the Don-Volga regions and eventually to obtain freedom and landownership. In April 1605, Czar Boris Godunov died. This was, no doubt, the turning point in the course of events for, as the strong man with authority, he most probably would have crushed the Pretender. The Pretender resumed his march on Moscow, where Fiodor, Boris' son, ascended the throne in name only, while his mother, Maria Maliuta-Skuratova, assumed the real authority. As the daughter of the once notorious *oprichnik*, Maria was rather unpopular and she also lacked the ability to handle the complicated affairs of state. Hence, the situation got out of hand quickly.

The Shuiskiis, Golitsins, and other nobles, after inciting the Moscow populace, took up the cause of the Pretender and, by a *coup d'etat*, overthrew the Godunovs' rule. Young Fiodor and his mother were cruelly murdered while Fiodor's sister, beautiful Ksenia, was first put into a monastery and then later forced to become Pseudo-Dimitrii's mistress. Even Boris Godunov's body was removed from the Archangels' Cathedral and entombed in an out-of-the-way and remote monastery. Prince Vasilii Shuiskii administered the oath of allegiance to the Pretender. Given this opportunity, Vasilii Shuiskii reversed himself and denied the credibility of his Uglich report about the death of Prince Dimitrii. At that time he denied the assassination attempt and Godunov's involvement in the plot. Now, Shuiskii was ready to admit that it was a conspiracy to murder young Prince Dimitrii and he accepted the popular belief that the prince miraculously escaped and was ready to assume the throne, having given his full endorsement to the Pretender's cause.

Meanwhile, mob rule prevailed in Moscow for several days, during which time many of Godunov's supporters and followers perished. Patriarch Yov was exiled. Thus, on June 20, 1605, Pseudo-Dimitrii triumphantly entered Moscow, accompanied by a heterogeneous crowd of supporters, each segment of which was looking for its own ends and was hoping for different rewards for assisting the Pretender. The nobles had used him against Godunov and now that Godunov was gone, they were ready to get rid of him as an imposter and fraud, having assumed that they were now fully able to protect their ancient class privileges alone.

The Cossacks from the Don regions wanted more freedom of action, more liberty from oppression, land ownership, and above all, the restriction of *boyar* class privileges. The peasant serfs wanted the abolition of serfdom, and looked toward the Pretender as the only guarantee of their hopes. Obviously, the nobles opposed any such demand of the lower classes. The mercenaries finally, wanted payments and booty even at the expense of the local population. The Catholic monks, brought to Moscow by Marina Mniszek a few weeks later sought to bring Catholicism to Muscovy against the universal will of the Muscovites to preserve their Orthodoxy at any price. Subsequent developments proved that these conflicting interests were irreconcilable and that they would cause major social and political upheavals. Above all, Pseudo-Dimitrii was unable to accomplish the miracle of making everybody happy and consequently pleased no one.

After the Pretender married Marina Mniszek and the Poles received more freedom of action, matters simply worsened. The Orthodox ecclesiastic circles were already antagonized by the Pretneder's becoming a Catholic. By now, national feelings were aroused. Furthermore, Pseudo-Dimitrii ignored the traditional royal ways by behaving in an unorthodox manner and thus hurting the conservative feelings of the Muscovites. His pattern of action was hard to understand: Godunov's favorites were allowed to return to the capital, the Romanovs were treated very kindly, while monk Philaret (Fiodor) Romanov was made the Metropolitan of Rostov. At the same time Vasilii Shuiskii, ardent supporter of the Pretender and the leader of the Moscow rebellion against Fiodor Godunov and his mother, was soon accused of treason and sentenced to death but his sentence was subsequently commuted to exile so that in a few months he was permitted to return to Moscow. Old Prince Simeon Bekbulatovich, who was politically harmless, was forced to take monastic vows. The Pretender, on the other hand, spent money lavishly making land grants, forcefully collecting funds from the Church without respect for its ancient rights. He surrounded himself with a new breed of low-class gentry, ignoring the old noble families, while his Cossack and Polish supporters continued to antagonize the Muscovites by almost every move they made.

Although most historians agree that Pseudo-Dimitrii did not really show any favoritism to the Poles and Catholics, the Muscovites were nevertheless deeply offended by his ways and accused him of being pro-Polish and pro-Catholic. This was enough to arouse them against him. On May 12, 1606, street disturbances erupted in Moscow, having been masterminded by Vasilii Shuiskii and other *boyars* under the slogan "the Poles are killing the *boyars*." Rioting and fighting continued for several days. On May 17, the Pretender was murdered in the Kremlin and his body dragged through the streets. It indicated the intense hatred the Moscow populace had for him. The *coup d'etat* succeeded, fitting very well into the long-range planning of the old *boyar* grandees: first to remove Godunov through the subterfuge of a prefabricated Pretender, and then, to liquidate the Pretender and to grab the power for themselves. Over two thousand foreigners (the Poles,

Lithuanians and Ukrainians) were massacred in the anti-foreign frenzy of the Muscovite mob. However, Marina Mniszek and her father, the chief sponsor behind the whole scheme, escaped liquidation, but were subsequently exiled to Yaroslavl. Two days after the Pretender's murder, Vasilii Shuiskii, a court operator of the first magnitude, managed to convene a mock council, and, with the help of would-be nobles, to elect himself the new Czar by virtue of his being related to the House of Rurik. Without much formality, he was proclaimed the Czar of Muscovy.

Czar Vasilii Shuiskii represented the conservative political outlook of the old boyardom, and attempted to continue the traditional Muscovite autocracy. Some historians believe that the promises Shuiskii had given to the *boyars* involved some constitutional limitations which he had agreed to accept. He apparently had promised not to apply any death penalties against the nobles without a trial by the Council of *Boyars,* an ancient but sometimes powerless institution. Furthermore, in case of sentencing the guilty, his family and friends were not to suffer nor be persecuted, as was the practice before, under Ivan the Terrible and Boris Godunov. Shuiskii allegedly promised to include guarantees against false informers and their subsequent punishment. This might have been simply the reaction to the legalized "lawlessness" of the terror regime of the *oprichnina* and the later period of Godunov's rule, when whoever was suspected or falsely denounced might have been executed, imprisoned or exiled. The promises given by Czar Shuiskii remained during his short reign but were mere tokens of no value, proving that his rule was essentially autocratic in nature and largely responsible for the social and political upheavals of the time, especially in view of the awakening revolutionary mood of the lower classes in Muscovite society.

Czar Vasilii was personally too mean to acquire any prestige and much too impolitic to pacify the situation. He was very uncertain of his power. To strengthen it, he sent the old and blind Prince Simeon Bekbulatovich, already abused beyond reason, to the distant Solovetskii monastery on the White Sea.

Then, he reversed himself once more on the Uglich story. This time he admitted that the plot to kill young Prince Dimitrii was masterminded by Godunov, that the plot succeeded, and that Dimitrii did not escape but died of the knife wound. He ordered Dimitrii's remains exhumed and brought to Moscow. The Muscovite Orthodox Church, to give credence to the official version of Dimitrii's death and to help the new Czar, canonized Dimitrii and included him among its saints under the patronage of Patriarch Hermogen, Shuiskii's appointee. This, however, was of little help to the Czar in the long run.

Meanwhile, new rumors persisted that Prince Dimitrii, for the second time, had miraculously escaped the assassin's dagger and was still alive and ready to claim the throne anew. The borderland peasant masses and the Don-Cossacks were excited about this prospect because Vasilii Shuiskii was considered to be a *"boyar* Czar," unwilling to help the lower social classes. The new Czar however did not act prudently. He turned sharply against the former supporters of the Pretender, although he had been one of them, and removed them from their positions. Then, he removed Patriarch Ignatii by appointing Metropolitan Philaret Romanov in his place. Soon he cancelled Philaret's appointment and made Hermogen the Patriarch of Moscow. The powerful and ambitious Romanov family as well as the influential Philaret were deeply offended and along with other nobles, opposed the new and unpopular Czar, whose government lacked both stability and prestige.

The country lacked stability for too long a period. The quick succession of four different Czars (Boris, Fiodor, Pseudo-Dimitrii and Vasilii) in the course of thirteen and a half months spoke for itself. Then, half of the country, especially the southern and south-eastern provinces, refused to recognize the *boyar* Czar. The country gentry refused to submit to Shuiskii, fearing revenge for their earlier support of Pseudo-Dimitrii. The peasant serfs and the Cossacks wanted a Czar who would give them freedom and land. The rebellious feelings prevailed throughout the land. Of course, the ultimate ends of both wings of the anti-Shuiskii movement (of the gentry, *boyars,* and other social strata) were diametrically opposed to each other. The gentry did not wish either freedom for the peasant serfs or liberty for the Cossacks. The rift had already existed at the Pretender's time and widened with each bloody encounter.

An open rebellion against Czar Vasilii Shuiskii was started in Putivl by his old adversary, Prince Gregorii Shakhovskoi, and in Astrakhan, by Prince Ivan Khvorostinin. It soon spread throughout the numerous Volga towns and into the countryside. The serfs, the slaves, and the Cossacks were on the move. Also, the Mordovians raised arms against their Muscovite oppressor, taking advantage of political instability. Although the populace of Moscow supported Shuiskii, it was, not to his advantage. He had been the one to incite the people into two rebellious *coups d'etats*, against Fiodor Godunov and Pseudo-Dimitrii. In the process, a lesson in anarchy and the taste of power were given to the Moscow mob. This interfered with Shuiskii's rule throughout.

The serf and Cossack uprising rapidly gained in strength and aggressiveness, after leadership was assumed by Ivan Bolotnikov, who gave it the character of an authentic national-social movement. From then on, Shakhovskoi and other nobles, who unfortunately joined the rebellious drive, became only the secondary figures in the general uprising. The Don-Cossacks, on the other hand, soon became the hard core of the Bolotnikov insurgents, championing the cause of the lower classes as well as developing a movement toward a separate national entity, different from that of the Muscovite people. Ivan Bolotnikov issued proclamations with the intent of inciting a definite social revolution. He called for violence against the rich and the noble oppressors of the poor and demanded that the wealth of the rich be distributed among the peasant serfs. Some gentry and *boyars*, blinded by their own hatred and fear of Shuiskii, helped Bolotnikov without fully realizing that such support might lead to their own eventual doom in the spreading wave of social revolution of the masses.

In October 1606, Bolotnikov's insurgent armies reached the gates of Moscow. The Muscovite autocracy was for the first time seriously threatened by a large-scale socially and ethnically motivated rebellion. However, the social-revolutionary character of Bolotnikov's uprising finally aroused the conservative circles of the *boyars* and country gentry to its dangers for their own cause, and they soon left the Don-Cossacks and revolting serfs and slaves and joined the Shuiskii armed forces. In this way, the government troops under the command of Prince Mikhail Skopin-Shuiskii, the Czar's relative and an able military leader, were capable of defeating Bolotnikov's insurgents almost at the very gates of the capital in December, 1606, and forced them to retreat to the cities of Tula and Kaluga. Nevertheless, the struggle of the Shuiskii forces against the rebels continued for more than a year, accompanied by utmost cruelty on both sides. Slaughter prevailed, people were tortured, killed and massacred, the countryside was pillaged, burned and ruined. No mercy for Shuiskii's followers was shown by the insurgents, nor any respite for the rebels from the government forces. Lastly, in October, 1607, Tula was taken by Shuiskii's armies and both Bolotnikov and Shakhovskoi were made prisoners. Subsequently, Ivan Bolotnikov and his chief lieutenants were executed, while Shakhovskoi was exiled.[10]

The quelling off the Bolotnikov uprising did not terminate the revolutionary fever in the least. Meanwhile, during 1607 and 1608, numerous rebels, calling themselves "czars" and "sons of czars," appeared in various parts of the country, and continued to lead the masses in the struggle against Muscovite autocracy and aristocracy. Peter, Fiodor, Lavrentii, Simeon, Vasilii or Martinka were their names, as Florinsky pointed out. Some of them claimed to be the sons of Czar Fiodor Ivanovich or made some other allegation concerning their connections with previous Moscow rulers to establish their rights to leadership against Shuiskii, the *"boyar* Czar." False Peter, allegedly Fiodor's son, born in 1592, was most outstanding from that array of imposters. He was captured in Tula by the government forces and executed. Even Bolotnikov and Shakhovskoi were connecting themselves with the cause of "Czar Dimitrii," the Pretender. The avalanche of pretenders and imposters and their considerable following indicated not only a deep social but also a far-reaching moral crisis of Muscovite society during the "Time of Troubles." Every principle of decency broke down in that class encounter between the conservative nobility and the revolutionary expression of the drive for social change and social reconstruction in the Muscovite state. The phenomenon of the second Pseudo-Dimitrii or Pretender condensed in itself, as it were, all the socially and morally destructive as well as constructive elements of that challenging era.[11]

The position of Czar Shuiskii was very difficult, but at that time he had still refused the Swedish assitance offered to him. He was aware of the nature of the social struggle, but having been a conservative *boyar* at heart, he was not ready for any reforms. He was driving a hard line and believed that the revolutionary movement could be suppressed by terror. Having fully forgotten his election promises, which actually pertained to the noble class only, he legalized plunder and murder in the rebel borderlands to squelch the opposition. Thousands were executed with elaborate cruelty, while the insurgents continued to repay in kind. The serfs who joined the insurrection, desiring freedom from bondage, after being captured by the government forces, were returned to their masters. Other prisoners were turned loose in the steppes without food and provisions and were allowed to perish. The discontent and hatred toward the "*boyar* Czar" grew steadily, but he was too narrow-minded to grasp the importance of the situation. In 1607, he issued several decress to strengthen the government control over the relationship between the landlords and their serfs and the landlords and the state, in order to prevent and to stop the flight of the serfs and slaves from their bondage and to suppress in this way the increasing social unrest. The effect of those decrees intensified the revolt of the masses and the turmoil. The Orthodox Church, reactionary and subservient to the state, did not help the situation.

In early summer of 1607, shortly before Tula fell and Bolotnikov's uprising was partially repulsed, the second Pseudo-Dimitrii or Pretender appeared on the social-political scene of the troubled Muscovite state. The intrigue had been hatched in Poland, where King Sigismund could not forget or forgive the slaughter of the Polish retinue in the Kremlin on May 17, 1606, during the *coup d'etat* to overthrow the first Pretender. Furthermore, Poland was just recovering from a domestic war and many unemployed warriors were roaming the country, producing unrest. The King decided to turn these war marauders upon the Muscovites and in this way to pacify the unrest in his own land. The second Pretender was a common imposter, of whom history records nothing. Who he was and from where he came is still a mystery. The first Pretender, allegedly Gregorii Otrepiev, might have believed he was Prince Dimitrii, but the second Pseudo-Dimitrii knew very well he was an imposter and his followers had no illusions in that respect. He relied mostly upon Polish support and simply intended to take advantage of the upheavals in the Muscovite state. However, the second Polish intervention in the domestic affairs of their country soon aroused the patriotic and religious feelings of the Muscovites, causing a new twist in the developments of the "Time of Troubles."[12]

The National and Religious Struggle; the Interregnum and the Election of Mikhail Romanov

The forces of the second Pretender were growing while Vasilii Shuiskii was still liquidating the last remnants of the Bolotnikov insurgents. Their composition was highly heterogeneous and included: (1) adventurous Polish and Lithuanian nobles and gentry under the leadership of Jan Sapieha and Roman Różynski, the Polish-Lithuanian rebels and war adventurers from the recent anti-Sigismund uprising, under the command of one of the prominent figures of that uprising, Aleksander Lisowski, (2) several thousands of the Ukrainian Cossacks, who participated in the assault by the first Pretender and since that time made plundering the Muscovite territories their favored occupation, (3) the Don-Cossacks under the leadership of their chieftains, of which Ivan Zarutskii was most prominent, and (4) the hordes of runaway serfs and slaves, who longed for recognition of their human dignity. Of course, some Muscovite nobles joined the new Pretender out of hatred for Shuiskii or for reasons of personal gains. But this time, just as before under Bolotnikov and other rebels, the motives and interests of those heterogeneous groups were diametrically and dramatically opposed to each other, and this made the second Pretender politically weak from the very beginning of his venture. The social interest of the *boyars* had nothing in common with the other groups or classes, as was emphasized before.

During the winter of 1607-1608, the opposing factions to the Pretender's following managed to some extent to amalgamate into one single force and became, at least on the surface, a cohesive force. The war started in the spring of 1608. The forces of the second Pseudo-Dimitrii began to move toward Moscow against the government troops of the Czar, Vasilii Shuiskii. Pseudo-Dimitrii reached the capital without much resistance and soon established his own capital in Tushino, close to Moscow. A military assault upon Moscow did not produce immediate surrender to the imposter, largely because of the able defense by Prince Mikhail Skopin-Shuiskii, who, however, was not strong enough at this point to defeat the Pretender completely.

By now the Czar was in a bad situation and he decided to negotiate an alliance with Sweden. The negotiations were conducted through Prince Mikhail Skopin-Shuiskii. Moscow agreed to surrender to Sweden the recently acquired territory, taken by Godunov, parts of the shores of the Gulf of Finland, with Ivangorod, Iam, Koporie, and Korela, in exchange for Swedish military assistance. Sweden sent some 6,000 men under Magnus de la Gardie to Novgorod, where Prince Mikhail Skopin-Shuiskii was gathering an army to resist the Pretender, commonly called the "Felon of Tushino." In the meantime, the military units of the Pretender of Tushino invaded the northern regions of Muscovy, where they behaved ruthlessly and with no respect for the traditions of self-government still remaining. The Ukrainian Cossacks, especially, who had no love for the rough northern land, were plundering the land thoroughly.[13] Soon, the Muscovites of those regions had to organize a people's militia to resist the invasion. The encounters between the militia troops and the Tushino dispatches were frequent and bloody throughout 1609. Then, after having completed the organization of his national army, Prince Mikhail Skopin-Shuiskii, aided by Swedish, French, Scottish and English mercenaries, advanced toward Tushino to face the Pretender's forces.

By now, however, Pseudo-Dimitrii's plight was highly precarious. He had lost his Polish support, since King Sigismund of Poland summoned the Polish units to his camp near Smolensk to support him in his war against Czar Shuiskii. The Muscovite-Swedish alliance of a few months ago had angered the King. In addition, the Pretender had a serious disagreement with Rozynski, one of the commanders of the Polish units. Hence, most of the Polish troops withdrew first to Volokolam and then to Smolensk. The Pretender was, thus, too weak to fight with Skopin-Shuiskii's army, and retreated to Kaluga in early 1610.

This was the end of the Tushino era. For two years the town was almost a second capital in Muscovy, rivaling Moscow itself. Tushino had its own council of boyars, its own system of administration, and made land grants to its followers while collecting another round of taxes for the court needs. Tushino also laid claim to being the lawful government of the land. The historical evaluation of that era reveals a deplorable time, during which the *boyars* and the gentry showed themselves at their worst. They had no loyalty to anybody, neither to Shuiskii nor to the Pretender, nor to their country. They frequently changed their allegiance from Shuiskii to Pseudo-Dimitrii and vice versa, whenever they could get a materially better deal for themselves without concern for anything else. Also, the merchants and the clergy speculated for more advantageous deals between the Czar and the Pretender, while neither of the two factions was strong enough to prevent or stop the indecent wheeling and dealing. Both contenders, in their weakness, clutched at support whenever they could find it, at whatever price. Those wheeler-dealers, who transferred their allegiance at every possible opportunity, were commonly and with disgust referred to as the "migratory birds." And this went on for some two years. Many noble clans had their representation in Moscow as well as in Tushino. For example, Metropolitan Philaret Romanov, considered by the insurgents to be their Patriarch, was there partially in the character of a "prisoner." Also, Marina Mniszek came there, accepted the second Pseudo-Dimitrii as her lawful husband and accompanied him almost until his death in Kaluga, late in 1610.

The flight of the second Pretender to Kaluga lifted the siege of Moscow. It was a great relief for Shuiskii's government, but the troubles were far from being over. The Polish bid for the Muscovite throne was by now official. The Polish troops were besieging Smolensk, revealing a clear intention to move against Moscow. King Sigismund prepared his assault upon Muscovy for several reasons. First of all, Prince Wladyslaw, Sigismund's son, was offered the Muscovite crown for the first time by secret negotiations in 1605, sponsored on the Muscovite side by the Shuiskiis and Golitsins. A personal union was contemplated between Poland-Lithuania and Muscovy.[14] Then, the plan was abandoned for a time because of the unfortunate developments with the first Pretender. Secondly, King Sigismund, an ardent Catholic, hoped by placing his son or himself on the Moscow throne to advance Catholicism. The idea was greatly dreaded by the Muscovites, themselves fervently Orthodox. Thirdly, Sigismund had not forgotten the massacre of the Polish retinue in the Kremlin, in May 1606. Fourthly and finally, Shuiskii negotiated an alliance with Sweden, Sigismund's bitter foe, and this was enough for the Polish king. Sigismund wanted to prevent that alliance by removing Shuiskii and getting the Moscow throne under his control.

In September 1609, Sigismund's army invaded the Muscovite territory and besieged Smolensk, from where the Polish troops in Tushino were ordered to leave the second Pretender's cause and to join the royal army. This actually killed the chances of the Pretender, as was indicated a while ago, and induced the leading Muscovite noble circles who were not able to patch up their differences with Czar Shuiskii largely because of their earlier associations with Pseudo-Dimitrii, to offer the Muscovite crown anew to Prince Wladyslaw of Poland, King Sigismund's son. Philaret Romanov, Ivan Saltykov, Prince Vasilii Golitsin were behind that pro-Polish scheme. The negotiations with the Polish court began as early as February, 1610. The Polish side of the agreement solemnly promised to respect the inviolability of the Muscovite socio-political institutions, especially the power of the noble landlords over their serfs and slaves and the rights of the noble courtiers, *dvorianie*, for promotions and advancements on the basis of merit. Also, the privileged position of the Orthodox Church in the spirit of past tradition was promised to be respected, while Prince Wladislaw was supposed to give up Catholicism and become Orthodox.[15] After the retreat of the second Pseudo-Dimitrii to Kaluga, many Muscovite nobles, including Metropolitan Philaret, undertook a voyage to Smolensk to join the camp of the new Czar-to-be. Philaret, however, was intercepted by Shuiskii's military detachment and brought back to the capital, allegedly as one being "liberated from the Tushino imprisonment." The Metropolitan did not feel very comfortable over the fact and secretly contacted the pro-Polish camp.

The situation of Shuiskii's government was again turning from bad to worse. Although there was a day of relief and joy when Prince Mikhail Shopin-Shuiskii freed and triumphantly entered Moscow, this outstanding military leader was soon poisoned, apparently by relatives who envied his popularity and support among the people. Hence the command of the Muscovite forces in the struggle against the advancing Poles was given to Prince Dimitrii Shuiskii, the Czar's brother, who soon proved to be a highly incapable military leader. He was badly defeated by the Polish armies at the Battle of Klushino in June, 1610, although he had a decisive manpower superiority over the outstanding Polish commander, Stanislaw Zólkiewski.

Czar Vasilii Shuiskii's fate was thereby decided. The foreign mercenaries in his service left him and went over to the Polish camp, the Swedish withdrew to Novgorod the Great, the Muscovite nobles went completely over to Wladyslaw or left the Czar's and their country's cause and scattered all over, attending their private business in their manors, villages and estates. Zólkiewski moved toward Moscow, while the Pretender advanced closer to the capital from his hide-out in Kaluga.

The populace of Moscow, already used to overthrowing its government on two occasions and having been twice incited to do so by Vasilii Shuiskii, and now agitated by Saltykov, Liapunov and others, ousted Vasilii from the throne on July 17, 1610. Vasilii Shuiskii and his wife were forced to take monastic vows, Prince Dimitrii Shuiskii, who fled from the battlefield of Klushino leaving behind his baton, sword and treasury, was arrested. The country was to be ruled from now on by a provisional body of the *boyar* council, headed by Prince Fiodor Mstislavskii until the election of a new Czar and his enthronement. The *interregnum* began. Shuiskii's cause, ardently championed by his appointee, Patriarch Hermogen, was lost.

Two forces stood at the gates of Moscow: the Polish army under Zólkiewski, and the Cossacks and rebellious serfs with the second Pretender. The temporary government, composed of conservative nobles, was rather quite prepared to accept the Polish contender for the throne, a foreigner of the aristocratic class in preference to the Pseudo-Dimitrii, backed up by the revolutionary "proletariat" of Cossacks and serfs. Hence, a landed council was hurriedly convened and Prince Wladyslaw of Poland was elected the new Czar. Zólkiewski accepted the crown in the name of the elect, and then promptly moved against the Pretender, defeating him and forcing him to retreat back to Kaluga again. The Poles then entered Moscow. In August, the Polish commander-in-chief concluded a new agreement with the Muscovite *boyars* in the name of the elect and King Sigismund, which was largely the repetition of the earlier one. It was supposed to bind the new Czar and safeguard the rights and privileges of the old Muscovite aristocracy. A delegation was dispatched to Smolensk to arrange Wladyslaw's arrival at the capital, his conversion to the Orthodoxy, and enthronement as the Czar of Muscovy. Things seemed to quiet down.

However, upon the arrival of the delegation at Sigismund's headquarters, a new and very serious complication developed. It became quickly quite apparent that King Sigismund wanted the Muscovite crown not for his son, but for himself. Wladyslaw was agreeable to the Muscovites but never the old King, whose Catholic fanaticism insulted their Orthodox religious feelings. Stanislaw Zólkiewski pleaded with the King to give up his insane and unrealizable plan, but in vain. He could not overcome Sigismund's stubbornness and therefore resigned as the commander-in-chief of the Polish forces. Serious frictions developed, during which time threats, briberies and other means of "persuasion" were employed by Sigismund. Finally, the leaders of the Muscovite delegation, Metropolitan Philaret Romanov, Prince Vasilii Golitsin and others, were imprisoned and taken to Poland.

The anti-Sigismund and anti-Polish movement caught fire rapidly because the Polish King began to favor the former Tushino men of low descent in the government and administration. Patriarch Hermogen agitated against the possibility of a "Catholic Czar," who usually broke promises.[16] Soon, the Patriarch was imprisoned by a Polish detachment and died in jail shortly thereafter either of starvation or by strangulation. Meanwhile in Riazan and Nizhnii-Novgorod uprisings erupted against the foreigners and Catholics. Patriarch Hermogen, when still alive, had kept in touch with the insurgents and had given them his moral support. But, in December, 1610, the second Pretender was murdered in Kaluga. Although some insurgents were campaigning to give the throne to Ivan, the infant son of Pseudo-Dimitrii and Marina Mniszek, yet the candidacy lacked strengh. Now, the national Muscovite forces aroused by religious anti-Catholic arguments, began to unite their defense of Orthodox Muscovy against the "threat" of a Catholic Czar.

The national and religiously motivated uprising spread quickly from Riazan and Nizhnii-Novgorod to other towns and regions. Even the remnants of the Tushino Don-Cossack and peasant-serf forces, under Ivan Zarutskii and Prince Dimitrii Trubetskoi, joined the uprising under Prokofii Liapunov, long very active in the anti-Shuiskii movement which had ousted the unfortunate Czar. In the spring of 1611, the Liapunov-Trubetskoi insurgent army, the country militia, the Cossacks and the peasant serfs, approached the capital to encourage an uprising that swept through Moscow, during which a large portion of the city was destroyed by the consuming fires, while a small armed detachment of Poles enclosed itself in the fortified Kremlin and Kitaigorod.

The leaders of the anti-Polish movement, gathered around Moscow, tried to patch up their traditional differences that divided the *boyars* from the Cossacks and from the peasant serfs, to produce some kind of united national government. Although they were one in their anti-Polish and anti-Catholic feelings, their deeply opposed social interests divided them. Prokofii Liapunov at first yielded to the demands of the Cossacks and serfs and promised, to the first, freedom and land grants and, to the latter, no reprisals and freedom from fear. The declaration alienated the conservative wings of the movement, producing the threat of a split and other serious complications. In June, 1611, the leaders of the uprising issued in the name of the whole land a joint document, called the Decisions, which was a reversal of the previous Liapunov declaration. Among other things, the Decisions provided for the return of the fugitive serfs and slaves to their original owners and placed the Don-Cossacks under the jurisdiction of the courtiers. By so doing, Liapunov sacrificed the national cause of an anti-Polish war for the sake of the *boyar* class interests, as Florinsky stated. For that he was killed by the Cossacks some weeks later. Subsequently, the nobles and the gentry deserted the cause, and left the leadership of the anti-Polish crusade in the hands of the extreme faction of the movement. Terror spread while the so-called temporary government under Prince Mstislavskii remained powerless.

The Liapunov experiment to combine various social segments for a common national action in Muscovy failed, as had similar attempts before. The conservative nobility was quite ready to accept foreign rule, as was pointed out above, rather than changes in the social or political structure of the country. The ecclesiastic leaders of the Orthodox Church were divided on the issue. Some of them, like Patriarch Hermogen before he had been liquidated by the Poles, were decidedly against the mob rule of the Cossacks, while others, like Abbot Dionisii of the Troitskii monastery, were ready to support the Cossacks and the mob revolt in their common fight against the Catholic Poles. The situation was chaotic and was getting worse.

Meanwhile, Smolensk surrendered and fell into King Sigismund's hands. A few months later, in Warsaw, the Polish capital, a celebration of the victory over the Muscovites was held at which former Czar Vasilii Shuiskii and his brother, Prince Dimitrii, were displayed as distinguished prisoners and symbols of the Polish victory.[17] Immediately after the fall of Smolensk, Novgorod the Great, always antagonistic to Moscow, gave up its allegiance to the state of Muscovy, and subsequently accepted Swedish supremacy.

The ruthless rule of the Don-Cossacks and the continuous presence of the Polish troops on Muscovite soil inspired a revival of the former national movement in the form of country militia. The Volga towns rose first, probably because they had suffered most. The new uprising began again in Nizhnii-Novgorod. Kuzma Minin-Sukhoruk, a meat dealer in that town, instigated a movement to re-establish law and order. He was a very able organizer and manager of the financial affairs of the movement. He combined his talents with the military know-how of Prince Dimitrii Pozharskii to give the insurrection a national character and to spur the rising tide of resistance to anarchy and terror. Soon, Minin and Pozharskii succeeded in uniting various Volga towns and regions in the drive to save Muscovy from foreign rule and from the Don-Cossack and mob terror regime. In 1612, already most of the northern and eastern provinces were backing up Minin and Pozharskii. The movement was essentially conservative, hence, joined by the nobles and the country gentry, who suffered most because of the revolutionary rule of the lower strata. The restoration of law and order became the main objective of the Minin-Pozharskii joint action. In their proclamation, issued early in 1612, Minin and Pozharskii denounced and repudiated the Don-Cossacks and their candidate for the throne, Ivan, the infant son of Marina Mniszek and the second Pseudo-Dimitrii, as well as the Polish candidacy of Wladyslaw. They intended to elect a new Czar. Prince Pozharskii established himself in Yaroslavl and gathered forces for a momentous strike.

Ivan Zarutskii and his Cossacks tried desperately to stop the Minin-Pozharskii insurgent movement, but in vain, because in the meantime he had to fight against Jan Chodkiewicz, another able Polish military man, who came to Moscow to rescue the Polish garrison, locked up in the Kremlin and Kitaigorod. Facing Chodkiewicz and demoralized by the Minin-Pozharskii movement, Zarutskii's forces began to disintegrate. His old associate, Prince Trubetskoi, also deserted him and went over with his gentry followers to the Minin-Pozharskii camp. Then, Ivan Zarutskii with the bulk of his armed force, retreated to Kolamna and Riazan, and subsequently to Astrakhan, hoping there in the wide steppes to secure freedom and land for the Cossack people.[18] Although the Cossacks finally took the Kitaigorod and forced the Kremlin to surrender and the Polish attempt to put Wladyslaw or Sigismund on the Muscovite throne was defeated, things were still in turmoil. It was up to Minin and Pozharskii to struggle against the odds and to re-establish order. The election of a new Czar had become the most important business of the day.

Hence, a landed council was convened in January, 1613. The impressive representation included over 700 elected delegates. They were not the appointees of a Czar or the pawns of any candidate for the throne. Several candidates came under consideration: Wladyslaw of Poland, who still was hopeful despite his many disappointments, a Swedish prince, with whom Pozharskii had kept in touch; some members of the Hapsburg dynasty with slim chances; Ivan, the second Pretender's son, acceptable to the masses but not to the nobility, and many hopeful candidates from among the Muscovite nobles, such as Vasilii Golitsin, Dimitrii Pozharskii and Mikhail Romanov.

It was a prevailing thought of the council that the new Czar should be an Orthodox Muscovite. The country had had too much trouble with foreign candidacies and so the notion was discarded. Finally, Mikhail Romanov, Metropolitan Philaret's son, was elected the new Czar on February 7, and proclaimed the Czar on February 21, 1613, after the general opinion of the country's provinces about the candidate was secretly checked. At that time, the landed council had no knowledge of the Czar-elect's whereabouts to be able to offer him the crown. After a short search, he was located in a Kaluga monastery, living there with his mother, who took the veil. At first, as the custom deemed proper, she refused the crown in the name of her minor son. Perhaps she was also terrified by the happenings of the "Time of Troubles" and desired to spare her son from similar misfortunes in the future. Then, on March 14, Mikhail himself accepted the throne and was solemnly crowned in Moscow on July 11, 1613. The fates deemed this to be the end of the "Time of Troubles."

Historians have given various reasons why Mikhail Romanov was elected the new Czar. Kluchevsky has asserted that the sixteen-year-old youngster, Mikhail, was chosen for this dignity because he seemed to the noble grandees and courtiers the easiest candidate to be handled. They wanted the power and looked for a Czar who would give them the opportunity. Experienced men on the throne, such as Godunov and Shuiskii, were hard to manage.[19] Then, Mikhail was related to the Rurik dynasty, being a nephew of Czar Fiodor, the last Rurik on the Muscovite throne. This made him acceptable for the conservative circles of the nobility. He was the son of Metropolitan-Patriarch Philaret Romanov, whose elevation had come from the hands of the two Pretenders, the symbols of the social struggle. Hence, Mikhail was acceptable to the broad masses of the people as well as to the separatist Don-Cossacks. Ivan, son of the second Pseudo-Dimitrii, might have been ideal for the populace but, of course, not for the nobility. Finally, the Romanov family, an old and prominent Muscovite clan, had produced Metropolitan Philaret who played a distinguished role in the recent developments and who suffered, it was assumed, a great deal as a prisoner of the Polish government. This added glamor and fame to the name and might have influenced the landed council considerably in deciding on Mikhail.[20]

Foreign affairs and the eastern expansion.

The era of the "Time of Troubles," as far as Muscovite foreign relations were concerned, was continually under the influence of the Polish push eastward, which seriously threatened Moscow's sovereignty. Sweden posed a similar threat for approximately the same reason. Nevertheless, in spite of the internal turmoil and foreign intervention in its domestic affairs, Muscovy seemed to be strong enough to continue an uninterrupted territorial expansion farther eastward and south-eastward by means of conquest and colonization.[21] Between the year 1584, the death of Ivan the Terrible, and the year 1613, the election of Mikhail Romanov (during the "Time of Troubles") significant progress was achieved by Moscow in extending its rule to Siberia and its political influence over the Caucasus. Bridgeheads were built to the Middle East and Central Asia.

At the time the Livonian war was over, having been brought to a close by a ten-year armistice, Poland-Lithuania was at the height of her political might. Her dynamic and militant ruler, King Stephan Batory, having the approval and the best wishes of the Holy See of Rome, planned an all-out anti-Turk crusade and wanted to draft Muscovy for the project. The project also had to involve the Caucasian lands, Persia and other lands of Asia Minor. But Moscow was a very reluctant partner. Then suddenly the situation changed substantially. In 1586, Batory, Moscow's number-one foe, died. Not only was the plan of an anti-Turk crusade gone, but also the Polish throne remained vacant for a time. Moscow was relieved. Subsequently, in order to get the "Polish threat" under control, Czar Fiodor's candidacy for the Polish throne was advanced by Moscow's court but with no success. Soon the situation worsened. Prince Sigismund, son of John III, King of Sweden, was elected the new King of Poland. Historically, Moscow had always feared the possibility of a political union between Sweden and Poland-Lithuania. Now the fateful union, so it seemed in 1592, was becoming a reality: King Sigismund of Poland was about to ascend the Swedish throne, following his father's death. Nevertheless, King Sigismund, an ardent Catholic, soon incurred the displeasure of the Protestant Swedes and was forced to give up the Swedish crown. His ambitions were limited to the Polish throne. Moscow felt a little safer once again.

Even before Sigismund's ascent to the Polish throne, a new fifteen-year armistice between Muscovy and Poland was negotiated, confirmed by the new King some four years later. Peace, however, did not last long. Along with the escapades of the first and second Pretender and the candidacy of Prince Wladyslaw, Sigismund's son, for the Muscovite throne championed by Shuiskii, Golitsin and other *boyars* as early as 1605, Polish-Muscovite relations became hopelessly snarled. This finally led to the outbreak of a new war between these two nations. In 1609, Sigismund's armed forces invaded Muscovite territory and besieged the city of Smolensk. King Sigismund himself reached for Moscow's throne. Eventually, in 1612, the last Polish strongholds in Moscow, the Kremlin and Kitaigorod, were taken by the Don Cossacks and the Muscovite adventure of the Polish goverment collapsed. In 1613, however, Wladyslaw's candidacy for the Muscovite crown was advanced once more in the landed council, but unsuccessfully. Yet, the Polish court could not remain reconciled with the fact of Mikhail Romanov's election as the new Czar.[22] Actually a permanent state of war continued between the two countries, in 1618 erupting into a shooting war, concluded by another armistice at Duelino near the end of the same year.

The conflict with Sweden was relatively permanent as well. Boris Godunov, as the "Lord-Protector" of Muscovy in Czar Fiodor's time, marched victorious against Sweden and recovered a portion of the territories on the shore of the Gulf of Finland, including the towns of Ivangorod, Iam, Orieshok and Korela with the exception of Narva. Although the annexation of that territory partially compensated Moscow for the losses of the Livonian war, yet its "window to Europe" remained closed to the Muscovites for some 125 years. Nevertheless, during the short and unfortunate rule of Czar Vasilii Shuiskii, Muscovite-Swedish relations grew friendlier. The Swedish troops even helped Shuiskii in his struggle against the second Pretender, for the price of returning to Sweden the districts of Ivangorod, Iam, Orieshok and Korela. A while later, however, after the Muscovite crown was offered to Wladyslaw of Poland, Sweden declared war on Muscovy for two main reasons: (1) because Muscovy had allied herself with Poland, Sweden's archenemy and (2) because the preference shown to Wladyslaw meant ignoring the candidacy of Swedish Prince Philip to the Muscovite throne. Sometime later, Novgorod the Great separated itself from Muscovy and accepted Sweden's suzerainty. The hostilities between Muscovy and Sweden actually lasted until 1617.

The perennial problem in Moscow's foreign policies was the relations with the Crimean Tartars. Although the Tartar raids upon the Muscovite lands became less frequent and less menacing, the Tartars still managed to harass the suburbs of Moscow in 1591. In 1592, they invaded and plundered Tula and Riazan. In order to stop these destructive Tartar raids for booty, the Muscovite government constructed along the country's southeastern frontiers new forts and towns and fortified the old settlements, such as Voronizh and Kursk in 1586, Bielgorod and Oskol in 1593, Valuiki in 1600, and a number of others. The Muscovites penetrated deeper into the Don-Volga steppe regions and proceeded with a policy of gradual colonization. The forts and towns were built there to make Moscow's mastery in those regions undisputed. Such iron-handed mastery was the cause of subsequent and at times violent, insurrections of the Don-Cossacks. Saratov was built between 1586 and 1589, Samara in 1586, several others followed. It was of utmost importance for the Muscovite state to secure unobstructed commercial navigation on the Volga River and toward the Caspian Sea. Thus the Caucasian lands, the Middle East and Central Asia, could be more easily controlled and eventually brought within the Muscovite sphere of political domination. The Don-Volga steppes, which in the sixteenth century were still sparcely inhabited, were progressively settled under Muscovite rule in the next century.

In 1586, the town of Ufa was built at the foot of the Ural mountains to strengthen Muscovite rule over Bashkiria. Nevertheless, during the "Time of Troubles," the Bashkirians rose several times against Moscow's oppression. Politically troubled and militarily weakened, Muscovy still prevailed over the primitive Bashkirians. The most essential move for Moscow's government to make at that time, with respect to future Muscovite territorial expansion in the east, was the reconquest of Western Siberia. After the initial success of Yermak's expedition there, Muscovite rule in Western Siberia was weakened by the local uprisings and bloody skirmishes of people seeking their own independence. Yermak himself perished during one encounter with the native tribes in 1585. Yet, Boris Godunov was determined to make Muscovite mastery over Siberia a permanent one. The native Tartars were finally subjugated and the towns of Tiumen and Tobolsk established, where territorial administration was centered and troops garrisoned as the stronghold of Moscow's power.

Once Western Siberia was tamed, the Muscovites began to penetrate southern and eastern Siberian regions. Numerous uprisings of the native Ostiaks and Voguls failed to cut down the speed of the Muscovite expansion eastward. Surprisingly, despite the torments of many internal and external misfortunes during the "Time of Troubles," the Muscovite people and government still had the energy and power to proceed with conquests and annexations. Between 1584 and 1613 all of the upper Ob and the lower Yenisei River regions were, for all practical purposes, completely under Moscow's supremacy. In 1604, the city of Tomsk was founded as the symbol of that supremacy. Lyashchenko writes that "by the time the first Romanovs came to the throne, the entire valley of the Yenisei was annexed and a number of fortified towns established."[23]

The Muscovite Russians proved to be outstanding empire builders, in this respect using a technique all their own. The process of conquest usually began with tradesmen, trappers and hunters exploring and penetrating the new territories farther and farther east. Then, the semi-private and para-military expeditions of Cossacks and other adventurers took possession of these territories by arms. In the third stage of the annexation process, Moscow sent its own military force there followed by its officials who imposed the *yasak* or tribute upon the natives as evidence of their subjugation. In the final phase, fortified garrisons were established, where troops were stationed and territorial administration set up and from which subsequently further penetration into ever more distant regions was sponsored until finally absorbed into the Muscovite Czardom. Briberies, gifts, promises, alcohol, intimidation, violence and outright extermination of the native chieftains and leaders were the "political" devices by which Muscovite conquest proceeded uninterruptedly and successfully.[24]

Muscovite tradesmen and industrialists, such as Stroganov, and later, Shelekhov, were looking in those distant regions for fur, hides, walrus oil, gold and silver. The natives of Eastern Siberia were themselves operating the gold and silver mines, which were soon taken away from them after the new masters established their rule. The economic motives of the tradesmen and industrialists not only preceded but also inspired all the more the subsequent official expansionist moves of the Muscovite government.[25] The rapid expansion of Muscovite Czardom toward the east, soon to reach the littorals of the Pacific Ocean, made farming an economic necessity in the newly acquired territories. The maintenance of troops and administration officials as well as the attempt to develop commerce and industry by means of Muscovite colonization and immigration required a steady supply of grain and other foods in these Asiatic regions. Shipments from European areas, sometimes beset by famines, were enormously difficult to maintain on a continuous basis. Hence, the Muscovite government began to sponsor agricultural setlements on vast governmental land properties (royal fields). The idle, except those under bondage and tax payment obligations, were encouraged to leave for Siberia. They were given land for their own use and their only duty was cultivating certain "royal fields" along with their own plots.[26]

At the same time Muscovite penetration was going in other directions with Astrakhan as the starting point. From Astrakhan, Muscovites spread their political and business influence toward Sub-Caucasia and the Caucasus Mountains and into Central Asia with rather modest success at first. In the North-Caucasian steppes, there lived the Nogay Tartars, vassals of the Turks, very antagonistic to Moscow. Also hostile toward Moscow were various tribes along the littorals of the Caspian Sea and the Kuma River for they also recognized Turkish suzerainty. Moscow nevertheless succeeded in developing friendlier relations with the Caucasian tribe of Kabarda, who wanted the Czar's protection precisely against the Nogai Tartars and the hordes living around the Caspian Sea. Ivan IV, the Dread, had already accepted the Kabarda as vassal of Muscovite Czardom and even married a Kabardian princess. The supremacy over the Kabarda enabled Moscow soon to penetrate into Georgia (or Gruzia) where it extended its influence over the feudal "kingdom" of Kakhetia.

Georgia had atracted the political attention of Moscow long ago. She had once been a great trading center between the West and the East. However, the discovery of the sea route from Europe to India and then the discovery of America had shifted trading routes and arteries away from Georgia. Thus the economic and the political power of Georgia declined, her political structure disintegrated into several feudal entities, and she became the victim of unending harassments by Persia, Turkey and various neighbor tribes. Moscow saw in Georgia the very avenue of its future expansion in the Near East. Soon, the Kingdom of Kakhetia, one of the Georgian feudal territories, asked Moscow for protection against the Persians and Turks, who were threatening its political independence. In 1586, a "cross-kissing" agreement was concluded between Alexander III, King of Kakhetia, and Fiodor, Czar of Muscovy, by which Moscow promised to protect the Kingdom against all external enemies, while Kakhetia became Muscovy's vassal state.[27] Although the arrangement had little if any practical value, still the later Czars renewed the agreement for some time which eventually led to the complete absorption of Georgia.

At first, Muscovy gained little in her endeavor to penetrate Central Asia, where several Khanates had been established, following the disintegration of Tamerlane's empire. Subsequently three of those Khanates, Khiva, Bukhara and Kokand, became strong political organisms in the area. The population of Central Asia was rather heterogeneous in origin and included the Turkmans, Uzbecks, Kazakhs, Tadzik, Kara-Kolpaks and others. All those people lived in various stages of economic development, ranging from hunting, trapping, cattle raising and fishing to farming and trading. Various Uzbeck dynasties ruled the Khanates of Khiva, Bukhara and Kokand. The northern parts of Central Asia were populated by the Kalmyks and Kazakhs, the latter being an ethnic branch of the Uzbecks. Moscow penetrated as far as the Ural River in the sixteenth century and there erected the township of Yaitskii-Gorodok. Nevertheless, the political power of the three Khanates of Khiva, Bukhara and Kokand, made any immediate Muscovite political gains in Central Asia quite impossible. By way of Astrakhan and the Caspian Sea, however, Muscovy succeeded in developing trading activities of considerable importance, meanwhile having postponed the political conquest.[28]

Evaluation

The era of Ivan, the Terrible or Dread, and the "Time of Troubles" have proven the tremendous vitality of the Muscovite people, who withstood the hardships, shocks and misfortunes of the period. Their society did not break down but soon recovered and resumed the structuring of its empire. The prolonged social ferment of the struggle between the conservatism of upper classes and the revolutionary nature of the lower strata brought upheavals, anarchy and bloodshed that marked the "Time of Troubles." At the end, law and order prevailed over chaos and the Muscovite-Russian patriotism superseded the materialist class interests. At the end, autocracy and centralism won the battle against democracy and decentralization. The *boyar* aristocracy, which was largely responsible for the upheavals, eventually lost a great deal of its old privileges, along with the classes of the "proletariat" such as the Cossacks and serfs, who did not gain personal freedom and land ownership.

Thus, the triumph of traditional Muscovite absolutism came at the culmination of a prolonged socio-political crisis. The defeat of the Don-Cossacks, who withdrew to the steppes, and the suppression of the Mordovian and Bashkirian uprisings, along with the taming of Siberia only proved the vitality of the Muscovite-Russian imperialist drive. Imperialism prevailed over the ethnic separatism and political particularism of the non-Muscovite peoples and made them victims of a growing empire. If those ethnic groups could not free themselves from the chains of the Muscovite oppression during the "Time of Troubles," when the Muscovite Czardom was convulsed with serious internal upheavals threatening a disintegration of the state and society, what chance would such groups have later on when the Czardom was consolidated in complete power. The ability of the Muscovite state to expand, conquer and annex during the "Time of Troubles" evidenced a rare strength even on the verge of a collapse, despite grave internal and external trials.[29] This ability should convince the greatest sceptics of the fact that Muscovy could overcome troubles only to emerge again greater in power.

On the other hand, the "Time of Troubles" was ominous in other respects. It was the time of an abortive social revolution and a victory for reaction. The aspiration for social changes and improvement could not be suppressed for all time. Hence, the outcome of the "Time of Troubles" had rooted within itself the germs of new social upheavals, revolts, misfortunes, and bloodshed. New ethnically and nationally motivated insurrections will try to overcome the forces of the reactionary Czarist oppression.

The rebellions of Bulavin, Riazin, Pugachov and numerous other insurgents seemed to be endless. The Decembrists, the Nihilists, the Anarchists, the Socialists and Communists, all in their time have attempted to destroy the Muscovite- Russian Czardom. The fall of that Empire some 300 years later through numerous non-Russian nationalities who declared their political sovereignties and built their own national states, came clearly as the consequence of an inability by Muscovy to cope with her social and national problems even as early as the "Time of Troubles." Then, however, the new Soviet imperialist reaction was set in motion to save the Russian empire anew.

CHAPTER THIRTEEN

THE WAY OF LIFE IN SIXTEENTH CENTURY MUSCOVY

Autocracy

Though not written but based on tradition and practical application, the existing Muscovite state constitution experienced some substantial modifications during the reign of Ivan IV and the "Time of Troubles." Some of those modifications such as those introduced by Ivan along the line of strengthening the autocracy, have been permanently built into the political life of Muscovy, while others, such as those initiated by the revolutionary turmoils of the years of the Troubles, did not leave any lasting imprint on the structure of the state or society. These two diametrically different periods of the Muscovite history also exhibited opposite tendencies in respect to constitutional changes.

Ivan's exceedingly long rule represented a further and a most definite trend towards an intensification and perfection of the constitutional principle of an hereditary, absolutist, all-comprehensive and limitless Muscovite autocracy, the foundations of which were already established. Its divine origin was made not only a matter of political doctrine but also almost a matter of religious beliefs. In order to strengthen the principle of autocracy of a divine origin, Ivan permanently assumed the title of the Czar, which previously was used only loosely and inconsistently by his predecessors. He insisted on his solemn coronation in the church in this way to stress the godly nature of his Czarist office, the solemn function that later on became a permanent institution initiating the reign of every new Muscovite or Russian sovereign.

The thought of this exalted view of a divine and absolute power of the Muscovite Czar over the state and the Orthodox Church might have been well impressed upon the mind of the young ruler by Metropolitan Makarii. Yet, it was not important who originated the idea. It was important that the constitutional developments were proceeding in this particular direction. Also assuming the so-called Kurbskii-Ivan correspondence had been a fabricated historical fraud does not change the situation. Perhaps Valdenberg's conclusion of Ivan IV deserving a prominent place among the medieval Muscovite political thinkers has been completely erroneous in view of the new findings, according to which the celebrated correspondence between Kurbskii and Ivan never existed.[1] Yet, Ivan the Dread thought and acted along the trend of ideas expressed in those assumed "letters" of his to Kurbskii.

He thought of himself as a representative of God on earth without limits to his divine authority. Neither any worldly nor ecclesiastic institution, landed or *boyar* council or the Orthodox Church, could put any checks upon his autocratic authority. In fact, Ivan thought that he had, as God's representative, full authority over the life and death of all his subjects. He certainly believed and by his actions impressed upon his contemporaries that "The beginning of our autocracy is of St. Vladimir. We were born and nurtured in the office of Czar, and do possess it, and have not ravished what is not our own. From the first the Russian autocrats have been the lords of their own dominions and not the *boyar* aristocrats.... Whereof should a man be named *samoderzhavets* if he himself shall not govern?.... With zeal I do ever strive to lead men toward truth and toward the light, that they may confess the One True God, as glorified in the Trinity, and, through the grace granted unto me as Czar, may cease from those feuds and perverse customs of living with which kingdoms are undone. If subjects submit not themselves unto their ruler, never shall strife cease in the land.... Let the Czar be a terror, not unto doers of good, but unto doers of evil. Wouldst thou not fear his power, then do thou good; wouldst thou fear him, then do thou evil; for the Czar beareth not the sword of cruelty, but for the punishment of wicked men and the heartening of the righteous.... We are free to reward our slaves, even as we are free also to punish them."[2]

The *oprichnina* institution indicated distinctly what was Ivan's interpretation of his autocratic power to reward or to punish. A mere resistance to any of his plans he considered a severely punishable crime, no matter that in the case of *oprichnina* the *boyars* only attempted to protect their ancient rights. Ivan, the autocrat, had other ideas in mind, and every subject had to submit no matter what. No doubt, the already established doctrine of Moscow as a "Third Rome" and a "Second Jerusalem" considerably contributed to Ivan's conviction about his infinite autocratic authority by adding to it a mystical and religious element. Any attempt to question or resist Ivan's all-comprehensive power was considered not only treason but also a mortal sin before God as well. Ivan called the landed council or *zemskii sobor* to convene. It was not, however, any manifestation of limiting the Czar's authority in any way. It was rather a politically motivated move during the first period of his reign to marshal the nobility around his throne by graciously giving the *boyars* the privilege to council and advise the sovereign, while the ultimate decision making was always his own.

Not only did Ivan the Terrible believe in that divine, all-comprehensive, boundless and hereditary autocracy of the Muscovite Czar, but many leading state and church men of Muscovy shared that belief for decades. Having been impressed upon the minds of the contemporaries, the autocratic ideology deeply affected the constitution of the Muscovite state and left an indelible imprint upon its future, although during the "Time of Troubles" some attempts were undertaken to limit that all-comprehensiveness of the autocracy.

During Fiodor's reign the Czar's authority was limited *de facto* because of his state of mind and illness. Yet *de jure* nothing was changed in the content of the high office of the autocrat, *samoderzhavets*. No doubt that Godunov, very early having had his eye on the throne for himself, tried to hold high the authority of the Czar. His own power as a "lieutenant of the empire" or a "lord-protector of Muscovy" was also a derivative of the fullness of the autocracy. Only by enhancing the prestige of the Czar could he hope to establish his office as being only a temporary state agency. He surrounded his office with an elaborate etiquette and dealt firmly with his adversaries and opponents in order to strengthen his position at the court. This was to lead him to the throne of which he had the identical concept as Ivan the Dread.

A *de jure* limitation of the Czarist authority came as a result of the convocation of the landed council to elect Boris Godunov the new Czar after Fiodor's death. The hereditary principle was interrupted, since there was no direct descendant of the Rurik house to assume the throne. Hence, the landed council was acknowledged as a supreme agency to elect a new Czar, in this way having acquired additional authority in the state. Godunov, as was pointed out, refused to accept the crown without the council's approval. It was a first step in placing the landed council constitutionally above the throne. If that trend had continued, the next prerogative of the council might have been the right to dethrone an unworthy sovereign. From that point on, after having handed down the crown to Boris Godunov, the landed council for a while continued to have an important place in the constitution of the Muscovite state. Later on it granted autocratic authority to Wladyslaw of Poland, and finally, to Mikhail Romanov. It was the council's historical mission to end the constitutional crisis on the verge of sixteenth century Muscovy and ultimately to uphold the autocracy for the future.

The cases of the Pseudo-Dimitriis introduced a new twist into the constitutional process of the Muscovite state. Though both Pretenders claimed their hereditary rights to mount the throne of Muscovy as direct descendants of the Rurik house, only the support of the populace, led by a few known nobles, could enable their fraudulent claims to survive and secure for them the office of Czar. Hence, the Muscovite mob, and in particular the mob of the city of Moscow, in this way acquired a constitutional chance to become instrumental in making Czars. (A very dangerous constitutional precedent for the orderly political development of a society was there in making). The proclamation of Vasilii Shuiskii, a new Czar followed approximately the same pattern. In that case also the hereditary right to the throne was stressed. Shuiskii was proclaimed the Czar by virtue of his being a member of a senior branch of the Rurik dynasty. Because of that, the landed council was left out entirely as superfluous, but the Muscovite populace added its authority to decide the issue of the succession to the throne.

Hence, the role of the Muscovite populace and nobility was increasing in the process of shaping up the office of the Czar during the "Time of Troubles." but the content of the autocratic authority was not essentially changed. All three of them, the two Pretenders and Shuiskii, enjoyed the fullness of absolute power, yet *de facto* only, because of the brevity of their rules allowed none of them really to establish himself as a true autocrat. Shuiskii's oath at the time of taking over the throne was certainly a political maneuver to gain an acceptance among the nobles, tired of the terror used by Ivan and Boris. This in no way indicated any of his intentions to abdicate any of his prerogatives as an absolute ruler. He called himself an "autocrat of all Russia." Although Shuiskii said, when taking the oath: "I do kiss the cross unto all the land, in token that ill shall unto no man be done without the council," yet in fact it meant his intention to play the *boyar duma* against the landed council in this way to attempt to rid himself of the tutelage and to secure for himself full autocratic power. It meant, however, granting to the landed council judicial authority over the major crimes, committed, of course, by the nobles.[3] It must be kept in mind that Shuiskii did not call upon the landed council to grant him the crown. He just ignored it and based his bid on hereditary right. By doing so, he actually raised the prestige of the *boyar duma*. All three "Czars" walked on a "tightrope" of their hereditary claims, though fraudulent in the case of Pseudo-Dimitriis, and moved between the "revolutionary" mob rule and the "conservative" *boyar* power. The situation produced a *de facto* limitation of their autocratic authority.

The election of Wladislaw of Poland to the Muscovite throne reversed the trend. Wladislaw had no hereditary rights to claim the Muscovite throne. Therefore, in order to establish him as a Czar and rightful autocrat, once again the authority of the landed council had to be called upon. The council, which convened in the summer of 1610 to elect Wladislaw, was not as formally assembled as before, yet, it did not matter. The reality was that only the landed council was recognized as a proper body to choose the ruler in case of the absence of a direct heir to the throne. The constitutional principle was apparent there. Wladyslaw's election however, introduced another important constitutional change. He certainly accepted some limitations of his future autocratic rule. He directly or indirectly promised by two subsequent agreements, one in Tushino in February and another in Moscow in August, 1610, to safeguard the inviolable rights of the Orthodox Church and to protect the ancient Muscovite institutions — in particular the rights of the nobles. The whole instance proved soon to be an abortive one because of the unreasonable tactics of King Sigismund of Poland. Soon, relying upon the authority of the landed council, Mikhail Romanov was made the new Czar, though his blood relationship with the house of Rurik was not left out of consideration.

Electing Mikhail Romanov was not connected or accompanied by any attempts either of the landed council or the *boyar duma* to limit the powers of autocracy. Of course, all concerned hoped that some *de facto* limitations would develop. Because of Mikhail's young age, he would be easily influenced. Yet, as Florinsky said, "The first Romanov ascended the steps of the throne of Ivan the Dread formally clothed with all the traditional and unlimited powers of Muscovite absolutism."[4]

General Government

A combination of autocracy with a great deal of regional and local self-government was a particular feature of sixteenth century Muscovite absolutism, while at the same time the self-governning agencies seemed to be the arm of the central government of the autocratic state. Furthermore, Muscovite absolutism afforded to introduce into the state machine during the earlier part of the century, under Ivan's rule, several worthwhile reforms in order to make that machine work administratively more efficiently and become socially more just. In the latter part of the sixteenth century, revolutionary movements attempted to carry on the reforms to an extreme. The earlier, "evolutionary" reforms of Ivan the Dread had been inspired by the writings of Ivan Peresvietov and the personal influence of the priest Sylvester, Aleksei Adashev and Prince Andrei Kurbskii.[5]

Because of its autocratic structure, the legislative, administrative and judicial powers in the Muscovite state of the sixteenth century were fully concentrated in the hands of the Czar. He, of course, at his will could have shared them with various government agencies, such as the inner or selected council, *izbrannaia rada*, which existed for about 12 years from 1543 to 1555, the traditional *boyar duma* or council, or finally, with the landed or territorial council, *zemskii sobor*, which was initiated by Ivan and met a few times during the sixteenth century. The new Code of Laws, *Sudebnik* of 1550 hinted in its article 98 on the right of the *boyar* council to be able to initiate some new legislation, which might have represented a certain limitation of the Czar's autocratic power as being the only source of law making. In fact, however, most historians agree that this "liberal" provision in the Code had no practical meaning whatsoever, and this was fully proven by the subsequent despotic and autocratic actions of the sovereign. Moreover, the new Code of Laws of 1550 was at Ivan's whim submitted for approval to the Church council, the so-called *Stoglav*, the ecclesiastic institution which was supposed to deal with Church matters only and actually having no immediate connection with state affairs. Yet, Ivan, the autocrat, wished to do so and he did. Apparently he meant in this way to add more prestige to the new Code, replacing or supplementing the old and long-accepted one from 1497.

By his legislative authority and in traditional consultation with the *boyars* (*boyar* council), Ivan adopted a new Code of Laws, the *Sudebnik* during the earlier period of his reign. He introduced several reforms of general administration, financial affairs, military matters and judiciary. The new Code of Laws, aside from its attempt to streamline the judicial and administrative procedures, also introduced some new provisions, related to the rights and responsibilities of landownership, and in particular with respect to the landownership in service tenure, *pomestie,* and hereditary ownership, *votchina,* to the state. Ivan also ordered the landed council to convene and then the Church council, *Stoglav,* to adopt some measures to improve the conditions in the Orthodox Church. Then, willfully and because of his mania of persecution, he introduced the terror of the *oprichnina,* the separate domain. During the "Time of Troubles," because of the social and political upheavals, the legislative and reform activity of the short-lasting sovereigns were not so fruitful.

The *boyar duma* or council was the oldest and the most traditional advisory governing body of the Czar, which for centuries was continuing to deal with pending legislation, a wide range of administrative matters, such as supervising the central administrative offices or departments, *prikazi,* making rulings in certain serious cases of crimes and offenses. Whenever the Czar wished the council to act or deal with any legislative matters or otherwise, he addressed it by a proclamation, *ukaz,* explaining the issue. Usually, every new piece of legislation or ruling was preceded by an unchangeable and traditional formula: "Thus hath the Czar commanded and the *boyars* ordained." The Code of Laws of 1550 certainly upheld that old advisory power of the council. At times its authority seemed at least theoretically strengthened, as happened under Vasilii Shuiskii who assumedly promised not to punish any noble suspected of a crime without consulting the *duma.* Historians largely agree that Shuiskii's promise actually had no real meaning.

Originally a *boyar* agency, the council expanded its membership with the progress of time and its membership became quite heterogeneous. There were in the *duma* first of all various *boyar* groups represented — the landed grandees and the minor *boyar* sons, heads of the central government departments or offices, upper level state functionaries, top level clerks, secretaries and other people, some of them even of a modest social background or origin. Hence, under Ivan the Dread and later on, the *boyar* council had a double-natured composition, it was in part aristocratic and in part bureaucratic. It included, in particular, the heads of the central government departments or offices, the so-called *prikazi* of the sixteenth century, some of them known as *puti* before that. Their particular responsibility was to supervise the functioning of those departments. The *boyar* council also had, therefore, an administrative jurisdiction in the name of the Czar, being to some extent an executive agency. Some top level problems of general administration, financial, military and judicial matters were discussed and decided there. It was a kind of a court or a court of appeals for certain major criminal offenses, as aforementioned.

Various central government agencies, departments or offices, the so-called *prikazi*, the supervision of which was in the jurisdiction of the *boyar* council, developed gradually until at one point there were more than thirty of them. Perhaps they could be, though distantly, compared with the present-day ministries. Their origin was highly heterogeneous. Some of them developed from the old departments, the *puti,* others were created for handling special problems arising with the development of the Muscovite empire, such as the Kazan and Siberian departments, and still others represented the over-all official attempt to centralize certain government functions. There were the following leading central government departments or offices, *prikazi*: the department or office of ambassadors, *posolskii prikazi;* the military office, *rozriadnii prikaz;* the office of landownership, *pomiestnii prikaz;* the department for slave affairs, *kholopii prikaz;* the office of felonies, *razboinii prikaz;*

the office of finances, *prikaz bolshavo prikhoda;* the department of supplications, *chelobitnii prikaz;* the book-printing office, *knigopechatnii prikaz;* the department of welfare, *prikaz stroienia bogadielen;* and various others attempting to attend numerous administrative functions of the growing state.[6]

The *boyar* council underwent certain evolutionary changes. At first, as mentioned, it was strictly a *boyar* class representation. Then it expanded to include other social elements. At times it was too large and too bulky a body and could not meet every day to advise the Czar or to attend to other business. Especially the landed grandees and high provincial or regional officers from the distant parts of the state were frequently absent from *duma's* daily meetings at sunrise. Hence, as in the previous periods of the Muscovite political history, some smaller, select or inner *boyar* bodies were assisting the duke or grand duke with its advice. During the early period of Ivan the Terrible's rule, an inner, select council, *izbrannaia rada,* took over many responsibilities of the traditional *boyar duma.* Yet, the select council was definitely not a *boyar* representation. This made it a novelty. The membership of the select council was determined by the Czar with the advice of his most trusted lieutenants. During its approximately 12 years of existence it was greatly influenced by the priest, Sylvester, who also was a successful businessman, by Aleksei Adashev, who originally was Ivan's valet and later on his trusted secretary or chancellor, by the head of the supplications department, Metropolitan Makarii; and by Prince Andrei Kurbskii. For that relatively short time, the selected council had a tremendously important impact on state affairs, and was responsible for most of the positive state measures of that era.

Along with the relatively new state departments and offices, there also still existed in the central administration the remnants of the old court offices, such as those of the court *boyar,* who managed the Czar's court, the horse *boyar,* who managed the stables, commissioned *boyars,* who collectively managed some aspects of the court and central administration, the *chashniks,* the *stolnkis,* the *lovchis,* and some other minor officials. On the whole, however, the separation of the reign's strictly "private" court affairs from those strictly "state" affairs was successfully progressing. Some of those court officials also joined the *boyar* council and select council, if the Czar so ordered.

Another constitutional novelty, introduced by Czar Ivan, was the so-called landed or territorial council, *zemskii sobor*.[7] Ivan most probably wanted to obtain a broad, cross country opinion about the needs of the land and about the possible ways to cope with those needs. In the course of time, the composition, the membership and the competence of the landed council was changing, but over-all it was evolving according to the following pattern: the members of the landed council were not elected by different lands or provinces but appointed by the Czar or Czar's agents. Yet, the membership was selected in such a way as to give every territory and various social groups, but not the serfs and slaves, a fair representation according to sixteenth century standards. The council embodied first of all the *Holy Synod* of the Orthodox Church, the boyar *duma*, the courtiers or *dvorianie*, the top officials, functionaries, and clerks of the state central administration, top military commanders, and representatives of trade and commerce, at times called the guests, *gosti*. Although the membership of the landed council were the government appointees, even those representing trade and commerce, it was still considered by the standards of the sixteenth century to be a fair, representative and popular assembly, as Kluchevsky said: "... which had authority to decide the fate of the nation."[8] There were in the council the representatives of all ends and all top strata of society and government of contemporary Muscovy; a very broad basis of consultation which could give the Czar reliable advice.

Ivan, when calling the assembly to convene in 1550 or 1556, intended to impose upon it the responsibility of deliberating the matters of administration, finances, judiciary and needed reforms from a nation-wide point of view. It was supposed to be simply an extension of the legislative power of the central government system. The council was by no means a representation of local or regional interests; not a body to resist the centralizing tendencies of Moscow, but an agency to deliberate, to arrive at certain conclusions and to make recommendations to be followed eventually by the government in the interest of the state. The official record of the landed council, the *prigavornaia gramota*, normally gave information about the membership, composition, recommendations and other details of the council's deliberations.

It is a common belief of historians that the first landed council convened in 1550, while Platonov insisted on the basis of his studies that the first one convened in 1556. Nevertheless, in 1556, the council's jurisdiction included in its deliberations the problems of Muscovite foreign policies. The Czar ordered it to discuss the Livonian war. He apparently wanted to get the council's backing on the controversial matter, which did cause some discord between the Czar and his initially trusted associates of selected council at an earlier date. The landed council supported by a prevailing majority a continuation of that doubtful military struggle in order to establish the Muscovite sovereignty over the Livonian "window to Europe." The council was an agency in this particular case to test the feelings, on the one hand, and to be used by the Czar as a rubber stamp for his political moves, on the other.

During the "Time of Troubles," the landed council widened its scope of jurisdiction by virtue of electing the new Czars, as was pointed out in the previous section of this discourse. It became somewhat a complementary electoral agency to supplement the traditional hereditary principle of succession to the throne in the Muscovite state whenever a direct heir to the throne was not available.

The regional and local authority in Muscovy was traditionally exercised by Czar's lieutenants or governors and their assistants. They all were the appointees of the central government, endowed with a compound, administrative, fiscal and judicial authority, and compensated by the notorious feed-themselves, *kormlenie*, system. The *kormlenie* system was badly abused by the office holders, mostly recruited from the *boyar* class, because of the selfish profit motives. Hence, a reform of the country's regional administration was needed. There was still another reason for the need of reforms. As pointed out above, the Muscovite government of the sixteenth century was a specific combination of autocratic centralism and local self-government. While the latter was quite chaotically structured, the principle of self-government was broadly applied to the territorial units and social groups, divided and subdivided in numerous independent self-governing elements. They developed and evolved over the decades in a very unsystematic way. For a long time all these self-governing rural, urban, class and sub-group communities, such as towns, townships, boroughs, villages and sub-villages, were not integrated or interdependent administratively or coordinated or supervised by certain intermediate level authorities. They all were rather directly responsible to various central *prikazi* according to their specific self-governing character.

Ivan initiated very early an attempt to streamline the regional and local administration for the purpose of more efficient government revenue collection, elimination of abuse of power by the local officials and safeguarding the people's interest. It was done on a small scale betwenn 1539 and 1541 along the line of widening local self-government. Several new fiscal-police-judicial, territorial units, *guba*, were established, headed by officials elected from among the landholders of the given *guba* region. Then, the *guba*, self-government arrangements were extended and the Code of Laws, *Sudebnik*, of 1550 granted to it broad authority and limiting the jurisdiction of the traditional appointees of the Moscow center, the *namiestniki*, the *volosteli* and their assistants.

In 1555, a sweeping landed or territorial reform was introduced. The new regions, called lands, the *zemstva*, were run by elected officials, vested with fiscal, police and judicial powers, having replaced the old appointees in the rural and urban communities. The traditional "feeding system," the *kormlienie*, was theoretically abolished and collection of all revised and consolidated taxes was made the responsibility of the elected land officials. Though the *zemstvo* reform represented a victory and the extension of the self-governing principle, it still had a serious loophole, since the elected officials were usually drawn from the *boyar* class, and so the opportunity of exploiting the socially and economically weaker was left wide open for the nobles. Individual lands were headed by the land elders, the *zemskii starosti*, the administratively divided, though not very systematically, into the regions, called the *uiezdi*, in turn headed by the regional elders, the *uiezdnii starosti*. Hence, the landed reform attempted on a self-governing basis to consolidate and to coordinate the regional and territorial government under some common authority of an intermediate level. Unfortunately, the original document, introducing the so-called *zemshchina* reform, was lost and today it is rather hard to reconstruct the full meaning of the act. Yet, because the local and regional, though elected, officials performed their functions in the name of the Czar and for the central government, the necessary connection between the principles of autocratic centralism and that of territorial self-government was preserved. It must be mentioned here again that, during the latter part of his reign, Ivan the Dread introduced the *oprichnina* administration of his special domains, and was progressively exempting numerous regions of the vast empire from the regular landed, *zemshchina*, administration and subjecting them to the *oprichnina* system. Consequently, for a number of years until the *oprichnina* police system went out of existence, the Muscovite state remained under a dual administrative structure.[9]

Finances, Judiciary and Military

The Muscovite empire continued to grow, hence its financial affairs were widely expanding to enable the maintenance of the huge state machine. Maintaining the expanding royal court, the general, central and local, administrations, the judicial and police protection, and the military forces to defend the country and to promote its imperial and imperialist expansion, were the main financial costs of running the government, and they were continually rising and getting more and more complex.

These were the main elements of the Muscovite public expenditures.

The ruling Orthodox Church was financed largely by means of its huge landholdings and numerous donations. The educational process, which was largely the Church's responsibility, was badly neglected. The main sources of public revenue to cover those growing expenditures were constituted by the vast state land possessions, which were either exploited by the state manorial enterprises, or leased or given in service tenure, *pomestie,* to the nobles in exchange for services, administrative, military and otherwise, to be rendered, the feeding or feed-themselves system, the *kormlienie,* and various other direct and indirect taxes, such as excises, tolls and duties. Along with the state manorial enterprises, the fisc or treasury received some income from its monopoly on salt, saltpetre, fisheries, and other similar sources. The decree of 1556 attempted to regulate the landholding in service tenure, the *pomestie,* in particular, the rights and duties of the landholders, toward streamlining the administration and military services. The feeding or *kormlienie* was the traditional, but an inefficient, outdated and highly abused source of public revenue to cover the costs of general administration and its specialized branches, such as judiciary and police protection. As in the previous century, appointed officials, governors and lieutenants, the *namiestmiki* and *volosteli,* in the urban and rural regions, and numerous other appointees and assistants, who were in charge of various state administrative functions, along with collecting taxes, court fees and charges, and penalties for committing crimes or trespassing the law, were allowed to retain a portion of those collections for themselves as the compensation for the services rendered. The privilege was transferred to them from the old *kormlienie* prerogative, in the past enjoyed only by the sovereign prince, duke or Grand Duke.

Having been backed by tradition and the authority of the state, those officials were abusing their power and their privilege to feed themselves out of the state collections by at times imposing unbearable financial or material burdens upon the population and, of course, often cheating the state treasury, the *prikaz bolshavo prikhoda,* of its lawful revenue or income. The major fault of the "feeding" system developed from the distortion of its basic philosophy, Kliuchevsky concluded. Actually the emphasis in the "feeding" system was supposed to be placed on services to be rendered by those state appointees, the compensation by the *kormlienie* being only the secondary and resultant aspect. Yet practically, the officials and appointees made the *kormlienie,* the "feeding," their end purpose, while the services were considered a nuisance and were rendered rather poorly. Still during the sixteenth century, some of those officials continued to undertake annual touring across their districts or provinces to collect the "feeding," as the princes did in the old times, while selfishness and self-interest was over-riding the public interest of serving the Tsar and the country's welfare.

The above abuses of the "feeding" system by the appointees of the government of any level of authority could not be checked or prevented as long as they were in office. Thereafter upon the complaints, the reappointment could be denied or even some restitution demanded by way of court proceedings. Very early during Ivan's reign an attempt was made to improve the situation. First of all, it was resolved to make the governors and lieutenants, administering the provinces of the realm, responsible for the irregularities committed by their subordinate officials. That rule was then upheld by subsequent laws and regulations of the Czar. The next step in the reform attempt ordered that the collection of taxes and all kinds of fees would be done not directly by the *kormlienie* officials, but rather by their assistants of a lower administrative level, who could not directly claim any "feeding" privilege. The collection, personally attended by the governors, lieutenants and other *kormlienshchiki,* compensated by the "feeding," was barred to avoid any direct abuses. Yet, not much relief was achieved in this way; the criminal abuses were simply reshifted. Other measures of reform included the supervision of the collection practices and shortening the collection period.

Finally, the abolition of the "feeding" system was undertaken along with the general landed reform. The *kormlienie* direct tax burden was then consolidated into one general tax, directly payable by individual self-governing communities to the state treasury or the office of revenue according to the established ratios. The elected officials of the lands, *guba* regions and *uiezd* districts were responsible for collection of direct taxes, having no claims on any "feeding" whatsoever, and were expected to be honest under the pain of possible heavy penalties for abuses. The higher officials were liable also for the actions of the subordinate ones. Those elected officials of the *Zemshchina* system were rewarded for their services by land-grants in service tenure, the *pomestie,* or by monetary compensations-salaries (which were at that time coming into use), according to their birth, fitness and service.

The commutation of the *kormlienie* into a general state was known as the redemption or *otkup,* certified by the so-called redemption charter or *otkupnia gramota,* and given to individual regions and localities as soon as they complied with the taxation requirements. The provincial elderlies, the *starosti,* were in charge of collecting all direct taxes and levies, among others, also of the so-called *cess,* a general levy on agricultural labor and farm produce, while all indirect taxes, such as excises and duties, tolls and revenues from the producing government establishments like manufacturing and sale of liquor, salt mining, fisheries and certain forest economies, were entrusted for collection to special government agents, called trust-men. The office of revenues, the *prikaz bolshavo prikhoda,* centrally managed the revenue affairs of the state.[10]

The judiciary of sixteenth century Muscovy was also a combination of the old judicial institutions cumulated with the new developments, undertaken by various reforms. Of course, the Czar continued to be the supreme judge, delegating his judicial authority to the *boyar* council and his agents throughout his realm. His also was the right of clemency. The monarch's judicial authority was unlimited, but during the "Time of Troubles" the *boyars* attempted to curb it somewhat by imposing upon him the obligation to consult the *boyar duma* in the criminal cases of the nobles, in order to avoid the abuses of the *oprichnina* and Godunov's terror measures in the future. Shuiskii's theoretical promise, given in his oath when ascending the throne, to consult the *boyar* council in the serious criminal cases, did actually reflect the trend which never materialized.

Then, great numbers of legal cases of major importance were left to the *boyar duma* to try and to place its decision before the Czar for his approval. In general, there were no appeal rights from the council's decisions. In the Moscow center there were also the departmental courts, the *prikaznii sudi,* handling the cases in their specific jurisdictions.

The territorial judiciary was exercised initially by the appointed governors for the urban regions, the *namiestniki,* and the lieutenants for the rural districts, the *volosteli,* and their agents. The jurisdiction of those governors and lieutenants extended over the major criminal matters, such as brigandage, murder, robbery, theft, and arson, generally called "the most villainous deeds," while most of the civil cases were tried by the minor court officials. The above mentioned severe crimes were punishable by confiscation of the properties of the criminals, their death by hanging or banishment from the country. Since the confiscation of property of the wrongdoer was a normal consequence of his "villainous deed," and since that confiscated property became the possession of the official, as his compensation for the apprehension of the criminal, persecution of the "most villainous deeds" represented an extremely lucrative source of income for the officials of the *kormlienie* system. Other minor crimes were punished by relatively insignificant monetary penalties, up to the full or the half value of the inflicted pain, and were unimportant sources of the *kormlienie* income. Hence, the government appointees were mostly interested in apprehension and punishment of the "villainous" criminals, in general, but not in crime prevention or criminals' correction, while minor crimes were poorly prosecuted throughout. That "materialistic" and self-interested approach to the judiciary twisted entirely the essence of justice in Muscovy of the sixteenth century.

The individual communities, where the crimes had been committed, had to search for the criminals, cooperate with the government officials and eventually deliver the criminals to justice as being responsible for common safety. If, however, those communities failed to do so, they could be punished by heavy monetary penalties up to three rubles, some 500 rubles according to the present monetary standards or equivalents. That money also went into the pockets of the state appointed officials as their "feeding." Income and not safety and prevention of crime was the end.[11] This produced deplorable conditions, urging some reforms to be undertaken.

In order to improve the situation, the office of special constables was established. The constables were supposed to hunt down the criminals, the "most villainous men." However, the novelty did not help much. It did not relieve the territorial communities from their duty to search for the criminals, but added to their financial burden to pay for the constables' services. First the introduction of the *guba* territorial system with elected officials, endowed with police and judicial authority to search, apprehend and punish the criminals, instead of delivering them to the state governors and lieutenants for punishment, improved the situation substantially. The first *guba* charters to establish these new territorial units of the police and judicial nature were granted in 1539 and 1541, while in the later years the *guba* system was extended over most of the state. In each *guba* district a number of police or prosecuting officials were supposed to be elected from among the lesser or minor *boyars*, *boyar* sons, who, assisted by other *guba* officers, were in charge of crime detection, punishment and prevention processes. The elected officials were compensated for their services, but they had no claim on any "feeding," of course. Then, the *guba* and *uiezd* police and judicial responsibilities were somewhat coordinated and consolidated on a regional basis, creating, as was pointed out before, some kind of an interdependent and intermediate level of the criminal and judiciary authority, which was completely lacking before. As a result of this, a fairly complex network of the head and subordinate police units developed, with local and regional police headquarters, police officers and houses of detention. The trend toward full understanding of the crime as a community problem was clearly apparent.

The trials of the criminals were upheld by proper government officials. Initially, those trials were started by private pleas, while later on they could be started as well by the official government initiative. The procedural steps included hearings, public inquiries, tortures either to get some incriminatory statement about the accomplices to the crime or to enforce the confession of guilt, and sentencing either to terminal or life imprisonment, confiscation of property, banishment, piercing the eyes or damaging other limbs of the body, or execution by hanging or decapitation.

Further reforms of the police and judiciary administration followed with the over-all landed reform, the *zemshchina*, which simply gave to the elected officials more authority and more responsibility. Of course, in the private hereditary landholdings of the nobles, the *votchina*, and partially in the landholdings in service tenure, the *pomestie*, the patrimonial judicial power of the nobles prevailed over their peasant tenants, serfs and slaves. The landlord-serf relationship in the *pomestie* possessions was to some extent supervised by the office of slaves, the *kholopii prikaz*. In the Church possessions, the ecclesiastic judiciary continued. However, major crimes were progressively becoming the matters for the state judiciary, limiting the jurisdiction either of the patrimonial or ecclesiastic judiciary.

The military force of sixteenth century Muscovy relied basically on the traditional *boyar* country militia, which included the *boyar* courtiers, the *dvorianie*, the provincial *boyar* grandees, and the lesser *boyars*, called to military duty whenever needed. All military duty-bound *boyars* were supposed to serve on horseback, fully armed at their own costs, and followed by their retinues, armed with swords, bows and arrows. The extent of the service was dependent upon the size of the landholdings in service tenure granted to the respective *boyars* or their *pomestie* possessions. Ivan's first military reform put the general military duty on all *boyars* of 15 years of age and older. Furthermore, since his wars were demanding, Ivan extended military duty in 1556 beyond the *pomestie* holdings only, and widened it over the hereditary landholdings, the *votchina*, as well. The number of men and their equipment to be provided for the army needs, were newly and uniformly regulated in accordance with the *boyar* land possessions, the *pomestie* and *votchina* together. That novelty, introduced by Ivan, subsequently contributed to the disappearance of the traditional difference between the hereditary and the in-service tenure landholdings of the previous historical era. Also the *boyar* daughters were expected, according to Ivan, to do their patriotic and paramilitary duty by bearing the sons and continuously supplying the ranks of the fighting men.

The *boyar* country militia was led by its regional leaders, the *voievodi*. Yet, that whole military system was hopelessly outdated and inadequate. Consequently, Ivan the Terrible undertook serious attempts to modernize his armed forces to make them cope with modern developments. First of all, the large, regionally organized units of the *boyar* country militia were split into smaller units, called the hundreds, and put under the command of appointed officers. In 1550, Ivan formed a special regiment of the "Moscow nobles," as opposed to the *boyar* country militia, as was mentioned in one of the preceding chapters. He evicted some of the *boyars* in the Moscow neighborhood and settled around the capital 1000 of carefully selected lesser *boyars*, making them bound to special military duty, a kind of "storm troopers" devoted to the Czar's service. Then, he organized well trained troops, equipped with cannons, artillery and engineering units according to modern war technology. However, perhaps the most important measure in modernizing the armed forces by Ivan was the establishment of the musketeer, *streltsy*, corps in 1550, too. The *streltsy* were recruited from among the taxpaying urban population, conscripted for life, armed with hand guns, sabers and halberds and commanded by the officers, chosen from among the ranks of the lesser *boyars*. Originally Ivan intended to have 3,000 musketeers as his bodyguard, yet by the end of his reign the *streltsy* corps amounted to over 20,000 men, stationed in various places throughout the empire. Like the artillery men, so also the musketeers were allowed during peacetime to carry out some kind of a semi-civilian way of life and to engage in trade and industry in their special, tax-exempt settlements or *slobodi*. Those trade activities of the conscripted military people supposedly had an adverse impact upon the development of the Muscovite free market. The *boyar* militia, having been an outdated institution, soon let the artillery and musketeer units become the most important combat force of the Muscovite state, the embryo of the future standing armed forces.

Of course, the Cossack detachments, in particular the Don-Cossacks, continued to be the important fighting force in Muscovy, largely defending the southern borderlands of the growing empire during the Ivan era, while during the "Time of Troubles" their role in the military actions of the Pretenders substantially increased. The Don-Cossacks continued to serve either under the command of the government appointed officers or of their own elected leaders, the *atamans*, as had been before, during the previous period of the Muscovite imperial development.[12] Also during the "Time of Troubles" the use of the mercenary troops by the Muscovite ephemeral rulers, the Pretenders and Vasilii Shuiskii, was expanding.

The Orthodox Church

The Muscovite empire was growing during the sixteenth century, and the Orthodox Church and religion developed there as one of the powerful forces, which kept it cohesive and united by way of controlling the Muscovite soul along the lines of the state and Czar's wishes. The Grand Dukes had already recognized that quality of Orthodoxy, and consequently, decided to build it into the empire as its inseparable spiritual arm. The grand-ducal *caesaropapism* was the very evidence of the successful subordination of religion to the imperial policies of the Muscovite rulers. It was not the intention of the Muscovite rulers to let Orthodoxy escape their domination and eventually become an independent, or perhaps even an anti-state force. The *caesaropapist* philosophy came to Muscovy from Constantinople, of course, but the imperial grandeur of the Muscovite autocrats caused this philosophy to permeate the entire religious, social and political thought of the Muscovite people.

Intentionally the Grand Duke, and especially Ivan the Dread, let the *caesaropapist* idea penetrate the political and ecclesiastic minds of their subjects, in order to make them more willing tools in the process of building the empire. Only for that very reason the hatred toward western Catholicism was nursed in the Russian North-East by the official ecclesiastic and political circles. Catholicism did not recognize any supremacy of the state over religion. The Catholic Church developed into an independent and sovereign religious institution, and as such it was feared by the Muscovites as a hostile, *anti-caesaropapist* force, which might endanger the very principles of Muscovite political thinking.[13]

Metropolitan Makarii, disciple of Joseph of Volokolam, was no doubt an outstanding representative of the *caesaropapist*, mystical and at the same time, highly political Muscovite Orthodoxy. Although he firmly believed in the ancient rights and privileges of the Church, and in particular in its right to possess land and wealth, which were not supposed to be suppressed by the state, he demanded a close cooperation of the Church with the state and recognized the elevated position of the Czar. For Makarii, Moscow was not only the "Third Rome" but the "Second Jerusalem" for the Christian world, as well. Moreover, being also a fanatic Muscovite patriot, Metropolitan Makarii, out of the religious and political motives, wanted and waited for an an exaltation of Moscow. Because of his personal influence on young Ivan, he imposed his belief on the Czar's mind, and from that point on, they both worked for the elevation of Muscovy and the Muscovite Orthodox Church.

Nevertheless, neither morally nor intellectually was the Muscovite Orthodoxy up to standards which would have justified its claims to self-styled leadership of Christianity in general, and of Eastern Christianity in particular. The clergy was in the most part not well educated, often illiterate, its ways of life were immoral and hypocritical throughout. Hence Ivan and

Makarii attempted various measures to raise the splendor of the Church externally and to improve its internal conditions.

Initiated either by Makarii or by Ivan, several Church councils, *sobors,* were held to bring about the needed changes. The Church councils of 1547 and 1549, in particular, and subsequent other councils held in the immediate later years, introduced a mass canonization of almost 60 new "saints," having taken into consideration their previous local venerations in various parts of the empire. This was done to raise the prestige of the Muscovite Church and to strengthen its position among and its influence upon other Eastern Churches. In the long run, the move, though an artificial one, really helped to establish the religious leadership of the Muscovite Orthodoxy. Nevertheless, the attempts at raising the spiritual, moral and intellectual standards in the Church largely failed, and lack of their success proved later on to be disastrous for the empire in the long run.

For the very purpose of the moral and intellectual renovation of the Muscovite Orthodox Church, the Council of 1551 was called to convene. Subsequently, it was named the "Council of One Hundred Chapters," the *Stoglav,* since all its proceedings, resolutions and decisions were compiled in one hundred chapters. At its convocation, the council was presented with a series of questions by the Czar, yet authored by Metropolitan Makarii, which it had to deliberate and to which it had to give answers. The questions and the resolutions of the council to these questions did supply an ample illustration of the most deplorable conditions of the Church, its moral and intellectual decadence, primitivism and immorality of the secular and monastic clergy, its abuses of the office, ignorance, indifference to poverty and human sufferings, neglect of duties, drunkenness, ignorance of the canon laws, neglect of spiritual education and numerous other fatal shortcomings, which were supposed to be corrected.

In order to introduce improvements to the Church, the council made various wholesome recommendations, such as condemnation of lending on usury terms by bishops, monasteries and clergy, revision of the ecclesiastic books, establishment of schools and homes for the poor and the needy, improvement of the

Church administration. Of course, along with the important matters, some very unimportant questions were discussed by the council, like the of shaving the beards of the clergy. Still in other matters, such as the redemption of the Muscovite captives in the Tartar lands, the council did not reach any decision. The problem of the ecclesiastic landhodings was also deliberated, since those holdings were already too vast and gave rise to some scandal. The council resolved that any future land grants to be given to the Church must first receive the Czar's approval.

However, most of the reforms recommended by the Council of 1551, due to the Church's own fault, were never put in practice and remained a dead letter on the books. The problem of the ecclesiastic landholdings was again resumed in discussions of the councils in 1573 and 1580. The new regulations were adopted in this respect, prohibiting the Church from accepting any new land grants in the future. Yet also in that case the council's resolutions were fully ignored. Hence the conditions within the Muscovite Church did not improve essentially, although some sincere efforts were undertaken in that direction by more enlightened Muscovites. They failed largely because of the ignorance and greed of the Church men and the primitive clergy. The clergy remained uneducated and stupid, immoral and hypocritical, as before, having continued to have a negative influence on the spiritual, moral and intellectual standards of the Muscovite people as a whole.[14] Only the external, ritual splendor of the Orthodoxy was raised, admired by those who did not know the troublesome truth. It had become the curse of the Muscovite-Russian Orthodox Church, centered around the external show-offs, to be completely shallow in matters of moral and religious substance.[15]

A very important development in the Moscovite Church, enormous in its political consequence, then took place during the reign of Czar Fiodor. Apparently Boris Godunov, still as "a Lord-Protector of Muscovy," was the moving force behind the development. In 1589, upon Godunov's initiative, the Patriarchate of Moscow, the fifth one of Eastern Christianity, was established. It added a great deal of prestige to the Muscovite-

Russian Church, and subsequently that prestige was successfully used by Moscow to enhance its imperial ends.

The legend of Moscow's being the "Third Rome" and the "Second Jerusalem" simply strengthened the Muscovite confidence and encouraged Moscow to reach for the dignity of a Patriarchate. The talks to the point were initiated in 1586, but the final opportune moment did not arrive until two years later, in 1588. That year, Yeremiah, Patriarch of Constantinople, first in the Eastern Churches, visited Muscovy to raise some funds for his Church, which was under the rule of the Turks. Then, he was persuaded by Godunov, while bribery, trickery and coercion helped the Muscovite too, to give his consent to the establishment of a Patriarchate in Moscow. Immediately, the Church council of the Muscovite bishops was induced to choose Yov, Metropolitan of Moscow, to become the first Patriarch. By 1589, the fact was accomplished; the Patriarchate of Moscow was already a reality. Subsequently, the patriarchs of the Eastern Churches reluctantly sanctioned the move, having given to Moscow's Patriarch the fifth, it meant the last, place among themselves. Moscow was not happy with the decision, demanding for its Patriarch the third place, a more proper one due to the Muscovite greatness. Yet, the Eastern Patriarchs insisted on their decision.

As it has been pointed out, the establishment of the Patriarchate of Moscow was very pregnant with political consequences, favorable to the growth of the empire. From the religious point of view, however, nothing really changed in the Muscovite Church. The Patriarch remained as subservient and subordinate to the throne as the Metropolitan and the whole Church were before. The political pressure of Muscovite *caesaropapism* was too great and the subservient attitude of the Church too traditional. Later attempts of some Patriarchs to free the Orthodox Church from state predomination failed completely.

Social Changes

A great many changes took place in the social and economic processes of Muscovite society of the sixteenth century. Some old social strata declined and faded away and some old forms of earning a living disappeared.

The upper class of society, the nobility, changed its composition and was newly differentiated internally. The urban population was slowly growing in number and importance, and continued to be separated into an urban upper class and an urban proletariat, rich and poor merchants, rich and poor industrialists and craftsmen. The peasant population underwent a very substantial change since the free peasantry was gradually disappearing and making room for the soil-bound peasant serfs. The peasant slaves were still in existence, slowly merging with the serf population. In the Muscovite borderlands, the Don-Volga regions in particular, a semi-social and paramilitary class of Cossacks was gaining in importance, also slightly stratified internally.

Perhaps the least change was experienced by the clergy, except that it was becoming exceptionally rich from the enormous land endowments and landholdings. Yet, its class autonomy was subject to a gradual reduction because of the growing absolutism of the Czars. The social differentiation of the sixteenth century Muscovy was not strictly related to the economic functions of the individual classes, since there were *boyars* who engaged in trade and commerce and there were townspeople who engaged in farming. Rather other factors, such as the legal status, military service, tax obligation and the degree of personal freedom, decided the class adherence more than agricultural, commercial or industrial activities of the subjects of the crown. Yet, transcending the social barriers and moving from one class to another was not easy.

Ivan's *oprichnina,* Godunov's terror measures, and also later developments of the Time of Troubles badly uprooted the upper class of the *boyardom.* Old princely and ancient *boyar* families were largely exterminated or socially and politically destroyed. Their members were either executed or purged, imprisoned or exiled, while some of them who managed to escape the purge and survive were forced into state service without having any political influence. Numerous newcomers were rising to the top of the social ladder. The class was changing from the *boyar* stratum to the courtier or *dvoriani* social segment, having been invaded by the new elements of the service tenure or *pomestie* people, lesser *boyars, boyar sons,* and others, who were rising from their previously very low social background, even from slavery. They all were receiving and holding lands in service tenure through the grace of the Czar, bound to state and military service. Not until the end of the next century did the courtiers succeed in developing into a cohesive class with a definite intention to limit an uncontrolled influx of newcomers of humble descent into their circles. Above all the sons of the priests and slaves were by now barred from acquiring lands in service tenure, *pomestie*, in the central provinces of the empire.

The courtiers or *dvoriani* were socially differentiated according to their economic status, which in turn was related to their individual standing in the service of the Czar. Some of them, who performed important functions either at the court or for the state, received huge landholdings in service tenure as a compensation and soon developed into a new segment of the aristocratic grandees, others held middle-sized or modest lands for their military and administrative functions, while still others held really small land plots and were almost on an equal level with the peasants as far as their economic plight was concerned. Only their social status was higher than that of the peasants. Of course, the courtiers, descendants of the ancient princely families, initially separated themselves from the "proletarian" newcomers of humble, urban, priestly, serf or slave descent. The service to the Czar and the state was initially the only common denominator of the courtier class, the *dvorianstvo*, while later on, in the seventeenth century, it melted into a socially more homogeneous group.

The landholding and land cultivation, either hereditary or in-service tenure, was the main economic occupation of the courtiers, the new nobility or *dvoriani*, and of the church people, the secular and monastic clergy to provide for living and accumulation of fortunes. The peasants, at first free and then serf and soil-bound in the noble and ecclesiastic possessions, were the main labor power to move the agricultural machine of the imperial economy. Then, the lower and poorer groups of the courtiers were exploited and economically ruined by the land grandees and the Church by the way of taking away from them the needed peasant labor power. As was pointed out above, the *oprichnina* terror and many wars depopulated the country. A shortage of labor developed especially in the small land possessions of the lesser courtiers, who pleaded for state assistance and tax exemptions in order to avert their economic and social ruin. The attempt to stop the Church accumulation of landholdings was also partially motivated by a desire to protect the middle-sized and small economies of the lesser courtiers.[16] Also the land-grandees by amassing their fortunes economically threatened the class.

The peasantry continued to be the largest, economically the most important and the most discriminated against social class of sixteenth century Muscovy. The peasantry was also internally differentiated, ranging from the fully free and well-to-do peasants, through the segment of the semi-soil-bound and serf peasants, to the outright slaves without any personal or property rights. On the whole, during that century the peasants experienced the most unfortunate change towards a general social and economic degradation and a sweeping soil bondage and serfdom, which became full-fledged in the next century, under the first Romanovs on the Muscovite throne. The unfortunate development was initiated by the *oprichnina* experiment and the prolonged foreign and civil war turmoil of the "Time of Troubles." The *oprichnina* era caused, as mentioned above, a large-scale recolonization process in the empire. Ivan uprooted many old aristocratic families, confiscated their properties and gave them to his faithful but primitive and at times cruel followers. Peasants in many cases did not like the new lords at all and ran away, deep into the eastern and south-eastern steppes or "wild fields." This left many central provinces without any adequate peasant labor.

Constant warfare only intensified the trend. Depopulated areas and a shortage of farm labor were rapidly producing a serious agricultural crisis, which combined with unfavorable natural developments, caused a widespread famine throughout the nation in 1601-1603. Especially, the small and lesser courtiers, *dvoriani*, were losing greatly. After the peasants left, they no longer had any use for the deserted lands, their farm economy drastically decreased. The approaching poverty then scared the remaining peasants away from those lands and could not attract any newcoming settlers. Eventually, the petty courtiers left too, either moving away to look for a better break or entering the services of the grandees or the Church. Also, many peasants preferred to move and live on the large landholdings of the grandees at times, where they could find better living conditions and better protection. Hence, the latifundia of the nobles and Church expanded and their fortunes accumulated, while frequently, and especially the Church, received the benefits of tax exemptions as well. Yet, the agricultural economy of the country suffered badly, because of the enormous instability in labor supply.

Although the state was interested in preserving the free and tax-paying peasantry, since the farming peasants paid the "cess," a general tax on land and land produce and other levies, the over-all trend proceeded in an opposite direction. The peasants were losing their freedom progressively. The difficult economic conditions forced the peasants into a heavy indebtedness. This usually induced the peasant to do one of two things, either to move to another landlord as his prospective tenant with the landlord's financial assistance, or to accept voluntary slavery. By becoming a slave, the peasant freed himself of any private debts or fiscal obligations. Of course, the state was losing a tax revenue, and it did not like that. However, the peasant, by forfeiting his personal freedom, could rid himself of bad material troubles and financial obligations he could not cope with. Any attempt to move somewhere else, where the living conditions could be more tolerable, was not easy and unobjectionable, either. As long as a peasant was indebted to his landlord, he could not legally move. First, the new landlord had to assume and to pay peasant debts to the old landlord. Then, usually the new landlord had to advance additional loans to the newcoming peasant tenant so that he could establish himself and start farming. The loan normally included the material to build living quarters, farm implements, grain for seeds, some food. Moving elsewhere meant, therefore, further and even greater indebtedness of the poor peasant.

Yet, the shortage of farm labor was so urgent at times that some landlords hired agents who moved around and persuaded primitive peasants to give up their old tenancies and to take up new tenancies with new landlords without any gurantees of being able to improve their living and working conditions. The rivalry to retain or to get needed farm labor sometimes was concluded by bloody encounters between the parties and agents involved. The chaos was spreading. The freedom of the peasants to abandon the old tenant and to assume a new one somewhere else with a new landlord, courtier, *boyar* or the Church, affected the agricultural process very badly. Hence, first some *de facto*, and then, *de jure* measures were undertaken to curtail the peasant's freedom to move and to make him soil-bound. So much more, because the financial indebtedness of the peasant tenants, though it restricted the resettlements to some extent, still gave the rich landlord an upper hand, they could assume the indebtedness of the new tenant prospects and leave the lesser courtier landlords without any farmhands. The latter asked the government for protection against the abuses of the rich.

At first the custom and then the law ruled, that the peasants could move only during certain and restricted time periods, namely, during the two weeks around St. Philip's and St. George's days, in the fall, after the field work had been completed, and of course, all debts paid and financial obligations met. The Codes of 1497 and 1550 affirmed the regulation concerning peasant renouncing of the old and accepting of the new tenant responsibilities. Whenever a peasant attempted to evade his responsibilities and moved illegally, the law provided for his compulsory return to the original tenancy and the original landlord.

With time another limitation of the peasant right to move developed. Those peasants, who for a long time did not make any use of their freedom to move, were simply considered to have forfeited their right to move for good and to have become sedentary and soil-bound. In this way a new peasant social subgroup of the semi-free, so-called "old-dwellers," or *starozhiltsi*, developed, which historically represented a definite evolutionary step toward a full serfdom and soil bondage of the entire Muscovite peasantry. The particular development was definitely motivated by fiscal and business considerations to keep the peasants on the state lands and private estates, so that the state would continue to get from those sedentary peasants taxes, rentals and labor services and the private landlords, *boyars, dvoriani* and the Church, would not suffer any pressing labor shortage and diminution of their receipts.

Either within the limits of the law or even outside the law, the landlord who suffered a shortage of labor and material loss because of that, attempted to vindicate the runaway peasants for an unlimited time. This produced a hardship on the peasants and the new landlords, multiplying economic difficulties. Moreover, because officially during the entire sixteenth century most of the peasants still had the freedom of moving and choosing new lords, the reclamation attempts for an unlimited time actually conflicted with the law.

Hence, Boris Godunov issued a decree in 1597, according to which a five-year limitation was imposed on any reclamation procedure on the fugitive peasants, beyond which time limit it could not be continued. Then, in 1586 and also in 1597, the procedures by which the free peasants could be accepted into slavery by their lords were newly regulated. Spreading the slavery was not welcome by the fiscal considerations, of course, but it could secure the supply of labor to the private estates to some extent. In 1601 and 1602, additional decrees were issued to keep the peasants bound to small estates, where the labor shortage was the most pressing for the reasons mentioned a while ago.

Along with the heavy indebtedness of the peasants, the time limitation on their right to move, the institution of the soil-bound "old-dwellers," the limitation of the reclamation time of the fugitives, and the attempt to keep the peasants on the small states, Godunov's favorable attitude to the Orthodox Church, granting it additional lands, tax exemptions and additional powers over the peasants in its estates constituted the gradual steps in the process of peasant enserfment. Once all peasants became soil-bound serfs, soon the distinction between the serfs and the slaves disappeared also. In addition, after the years of famine, 1601-1603, Godunov ruled that those peasants whose landlords kept them on their estates and helped to survive the crisis at their own expense, were not allowed to leave those landlords after conditions improved. It was still another step toward enserfment. Finally, then, the landlords, accepting new peasant settlers on their estates, began to include in the tenancy contracts a "no leave" clause to insure a labor supply in their landholdings. The whole enserfment process was then crystallized and completed in the next century, as indicated.

The peasant social and economic position was differentiated, of course, according to their tenancy dependence, whether being dependent upon the state in the fiscal lands, or the Church in the ecclesiastic possessions, or upon the aristocratic landlords in their in-service tenure or hereditary latifundia and small landholdings. The peasant tenant burdens, the rents in kind, the *obrok*, or labor services, the *barshchina*, or the monetary payments, varied from locality to locality and in relation to the landholding, fiscal, ecclesiastic or courtier, they were living on. Also the whole enserfment process toward the all-out soil-bondage was not evolving uniformly throughout all Muscovy. It was a most intense and aggressive process in the central Muscovite provinces, where the problem of the labor shortage was most acute for most of the time.

In general, a peasant entering into the tenant relationship with a landlord, the state, the Church or the nobleman, normally concluded a verbal contract by which he received a loan and material subsidy from the landlord (money, equipment and seeds) to start his farm business, and by which he also pledged to the landlord to plow the land, to sow the seeds, to harvest the crops, to mow the hay, to keep up the fallow land, to carry the manure to the fields, to plot the garden, to fish, and to do other work around the farm. Furthermore, the agreement also included provisions about paying the rental in kind (in produce), the *obrok*, to render labor services, the *barshchina*, which normally exceeded the regular farm work and called, for example, for constructing boats for fishing, working in the flour mills, distilleries, lumber yards and furnishing transportation, and also paying some money rentals. The new tenants were often freed from all the burdens, even the state taxes, for a certain period to help them to get started.[17]

Slaves were still an important source of labor in sixteenth century Muscovy. Yet, initially even the slave had some freedom of motion and departure, after he had paid all his debts to his master. Then, as in the case of the free peasantry, the pressing shortage of labor and the economic crisis contributed to a progressive restriction of the slave's relative "freedom" of movement altogether and bound him to the soil and to his master. The free and slave peasantry lived in all kinds of settlements, the villages, comprising a few peasant households, the small hamlets and the scattered homesteads. They were largely communes, the *mir*, which were, however, quite different in their organizational structure from the later, nineteenth century communes, called *obshchina*. In the *mir* commune, the land was not compulsorily apportioned to its members, nor were the corporate responsibilities of the same nature and degree, as in the *obshchina*, Kluchevsky concluded. The plots of land, cultivated by a given peasant family, were fixed according to the tenancy contracts, "wheresoever the plough and the sicle and the axe may pass." Neither was the peasant in the *mir* bound to his plot of land or to his commune.[18]

The townspeople represented another traditional social segment of Muscovite society of that era, which was, however, much less developed socially, politically and economically, than the urban class in Western Europe. Most towns were rather small commercial and industrial centers, growing around the military forts and posts. There were only a few really large cities of the Western style, such as Moscow, Smolensk, Vitebsk Polotsk and Perm, in the whole vast empire, and only Moscow's urban populace had any political influence on a *de facto* basis. State regimentation of trade out of fiscal reasons actually retarded the growth of commerce and handicraft, also having held down the social and political significance of the urban population in Muscovy. First of all, in order to expedite the collection of taxes on trade and exchange, the pursuit of trade was restricted by the government to certain localities only. Secondly, the government contributed also for fiscal reasons to the social stratification of the urban population. The fisc made some wealthy merchants its agents for expediting the tax collection of levies on trade and commerce. Those agents were not paid for their fiscal services but were given tax exemption and an exemption from the local judiciary, which made them a kind of privileged people, who, being rich, grew still richer as a result of their special status. The tax exemption of the agents actually aggravated the material position of other townspeople who had to assume the tax burdens of the former in order to meet the fiscal responsibility of their city toward the state. This obviously caused some frictions among all concerned and unfavorably affected the development of trade and commerce. Third, also the courtiers, the *dvoriani*, as well as the military men, the musketeers and artillery men, stationed in various towns, were tax exempt when performing their trade and commercial activities. In addition, the trades and commercial dealings of the monasteries enjoyed a privileged and tax exempt status too.

These discriminatory government measures placed the townspeople in a definitely disadvantaged position, in the long run suppressing and retarding the economic growth of the Muscovite town. The taxpaying urban population, *par excellence*, had to suffer the unfair competition of the privileged groups. The town did not grow, while its population was gradually declining during the sixteenth century. The depopulation of the town hurt the fisc. Consequently, the government was undertaking some measures to permanently attach the urban population to the cities and towns, yet without much success. Of course, the social process of the town developed differently in various parts of the empire.

In the cities and large towns there were, however, numerous trades developed along the lines of food processing, clothing production, metal processing and home construction and furnishing. In Moscow alone at that time there were some 2,367 different craftsmen. Exercising any trade was rather free, except for some government restrictions. There were no rigid and powerful guild organizations in Muscovy to regiment the economic life of the town. Furthermore, townspeople were free to engage in other pursuits, such as farming, cattle raising and fishing, they plowed the fields, leased the meadows and maintained artificial fish ponds. Of course, the economic status of the townspeople largely contributed to their social differentiation as well. There were some merchants and industrialists who possessed wealth amounting to several thousands of rubles, and there were some very poor city proletariat who sought alms in order not to perish and were held in contempt by the rich.[19]

The Cossacks, living in the south-eastern borderlands of the Don-Volga area of the empire, continued to develop into a separate national group, different from the Muscovites. During peace time, the Cossacks lived in their farmsteads in the steppe regions, engaged in hunting, fishing, cattle raising and some farming, always ready for some military expeditions, especially against the Tartars, and warlike adventures, under the leadership of their chieftains, the *atamans*. Also during peaceful times, the *atamans* exercised some ruling functions to provide law and order in the Cossack communities on a self-governing basis. The war requisitions and booty, acquired during the military expeditions and raids, considerably added to the Cossack standard of living, which would have been rather low when relying on their extensive economy of hunting, fishing, cattle raising and a little farming. In particular during the "Time of Troubles", the Don-Cossacks attempted to establish themselves as a separate class or national group of the empire, with special rights and privileges, as tax exemption, their own separate judiciary and the right to own land, along with the courtiers. They demanded these privileges as a reward for defending the borderlands of the empire. Nevertheless, their struggle for a more elevated social status largely failed during the revolutionary turmoils of the "Time of Troubles." Somehow the Czardom recognized the potential threat of the Cossacks developing into a separate national entity, for the future interests of the Muscovite-Russian empire and suppressed their political and social aspirations, which received their first, though not yet fully definite, expression in Bolotnikov's uprising.

The people around the Church, the secular and monastic clergy, the religious, the peasants, townspeople and serfs in the ecclesiastic possessions, villages and townships, continued to have a special status to some extent, such as tax exemption or different tax treatment, and separate Church courts for minor offenses. Yet, the growing power of the Czarist autocracy progressively reduced that special status of the Church, subject to the regular state authorities. The *oprichnina* system obviously did not spare the Church lands in some cases.

Economic Process

The economic process of sixteenth century Muscovy was dominated by agricultural pursuits, supplemented by hunting, trapping, fishing, mining, manufacturing, and trading, to enable the political growth of the young empire. Of course, hunting lost a great deal of its previous importance since the forest and steppe regions were no longer full of animal resources, which could amply supply skins, meat, and fat. Cattle raising had to make up for the difference. The two-field system in farming was slowly making room for a more advanced three-field technique but not in a pure sense of the term. Rather, the fallow system without any correct three-field practice, a "mixed field" approach, prevailed. In the remote parts of the country, a backward and irregular tilling of lands was applied. Therefore, the official registers of lands for tax purposes, the *cadastres*, having described the arable fields, usually applied the following classification of lands as Lyashchenko stated: the plowed or living fields, which were regularly tilled, "visited" fields, irregularly cultivated, fallow fields, left to recuperate, and fields overgrown with brush and woods, requiring additional effort to be used in farming.[20] Then, in the wooded regions the so-called *podsiechna*, and in the steppe areas the so-called *perelozhna* techniques of tilling the soil were used, each having been a proper technique for the specific geographical and climatic conditions.

From among different crops, rye, oats, and barley were most popularly cultivated, while in the southern borderlands some wheat and millet, and in the western regions of Smolensk and Pskov some hemp and flax were raised.[21] The farm implements were still simple: wooden plow, perhaps with an iron share, used by the peasants, and iron plow, mostly used in the manorial economies of the state, Church, and the nobility. Also in some parts of Muscovy, a heavy, double-share plow was known too. Sickle, scythe, hoe, and sometimes harrow, mostly of wood and rarely with iron parts, were used. The use of draft-animals, horses, oxen, and cows at times, and fertilizing soil with animal manure were known already in the central Muscovite regions and also among some peasants, while in the manorial economies, hundreds of draft-animals and a large-scale fertilizing by animal manure were applied to raise the agricultural productivity of the rather poor quality lands.[22] Only in the large estates, cows, sheep, hogs, and poultry were raised, the activity which was little known among the peasants. Most of the agricultural work was done by the peasant tenants, while in the manorial estates, serfs and slaves were employed to attend the field work and the first stage of processing the crops. The slaves, who voluntarily sold themselves into slavery in order to avoid their debts and other financial burdens, actually represented an important and novel source of labor supply at that time.

The *oprichnina* terror, the years of oppression under Godunov and the wars provoked a mass flight of peasants from the central regions of Muscovy, as pointed out before, causing a dramatic decline of the agricultural efficiency. The land was deserted by labor. This together with poor harvests due to weather conditions, resulted in an agricultural crisis and a terrible famine in Muscovy in 1601-1603. Masses of unprovided for slaves and serfs roamed the countryside, attacked Churches, monasteries, and noble possessions, especially the granaries, indulged in theft and robbery, rape and murder. The state used most severe measures to liquidate the disorders. The landlords, who were partially ruined during the agricultural crisis and the three years of famine, received subsidies and tax privileges to overcome the era of prolonged depression. State penalties were introduced for harboring fugitive serfs. The peasants who were kept and provided for by the landlords during the famine became soil-bound by law to compensate those landlords for their material sacrifice by feeding and sheltering the unneeded surplus of farm hands in those terrible years.

Handicrafts developed in three ways: in the towns as specialized trades, in the manorial economies as their supplementary services, and in the peasant households to supplement their meager livelihood. The urban crafts which developed very well in Western Europe could not do so in Muscovy because they suffered not only from competition of manorial and peasant craftsmen, but also the competition of the musketeers and artillery men, who had been settled in various localities and were allowed to indulge in various trades in peacetime and had been enjoying a privileged status of tax exemption.

The Muscovite craftsmen used rather simple tools, carpenters used axes and hammers, while the saw was yet largely unknown; textile crafts used only human power-run looms; in the iron industry only hand-operated smelters were known; blacksmiths applied raw-air blowing, hammers, tongs, and bellows. Yet, in Moscow at that time there were some 210 different trade professions in existence already, which showed a considerable progress in the development of the crafts there in comparison to the previous era. There were numerous trades in food processing, such as bakers, cake bakers, fish men, brewers, and distillers; in clothing production there were fullers, tanners, bootmakers, tailors, furriers, coat makers, hatters, hosiery makers, linen drapers, spinners, and weavers; in metal processing and production of metal articles, there were locksmiths, sword makers, armory makers, ax makers, smiths, goldsmiths, tin makers, needle makers, pan makers, and various other specialized jobs.[23] Ivan the Dread and Boris Godunov had invited numerous foreign craftsmen to come to Muscovy. They lived in separate quarters and were involved in production of luxury articles, an art not yet well known to the native Muscovites. They were silversmiths, goldsmiths, painters, lace makers, apothecaries and others, who, for some time had to be protected by the government against the hostile Muscovites.[24]

The town crafts could not supply all the country's needs, since their development was retarded by discriminatory state tax policies. Hence the village craftsmen had to procure, to a great extent, the needed articles of industry for the peasant population. In the peasant households at times crude and sometimes a quality *kustar* craftsmanship developed, which included making clothing and household articles and building huts. The needs of the manor and the population in the latifundia estates of the royalty, nobility, and Church were supplied by the manorial craftsmen and artisans, such as carpenters, smiths, stone masons, bootmakers, weavers, and spinners, tailors, icon painters, and engravers. They were either free craftsmen hired by the manor for wages, or slave artisans. The manor also covered its needs in part by the work of the peasant *kustar* craftsmanship, counted as a form of the *barshchina* service obligation of the peasant tenant or serf toward the landlord.[25]

In the sixteenth century large-scale manufacturing emerged in Muscovy. The workshops sometimes employed as many as a few hundred workers, who were again either "free" artisans, serfs, or slaves. Such large-scale manufacturing was first developed in the salt-boiling and mining industries, potash manufacturing and metallurgic production, and it was by no means confined to the manorial economies of large landholders. It was rather done in the form of "free enterprising" of wealthy merchants, like Stroganov and Morozov. Salt-boiling and ironworks, the oldest branch of the large-scale, privately owned manufacturing, started on the "lease" basis by independent enterprisers usually on the manorial grounds, against certain rental payments.[26] Then, they became fully separate business projects. Stroganov's family enterprises were apparently the largest of the kind and included numerous salt mines and salt-boiling establishments in the Ural mountains and along the Kama River, potash works, bristle works and iron works in Solvychegodsk, Cheredin, Perm, on the banks of the Irtysh River, and farther east. Stroganov's wealth developed over a few generations out of rich peasant estates which at a later time employed some 15,000 people, free, serf and slave workers.[27] There were other industrial enterprises though not as big, where the exploitation of the serfs and slaves was considerable and even inhuman, through which large fortunes were accumulated.

In sixteenth century Muscovy a large-scale exchange economy, based on the territorial and product specialization and division of labor, emerged, inducing an extensive use of money and growing application of credit. Hence, commercial and marketing activities were extending their volume and their radius, in which the town merchants, the courtiers, the Church, the peasants and other social groups were busily engaged to some extent. The landowners entered the marketing process with their surplus goods, coming from the peasant rental payments and from the output of their own manorial economies, run by use of the serf and slave labor and the peasant *barshchina* services. Grain, livestock, leather, butter, lard, vegetables and fruits and the products of the manorial handicrafts were delivered either to the domestic and local markets for home consumption or diverted to exports, especially grain and lumber.[28] The peasants sold, in most part locally, some produce of their farming or their other occupations, such as fishing, trapping, and handicraft. Herberstein reported that during the winter months the city of Moscow received about 700 to 800 carloads of grain, fish, and other foodstuffs, some delivered from such distances as over 1000 miles away.[29] Unfortunately other writers of that time asserted that the Muscovite peasant, himself living in real poverty, was trying to sell whatever had any market value. The urban crafts and the military settlements largely produced for the market.

The marketing or distribution process operated through the small local markets in the towns and townships, large periodic fairs in the well-known commercial centers, peddling the products of handicrafts, and small stores in the towns and cities. The small local markets were held daily in the cities, towns, townships, and even villages, on the monasterial and Church grounds as well, where primarily agricultural produce and foodstuffs were sold along with some manufactured articles of the "professional" trades and the military men, like the *streltsy*. Contemporary documents enumerated a great many items, which were sold and bought in these local market places, such as meat, eggs, fish, skins, fur, cows, lambs, geese, ducks, pigs, wheat, rye, barley, oatmeal, peas, garlic, onions, hops, flax, hemp, fruit, poppy seeds, honey, footwear, wood and lumber, boards, baskets, sleds, wheels, spades, iron and many other items.[30] Some craftsmen indulged in a direct peddling of the articles of their skilled work during certain months of the year when traveling was relatively easy. They sometimes traveled considerable distances to reach famous fairs, held periodically in certain places, especially on specific holidays. In those fairs everything salable was sold.

In the commercial centers of Muscovy at that time, such as Moscow, Tula, Kolomna, Novgorod, Pskov, Arkhangelsk, Nizhnii-Novgorod, Smolensk, and Riazan, goods from all parts of the empire were delivered, sold, and bought. There were several major trade routes by which the nationwide commercial exchange was carried out, one from Moscow through Smolensk or Vitebsk to Riga, another one from Moscow through Vologda, Sukhoma, Ustiug and along the Northern Dvina River to Arkhangelsk, still another from Moscow along the Volga River to Astrakhan, an overland route ran along the Kama River towards the Ural Mountains and the southern Siberian regions. There were numerous roads of rather local importance running from Moscow to various commercial centers, such as Vladimir, Kostroma, Kaluga, Tula or Riazan. The volume of trading was considerable for the time as recorded by the tax collection registers. It amounted to some 450,000 rubles for Moscow on an annual average, some 140,000 for Kazan, and some 50,000 for Nizhnii-Novgorod.[31]

To a rather limited extent trading was also done in the small stores and shops, which were permanently established in large cities. These stores were not very sizeable, with scarcely room enough for the salesman to move around. A variety of items were usually sold, each group of articles placed in a separate row.[32]

Foreign trade was largely maintained and managed by the Dutch, German, Swedish and English merchants, living in separate quarters or settlements in larger cities and commercial centers. The Muscovite merchants traditionally disliked the foreigners and were very hostile towards the foreign competition. As before, they attempted to limit the freedom of movement of the foreign merchants and to restrict their trading activities in order to concentrate the commercial operations in Russian hands and to maximize their own material gains. The foreigners were largely prohibited from engaging in retail trade in Muscovy and were not allowed to visit local markets and fairs. Largely wholesale imports and exports were attended by the foreign mercantile group. Grain, valuable furs, leather, linen, lard, caviar, wax and honey were the main articles of Muscovite exports, while gold and silver articles, diamonds, paper, hats, needles, wine, pepper, arms, drugs, woolen clothing, and luxuries were among the leading import items.[33]

It must be emphasized here also, that in sixteenth century Muscovy the financial and money lending operations were already quite developed in order to maintain the large-scale trading and the emerging large-scale manufacturing. The Church, and especially the wealthy monasteries, courtier grandees and rich merchants were substantially involved in supplying financial means for business operations on the credit basis and charged considerable interest rates. Several Church councils, and in particular the *Stoglav*, condemned the credit operations conducted by numerous churchmen and church institutions as usury.

Cultural Developments

An intellectual primitivism continued to prevail in the Muscovite empire during the sixteenth century. The Orthodox Church, which was actually supposed to initiate and sponsor the spiritual and intellectual progress of society, as it did in the Kievan empire of the eleventh and thirteenth centuries or as the Catholic Church did in the West at the same time, rather promoted intellectual retardation and primitivism, having been permeated by the Byzantinian and Oriental religious mysticism and not by the Occidental drive for logical arguments in the sphere of religion.[34] Muscovite Orthodoxy considered itself to be the standard-bearer of the true Christianity, but because of its practical primitivism, formalism and almost barbarism it made Muscovite society to seem to foreign visitors scarcely Christian at all and rather pagan.

In its alleged defense of the Orthodox purity, the Muscovite Church was driving a hard campaign against any progress and any intellectual innovation, in particular when originating in the West, no matter whether in the field of religious thinking, social life, or literary and educational areas, including the new technique of printing books. Grot asserted the following: "... the majority of Russian people did not receive an education and entered into active life directly from childhood on in a mental and ethical state of minors, and there was no family in a true meaning of the word, nor a school... and not even the *boyars* knew how to read, ..."[35] Almost a Chinese wall was established by the sixteenth century Muscovites in order to separate themselves from the "sinful and damaging" influences of the Catholic West, which was actually at that time a hotbed of cultural growth. Of course, there were a few enlightened men in Moscow, such as Ivan the Dread, Metropolitan Makarii and Boris Godunov, who wanted to tear away their people from that utterly reactionary primitivism, but to no avail. They either did not know how to do it, or did it the wrong way. The *Stoglav*, for example, exposed the illiteracy and backwardness of the clergy. Yet, practically nothing was done to remedy the situation, and for many more years the intellectual life in Muscovy remained stagnant. Hence, contemporary Western visitors to Muscovy described it as weird, primitive, sumptuous, colorful and quite different from anything they ever saw before, a barbarian land, full of inequalities and contradictions, where tremendous riches bordered on utter misery, self-righteousness cumulated with an utter suspicion toward the outside world, self-satisfied pride and an inferiority complex, lavish banquets and elaborate ceremonial for the royalty and the nobility and a below-subsistence minimum for the low social segments, while tremendous drinking was a way of life for all, the rich and the poor.[36]

While pathologically afraid of "sinful" foreign novelties in defense of its Orthodox self-righteousness, the Muscovite Church, state administration and upper crust of society refused even to accept without reservations the books and written materials published in the neighboring Orthodox Ukraine, not to mention Western publications. Consequently, there was a shortage of books in Muscovy, and those available were rarely read. When book printing, a novelty, was introduced to Moscow in 1553, the ignorant and reactionary clergy caused the burning of the printing press and all newly printed literature as a work of "the devil." Though printing of books was resumed there in 1568, only a few books were published before 1613. After the "Time of Troubles," the printing and publishing of books in Muscovy was begun, but didn't really develop until the next century. Or course, a shortage of books substantially hindered any development of education to which the primitive Muscovite almost had an aversion anyway. The Muscovite state administration, partially brainwashed by the Orthodox clergy and partially afraid of it, did not dare to initiate any breakthrough in the educational stagnation and cultural isolation on any large scale, or to start the organization of schools and other institutions of learning of a middle or higher level. During the sixteenth century there were only elementary schools in Muscovy around the monasteries and in various towns, which gave just very basic instruction. Libraries, as in the previous two centuries, were very few.

Bringing foreign professionals, doctors, apothecaries, painters, and skilled artisans to Muscovy by Ivan IV and Boris Godunov in order to raise the civilization standards of the country and to boost it economically, did not really help much. It just strengthened the aversion of the Muscovites toward the foreigners. Godunov thought of establishing an institution of higher learning. For that purpose he sent a number of young Muscovites abroad to study to bring wisdom and enlightenment back home. Yet the project failed because of the opposition of the leading churchmen and politicians. It took almost another one hundred years until an institution of higher learning was established in Muscovy, some time toward the end of the seventeenth century.[37]

On the basis of that general backwardness of the Muscovite society of the sixteenth century, letters scarcely developed at that time, with only a few exceptions, having presented very little progress over the immediate post-Mongolian years of Muscovite history. Some translations of foreign works, with patriotic and moral teachings, at times adapted for the Muscovite conditions, were written. The hagiographic writings, including compilations of lives of saints or believed-to-be saints, organized in a calendar-wise order under the dates of their respective feasts, were rather numerous, corresponding with the aggressive but mystical Orthodox religiosity of the era. *The Menaea,* written by Metropolitan Makarii, was an outstanding example of that kind of literature. Also Ivan the Dread was supposedly writing hagiographic stories. Reflecting the historical events, tales were written down according to the tradition of the previous centuries, such as the *Tale of the Taking of Pskov* by Prince Vasilii or the *Tale of the Siege of Pskov* by the Polish king, Stefan Batory, and many others, less famous. Pskov seemed to be a leader in that kind of literary writing. The growth of the Muscovite empire during the sixteenth century could not help but have an impact upon the thinking of the small intellectual, crust of its society, which was again reflected in rather rich chronicle writing. The *Novgorodian Chronicle,* the *Pskovian Chronicle* and the *Second Novgorodian Chronicle,* recorded the events until the last days of Vasilii III and of the earlier rule of Ivan the Dread, and the *Nikon Chronicle* of a great historical value. The *Kazan Chronicle,* or rather the *History of the Kazan Empire,* relating in detail the capture of Kazan by the Muscovites, is an historical narrative.

Religious dissent of the time was projected by some polemical writings mainly represented by such men as Vassian Patrikeiev, perhaps the greatest author of the sixteenth century, Joseph of Volokolam, Metropolitan Daniel and a few others. Ivan Peresvietov wrote his *Little and Great Petitions* to Czar Ivan without much success, having proposed in them several reforms for the empire, such as the abolition of slavery and limitation of the numerous *boyar* abuses. In general, however, both petitions were written in the spirit of a humble submission to autocracy. Peresvietov was saluting Czar Ivan by the words: "Thou art a sovereign terrible and wise." Another work in the area of political science was the long celebrated alleged correspondence between Kurbskii and Ivan the Dread. Yet, this is apparently a fabrication of later decades. It had been a dialogue, raising charges against (Kurbskii) and arguments for autocracy (Ivan).[38]

The *Domostroi* or House Management is an example of writing in the area of social morality. Some thought that priest Sylvester was the author of the work. In fact, however, it is a conglomeration of some 63 independent literary units put together without any system, written down between 1556 and 1563. The *Domostroi* instructed the Muscovites on how to run their family life according to their ancient tradition, based on patriarchalism, ritualism, formalism, true Orthodoxy and severity of the family regime. The language of those writings, especially of the chronicles, slowly departed from the old Slavonic and was gradually penetrated by the idioms of the colloquial Muscovite-Russian, following the official language of the court and administration, the so-called "chancery Russian."[39]

In the area of arts, icon painting continued throughout the sixteenth century. Around 1580, a special school of icon painting with bright background, rich colors, minute and elaborate decorations and designs and decorative elements in gold, developed, known as the so-called Stroganov school. Fresco painting continued on a very small scale. Music did not experience any notable change or progress during the sixteenth century.

However, a truly Muscovite architectural style began to develop at that time, freed to some extent from the Byzantinian architectural rigor but with some Oriental influence. It became truly national and corresponding to the contemporary tastes. That architectural style was a conglomeration of many independent, structurally different, and incoherent building units, without a symmetry and system, with little esthetics, connected into one clumsy whole. The style was used first for the wooden construction of mansions of the royalty and nobility.

Then, stones were used to build the same style of the so-called *khoromy* according to the same patterns. The mansion or *khoromy* of the Stroganov family in Solvychegodsk and the summer palace of the Czars in Kolomenskoie, near Moscow, may be considered as classic examples of that Muscovite architecture. The style was also manifested in church construction, of which the Church of St. Basil on the Red Square, in Moscow, and the church in Diakovo were leading monuments. Riasanovsky depicted these two examples of Muscovite church building in order to illustrate the style.

The first is a wooden construction in stone, erected in 1555-1560 by two architects from the city of Pskov. It consists of nine separate church units on a common foundation, one central one and eight others around the central, all with different tops, the *cupolas*, stressing in this way the independence and singularity of each component construction. The church was painted in bright colors and richly decorated also in the way that strengthened the individuality of each unit. The church in Diakovo consisted of five component units on the same foundation with all the characteristics of the Muscovite taste. In fact, the Kremlin, the traditional seat of the Czars, the construction of which was under way already under Ivan III and continued to be built in its main body under Vasilii III, bears the features of Muscovite architecture of the time.[40]

BIBLIOGRAPHY

General works on history:

Bestuzhev-Riumin, C., *Russkaia istoria*, St. Petersburg, 1872.
Bobrzynski, M., *Dzieje Polski w zarysia*, 3 volms. Warsaw, 1927-31.
Brückner, A., *Geschichte Russlands bis zum Ende der XVIII Jhrh.*, Gotha, 1896.
Chase, T., *The Story of Lithuania*, New York, 1946.
Chirovsky, Fr.-, N., *An Introduction to Russian History*, New York, 1967.
Clarkson, J., *A History of Russia*, New York, 1961.
Doroshenko, D., *Narys istorii Ukrainy*, Volms. I-II, Munich, 1966.
Florinsky, M., *Russia, A History and an Interpretation*, Volms. I-II, New York, 1953.
Halecki, O., *History of Poland*, New York, 1942.
Harcave, S., *Russia, A History*, Chicago-Philadelphia-New York, 1952.
Hrushevsky, M., *Istoria Ukrainy-Rusi*, Volm. I-X, New York, 1954-1958.
Hrushevsky, M., *Istoria Ukrainy-Rusi*, Volms. I-X, New York,
Kluchevsky (Kliuchevsky), V., *A History of Russia*, Volms. I-V, London-New York, 1911-1914.
Karamzin, N., *Istoria gosudarstva rossiiskavo*, Volms. I-XII, St. Petersburg, 1851-1853.
Karamzin, N., *Primiechania k istorii gosudarstva rossiiskavo*, St. Petersburg, 1852-1853.
Manning, G., *The Forgotten Republics*, New York, 1952.
Mazour, A., *Russia, Tsarist and Communist*, Princeton-Toronto-New York-London, 1962.
Nahayevsky, I., *History of Ukraine*, Philadelphia, 1962.

Pares, B., *A History of Russia*, New York, 1949.
Platonov, S., *History of Russia*, Bloomington, 1964.
Pokrovsky, M. *Brief History of Russia*, Volms I-II, London, 1933.
Presniakov, A., *Lektsii po russkoi istorii, Kievskaia Rus'*, Vol. I, Moscow, 1938.
Riasanovsky, N., *A History of Russia*, New York, 1963.
Soloviov, S., *Istoria Rossiis drevnieiskikh vriemen*, Volms. I-XXIX, St. Petersburg, 1894-1895.
Stukas, J., *Awakening Lithuania*, Madison, 1966.
Vernadsky, G., and Karpovich, M., *A History of Russia*, Vol. I, *Ancient Russia*, New Haven-London, 1952; Vol. II, *Kievan Russia*, New Haven-London, 1951; Vol. III. *The Mongols and Russia*, New Haven-London, 1953; Vol. IV *Russia at the Dawn of the Modern Age*, New Haven-London, 1959.
Vernadsky, G., *A History of Russia*, New Haven-London, 1951.

Monographic works and special subject matters:

Abraham, G., *On Russian Music*, New York 1939.
Abraham, J., *Organizacia kosciola lacinskiego na Rusi*, Lwow, 1904.
Akulin, I., *Yermak i Stroganovi*, Paris, 1933.
Alpatov, N. and Brunov, N., *Geschichte der Altrussischen Kunst*, Augsburg, 1932.
Artsikhovskii, A., *Vvedienie v arkheologiu*, Moscow, 1940.
Bagalei (Bahalii), D., *Ocherki po istoril kolonizatsii i byta stepnoi okrainy Moskovskavo gosudarstva*, Moscow, 1887.
Bagalei (Bahalii), D., *Materialy dlia istorii kolonizatsii i byta*
Bakhruskin S., *Pamiatki Vielikavo Novgoroda*, Moscow, 1909.
stepnoi okrainy Moskovskavo gosudarstva, Moscow, 1886.
Bakhrushin, S., and Cherepnin, L., *Dukhovniie i dogovorniie gramoty vielikikh i udielnikh kniazei XIV-XVI viekov*, Moscow-Leningad, 1950.
Balzak, S., Vasyutin, V., and Feigin, Ya., *Economic Geography of the U.S.S.R.*, New York, 1952.
Berdiaiev, N., *Dusha Rossii*, Moscow, 1915.
Berdiaiev, N., *The Russian Idea*, London, 1947.

Bradovich, M., *Derzhava bez natsii,* New York, 1952.
Buxton, D., *Russian Medieval Architecture,* Cambridge, 1934.
Chamberlin, W., *The Russian Enigma,* New York, 1943.
Chechulin, N., *Goroda Moskovskavo gosudarstva v XVI v.,* St. Petersburg, 1899.
Chirovsky, Fr.-, N., *Old Ukraine, Its Socio-Economic History prior to 1781,* Madison, 1963.
Chirovsky, Fr.-, N., *The Economic Factors in the Growth of Russia,* New York, 1957.
Chubaty, N., *Kniazha Rus' — Ukraina ta vyneknennia triokh skhidnio-slovianskykh natsii,* New York-Paris, 1964.
Chyzhevsky, D., *Istoria ukrainskoi literatury,* New York 1956.
Chyzhevsky, D., (Cizevskij), *History of Russian Literature,* 'S-Gravenhage, 1960.
Coates, W. and Zelda, K., *Six Centuries of Russo-Polish Relations,* London, 1948.
Cresson, W., *The Cossacks,* New York, 1919.
Cross, S., *Medieval Russian Churches,* Cambridge, 1949.
Curtin, J., *The Mongols in Russia,* Boston, 1908.
Czaplicka, K., *The Evolution of the Cossack Communities,* 1919.
Czaplicka, M., *Aboriginal Siberia,* Oxford, 1914.
Dankevych, M., *Future Potentials of Siberia,* Washington, 1965.
Day, C., *Economic Development of Europe,* New York, 1942.
Diakonov, M., *Vlast' moskovskikh gosudarei; ocherki po istorii politicheskikh idei drevniei Rusi do kontsa XVI vieka,* St. Petersburg, 1889.
Dmitrieva, R., *Skazania o kniaziakh vladimirskikh,* Moscow-Leningrad, 1955.
Dobriansky, L., *The Vulnerable Russians,* New York, 1967.
Dolgorukov, P., *Rossiiskaia rodoslovnaia kniga,* 4 volms., St. Petersburg, 1857.
Dovnar-Zapolsky, M., *Istoria russkavo narodnavo khoziaistva,* Vol. I, Kiev, 1911.
Eckard, H., *Ivan the Terrible,* New York, 1949.
Ekzemplarskii, A., *Vielikie i udielnie kniazia sieviernoi Rusi v tatarskii period,* St. Petersburg, 1889-1891, Volms. I-II.
Fennel, J., *Ivan the Great; Expansion of the Muscovite State,* London, 1961.

Fennel, J., *The Correspondence between Prince A. M. Kurbskii and Czar Ivan IV of Russia, 1564-1579*, New York, 1955.
Findeizen, N., *Ocherki po istorii muzyki v Rossii*, I Moscow-Leningrad, 1928.
Fisher, R., *The Russian Fur Trade 1550-1700*, Berkley, 1943.
Golobutskii, V., *Zaporozhskoie kazachestvo*, Kiev, 1957.
Golubinskii, E., *Istoria russkoi tserkvi*, Vols. I-II, Moscow, 1901-1917.
Gotie, Yu., *Ocherki po istorii materialnoi kultury vostochnoi Yevropy*, I, Moscow, 1925.
Gotie, Yu., *Zheleznii viek v vostochnoi Yevropie*, Moscow-Leningrad, 1930.
Graham, S., *Boris Godunov*, New Haven, 1933.
Graham, S., *Ivan the Terrible; Life of Ivan IV of Russia, Called the Terrible*, New Haven, 1933.
Grekov, B., *Kiev Rus'*, Moscow, 1959.
Grekov, B., *The Culture of Kiev Rus'*, Moscow, 1947.
Gudzii, N., *Istoria drevniei russkoi literatury*, Moscow, 1941.
Hamilton, G., *The Art and Architecture of Russia*, London, 1954.
Keenan, E., *The Kurbskii-Groznyi Apocrypha; The 17th Century Genesis of the "Correspondence" Attributed to Prince A. M. Kurbskii and Tsar Ivan IV*, Cambridge, 1971.
Kerner, J., *Urge to the Sea; the Course of Russian History*, Berkley and Los Angeles, 1942.
Khara-Davan, E., *Chingis-Khan kak polkovodiests i yevo nasliedie*, Belgrade, 1929.
Kluchevsky (Kliuchevsky), V., *Istoria soslovi v Rossi*, Moscow, 1913.
Kluchevsky (Kliuchevsky), V., *Boyarskaia duma drevniei Rusi*, Moscow, 1909.
Kolarz, W., *Russia and Her Colonies*, New York, 1952.
Kondakov, N., *The Russian Icon*, Oxford, 1927.
Korduba, M., *Najnowsze teorje o poczatkach Rusi*, Warsaw, 1932.
Korchmaryk, F., *Dukhovni vplyvy Kyieva na Moskovshchynu v dobi hetmanskoi Ukrainy*, New York, 1964.
Kulisher, J., *Russische Wirtschaftgeschichte*, Jena, 1925.
Lamb, H., *The March of Muscovy: Ivan the Terrible and the

Growth of the Russian Empire, 1400-1648, Garden City, 1948.
Lamb, H., *Tamerlane the Earth Shaker*, New York, 1928.
Lengyel, E., *Siberia*, New York, 1943.
Lantzeff, G., *Siberia in the Seventeenth Century*, Berkeley, 1943.
Luzhnytsky, H., *Ukrainska tserkva mizh skhodom i zakhodom*, Philadelphia, 1954.
Lyashchenko, P., *History of the National Economy of Russia*, New York, 1949.
Malinin, V., *Starets Yeleazarova monastiria Filotei i yevo poslania*, for Moscow, 1901.
Marx K. and Engels, F., *The Russian Menace to Europe*, Glencoe, 1952.
Mavor, J., *The Economic History of Russia*, Volms. I-II, New York, 1925.
Miliukov, P., *Outlines of Russian Culture*, Philadelphia, 1948.
Miller, V., *Ocherki russkoi narodnoi slovesnosti*, Vol. I, Moscow, 1897.
Mirov, N., *Geography of Russia*, New York, 1951.
Mirskii, D., *Russia, a Social History*, London, 1942.
Mitchell, M., *The Maritime History of Russia, 848-1948*, New York, 1950.
Nasonov, A., *Mongoly i Rus'*, Moscov-Leningrad, 1940.
Niekrasov, A., *Ocherki po istorii drevnie-russkavo zodchestva XI-XVII viekov*, Moscow, 1936.
Nikitskii, A., *Istoria ekonomicheskavo bita Vielikavo Novgoroda*, Moscow, 1893.
Nikitskii, A., *Ocherk vnutrenniei istorii Pskova*, St. Petersburg, 1873.
Ohloblyn, O., *Moskovska teoria III Rymu v XVI-XVII stolittiakh*, Munich, 1951.
Orlov, A., *Drevniaia russkaia literatura XI-XVI vv.*, Moscow-Leningrad, 1945.
Paszkiewicz, H. *The Origin of Russia*, New York, 1954.
Platonov, S., *Proshloie russkavo sieviera*, Berlin, 1923.
Platonov, S., *Boris Godunov*, Prague, 1924.

Platonov, S., *Sotsialnii krisis Smutnavo Vriemini*, Leningrad, 1924.

Platonov, S., *Moskva i Zapad v XVI-XVII viekakh*, Leningrad, 1925.

Priesniakov, A., *Kniazhoie pravo v drevniei Rusi; ocherki po istorii X-XII stolietiia*, St. Petersburg, 1909.

Priesniakov, A., *Obrazovanie vielika-russkavo gosudarstva*, Petrograd, 1918.

Reischauer, E. and Fairbank, J., *East Asia; the Great Tradition*, Boston, 1960.

Rice, D., *Russian Icons*, London-New York, 1947.

Rostovcev, M., (Rostowcew, Rostovzeff), *Skythien und der Bosforus*, Berlin, 1931.

Rostovcev, M., *Iranians and Greeks in South Russia*, Oxford, 1922.

Rozhdenstvienskii, S., *Sluzhiloie ziemlievladanie v Moskovskom gosudarstvie XVI vieka*, St. Petersburg, 1897.

Rozhkov, N., *Sielskoie khoziaistvo Moskovskoi Rusi XVI v.*, St. Petersburg, 1899.

Rozhkov, N., *Obzor russkoi istorii s sotsiologicheskoi tochki zrienia*, St. Petersburg, 1905.

Schaeder, H., *Moskau das Dritte Rom*, Hamburg, 1929.

Schwartz, H., *Russia's Soviet Economy*, New York, 1954.

Sergeievich, V., *Lektsii i izliedovania po drevnii istorii russkavo prava*, St. Petersburg, 1910.

Sergeievich, V., *Russkaia Pravda v cheteriokh redaktsiakh*, St. Petersburg, 1904.

Sergeievich V., *Drevnosti russkavo prava, Volms. I-III*, St. Petersburg, 1908-1911.

Shelukhin, S., *Ukraina*, Prague, 1936-1937.

Sirelius, U., *The Geneology of the Finns*, Helsinki, 1925.

Skrynnikov, P., *Nachalo oprichninoie i oprichnii terror*, Leningrad, 1966-69, 2 volms.

Smirnov, I., *Les populations Finnoises des bassins de la Volga et de la Kama*, Paris, 1898, vol. I.

Smirnov, P., *Volzhzkii shliakh i starodavni rusy*, Kiev, 1928.

Smirnov, S., *Istoria moskovskoi Sloviano-Greko-Latinskoi Akademii*, Moscow, 1885.

Smirnov, V., *Krimskoie Khanstvo pod vierkhovienstvom Ottomanskoi Porty*, St. Petersburg, 1887.

Soloviov, S., *Istoria otnoshenia mezhdu russkimi kniaziami Rurikavo doma*, Moscow, 1847.

Spuler B., *Die Goldene Horde*, Leipzig, 1943.

Stalin, J., *Marksizm i natsionalno-kolonialnii vopros*, Moscow, 1937.

Svatikov, S., *Rossia i Don*, 1919.

Tikhomirov, M., *The Towns of Ancient Rus'*, Moscow, 1959.

Tizengauzen, V., (Tiesenhausen), *Sbornik materialov otnosiashchikhsia k istorii Zolotoi Ordy*, I, St. Petersburg 1884; II, Moscow-Leningrad, 1941.

Tolstoi, I., and Kondakov, N., *Russkie drevnosti*, St. Petersburg, 1889-1899, Volms. 6.

Tolstoi, Yu., *Piervia sorok liet snoshenii mezhdu Rossieiu i Anglieiu*, St. Petersburg, 1875.

Tretiakov, P., *Vostochno-slovianskie plemena*, Moscow, 1953.

Trubetskoi, N., *Nasliedie Ginghiskhana*, Berlin, 1925.

Trubetskoi, N., *K probliemie russkavo samopoznania*, Prague, 1927.

Vladimirskii-Budanov, M., *Obzor istorii russkavo prava*, Petrograd-Kiev, 1915.

Vladimirskii-Budanov, M., *Khristomatia po istorii russakvo prava*, St. Petersburg-Kiev, 1908.

Vladimirstsov, B., *Chingis-Khan*, Berlin-St. Petersburg-Moscow, 1922.

Vozniak, M., *Istoria ukrainskoi literatury*, Lviv, 1920, Vol. I.

Vviedenskii, N., *Torgovii dom XVI-XVII vv.*, Leningrad, 1924.

Wanstrat, L., *Beitraege zur Charakteristik des russischen Wortschatzes*, Leipzig, 1933.

Wipper, R., (Vipper), *Ivan Groznyi*, Moscow, 1947.

Chronicles, documents, articles:

Akty Arkheograficheskoi Ekspeditsii, St. Petersburg, 1836, Vols. I-II.

Biblioteca Innostrannikh Pisatelei o Rossii XV-XVIII vv., St. Petersburg, 1863.

Bond, E., sir, edt., *Russia at the Close of the Sixteenth Century, Comprising the Treatise "Of the Russe Common Wealth", by Dr. Giles Fletcher, and the Travels of Sir Jerome Horsey*, London, 1856.

Bouvat, L., "Timur Lang (Tamerlane)", *Encyclopedia of Islam*, London, 1913-1936, Vol. IV.

Chubaty, N., "The Meaning of 'Russia' and 'Ukraine'," *Readings in Russian History*, edt. by S. Harcave, New York, 1962.

Cross, S. and Sherbowitz-Wetzor, O., eds., *The Russian Primary Chronicle*, Cambridge, 1953.

Dewey, H., "The 1497 Sudebnik", *American Slavic and East European Review*, 15, 1956.

Dombrovsky, A., "The Spiritual Trend of Ukraine in Antiquity", *Proceedings*, Shevchenko Scientific Society, Historical-Philosophical Section, New York-Paris, 1951.

Doroshenko, D., "Die Namen 'Rus', 'Russland' und 'Ukraine' in ihrer historischen und gegenwaertigen Bedeutung", *Abhandlungen des Ukrainischen Wissenschaftlichen Instituts*, Berlin, 1939, Vol. III.

Fletcher, G., *Of the Rus Commonwealth*, Ithaca, 1966.

Garkavi, A., ed., *Skazania muzulmanskikh pisatielei o slovianakh i russkikh*, St. Petersburg, 1870.

Grammaticus, Saxo, *Gesta Danorum*, edt. by Olrik, j., and Reader, M., Copenhagen, 1931, 2 volms.

Harcave, S., edt., *Readings in Russian History*, New York, 1962, 2 volms.

Herberstein, S., *Notes upon Russia*, edt. by Major, R., London, 1851-52.

Herodotus, *Historiae*, ed. by H. Stein, Berlin, 1884.

Hrushevsky, M., "Zvychaina skhema russkoi istorii i sprava ratsionalnoho ukladu istorii skhidnioho slovianstva", *Sbornik statiei po slavianovidiniu*, St. Petersburg, 1904, Vol. I.

Karskii, E., *Russkaia Pravda, po drevnieishemu spisu*, St. Petersburg, 1930.

Kazachii Slovar-Spravochnik, edt. Skrylov, A, and Gubariev, H., Cleveland, 1966, Vol. I. Pts. i-2.

Kulakovskii, Yu., *Alany po sviedieniam klasicheskikh i vizantiiskikh pisatielei,* Kiev, 1899.

Kostomarov, N., "Mysli o federativnom nachali v drevniei Rusi", *Sobranie sochinienii,* St. Petersburg, 1903, Vol. I.

Kostomarov, N., "O znachenii Vielikavo Novgoroda", *Sobranie sochinienii,* St. Petersburg, 1903, Vol. I.

Kostomarov, N., "Sieviernorusskiia narodopravstva", *Sobranie sochinienii,* St. Petersburg, 1904, Vol. III.

Kotkowski, J., *Letopis Nestora,* Kiev, 1860.

Krypiakevych, I., "Pobut", *Istoria ukrainskoi kultury,* edt. *Tyktor,* I, Winnipeg, 1964, Vol. I.

Kurtz, B., *Sostoianie Rossii v 1650-1655 po donosieniam Rodesa,* Moscow, 1914.

Makarenko, M., "Skulptura i rizbarstvo Kyiivskoi Rusy", *Kyivskyi zbirnyk istorii i arkheolohii, pobutu i mystetstva,* Kiev, 1931, Vol. I.

Maksimovich, E., "Piervosovietniki dumy boiarskoi", *Zapiski Russkavo Istoricheskavo Obshchestva v Prage,* Prague, 1930, Vol. II.

Malinovskii, I., "Drevneishaia russkaia aristokratia", *Sbornik statei po istorii prava posviashchenii M. F. Vladimirskamu-Budanovu,* Kiev, 1904.

Mansikka, V, "Die Religion der Ostslaven," *Folklore Fellows, Communications,* 43, Helsinki, 1922.

Mitchell, R. and Forbes, N., "The Chronicle of Novgorod", *Royal Historical Society Publications,* Camden, Third Series, Vol. XXV, London, 1914.

Miklosich, F., "Die Türkischen Elemente in den Südost-und Osteuropaeischen Sprachen", *Denkschriften,* Phil.-Hist. Klasse, Akadedemie der Wissenschaften, Vienna, 1884-1890.

Narodnoie Khoziastvo SSSR v 1970 g., Staticheskii Yezhegodnik, Tsentralnoie Statisticheskie Upravlenie pri Sovietie Ministrov SSSR, Moscow, 1971.

Nasonov, A., ed., *Pskovskaia piervaia letopis',* Moscow-Leningrad, 1941.

Nestor, monk, *Poviest' vrieminnikh let po lavretievskamu spisku,* St. Petersburg, 1910.
Olearius, A., *Voyages and Travels,* London, 1662.
Platonov, S., "Ivan Groznyi v russkoi istoriografii", *Russkoie Proshloie,* 1923, Vol. I.
Polnoie sobraine russkikth letopisei: 1, *Lavrentievskaia letopis,* Leningrad, 1927; 2, *Ipatievskaia letopis,* Petrograd, 1923; *Novgorodskaia letopis po sinodalnomu kharateinomu spisku,* St. Petersburg, 1888; 3, *Novgorodskie letopisi,* ed. by A. Bychkov, St. Petersburg, 1879; 9-13, *Patriarshia ili Nikonovskaia letopsis,* St. Petersburg, 1862-1906.
Procopius, *History of the Wars,* ed. Dewing, H., "Loeb Classical Library", 5 volms.
Sbornik, Russkoie Istoricheskoie Obshchestvo, CXLII.
Shakhmatov, A., "Ocherk drevnieishevo perioda istorii russkavo yazika", *Entsyklopedia slovianskoi filologii,* Petrograd 1915, XI.
Shcherbakivsky, V., "Ukrainska praistoria", *Nasha Kultura,* Warsaw, 1935-37, Vol. I.
Sherekh, Yu, "Nazva 'Rus'", *Entsyklopedia ukrainoznavstva,* Munich-New York, 1949, Vol. I.
Smirnov, P., "Obrazovanie russkavo tsentralizovanovo gosudarstva v XIV i XVI viekakh", *Voprosy istorii,* 1946, 2-3.
Sibirskia letopisi; Stroganov, Episov and Remezov chronicles, St. Petersburg, 1907.
Soloviov, A., "Sviataia Rus'", *Sbornik Russkavo Arkheologicheskavo Obshchestva v Korolevstvie S.Kh.S.,* 1927, I.
Trautmann, R., *Die Nestor Chronik,* Leipzig, 1931.
Vasmer, M., "Wikingerspuren in Russland", *Sitzungsberichte,* Preussische Akademie der Wissenschaften, Phil.-Hist. Klasse, Berlin, 1931, XXIV.
Vernadsky, G., "The Scope and Contents of Chingis-Khan's Yasa", *Harvard Journal of Asiatic Studies,* 3, 1938.
Vernadsky, G., "Juwaini's Version of Chingis-Khan's Yasa", *Annales de l'Institut Kondakov,* II, 1939.
Vernadsky, G., "Feudalism in Russia", *Speculum,* 14, 1939.

Vernadsky, G., "The Death of the Tsarevich Dimitry; A Reconsideration of the Case", *Oxford Slavonic Parers,* V, 1954.
Vesielovskii, N., "Tatarskoie vliianie na posolskii tseremonial v moskovskii period russkoi istorii", *Otchet St. Petersburskavo Univiersitieta za 1910 god,* St. Petersburg, 1911.
Wiklund, K., "Finno-Ugrier", *Reallexikon der Vorgeschichte,* 3.
Zbruieva, A., "Ananinskii mogilnik", *Sovietskaia Arkheologia,* II, 1937.
Zimin, A., *Pamiatki prava Kievskavo gosudarstva, Russkaia Pravda prostrannoi redaktsil,* Moscow, 1952.

FOOTNOTES TO CHAPTER ONE

1. *Narodnoie Khoziaistvo SSSR v 1970, Statyscheskii Yezhegodnik,* Centralnoie Statystycheskoie Upravlenie Pry Sovietie Ministrov SSSR, Moscow, 1971, pp. 1-15; basic data.
2. *Ibid.*
3. D. Doroshenko, *Narys storii Ukrainy,* vol. 1, Munich, 1966, pp. 64-68; also, A. Priesniakov, *Obrazovanie Velikorusskavo Gosudarstva,* Petrograd, 1918; and M. Pokrovskii, Brief *History of Russia,* London, 1933, Vol. I, pp. 30-38; also the same, *Istorik Marksist,* 1930, No. 18-19, p. 28; S. Platonov, *History of Russia,* Bloomington, 1964, pp. 8-10.
4. M. Chubaty, *Kniazha Rus'-Ukraina ta vynyknennia triokh skhidnoslovianskykh natsii,* New York-Paris, 1964, p. 94.
5. P. Struve, *Sotsialnaia i ekonomicheskaia istoria Rossii,* Paris, 1952, p. 26.
6. C. Day, *Economic Development in Europe,* New York, 1942, p. 478; Vernadsky, *A History of Russia,* Vol. III, *The Mongols and Russia,* New Haven-London, 1953, pp. 333-390.
7. A. Sobolevskii, *Ocherki iz istorii russkavo yazika,* 1884, first chapters, and his other works; The discussion of the theory; *Doroshenko, loc. cit.,* pp. 63-68.
8. P. Tretiakov, *Vostochno-Slovianskie Plemena,* Moscow, 1953, pp. 121-128, 145, 157, 210, 212; B. Rybakov, "Anty i Kievskaia Rus'," *Viestnik drevnostiei istorii,* part I-II, Moscow, 1939; also Chubaty, pp. 27-38.
9. Chubaty, pp. 60-104 and 125-131.
10. G. Fedotov, *Russian Religious Mind-Kievan Christianity,* Cambridge, 1946, pp. 330 and 405; B. Shulgine, "Kiev the Mother of Russian Towns," *The Slavonic and East-European Review,* Vol. XIX, 1939-1940, pp. 71-72; Chubaty, *loc. cit.;* Comprehensive analysis of the issue: M. Hrushevsky, "Zvychaina skhema russkoi istorii i sprava ratsionalnoho ukladu istorii skhidnioho slovianstva," *Sbornik statei po slavianovidinii,* Vol. I, St. Petersburg, 1904.

FOOTNOTES TO CHAPTER TWO

1. P. Lyashchenko, *History of the National Economy of Russia,* New York, 1949, pp. 35-36.
2. G. Vernadsky and M. Karpovich, *A. History of Russia,* Vol. 1,

Ancient Russia, New Haven-London, 1952, p. 15.

3. The cultural, social, economic and political niveau in the development of any people represents an accumulation of achievements and experiences of all their preceding generations from earliest times. Every detail is important, such as how early man lived in the given area, how early (having gotten used to the environment) he began to create new material and spiritual values there.

4. Historical references to the Ukrainian past go as far back as the fifth century B.C. A number of Greek authors, including Herodotus, the historian, wrote about the peoples in the Pontic area, the Scytians and the Sarmatians: Herodotus, *Historiae,* Loeb Classical Library, ed. by A. Godley, Berlin 1884, IV, 17-22, 110-117 and other places. In the sixth century. A.D. other Greeks, Procopius and Emperor Mauricius, and Jordanis, the historian of the Goths, again conveyed information about the Slavs: *Procopius, History of the Wars,* Loeb Classical Library, VII, 14, 22; VIII, 4, 9; Jordanis, *Romana et Getica,* ed. by Th. Mommsen, in *Monumenta Germaniae Historica,* Berlin, 1882, Vol. 5 sec. 34 and 35. These references do not pertain to the Russian North-East, of which the above authors knew nothing. First, *The Story of Ancient Years,* the first chronicle in East Europe clearly conveyed references about future Russian areas, mentioning there the Slavs and Finns. The information about the Slavs, related by Arab and Jewish travelers, merchants and writers from the ninth and tenth centuries, basically concerns Ukraine and the Ukrainian Slavs: V. Sichynsky, *Ukraine In Foreign Comments and Descriptions From the VIth to XXth Century,* New York, 1953, pp. 31-36, also, A. Garkavi, *Skazania muzulmanskikh pisatelei o slovianakh i russkikh,* St. Petersburg, 1870; relations of Ibn-Dasta, Ibn-Fadlan, Ibn-Hawkal, Al Massudi, Ibn-Yakub and others.

5. Pre-history: A brief coverage, Lyashchenko, pp. 17-34, Vernadsky, Vol. I, pp. 14-48; A. Artsikhovskii, *Vvedienie v arkheologiu,* Moscow, 1940; Yu. Gotie, *Zheleznii viek v vostochnoi Yevropie,* Moscow-Leningrad, 1930; the same, *Ocherki po istorii materialnoi kultury vostochnoi Yevropy,* 1, Moscow, 1925.

6. Gotie, IX, pp. 81-82 *(Fatianovo culture),* chapter X, *(Ananyino culture);* Vernadsky, Vol. I, pp. 23-24 and 47-48; A. Zbruieva "Ananinskii mogilnik," *Sovietskaia arkheologia,* II, 1937, pp. 95-110.

7. Saxo Grammaticus, *Gesta Danorum,* ed. by J. Orlik and H. Reader, Copenhagen, 1931, Vol. 1, p. 138; also Lyashchenko, p. 40.

8. About the Finns: K. Wiklund, "Finno-Ugrier," *Reallexikon Der Vorgeshicht,* by M. Ebert, 3, 354-383; I. N. Smirnov, *Les Populations Finnoises Des Bassins De La Volga Et De La Kama,* Vol. I, Paris, 1898; U. Sirelius, *The Genealogy of The Finns,* Helsinki, 1925; also briefly, Vernadsky, Vol. I, pp. 233-239.

9. R. Meckelein, *Die Finnisch-Ugrischen Elemente in Russischen,*

Diss., Berlin, 1913; D. Doroshenko, *Narys istorii Ukrainy* Munich, 1966, pp. 62-68; M. Vieske, "Slaviano-finskie kulturnie otnosheniia," *Izviestia*, Obshehestvo Arkheologii, Istorii i Etnografii, Kazan, 1890.

10. Procopius, VII, 4, 9; Jordanis, Vol. 5, secs, 34 and 35.

11. Garkavi, Relations of Ibn-Khordadbeh, p. 48; of Ibn-Fadlan, p. 85; of Al Massudi, p. 125; of Ibn Dasta, p. 262, and others.

12. *Poviest Vriemennikh Let*, po Lavrentievskamu spisku, St. Petersburg, 1910; P. Trestiakov, *Vostochno-slovianskie plemena*, Moscow, 1953.

13. N. Chirovsky, *Old Ukraine*, Madison, 1963, pp. 8-9; Vernadsky, Vol. I, pp. 84-100, 191-199; V. Shcherbakivsky; "Ukrainska praistoria," *Nasha Kultura*, I, Warsaw, 1935-37; A. Dombrovsky, "The Spiritual Trends of Ukraine in Antiquity," *Proceedings*, Shevchenko Scientific Society, Historical-Philosophical Section, Vol. 1, New York-Paris, 1951, pp. 52-55.

14. Chirovsky, pp. 38-49; about the early economic development of the eastern Slavs: Lyashchenko, pp. 36 and 41: "In cultural relations the Slavs ranked not lower but instead above the cultural levels of the peoples among whom they settled and to whom they began to transmit their culture,... the influence of the Chuds on the Russian Slavs was revealed more in customs, ethnography, and even language, than in economic respects."

15. *Ibid.*, pp. 61-81.

16. "From the East they obtained silk, silver objects, spices, luxury articles; and sold to the East furs and slaves..., the Russian merchants came with their goods by way of the Volga to the capital of the Khazar Kingdom, Ityl,...": *Ibid.*, p. 77; Fur trade being traditional in Russia: R. Fisher, *The Russian Fur Trade*, Berkeley, 1943.

17. "Our people are permeated in the large majority... with the principle of communal property; they are, if I may say so, instinctively, traditionally communist. The idea of collective property is... deeply rooted in the whole world philosophy of the Russian people..." said Tkachov, a Russian socialist: quoted after K. Marx and F. Engels, *The Russian Menace to Europe*, Glencoe, 1952, pp. 210-211. The same opinion was shared by other students of Russian social and economic institutions, such as Bakunin, Haxthausen and Wallace: H. Schwartz, Russia's Soviet Economy, New York, 1954, pp. 40-41.

18. Gotie, I, pp. 226-227; Lyashchenko, pp. 68-69.

19. M. Chubaty, *Kniazha Rus'-Ukraina ta vynyknennia triokh skhidnioslovianskykh natsii*, New York-Paris, 1964, pp. 60-104 and 125-131: Chubaty has discussed the differential development of the three East-European Slavic nationalities: the Russians, Ukrainians and Byeloruthenians in detail.

20. V. Kluchevsky, *Istoria soslovii v Rossii*, Moscow, 1913, pp. 41-42 and other; also Chirovsky, pp. 35-38.

21. About the evolution of the family, clan, and tribe: E. Jarra, *Ogolna teorja prava*, Warsaw, 1920, pp. 75-80; Also M. Hrushevsky, *Istoria Ukrainy-Rusy*, New York, 1954, Vol. 1, pp. 350-358.

22. "Because they have many princes who quarrel among themselves, it would benefit us to play one against the other...., especially those who live in the border zone," said Emperor Mauricius of Byzantium, from 582-601 A.D.: quoted after Sichynsky, p. 28. On the evolution of the princely and people's meeting institutions by Kluchevsky, Platonov, pp. 368-270, also Vernadsky, briefly, p. 178. On the ancient institution of people's meeting (*vieche*); Procopius, *loc cit.*, and *De bello Gotico*, III, 14: "All affairs, good and bad, are submitted to the people's decision"; Hrushevsky, pp. 350-378: The *Vieche* became an assembly of the householders of a given district, regardless of whether there was any blood relationship among them or not. Brought together by some common interest, they formed a commune (*zadruga, verv*) and chose their elders to attend to their communal affairs. In this manner the original clan organization was gradually superseded by the [territorial] commune,...

The relations of Procopius and Mauricius, as well as the analysis of the princely and people's meeting institutions by Kluchevsky, Platonov, Hrushevsky and others refer primarily to the South-Eastern Slavs, because of the available historical source material. Through the analogy, however, the analysis can be referred to the pre-Russian Slavs, whose mode of life was very similar.

23. *Hypatian Chronicle*, col. 15, in *Polnoie sobranie russkikh lietopisei II*, Petrograd, 1923.

24. Vernadsky, Vol II, *Kievan Russia*, 1951, p. 181; M. Florinsky, *Russia, A History and An Interpretation*, New York, 1953, Vol. 1, pp. 71-100: "The Growth of Moscow Absolutism."

25. In old Ukraine, for example, there were such super-tribal organizations as *Valinana, V-a-i,* and *Chervenski Horody, preceding* the growth of the Kiev state. *Valinana* was mentioned by Al Massudi: Garkavi, pp.125-141.

26. Procopius, VII, 14, 23; *The Song About Ihor's Host* (*Slovo o Polku Ihoreve*) has many references to the pagan deities; apocryphal *Revelation of the Apostles*: V. Mansikka "Die Religion der Ostlaver", *Communications*, Folklore Fellows, Helsinki, 1922; and others, like *The Word of St. Gregory* and *The Holy Virgin's Journey Through Inferno*.

27. Vernadsky, pp. 48-56.
28. *Ibid.*, p. 55.
29. Garkavi, pp. 85-102, 262-270.

FOOTNOTES TO CHAPTER THREE

1. References to the point: 1. Tikhomirov, "Kto nasypal yaroslavskie kurgany," *Trudy*, The Second Tver Region Archeological Congress, Tver,

1906; P. Smirnov, *Volzhskyi shliakh i starodavni Rusy*, Kiev, 1928, p. 145; a conclusion in: G. Vernadsky and M. Karpovich, *A History of Russia*, Vol, 1, *Ancient Russia*, New Haven and London, 1952, p. 326.

2. *Hypatian Chronicle*, col. 15, *Polnoie sobranie ruskikh letopisei*, Vol. II, 3rd edition, Petrograd, 1923: The arrival of the Danes in the Novgorod vicinity (*in finibus Slavorum*) has been reported by Rimbert, *Vita Ankarii*, ed. by G. Waitz, Hannover 1884, p. 43.

3. *Hypat. Chronicle, Ibid.*

4. Hapsburgs in the Holy Roman Empire of the German Nation, in Austria, Spain, Hungary, Bohemia, Sardinia, Sicily, Burgundy, Naples, Luxemburg, the Netherlands and some other lands.

5. It means that they were thinking of opposed interests either in the Ukrainian South or the Russian North. Florinsky made a very distinct reference to the point, that Ukraine and Kiev, "...as such, made no special appeal to the Grand Dukes of Vladimir, and their sporadic interference in Southern affairs, inspired by [their] narrow regional considerations, merely added to the political confusion and disintegration of the south." Also the the continual Cuman raids in Ukraine were in the interest of Vladimir separatism: M. Florinsky, *Russia, A History And Interpretation*, New York, 1953, Vol. 1, pp. 51.

6. On the Normanistic and Anti-Normanistic approaches: N. Riasanovsky, *A History of Russia*, New York, 1963, pp. 25-30; M. Hrushevsky, *A History of Ukraine-Rus*, Vol. I, New York, 1954, pp. 602-624; M. Vasmer, "Wikingerspuren in Russland," *Sitzungsberichten*, Preussische Akademie der Wissenschaften, Phil. -Hist. Klasse, Berlin, 1931.

7. All Kievan princes were theoretically equal; their actual differences made for their being referred to as "senior" and "junior" princes. That principle of "equality" was broken essentially first by Vsievolod III, of Vladimir, who began to call himself Grand Duke, on the one hand, to strengthen in this way Vladimir's separatism from Kiev, and on the other, to place himself over the lesser princes of the Russian North, and to strengthen at the same time Vladimir's Russian centralism: Vernadsky, Vol. II, *Kievan Russia*, New Haven and London, 1951, pp. 178-182; Hrushevsky, Vol. III, pp. 194-196. Various versions of the *Primary Chronicle* fully support in their wording the absence of the grandducal title among the Kievan princes; compare: S. Soloviov, *Istoria otnoshenia mezhdu kniaziami riurikova doma*, Moscow, 1847.

8. Compare: N. Chirovsky, *An Introduction To Russian History*, New York, 1967, pp. 15 and 18.

9. N. Karamzin, *Istoria Gosudarstva Rossiiskavo*, St. Petersburg, 1851, III, pp. 192-193; the same, *Primichaniia k Istorii Gosudarstva Rossiikavo*, St. Petersburg, 1852, III, no. 200; Vernadsky, II, 233.

10. Riasanovsky, p. 88.

11. N. Kostomarov, "O znachenii Velikavo Novgoroda," *Sobranie Sochinienii*, Vol. I, St. Petersburg, 1903; the same, "Sieviernorusskiia narodo-

pravstva," *Sobranie Sochinienii,* Vol. III, St. Petersburg, 1904; briefly, on the survival of democratic institutions in the Russian North-East: Florinsky, Vol. I, pp. 110-125.

12. On the formation of the Russian, Ukrainian and Byeloruthenian nationalities: M. Chubaty, *Kniazha Rus-Ukraina ta vynyknennia triokh skhidnioslovianskykh natsii,* N. York and Paris, 1964; pp. 60-68 and 88-104; also, Vernadsky, Vol. II, p. 215: "To be sure, differences in the language of various groups were still slight but the tendency was to divergency rather than unity.... The opposition of the Kievan population to the Suzdalian *boyars* brought into Kiev by Prince Iuri Dolgoruky in 1154 may be considered one of the first expressions of Russo-Ukrainian rivalry." This ethnic divergency did not exist to that extent between Novgorod and Rostov-Suzdal; also Dombrovsky to that point: ". . . (Hellenism) appears to be one of the most important factors in the formation of Ukrainian spiritual individualism, hence of the Ukrainian people... " A. Dombrovsky, "The Spiritual Trend of Ukraine in Antiquity," *Proceedings,* Shevchenko Scientific Society, Histo. Phil. Section, Vol. I, New York and Paris, 1951, p. 54.

13. Chirovsky, p. 15.

14. J. Clarkson, *A History of Russia,* New York, 1961, p. 63.

15. P. Lyashchenko, *History of the National Economy of Russia,* New York, 1949, p. 168; S. Bakhrushin, *Pamiatniki Vietlikavo Novgoroda,* Moscow, 1909.

16. Lyashchenko, pp. 164-169; A. Nikitskii, *Istoria ekonomicheskavo bitia Vielikavo Novgoroda,* St. Petersburg, 1893; also briefly, Florinsky, Vol. I, pp. 111-114.

17. In 1141 there was a famine in Novgorod because Ukrainian grain shipments did not arrive on account of some military developments in the South: I. Krypiakevych, "Pobut," *Istoria ukrainskoi kultury,* Lviv, 1937, p. 16.

18. On the prince and the people's meeting; the origin and the development: Hrushevsky, Vol. III, pp. 194-227; V. Kluchevsky, *A History of Russia,* London and New York, 1911, Vol. I, pp. 115-116 and 221-238; R. Michell and N. Forbes, "The Chronicle of Novgorod, 1016-1471," translation in *Royal Historical Society Publications,* Camden Third Series, Vol. XXV, London, 1914; the Novgorodians were free "where it pleased them, there they might take to themselves a prince" (p. 36); or "... let the men of Novgorod worry as they like, and get themselves a prince where they like": *Nikonovskaia letopis, Polnoie Sobranie Russkikh Letopisei,* Moscow, 1841-1930, Vol. IX, p. 165.

19. On the development of the upper class: N. Fr. Chirovsky, *Old Ukraine, Its Socio-Economic History Prior to 1781,* Madison, 1963, pp. 35-38 and 61-66; Vernadsky, Vol. II, *Kievan Russia,* pp. 135-140; also Florinsky, Vol. I. pp. 119-120.

20. N. Porfiridov, *Drevnii Novgorod,* Moscow and Leningrad, 1947; also briefly, Clarkson, *op. cit.,* p. 66, S. Platonov, *History of Russia,* Bloom-

ington, 1964, pp. 59-66; The Russia of Novgorod. The last decades of Novgorod and its submission: G. Vernadsky and M. Karpovich, *A History of Russia*, Vol. IV, *Russia at the Dawn of the Modern Age*, New Haven-London, 1959, pp. 42-63; Florinsky, I, pp. 114-122.

FOOTNOTES TO CHAPTER FOUR

1. G. Vernadsky and M. Karpovich, *A History of Russia*, Vol. I, *Ancient Russia*, New Haven-London, 1952, pp. 23-24, 43-37 and 47-48; Yu. Gotie, *Ocherki po istorii materialnoi kultury vostochnoi Yevropy*, Moscow, 1925, pp. 81-82, Chapters IX and X.

2. *The Russian Primary Chronicle, Laurentian Text*, by S. Cross and O. Sherbowitz-Wetzor, Cambridge, 1953, p. 142: "My sons, I am about to quit this world. Love one another, since ye are brothers by one father and mother.... The throne of Kiev I bequeath to my eldest son, your brother Iziaslav. Heed him as ye have heeded me, that he may take my place among you. To Sviatoslav I give Chernigov, to Vsievolod — Pereyaslavl, to Igor the city of Vladimir, and to Viacheslav-Smolensk"; Brief analysis of the testament: M. Hrushevsky, *History of Ukraine-Rus'*, New York, 1954, Vol. II, pp. 44-46.

3. S. Shelukhin, *Ukraina*, Prag, 1936-1937, Introductory chapter.

4. S. Platonov, *History of Russia*, Bloomington, 1964, pp. 67-68; also M. Florinsky, Russia, *A History and an Interpretation*, New York, 1953, Vol. I, pp. 44-51.

5. Platonov, pp. 66-69.

6. Hrushevsky, Vol. II, p. 181; The wording of the chronicle; *Ipatievskaia letopis, Polnoie sobranie russkikh letopisei, 3rd edition*, Petrograd, 1923, under the year 1157.

7. *Ipatievskaia letopis,* as above, under the year 1169.

8. *Idem.*, under the years 1170 and 1172; also, Hrushevsky, Vol. II, p. 199.

9. Andrei built a beautiful church of the *Assumption of Virgin* Mary, to serve as a future metropolitan cathedral. E. Golubinskii, *Istoria Ruskoi Tserkvi*, Moscow, 1901-1904, I, pt. 2; the Patriarch of Constantinople refused to cooperate with Andrei's request: Hrushevsky, Vol. III, pp. 268-269; Patriarch's letter of refusal; *Russkaia Istoriecheskaia Biblioteka*, VI, nr. 3.

10. An excellent analysis of Andrei's character and his rule: V. Kluchevsky, *A History of Russia*, London-New York, 1911, Vol. I, pp. 221-229.

11. Kluchevsky, Vol. I, p. 234; Analysis of Vsievolod's intrigues to spread chaos in Ukraine: Hrushevsky, Vol. II, pp. 216-219.

12. Platonov, p. 71; excellent characteristics of Vsievolod III: Kluchevsky, Vol. I, pp. 234-238.

13. Compare: Hrushevsky, *op. cit.*, Vol. II, pp. 71-73.

14. Being harrassed by political misfortune, chaos and dynastic strife and then, due to the Mongol invasion, the Dukes of Vladimir and later on, of Moscow could not, until the days of Ivan III, effectively resume their dynastic claims to Ukraine. These claims served later as a smoke screen for Muscovite political expansion beyond Russian ethnic territory in East Europe.

FOOTNOTES TO CHAPTER FIVE

1. On the constitution of the Kievan realm: N. Kostomarov, "Mysli o federativnom nachale v drevniei Rusi," *Sobranie sochinienii*, Book 1, St. Petersburg, 1903; A. Priesniakov, *Kniazhoie pravo v dreviniei Rusi. Ocherki po istorii X-XII st.*, St. Petersburg, 1909; V. Kluchevsky, *A History of Russia*, London-New York, 1911, Vol. I, pp. 94-109; a brief summary: D. Doroshenko, *Narys istorii Ukrainy*, Munich, 1966, Vol. I, p. 49-53.

2. Kluchevsky, p. 235.

3. M. Florinsky, Russia, *A History and An Interpretation*, New York, 1953, Vol. I, p. 45.

4. M. Vladimirskii-Budanov, *Obzor istorii russkavo prava*, Petrograd-Kiev, 1915, pp. 44-51; V. Kluchevsky, *Boiarskaia duma drevniei Rusi*, Moscow, 1909 chpts. I-II, V. Sergeievich, *Drevnosti russkavo prava*, St. Petersburg, 1908-1911, Vol. II, pp. 371-504.

5. Vladimirskii-Budanov, pp. 51-60; Sergeievich, pp. 1-118.

6. A. Presniakov, *Obrazovanie vielikarusskavo gosudarstva*, Petrograd, 1918, p. 44.

7. *Mir* in the Russian village: H. Schwartz, *Russia's Soviet Economy*, New York, 1954, pp. 39-53.

8. Sergeievich, Vol. III, pp. 164-313; Presniakov, *Lektsii po russkoi istorii*, I, pp. 205-207; also N. Chirovsky, *Old Ukraine*, Madison, 1963, pp. 122-125.

9. G. Vernadsky and M. Karpovich, *A History of Russia*, Vol. II, *Kievan Russia*, New Haven-London, 1951, pp. 189-192 and 194-196.

10. On the judiciary: Vladimirskii-Budanov, pp. 610-629.

11. Sergeievich on the Ruska Pravda: "Who in the world would have cared to learn how to read *Rus'ka Pravda*? Everyone profited by reading the Holy Bible; it was read and even memorized. But *Rus'ka Pravda*? Who needed it?... It interested no one but a professional copyist"; V. Sergeievich, *Russkaia Pravda v cheteriokh redaktsiiakh*, St. Petersburg, 1904, p. xx. Even less importance had the code in the Russian North-East; it was largely alien to the Russian Slavs (transl. by Florinsky).

12. "... Also food supplies — these, however, were not ample, since the army as a rule lived off the country it passed through": Vernadsky, II, p. 193.

13. Vladimirskii-Budanov, op cit., pp. 25-31; I. Malinovskii, "Drevnieishaia Russkaia aristokratia," *Sbornik statiei po istorii prava posviashchennii M. F. Vladimirskomu-Budanovu*, Kiev, 1904, pp. 256-274; also, Chirovsky, pp. 61-66.

14. Vladimirskii-Budanov, pp. 31-33; V. Sergeievich, *Drevnosti russkavo prava*, St. Petersburg, 1908-1911, Vol. I, pp. 335-338; also, Chirovsky, pp. 69-71.

15. V. Kluchevsky, *Istoria soslovii v Rossii*, Moscow, 1913, p. 49.

16. On the position of the peasants and slaves: Vernadsky, Vol. II, pp. 143-151; Vladimirskii-Budanov, pp. 33-35 and 395-408; Sergeievich, I. pp. 105-159, 203-214 and 215-225.

17. P. Lyashchenko, *History of National Economy of Russia*, New York, 1949, p. 166.

18. Vernadsky, Vol, II, pp. 159-161; Kluchevsky, *A History of Russia*, London-New York, 1911, Vol. I, pp. 203-220: on the Russian colonization of the upper Volga regions.

19. N. Chirovsky, *The Economic Factors in the Growth of Russia*, New York, 1957, pp. 1-7, chapter on the economic background of the emerging empire.

20. *Ibid.*

21. The analysis of economic conditions was heavily based on author's two other books, the quoted above one, and *Old Ukraine*, Madison, 1963, pp. 66, 68-69, 81-92, 97-98.

22. Vernadsky, Vol. II, pp. 163-172; also, J. Clarkson, *A History of Russia*, New York, 1961, pp. 73-76; strictly a Marxian view: Lyashchenko, pp. 83-94 and 136-138.

23. Saxo Gramaticus, *Gesta Danorum*, ed. by J. Olrik anh. Reader, Copenhagen, 1931, 2 vols., p. 138; Also, Yu. Fedoriv, *Istoria tserkvy v Ukraini*, Toronto, 1967, p. 43.

24. Vernadsky, Vol. II, p. 269.

25. A. Niekrasov, *Ocherki po istorii drevnierusskavo zodchestva XI-XVII viekov*, Moscow, 1936; I. Tolstoy and N. Kondakov, *Russkie drevnosti*, St. Petersburg, 1889-1899, 6 vols.; sections on the Suzdalian and Vladimirian architecture.

26. N. Trubetskoi, *K problemie russkavo samopoznania*, Prague, 1927, pp. 29; M. Pekelis ed., *Istoria russkoi muzyki*, I, Moscow-Leningrad, 1940, chs. 1-11.

27. A. Shakhmatov, "Ocherk drevnieishevo perioda istorii russkovo yazika," *Entsiklodediia slovianskoi filologii*, Petrograd, 1915, XI, pt. 1; also, St. Petersburg, 1919, ed. II.

28. Vernadsky, Vol. II, pp. 279-280.

29. *Ibid.*, p. 283.

FOOTNOTES TO CHAPTER SIX

1. Herodotus, *Historiae*, ed. H. Stein, Berlin, 1884, IV, 11-13. G.

Vernadsky and M. Karpovich, *A History of Russia*, Vol. I, *Ancient Russia*, New Haven-London, 1952, pp. 40-51; D. Doroshenko *Narys istorii Ukrainy*, Vol. I. Munich, 1966, pp. 29-30; M. Rostovtsev, *Davno-mynule nashoho pivdnia*, Petrograd, 1916.

2. M. Rostovtsev, *Skythien und der Bosporus*, Berlin, 1931; the same (Rostovtzeff), *Iranians and Greeks*, Oxford, 1922; Vernadsky, Vol. I, pp. 51-73; also, Doroshenko, p. 30.

3. A. Dombrovsky, "The Spiritual Trend of Ukraine in Antiquity," *Proceedings*, Shevchenko Scientific Society, Historical-Philosophical Section, New York-Paris, 1951, Vol. I, pp. 52-55; Doroshenko, Vol. I, pp. 33-35; also, N. Chirovsky, *Old Ukraine*, Madison, 1963, pp. 8-12; V. Shcherbakivsky, "Ukrainska Praistoria," *Nasha Kultura*, I, Warsaw, 1935-37.

4. Vernadsky, Vol. I, pp. 175-201; *The Russian Primary Chronicle*, by S. Cross and O. Sherbowitz-Wetzor, Cambridge, 1954, p. 55: "They made war upon the Slavs, and harrassed the Dulebians, who were themselves Slavs. They were even violent to Dulebian women. When an Avar made a journey, he..., but gave the command... that three or four or five women should be yoked to his cart...."

5. M. Korduba, *Najnowsze teorje o poczatkach Rusi*, Warsaw, 1932; Yu. Sherekh, "Nazva' Rus'." *Entsyklopedia Ukrainoznavstva*, Munich-New York, 1949, Vol. I, pp. 13-14.

6. D. Doroshenko, "Die Namen' Rus', 'Russland' und 'Ukraine' in ihrer historischen und gegenwärtigen Bedeutung," *Abhandlunger des Ukrainischen Wissenschaftlichen Instituts in Berlin*, Vol. III, Berlin, 1931; also Sherekh, *loc. cit.*

7. *The Russian Primary Chronicle*, pp. 86-87; *Vernadsky*, Vol. II, *Kievan Russia*, New Haven-London, 1951, pp. 42-47.

8. *The Russian Primary Chronicle*, p. 133: "..., and Sviatopolk fled. As he fled, a devil came upon him and his bones were softened, so that he could not ride, but had to be carried in a litter.... Upon reaching the wilderness between Poland and Bohemia, he died a miserable death. When judgment thus rightly fell upon him as a sinner, torments seized this impious prince after his departure from this world."

9. *Ibid.*, p. 142: Yaroslav's Testament.

10. Compare: Chapter Four, p. 86.

11. On the history of Ukraine and the Galician-Volhinian principality: D. Doroshenko, *Narys istorii Ukrainy*, Munich, 1966. Vol. I. and M. Hrushevsky, *Istoria Ukrany-Rusi*, New York, 1954-1955, Vols. I-IV.

12. *Rus'ka Pravda* as a piece of legislation: A. Zimin, *Pamiatki prava Kievskavo Gosudarstva, Russkaia Pravda prostrannoi redaktsii*, Moscow, 1952; its analysis: V. Kluchevsky, *A History of Russia*, London-New York, 1911, Vol. I, pp. 144-164.

13. Vernadsky, Vol. II, *Kievan Russia*, pp. 251-256; N. Findeizen, *Ocherki po istorii muzyki v Rossii*, I, Moscow and Leningrad, 1928.

14. Cultural life in the Kievan state: Hrushevsky, Vol. III, pp. 401-504; Vernadsky, Vol. II, pp. 241-316; A Niekrasov, *Ocherki po istorii drevnierusskavo zodchestva XI-XVII viekov*, Moscow, 1936; D. Chyzhevsky, *Istoria ukrainskoi literatury*, New York 1956, pp. 24-211; M. Vozniak, *Istoria ukraiskoi literatury*, Lviv, 1920, Vol. I; M. Makarenko, "Skulptura i pizbarstvo Kyiivskoi Rusy," *Kyiivski zbirnysky istorii i arkheologii, pobutu i mystetstva*, Kiev, 1931, Vol. I; V. Miller, *Ocherki russkoi narodnoi slovesnosti*, Moscow, 1897-1910, 2 vols.

FOOTNOTES TO CHAPTER SEVEN

1. E. Reischauer and J. Fairbank, *East Asia: The Great Tradition*, Boston, 1960, pp. 94-95; G. Vernadsky and M. Karpovich, *A History of Russia*, Vol. I, *Ancient Russia*, New Haven-London, 1952, pp. 50, 80-81, 122-124.

2. M. Paris, *English History*, tr. by J. Giles, London, 1852-1854, Vol. I, p. 312; also Vernadsky, Vol. III, *The Mongols and Russia*, New Haven-London, 1953, p. 12.

3. N. Chirovsky, *An Introduction To Russian History*, New York, 1967, pp. 52, 171-172, 218; *Krasnaia Nov*, June 1927, Bukharins polemic article.

4. Vernadsky, Vol. III, p. 59.

5. Reischauer, pp. 267-280; China under the Yuan dynasty, also Vernadsky, Vol. III, pp. 80-92: The Yuan Dynasty.

6. B. Spuler, *Die Goldene Horde*, Leipzig, 1943; Vernadsky, Vol. III, pp. 138-232; V. Tizengauzen (Tiesenhausen), *Sbornik materialov otnosiashchikhsia k istorii Zolotoi Ordy*, Moscow-Leningrad, 1941, on the life and reign of Genghis-Khan: B. Vladimirtsov, *Chingis-Khan*, Berlin- Petrograd-Moscow, 1922; also R. Fox, *Genghis-Khan*, New York, 1936. The Khanate of Kipchak was also called the White Horde from the colors of Juchi's clan. The name of the "Golden" Horde was apparently derived from the yellow colors, the symbol of the Mongol imperial power in general: E. Khara-Davan, *Chinghis-Khan kak polkovodets i yevo nasledie*, Belgrad, 1929, p. 199 and others; also Vernadsky, Vol. III, pp. 138-140.

7. Chirovsky, p. 40; also, the same, *Old Ukraine*, Madison, 1963, pp. 12-13.

8. A. Nasonov, *Mongoly i Rus'*, Moscow-Leningrad, 1940, pp. 51-53.

9. L. Bouvat, "Timur Lang (Tamerlane)," *Encyclopedia of Islam*, 1930, 4, 777-779; H. Lamb, *Tamerlane the Earth Shaker*, New York, 1928.

10. V. Smirnov, *Krimskoie Khanstvo pod vierkhovenstvom Ottomanskoii Porty*, St. Petersburg, 1887.

11. N. Karamzin, *Istoria gosudarstva rossiiskavo*, St. Petersburg, 1851-53, Vol. V, pp. 365-384.

12. N. Trubetskoi, *Nasledie Genghis-Khana* Berlin, 1925; also, Vernadsky, Vol I.II, *The Mongols and Russia*, 1953, pp. 333-390, Chapter V, The Mongol Impact on Russia; also, Khara-Davan, *op. cit.*

13. "To say, however, that the Tsardom of Moscow merely followed the tradition of Andrew Bogolubsky and some of other Suzdalian princes would be to underestimate the significance of the change. (Under the Mongol impact). With all their monarchic tendencies the Suzdalian princes never succeeded in becoming absolute rulers of their land" (and on their own alone): Vernadsky, III, p. 336.

14. G. Fletcher, *On the Rus Commonwealth*, London, 1856, p. 26; also S. Herberstein, *Zapiski o moskovitskikh dielakh*, St. Petersburg, 1908; He felt he entered a different world when he arrived in Moscow in 1517 as the Austrian envoy. He remarked that Grand Duke Vasilii III had much more comprehensive authority over his subjects than any other European ruler of his time (p. 20).

15. According to Zagoskin's computation of the origin of the princely and *boyar* noble families for the later post Mongol era (the 17th century) indicated that over 17% of them were of the Tartar or other Oriental descent; some 156 families out of the total number of some 915; M. Vladimirskii-Budanov, *Obzor istorii russkavo prava*, St. Petersburg-Kiev, 1915, p. 123, nt. 1.

16. G. Vernadsky, "The Scope and Contents of Chingis-Khan's Yasa," *Harvard Journal of Asiatic Studies*, 3 (1938), pp. 337-360; the same, "Juwaini's Version of Chingis-Khan's Yasa," *Annales de l'Institut Kondakov*, II (1939), pp. 33-45.

17. Karamzin, Kostomarov, Leontovich, Sergeievich, Trubetskoi, Khara-Davan and Vernadsky admitted the significant impact of the Mongols upon Russian society, while Soloviov, Diakonov, Vladimirskii-Budanov, Riasanovskii, Grekov and Kluchevsky either denied or, at least, minimized its effects.

18. N. Vesielovskii, "Tatarskoie vliianie na posolskii tseremonial v moskovskii period russkoi istorii," *Otchet St. Petiersburgskavo Universtieta za 1910 god*, St. Petersburg, 1911, suppl. pp. 1-19; also Khara-Davan, p. 199; G. Vernadsky and M. Karpovich, *A History of Russia*, Vol. III, *The Mongols and Russia*, New Haven-London, 1953, pp. 387-389.

19. M. Hrushevsky, *Istoria Ukrainy-Rusy*, New York, 1954, Vol. III, pp. 301-312.

20. Vernadsky, Vol. III, pp. 367-372.

21. *Gramoty Vielikavo Novgoroda i Pskova*, ed. S. Valk, Moscow-Leningrad, 1949, pp. 11 and 57; Vernadsky, III, pp. 171-172. P. Smirnov, "Obrazovanie russkavo tsentralizovanovo gosudarstva v XIV-XVI viekakh," *Voprosy istorii*, 1946, Facs. 2-3, pp. 76-79; N. Rozhkov, *Obzor russkoi istorii s sotsiologicheskoi tockhi zrenia*, St. Petersburg, 1905, 2, pp. 137-138; also references to the farm economy: *Dukhovniie i dogovorniie*

gramoty vielikikh i udielnikh kniazei XIV-XVI viekov, eds. S. Bakhrushin and L. Cherepnin, Moscow-Leningrad, 1950, pp. 8, 14, 16.

22. At that time, also, the famous monastery on the Solovki Islands in the White sea was founded. It became a notorious Soviet concentration camp during the Stalin era.

23. F. Miklosich, "Die Türkischen Elemente in den Südost und Osteuropaischen Sprachen," *Denkschriften*, Phil-Historische Klasse, Akademie der Wissenschaften, Vienna, 1884-1890, pp. 34-35, 37-38; also, L. Wanstrat, *Beiträge zur Charakteristik des russischen Wortchatzes*, Leipzig, 1933, pp. 63-82, 97-98; N. Karamzin, a famous historian, P. Chaadaiev, a famous philosopher, and many other outstanding Russians were of the Tartar descent: P. Dolgorukov, *Rossiiskaia rodoslovnaia kniga*, 4, St. Petersburg, 1857, pp. 44, 71, and other; also on the literary inspiration: A. Orlov, *Drevnaia russkaia literatura XI-XVI viekov*, Moscow-Leningrad, 1939, pp. 141-145; D. Cizevskij (Chizhevsky), *History of Russian Literature* 'S-Gravenhage, 1960, pp. 124-131, 141-162.

FOOTNOTES TO CHAPTER EIGHT

1. That dualism of the Russian character was identified by N. Gogol in his famous comedy-satire, *The Inspector General*, published in 1836, and his masterpiece, *Dead Souls*, published in 1842.

2. For the Swedes and the German Knights there was little difference between the "non-Christian infidels" and the Orthodox "schismatics"; they were in need of "salvation." This was the smokescreen of the Swedish and German military exploits in the European North-East during its difficult days of the Mongol invasion, having attacked Novgorod and Pskov in 1240: G. Vernadsky and M. Karpovich, *A History of Russia*, Vol. III, *The Mongols and Russia*, New Haven-London, 1953, pp. 54-55.

3. *Idem.*, pp. 168-170; also, A. Nasonov, *Mongoly i Rus'*, Moscow-Leningrad, 1940, pp. 59, 62 and others.

4. *The Patriarch Nikon Chronicle, Polnoie sobranie russkikh letopisei*, 9-13, 1862-1906, 10, 155; also, Yu. Kulakovskii, *Alany po sviedieniiam klassicheskikh i vizantiiskikh pisatielei*, Kiev, 1899, p. 60.

5. *The Patriarch Nikon Chronicle*, 10, 138, indicated, that Andrei went with his *boyars* to Novgorod, after being defeated by the Mongols. Then, there were no *boyars* from Vladimir mentioned in attendance to greet Alexander upon his arrival in the city; *Nikon's Chronicle*, 10, 139. This suggests the conclusion of the noble support for Andrei's and opposition to Alexander's policies toward the Mongols; check also Vernadsky's commentary: Vol. III, p. 148.

6. It was a general indignation in Novgorod at Alexander's servile

policy toward the Tartars: *The First Novgorodian Chronicle, Polnoie sobranie russkikh letopisei*, 3, 1841, pp. 310-311.

7. Vernadsky, III, pp. 159-161; also, Nasonov, pp. 52-53; the chronicles gave a rather confusing account about the princely participation or non-participation in the uprisings.

8. V. Kluchevsky, *A History of Russia*, London-New York, 1911, Vol. I, pp. 254-271. The author gave a comprehensive analysis of those relations and developments; also, J. Clarkson, *A History of Russia*, New York, 1961, pp. 73-76: The question of feudalism.

9. N. Riasanovsky, *A History of Russia*, New York, 1963, pp. 119-124, on why Moscow succeeded.

10. "The primary cause of the ascendancy of Moscow was its exceptionally favorable geographical position."... "Another reason for the rise of Moscow was the ability and cleverness of the first Moscow rulers": S. Platonov, *History of Russia*, Bloomington, 1964, pp. 89-90; the chronicles called the place either *Moskva or Kuchkovo*; Kluchevsky, I, pp. 272-294.

11. Kluchevsky, Vol. I, pp. 289-293. M. Florinsky, *Russia, A History and an Interpretation*, New York, 1953, Vol. I, pp. 85-86 and 92-93; an over-all analysis: E. Golubinskii, *Istoria russkoi tserkvi*, two vols., Moscow, 1900-1911.

12. S. Soloviov, *Istoria Rossii s drevnieishikh vremien*, Moscow, 1851-1879, 29 vols., Vol. III, pp. 287-289. Apparently Khan Uzbeg did not trust Ivan yet or did not want to see a powerful Moscow. Hence, not Ivan but Alexander was made the Grand Duke, and the first was constantly watched by Khan's commissioner: Nasonov, pp. 107-110.

13. The autocracy of the Muscovite rulers and the Orthodox Church: Platonov, pp. 114-117; Florinsky, Vol. I, pp. 92-93, 96, 136-142: "The idea of the subservience of the Church to the state... had been transplanted from Byzantium to Russian soil"; also on the subject, H. Luzhnytsky, *Ukrainska tserkva mizh skhodom i zakhodom*, Philadelphia, 1954, pp. 150-160, Comprehensively: Golubinskii, *op. cit.*

14. Florinsky, Vol. I, p. 89; Kluchevsky, Vol. I, p. 297; the term "votchina" instead of "udiel" was used. Kluchevsky said that five principal methods were employed by the Muscovite princes for extension of their territories; purchase, seizure by military force, diplomatic acquisition, treaty of the in tenure-service with other appanage princes, and colonization (p. 284).

15. Platonov, p. 92, as he quoted a chronicle.

16. Luzhnytsky, pp. 149-150.

17. N. Chirovsky, *An Introduction to Russian History*, New York, 1967, pp. 39-41; also Vernadsky, Vol. IV, *Russia at the Dawn of the Modern Age*, New Haven-London, 1959, pp. 169-170.

18. On the battle of Kulikovo plain: *The Patriarch Nikon Chronicle*,

II, pp. 55-66; *The Trinity Chronicle*, reconstructed by M. Priselkov, pp. 419-420; Platonov, pp. 93-98; Soloviov, Vol. III, pp. 358-360; also, N. Karamzin, *Istoria Gosudarstva Rossiiskavo*, St. Petersburg, 1851-1858, Vol. V, pp. 70-76.

19. "... the victory on the Don consisted in that it destroyed the idea that the Tartar was invincible, and demonstrated that Russia had grown sufficiently strong for an open struggle for independence... in that it gave an impetus toward a vigorous national consolidation under a single ruler, the prince of Moscow": Platonov, p. 97; also a commentary by Florinsky, Vol. I, pp. 65-66.

20. On the princely testaments: Kluchevsky. Vol. I, pp. 294-308.

FOOTNOTES TO CHAPTER NINE

1. V. Kluchevsky, *A History of Russia*, London-New York 1911, Vol. I, p. 314.

2. *Ibid.*, pp. 303-304.

3. On the Lithuanian-Ruthenian (Ukrainian) Commonwealth: M. Hrushevsky, *Istoria Ukrainy-Rusy*, New York, 1955, Vols. IV and V; also, D. Doroshenko, *Naris istorii Ukrainy*, Munich, 1966, Vol. I, pp. 97-144; briefly, N. Riasanovsky, *A History of Russia*, New York, 1963, pp: 146-154: The Lithuanian-Russian state; also, N. Fr. Chirovsky, *Old Ukraine*, Madison, 1963, pp. 129-135; The terminology of deacon Yakim, *Moskovskie chtenia*, 1883, I, p. 2: "Our Christian Rus' Commonwealth, the Lithuanian Grand Duchy"; also, J. Stukas, *Awakening Lithuania*, Madison, 1966, pp. 1-20.

4. *The Patriarch Nicon Chronicle*, II, p. 160, in *Polnoie sobranie russkikh letopisei*, 9-13 (1862-1906).

5. M. Florinsky, *Russia, A History and an Interpretation*, New York, 1953, Vol. I, p. 99: "No such things have ever been heard of or seen,' one chronicler added, although it seems difficult to imagine tortures and savagery to which the Russians had not become accustomed during the course of the preceding centuries."

6. *The Fourth Novgorodian Chronicle*, p. 443, in *Polnoie sobranie russkikh letopiesi*, 4, 1848; G. Vernadsky and M. Karpovich, *A. History of Russia*, Vol. III, *The Mongols and Russia*, New Haven-London, 1953, p. 322.

7. About the Church union: Hrushevsky, Vol. V, pp. 508-528; Vernadsky, Vol. III, pp. 307-311; E. Golubinskii, *Istoria russkoi tserkvi*, Moscow, 1900-1917, Vol. II, pp. 433-441.

8. Grand Duke Ivan III: Vernadsky, Vol. IV, *Russia at the Dawn of the Modern Ages*, New Haven-London, 1959, pp. 67-133; Kluchevsky, Vol. II, pp. 1-37.

9. Vernadsky, Vol. IV, pp. 101-116; Florinsky, I, pp. 155-162.

10. On annexation of Novgorod: S. Soloviov, *Istoria Rossii s drevnieishikh vriemen*, Moscow, 1851-1879, Vol. V, pp. 37-40; also, N. Karamzin, *Primiechaniia k istorii Gosudarstva Rossiiskavo*, St. Petersburg, 1852-1853, Vol. VI, nts. 147, 182, 198 and other; J. Dlugosh, a Polish scholar, told the story of enormous booty, Ivan raised in Novgorod: *Opera omnia*, Krakow, 1873-1878, Vol. 14, pp. 697-698; also, *The Fourth Novgorodian Chronicle*, pp. 448-516, in *Polnoie sobranie russkikh letopisei*, 4, 1925.

11. The text of the treaty: S. Bakhrushin and L. Cherepnin, eds. *Dukhovnie i dagovornie gramoti vielikikh i udielnikh kniazei XIV-XVI viekov*, Moscow-Leningrad, 1950, pp. 207, 277, 295-301, 319-322, and other pages.

12. *Sbornik Imperatorskavo Russkavo Istoricheskavo Obshchestva*, Vol. 35, pp. 398-402.

13. Nevertheless, gifts and monetary payments were still going for some time from Moscow mainly to the Crimean Horde, and to other Hordes, to buy peace and friendship. These were no more, however, a sign of a political submission: Vernadsky, Vol. IV, p. 77.

14. S. Platonov, *History of Russia*, Bloomington, 1964, p. 102.

15. *Pskovskie letopisi*, A. Nasonov, ed., Moscow-Leningrad, 1941, I, pp. 92-97.

16. Florinsky, Vol. I, p. 158; also Filotei's letters to Vasilii III and the Pskovians: V. Malinin, *Starets yeleazarova monastiria Filotei i yevo poslania*, Moscow, 1901, pp. 49-56 and 7-24.

17. W. Pociecha, "Daszkiewicz," *Polski slownik biograficzny*, 1938, 4, pp. 444-447, Hrushevsky, Vol. VII, pp. 91-93.

18. Platonov, p. 114.

19. R. Dmitrieva, *Skazanie o kniaziakh Vladimirskikh*, Moscow and Leningrad, 1955, pp. 159-178, and S. von Herberstein, *Zapiski o moskovitskikh dielakh*, trans. by A. Malein, St. Petersburg, 1908, pp. 4 and 32.

20. Imperial ideology: Vernadsky, Vol. IV, pp. 165-168.

21. Malinin, pp. 49-56; also, H. Schaeder, *Moscau, das Dritte Rom*, Hamburg, 1929.

22. Von Herberstein related the story, that Vasilii's lieutenant, Peter, under whose command Vasilii left Moscow in the presence of the Mongol menace, supposedly gave the promise to Mohammed-Girey in the name of his sovereign government to resume the regular tribute payment to the Khan. Vernadsky, found, however, the story to be of little credibility. S. von Herberstein, *Commentaries on Muscovite Affairs*, ed. and trans. by O. Backus, Lawrence, 1956, pp. 107-109; Vernadsky, Vol. IV, p. 153, also Soloviov, Vol. V, pp. 365-369.

23. Karamzin, Vol. VI, n. 370; About the text of the quoted letter.

FOOTNOTES TO CHAPTER TEN

1. Compare: Chapter Seven, the last section, dealing with the Mongol impact upon the Russian society.
2. Compare: G. Vernadsky and M. Karpovich, *A History of Russia*, Vol. III, *The Mongols and Russia*, New Haven-London, 1953, pp. 349-354, 385-389; also, but comprehensively, M. Diakonov, *Vlast' moskovskikh gosudarei*, St. Petersburg, 1889; V. Kluchevsky, *Skazania inostrantsev o moskovskom gosudarstvie*, Moscow, 1918, p. 18 and other.
3. E. Maksimovich, "Piervosovietnik dumy boyarskoi," *Zapiski Russkavo Istoricheskavo Obshchestva v Prage*, 2, 1930, pp. 141-162; Compare: The *duma* in the pre-Mongol era: V. Kluchevsky, *Boyarskaia duma dreviei Rusi*, Moscow, 1909; also Vernadsky, Vol. III, pp. 347-348, and Vol. IV, *Russia at the Dawn of the Modern Ages*, New Haven- London, 1953, 1959, pp. 117-119.
4. The text of the *Sudebnik* may be found in *Pamiatniki russkavo prava*, 3, pp. 346-357; the general characteristics: H. Dewey, "The 1497 Sudebnik," *American Slavic and East European Review*, 15, 1956, pp. 325-338; also, L. Cheriepnin, *Russkie feodalnie arkhivy XIV-XV viekov*, Moscow, 1949-1951, 2, pp. 273-310.
5. M. Vladimirskii-Budanov, *Khristomatia po istorii russkavo prava*, St. Petersburg-Kiev, 1908-1915, Vol. II, p. 85-94; *The Sudebnik*, art. 9.
6. On the "kormlenie": M. Vladimirskii-Budanov, *Obzor istorii russkavo prava*, St. Petersburg-Kiev, 1951, pp. 192-194; Vernadsky, Vol. III, pp. 359-360; Vol. IV, pp. 102-103.
7. P. Lyashchenko, *History of the National Economy of Russia*, New York, 1949, pp. 163-164.
8. *Ibid.*, pp. 183-188.
9. A concise, but a very good presentation of the government and administration in the old Muscovy-Russia: Vernadsky, Vol. III, *The Mongols and Russia*, pp. 344-366; also, Vladimirskii-Budanov, *op. cit.*, respective pages.
10. D. Doroshenko, *Naris istorii Ukrainy*, Munich, 1966, Vol. I, pp. 149-160 and 186-195; also, N. Fr.-Chirovsky, *Old Ukraine, Its Socio-Economic History prior to 1781*, Madison, 1963, pp. 232-234.
11. The *boyars* and the *miestnichestvo*: V. Kluchevsky, *A History of Russia*, London-New York, 1912, Vol. II, pp. 38-57: "..., in the *miestnichestvo* system, *miestnichestvo* was the inherited service relation of a given individual or a given family, of the official class to all other individuals or families of that class. (p. 46).
12. The urban and rural population: Lyashchenko, pp. 136-165; also, Vernadsky, Vol. III, pp. 372-377; Vladimirskii-Budanov, *Obzor*, pp. 129-130 and other, on the social classes in old Muscovy.
13. On feudalism in the North-East Russia: Lyashchenko, *Ibid.*, "In

the northeastern Rostov-Suzdal, Vladimir and Moscow Rus' of the twelfth century, and especially in the thirteenth and fourteenth centuries, this process of feudalization achieved its final fruition, affecting decisively the entire political and economic order of the land (p. 138); G. Vernadsky, "Feudalism in Russia," *Speculum*, 14, 1939, pp. 300-323; Chirovsky, pp. 152-153.

14. The extent of the property rights on land was determined by the legal character of the land ownership or possession, having been either the hereditary and traditional *votchina* (patrimonium) or the newer form of the *pomiestie* (service-tenure): Lyashchenko, pp. 189-190. About their natural character: *Ibid.*, pp. 148-150.

15. B. Rybakov, *Remeslo drevniei Rusi*, Moscow, 1948, pp. 525-538, 595 (f), 640-645; also briefly, Vernadsky, Vol. III, pp. 339-340.

16. N. Fr.-Chirovsky, *The Economic Factors in the Growth of Russia*, New York, 1957, pp. 17-24; *Novotorgovii Code* of 1667 read as follows: "Any foreigners shall not sell any goods in retail... and they shall not visit the fairs or travel with their goods and money into any town or send any salesmen.": Lyashchenko remarked to the point: "On the whole this measure was double-edged and disadvantageous from the standpoint of the volume of trade, but profitable for the Russian merchants," p. 227.

17. B. Pares, *A History of Russia*, New York, 1949; pp. 87 and 92.

18. A. Soloviov, "Sviataia Rus'," *Sbornik Russkavo Arkheologicheskavo Obshchestva v Korolevstvie S. Kh. S.*, 1927, I, pp. 77-113; O. Ohloblyn, *Moskovska teoria III Rymu v XVI-XVII stolittiakh*, Munich, 1951.

19. Comprehensively on the Russian Orthodox Church of that era: E. Golubinskii, *Istoria russkoi tserkvi*, Moscow, 1900-1917, Vol. II; Ohloblyn, *op. cit.*

20. "Departure of the national architectural style from the Byzantine tradition provoked a strong reaction among churchmen and government officials, for departure from tradition was considered nothing short of heresy": M. Florinsky, *Russia, A History and an Interpretation*, New York, 1953, Vol. I, p. 148.

21. Muscovite painting: M. Alpatov and N. Brunov, *Geschichte der Altrussischen Kunst*, Augsburg, 1932, pp. 285-346; also, D. Rice, *Russian Icons*, London-New York, 1947.

22. *The Laurentian Codex, The Trinity Chronicle, The Patriarch Nikon Chronicle, The Voskresenski Chronicle*, and others, all can be located in the *Polnoie sobranie russkikh letopisei*, 1846-1906.

23. N. Gudzii, *Istoria drevniei russkoi literatury*, Moscow, 1941, pp. 225-226, 318-321; D. Chizhevskii (Čiževskij), *History of Russian Literature*, 'S-Gravenhage, 1960, pp. 145-230.

FOOTNOTES TO CHAPTER ELEVEN

1. The ethnic composition; V. Kluchevsky, *A History of Russia* London-New York, 1911, Vol. 1, pp. 203-220; also, N. Fr.-Chirovsky, *An Introduction to Russian History*, New York, 1967, pp. 8-16.

2. H. Kohn, *Pan-Slavism; Its History and Ideology*, University of Notre Dame, Indiana, 1953, in particular Part II, "Pan-Slavism and Russian Messianism"; W. Chamberlin, *The Russian Enigma*, New York, 1943, Chap. II.

3. Chamberlin, p. 19: "The Soviet Union cannot escape Russian history. The roots of many Soviet actions and institutions may be sought and found in events and developments as far back as the days of Ivan the Terrible (1547-1584) and Peter the Great (1689-1725)... Stalin is indebted to both rulers for many models of policy"; then, M. Bradovich, *Derzhava bez natsii*, New York, 1952, p. 36 added to the very point: "It would be a mistake to look upon the Russian Bolshevism as something entirely new, original and revolutionary.... Everything which is essential for Bolshevism, had been originated, beyond any doubt, long ago in the time of the Czars, and has been only a heritage of the Czarate, taken over and utilized by the present rulers of the Kremlin to the utmost."

4. Compare, Fr.-Chirovsky, p. 133-146.

5. The story of Ivan IV, the Terrible or Dread: R. Wipper, *Ivan Groznyi*, Moscow, 1947; Eckhard, H., *Ivan the Terrible*, New York, 1949; J. Fennel, *Ivan the Great: Expansion of the Muscovite State*, London, 1961; also, Kluchevsky, Vol. II, pp. 91-103.

6. A brief but a penetrating analysis of Ivan's character: M. Florinsky, *Russia, A History and an Interpretation*, New York, 1953, Vol. I, pp. 182-190; More recently the Soviet historians, in order to follow the official scheme, have attempted to present a more favorable evaluation of Ivan himself and his epoch, also including there the "Time of Troubles": P. Skrynnikov, *Nachalo oprichninoie i oprichnii terror*, Leningrad, 1966-69, 2 volms. Then some western historians have also followed the new trend: J. Culpepper, "The Kremlin Executions of 1575 and the Enthronement of Simeon Bekbulatovich," *Slavic Review*, Sept. 1965.

7. On Ivan's political theory of Muscovite absolutism: V. Valdenberg, *Drevnierrusskiie ucheniia o predielakh tsarskoi vlasti*, Petrograd, 1916, sections referring to Ivan IV; also briefly, Florinsky, Vol. I, pp. 185-186.

8. Wipper, *op. cit.*; Eckhard, *op. cit.*

9. Kluchevsky, Vol. II, pp. 74-90; also on *oprichnina*: Florinsky, Vol. I, pp. 199-202.

10. Kluchevsky, Vol., II, p. 80.

11. The correspondence between Prince Kurbskii and the Czar shed a great deal of light on many problems of politics of the time: J. Fennel,

The Correspondence Between Prince A. M. Kurbsky and Tsar Ivan IV of Russia, 1564-1579. New York, 1955; Yet recently Keenan from Harvard shed considerable doubt with respect of the correspondence. He doubts whether such correspondence ever existed, being largely a forgery of a later time: Keenan, Ed., *The Kurbskii-Graznyi Apocrypha; The 17th Century Genesis of the "Correspondence" Attributed to Prince Kurbskii and Tsar Ivan IV*, Cambridge, 1971.

12. Chamberlin, Bradovich; also to the point: W. Kulski, *The Soviet Regime; Communism in Practice*, Syracuse, 1954; all referring to the historical genesis of modern Russia.

13. S. Platonov, *History of Russia*, Bloomington, 1964, p. 133.

14. Kluchevsky notably understimated the impact of the *oprichnina* institution. Above all, he thought that the *oprichnina* failed to accomplish what Ivan expected to achieve by it; that is, to overhaul the whole administration system of the land: Vol. II, in particular, pp. 86-87.

15. Yu Tolstoi. *The First Forty Years of Intercourse between England and Russia, 1553-1593 (Piervia sorok liet snoshenii mezhdu Rossieiu i Anglieiu)*, St. Petersburg, 1875.

16. On the Livonian war: J. Clarkson, *A History of Russia*, New York, 1951, pp. 112-115; Platonov, pp. 135-137: "Ivan's successors during the seventeenth century renewed the attempt to get possession of it (the Baltic Sea shore), and Peter the Great at last succeeded in bringing this about."

17. Florinsky, Vol. II, pp. 186-188.

18. Platonov, p. 133.

19. P. Lyashchenko, *History of the National Economy of Russia*, New York, 1949, pp. 230-232; as far as the colonization of the south-eastern borderlands was concerned; D. Bagalei, *Ocherki po istorii i byta kolonizatsii stepnoi okrainy Moskovskavo gosudarstva*, Moscow, 1887; about the Muscovite exploitation of the borderlands: S. Balzak, V. Vasyutin, and Ya Feigin, eds., *Economic Geography of the USSR*, New York, 1952, pp. 122-131.

20. A. Nikitskii, *Istoria ekonomicheskavo byta Velikavo Novgoroda*, St. Petersburg, 1893; Lyashchenko, p. 232: 'In the course of the thirteenth century, the Novgorod people had come to consider Yugra and Odobrino as practically their own volosts.... In the wake of these Novgorod river pirates and "prospectors" if not together with them, also came the Moscow traders and industrialists."

21. R. Fisher, *The Russian Fur Trade, 1550-1700*, Berkeley, University of California Press, 1943; Lyashchenko, pp. 237-240: An excellent, brief coverage; Dankevych, M., *Future Potentials of Siberia*, Washington, 1965, pp. 13-15.

22. I. Akulinin, *Yermak i Stroganovi*, Paris, 1933; Dankevych: *Ibid;* Lyashchenko, *loc. cit.*

FOOTNOTES TO CHAPTER TWELVE

1. "Donskie kazaki," in *Kazachii slovar-spravochnik*, A. Skrilov and G. Gubarev, eds., Clevland, 1966, Vol. I, pt. 2, pp. 173-204; W. Cresson, *The Cossacks*, New York, 1919; K. Czaplicka, *The Evolution of the Cossack Communities*, 1919; S. Svatikov, *Rossia i Don*, 1919. A sharp distinction must be made between the Don-Cossacks, who were under the Muscovite supremacy, and were ethnically alien to the Ukrainian Zaporozhe Cossacks. Their political aims were different from those of the Ukrainian Cossacks, whose chief political end was in fighting against the Polish rule and in liberating Ukraine from the Polish oppression; D. Doroshenko, *Narys Istorii Ukrainy*, Munich, 1966, Vol. I, pp. 144-161. The Russian historiography preferred to ignore the difference and treated both the Cossack phenomena as identical to support its "general line" of everything being Russian. About the struggle of the Don-Cossack nation, denied largely by the Russian history writing: *Kazachii istoricheski kalendar* - 1953, by S. Boldirev, Philadelphia, 1953; also, N. Chirovsky, *The Economic Factors in the Growth of Russia*, New York, 1957, pp. 27, 81-89.

2. V. Kluchevsky, *A History of Russia*, London-New York, 1913, Vol. III, pp. 15-16.

3. S. Platonov, *History of Russia*, Bloomington, 1964, pp. 144-145; also the same more extensively on the subject matter: the same, *Boris Godunov*, Prague, 1924; from among the modern historians, M. Florinsky, *Russia, A History and an Interpretation*, New York, 1953, Vol. I, p. 226.

4. Florinsky, *Ibid*.

5. It was particularly indicative of Shuiskii's character, in general. He had no morals and scruples, and he reversed his official statements whenever it only served his purpose. He incited twice the Moscow mob to revolt and to overthrow the government. There was little wonder, therefore, that he himself as a Czar could scarcely provide law and order, and succeed as a ruler: Kluchevsky, Vol. III, p. 32.

6. Giles Fletcher, Queen Elizabeth's ambassador, described the situation in Muscovy at that time as follows: "...this wicked policy and tyrannous practice... hath so troubled that country, and filled it so full of grudge and mortal hatred ever since, that it will not be quenched (as it seemeth now) till it burne againe into a civil flame": Sir E. Bond, *Russia at the Close of the Sixteenth Century, Comprising the Treatise "of the Russe common wealth" by Dr. Giles Fletcher; and the Travels of Sir Jerome Horsey...*, London, 1856, p. 34; Platonov, p. 146; also, N. Riasanovsky, *A History of Russia*, New York, 1963, p. 178.

7. Kluchevsky, Vol. III, p. 28: "..., as soon as Boris heard of the false Dimitrii, he told the boyars that it was their work — that it was they who had put forward the Pretender"; also *Ibid.*, p. 31: "The 'great' boyars were forced to create a pretender for the purpose of dislodging

Boris, and thereafter to dislodge that pretender for the purpose of clearing the road to the throne for a member of their own circle." Also Platonov believed, that the whole episode of Pseudo-Dimitrii was a Muscovite phenomenon, and that the whole conspiracy was evolved in the *boyar* circles; G. Vernadsky, "The Death of the Tsarevich Dimitry: A Reconsideration of the Case," *Oxford Slavonic Papers*, V, 1954.

8. S. Platonov, *Boris Godunov*, Prague, 1924, p. 162: "Boris dreamed of introducing into Russia European scholars (even, perhaps, a university); he ordered scholars sought out abroad and brought to Moscow;..."

9. On the over-all evaluation of Boris Godunov's reign: Platonov, in particular, the pages 150 to 166; Briefly on the subject matter, J. Clarkson, *A History of Russia*, 1961, pp. 131-133; also about Godunov; S. Graham, *Boris Godunov*, New York, 1933.

10. The Bolotnikov episode: Kluchevsky, Vol. III, pp. 45-46: "Bolotnikov himself was killed, but his effort found a universal echo. Everywhere the peasantry, slaves, and alien settlers of the Volga region — in short, everyone who was either fugitive or without substance — rose for the Pretender.... In short, Bolotnikov summoned to his standard all who desired to attain freedom, distinction, and wealth"; S. Platonov, *Smutnoie Vremia*, St. Petersburg, 1923.

11. S. Platonov, *Sotsialnii krizis Smutnavo Vremeni*, Leningrad, 1924; Platonov has been the leading scholar of the era of "Time of Troubles."

12. More recent history works, published in the United States, on the subject matter: Florinsky, Vol. I, pp. 231-243; Clarkson, pp. 135-144; Riasanovsky, pp. 181-192; A Mazour, *Russia, Tsarist and Communist*, Toronto-New York-London, 1962, pp. 65-74.

13. M. Hrushevsky, *Istoria Ukrainy-Rusi*, New York, 1956, Vol. VII, pp. 322-325, 332-333. Hrushevsky made a clear distinction between the Don-Cossacks and the Ukrainian Zaporozhe Cossacks: "..., and they [the Zaporozhe Cossacks] took substantial part in the Muscovite troubles and in the plunder of the Muscovite territories..., and made that their trade." (325).

14. Florinsky, Vol. I, p. 235.

15. The text of the agreement: *Sbornik, Russkoie Istoricheskoie Obshchestvo*, CXLII, pp. 64-73, 93-113.

16. That the Poles, and in particular King Sigismund, were evasive with respect of Prince Wladyslaw 'becoming Orthodox,' angered the Orthodox Muscovites very much. It was the reason why Patriarch Hermogen opposed a "Catholic Czar" who broke promises.

17. "..., and Sigismund yielded to the temptation to hold in Warsaw in October an elaborate celebration at which the former Czar Vasilii Shuiskii and his brother, now Polish prisoners, were ostentatiously displayed with little good taste as living examples of the vicissitudes of human fortune": Florinsky, Vol. I, p. 241.

18. The Don regions at the end of the fifteenth century: "Putieshchestvie Kontarini," *Biblioteka inostrannikh pisatielei o Rossii XV-XVII, vv,* St. Petersburg, 1863, pp. 102-104. In the next century the Don-Cossack formation began to develop in the steppes of the Don-Volga regions. During Batory's war against Ivan the Dread, the Don-Cossacks were helping the Pskovians to defend the city against the Polish onslaught: V. Golobutskii, *Zaporozhskoie Kazachestvo,* Kiev, 1957, p. 94; G. Vernadsky and M. Karpovich, *A History of Russia,* Vol. IV, *Russia at the Dawn of the Modern Age,* New Haven-London, 1959, p. 262; *"Kazachii slovar-sprovochnik,* pp. 175-180.

19. Kluchevsky, Vol. III, p. 63; "An item exists that a certain Sheremietiev wrote to prince Golitsin, in Poland, the words: 'Our Mikhail is as yet but young, and has not come unto understanding: yet is he such a one as will be familiar unto us...' and Boris Godunov would never be repeated."

20. *Ibid.,* pp. 59-63; also, Florinsky, Vol. I, pp. 244-246.

21. S. Platonov, *Boris Godunov,* Prague, 1924, p. 98: "After surviving a series of grievous military and diplomatic failures, ..., the Moscow government did not lose its vigor of spirit and its will power."

22. In March 1613, an embassy was sent to Poland in order to arrange for an exchange of prisoners, was instructed to deny Mikhail's election not to aggravate the situation. In 1618, an armistice agreement was concluded between Muscovy and Poland, at which Wladyslaw refused to renounce his claim to the Muscovite throne; Florinsky, I, p. 254.

23. P. Lyashchenko, *History of the National Economy of Russia,* New York, 1949, p. 239.

24. *Ibid.,* p. 241.

25. W. Kolarz, *Russia and Her Colonies,* New York, 1952, p. 4: "Official Russian policy and Russian state imperialism often lagged behind the people's initiative. Frequently, official Russia did no more than endorse the facts which the people had created. Even the greatest figures of Russian history, like Ivan the Terrible and Peter the Great, on several occasions simply followed in the wake of lawless bands of fugitive peasants, the famous Cossacks, who had enlarged the boundaries of Russia without even knowing it. In this way Russia lived a double life and had a double history"; The element of enterprising and trading in the territorial expansion of Muscovy; R. Fisher, *The Russian Fur Trade,* Berkeley, 1943; J. Kerner, *Urge to the Sea,* Berkeley and Los Angeles, 1942; also, Chirovsky, pp. 91-101; Lyashchenko, pp. 238-241.

26. The charter for the town of Solvichegodsk from 1590: *Akty Arkheograficheskoi, Ekspeditsii,* Vol. I, Nr. 349.

27. Georgia during the feudal era: J. Stalin, *Marksizm i natsionalnokolonialnii vopros,* Moscow, 1937, pp. 5-6.

28. Kolarz, pp. 255-302; Lyashchenko, pp. 243-246.

29. Platonov, pp. 98 and others; also, Clarkson, p. 128.

FOOTNOTES TO CHAPTER THIRTEEN

1. The whole case of the celebrated so long, alleged correspondence between Ivan the Dread and Prince Andrei Kurbskii has been put in doubt by a recent study of Keenan: Compare: Note 11, Chpt. 11.

2. V. Kluchevsky, *A History of Russia*, London-New York, 1912, Vol. II, pp. 70-71: various quotations from the writings of Ivan; the growth of the doctrine of the Muscovite autocracy: *ibid.*, pp. 16-37 and 91-103; also, G. Vernadsky and M. Karpovich, *A History of Russia*, Vol. IV, *Russia at the Dawn of the Modern Age*, New Haven-London, 1959, pp. 165-170; G. Flecher, *Of the Rus Commonwealth*, ed. by A. Schmidt, Ithaca, 1966, pp. 30-33: Chapter VII, The State or Form of their Government. Equally interesting are the chapters XII, on Tsar's revenues (pp. 64-70) and XXI, on the Church and clergy (pp. 107-124).

3. Kluchevsky, Vol. III, pp. 32-34; also, M. Florinsky, *Russia, A History and An Interpretation*, New York, 1953, Vol. I, p. 230.

4. *Ibid.*, p. 246.

5. J. Fennel, *Ivan the Great's Expansion of the Muscovite State* London, 1961; R. Wipper, *Ivan Groznii*, Moscow, 1947; and S. Graham, *Ivan the Terrible*, New Haven, 1933.

6. Administration of the Muscovite state: Kluchevsky, Vol. II, pp. 242-264, chapter XIV.

7. The very origins of the landed council, the *ziemskii sobor*, may go as far back as Grand Vsievolod III of Suzdal, who ordered in 1211 a gathering of his *boyars*, abbots, priests, courtiers, merchants and "all the people" to deliberate the matters of the state: A. Priesniakov, *Obrazovanie velikorusskavo gosudarstva*, Petrograd, 1918, p. 44; also, Vernadsky, Vol. II, *Kievan Russia*, New Haven-London, 1951, p. 187.

8. The formation and the evolution of the council: Kluchevsky, Vol. II, pp. 288-318: chapter XVI; also, H. von Eckard, *Ivan the Terrible*, New York, 1949, pp. 76-100, 336-337.

9. The *oprichnina* institution: compare, chapter eleven, section on domestic affairs and the *oprichnina* institution in this work; also, Eckard, pp. 241-300; compare, chapt. II, ft. 6.

10. Kluchevsky, Vol., II, pp. 265-286; P. Lyashchenko, *History of the National Economy of Russia*, New York, 1949, pp. 212, 221, 223 and other pages mentioned all kinds of taxes collected by the Muscovite government; also, J. Clarkson, *A History of Russia*, New York, 1961, pp. 110-111 and 161; *Tamozhennie gramoty, Akty Arkheograficheskoi Ekspeditsii*, Vol. I. No. 230, 263, Vol. II, No. 65.

11. Kluchevsky, Vol. II, p. 272; Florinsky, Vol. I, pp. 192-194.

12. The Don-Cossacks: *Kazachii slovar-spravochnik*, Cleveland, 1966, Vol. I, pt. 2, pp. 173-186; also briefly: M. Pokrovsky, *Brief History of Russia*, London, 1933, Vol. I, pp. 70-71.

13. F. Korchmaryk, *Dukhovi vplyvy Kyieva na Moskovshchynu v dobi hetmanskoi Ukrainy*, New York, 1954, pp. 9-20; P. Miliukov, *Outlines of Russian Culture*, Philadelphia, 1948, pp. 9-26.

14. Miliukov, *ibid.*, Korchmaryk, *ibid.*, Fletcher, pp. 116-117: "They are men utterly unlearned, which is no marvel, forasmuch as their makers, the bishops themselves, as before was said, are clear of that quality and make not further use of any kind of learning..., not of the scriptures themselves, save to read and to sing them." The same witness to the primitivism of the Muscovites in general: S. Herbertstein, *Rerum Moscovitacarum Commintarii*, Antwerp, 1557, p. 32: He related, that living in a utter primitivism, the Muscovites thought they were only true Christians and severely condemned the Western Catholicism as a sinful deviation from the ancient Church and the ancient holy rules.

15. S. Platonov, *Moskva i Zapad v XVI-XVII viekakh*, Leningrad, 1925; Florinsky, Vol. I, pp. 196-197; N. Berdiaiev, *Dusha Rosii*, Moscow, 1915; Fletcher, Herbertstein and Olearius, among many others, testified to the point of a traditional Russian ritualism and formalism.

16. The *boyars* and *dvoriani*: Florinsky, Vol. I, pp. 209-214; Kluchevsky, Vol. II, pp. 104-121; Pokrovsky, Vol. I, pp. 51-52, 64, 67, 83-85; Lyashchenko, pp. 180-199; comprehensively: S. Rozhdenstvienskii, *Sluzhiloie zemlievladanie v moskovskom gosudarstvie XVI vieka*, St. Petersburg, 1896.

17. Kluchevsky, Vol. II, pp. 197-241; Florinsky, Vol. I, pp. 214-219; Lyashchenko, pp. 51-52, 63-64, 67-69, 86; Rozhdenstvienskii, *op. cit.*

18. Kluchevsky, p. 207.

19. Fletcher, pp. 67-68; about the accumlation of wealth: Lyashchenko, pp. 211-212, 223-226; "There also were frequently examples of artisans who lacked their 'own livelihood' and sought 'for alms' ": p. 209; M. Dovnar-Zapolsky, *Torgovlia i Promishlennost Moskey VI-XVII*, vv., Moscow, 1910, p. 84 and other.

20. N. Rozhkov, *Sielskoie khoziaistvo Moskovskoi Rusi XVI v.*, St. Petersburg, 1899.

21. Fletcher, pp. 15-16; flax was grown also in Novgorod, Vologda and Iaroslal according to other foreign accounts.

22. Lyashchenko, p. 181.

23. N. Chechulin, *Goroda Moskovskavo gosudarstva*, St. Petersburg, 1899, p. 339 and others; also Lyashchenko, p. 206.

24. "...they formed a separate suburban settlement... a type more closely related to the guild crafts of western Europe"; Lyashchenko, p. 209; "Vriemiennik diaka Ivana Timofieieva," in *Pamiatniki drevniei russkoi pismiennosti otnosiashchiiesia k Smutnomu Vriemini*, 3rd edition, Vol. XIII, Part I, p. 271-2, as quoted by Clarkson, p. 122.

25. I. Kulisher, *Istoria russkavo narodnavo khoziastva*, Moscow, 1925, Vol. II, pp. 211-223; Lyashchenko, pp. 209-210.

26. *Ibid.*, p. 211.

27. About the Stroganov family: N. Vviedenskii, *Torgovii dom XVI-XVII vv.*, Leningrad, 1924; also, G. Akulinin, *Yermak i Stroganovi*, Paris, 1933.

28. *Akty Arkheograficheskoi Ekspeditsii*, Vol. I, Nrs. 97, 258, 271 and others.

29. S. Herbertstein, *Notes upon Russia,* tr. and edt. by R. Major, New York, 1851-52, Vol. I, pp. 109-116, 242-244, Vol. II, 187-188, 198, 229-230 and others.

30. *Akty Arkheograficheskoi Ekspeditsii*, Vol. I, Nrs. 230, 263, and Vol. II, Nrs. 65 and others.

31. "Piatina 142 goda," by Staschevskii, *Zhurnal ministerstva narodnavo prosvieshchenia*, Vols. IV-V, p. 99 ff, as quoted by Lyashchenko, p. 221.

32. Dovnar-Zapolsky, p. 55.

33. B. Kurtz, *Sostoianie Rossii v 1650-1655 po donesienian Rodesa*, Moscow, 1914, p. 166 ff; Lyashchenko, pp. 226-227.

34. Yu. Fedoriv, *Istoria Tserkvy v Ukraini*, Toronto, 1967, p. 77: "..., that in the Eastern Christianity the elements of the Oriental culture with their leanings to the mysticism, while in the Western — its preference for a strict judicial and cool logic were reflected."

35. Ya. Grot. "Piotr Vielikii, kak prosvietitiel Rossii," *Atdielenia Russ-kavo Yazika i Sloviesnosti Imperatorskoi Akademii Nauk*, St. Petersburg, 1872, Vol. X, p. 18-20.

36. Korchmaryk, pp. 18-19: he quoted several foreign visitors, who testified to the very point of the popular drunkenness in Muscovy.

37. S. Smirnov, *Istoria Moskovskoi Slaviano-Greko-Latinskoi Akademii*, Moscow, 1885; Korchmaryk, pp. 23-30.

38. J. Fennel, *The Correspondence Between Prince A. M. Kurbsky and Tsar Ivan IV of Russia*, 1564-1579, New York, 1955; The authenticity of the correspondence challenged: Keenan, E., *The Kurbskii-Groznyi Apocrypha, The 17th Century Genesis of the "Correspondence" Attributed to Prince Kurbskii and Tsar Ivan IV*, Cambridge, 1971.

39. The Muscovite literature of the sixteenth century: D. Cizivskij, *History of Russian Literature,* 'S-Gravenhage, 1960, pp. 230-306; on the Muscovite culture: Miliukov, pp. 9-39.

40. Compare: N. Riasanovsky, *A History of Russia*, New York, 1963, pp. 225-226; on the architecture and arts: G. Hamilton, *The Arts and Architecture of Russia*, London, 1954: corresponding chapters on the sixteenth century.

INDEX

Adashev, A., 292-293, 295-298, 306, 363, 366
Agapetos, 242
Akhmad, 172, 229, 234
Aleksei, Metropolitan, 212-214, 277
Alexander I, 13
Alexander II, 13
Alexander III, 13
Alexander, of Kakhetia, 247, 354
Alexander Nevskii, 56-57, 166-168, 189-198, 202, 205, 282, 429 f
Alexander of Twer, 204-206, 430 f
Alexander, of Lithuania, 233
Al Massudi, 418 f- 420 f
Anastasia, Czaritsa, 291, 298
Anastasii, Metropolitan, 290
Andrei Bogolubskii, 50, 54-55, 81, 83-89, 92, 95-98, 107, 110, 129, 147, 236, 423 f, 428 f
Andrei II, of Vladimir, 166-167, 185, 190-192, 194, 429 f
Andrei III, of Vladimir, 190, 197-198, 202
Andrei, of Galicia, 148
Andrei, Junior, 229-230
Andrei, Senior, 229-230
Andrew, Apostle, St., 243
Antonovych, V. 9
Arik-Buka, 168
Aristotle, 132
Askold, 52, 138-139
Attila, 135
Augustus, Caesar, 241, 293

Bakunin, M., 419 f
Barbarossa, Frederick, 129
Basenok, F., 224
Basil, of Galicia, 148
Basmanovs, the, 292, 301

Batory, Stefan, of Poland, 308, 348, 402, 439 f
Batu, 90, 158-159, 161-167, 173, 189
Bayer, G., 49
Bekbulatovich, Simeon, 304, 324-326, 331-332, 435 f
Bela, of Hungary, 163
Berdibeg, 171
Berke, 168, 194-195
Bielskii, I., 296
Bielskii, B., 324-325
Bielskiis, the, 287, 296
Bitiagovskii, M., 322-323
Boleslav, of Poland, 144
Bolotnikov, I., 319, 334-338, 392, 438 f
Boretskiis, the, 59
Boretskii, M., 59
Boris, Prince, 75, 144
Boris, of Rostov, 194
Boris Vasiliivich, 229-230
Brezhniev, L., 13, 285
Bukharin, N., XIII
Bulavin, K., 356

Casimir, see Kazimierz
Catherine, Princess, 311
Catherine II, 286, 290
Chaadaiev, P., 429 f
Chancellor, R., 307
Cherkasskii, B., 328
Chinghis-Khan, see Genghis-Khan
Chodkiewich, J., 346
Chubaty, N., XII, 7
Clarkson, J., 62
Constantine, Monomakh, 241
Constantine, of Nizhnii-Novgorod, 211
Constantine, of Vladimir, 90, 132, 189

Constantine, Dimitrovich, 220
Cyprian, Metropolitan, 214, 220
Czech, 37
Cyril, of Turiv, 151

Daniel (Danilo), of Galicia, 148, 163, 193
Daniel, of Moscow, 190, 198-199, 202
Daniel, Metropolitan, 239, 242, 277, 287, 402
Danilevskii, M., XI
Dashkevych, O., 238
Davlet-Girey, 305
Day, C., 9
Dazhbog, deity, 43
Diakonov, M., 173, 428 f
Dimitrii Donskoi, 180, 201, 205, 209-219, 277
Dimitrii, son of Ivan III, 236, 294
Dimitrii, son of Ivan IV, the Dread, 322-323, 327, 329-330, 333, 337
Dimitrii, of Suzdal, 211
Dimitrii Shemiaka, 219, 223-226
Dimitrii, of Twer, 204
Dimitrii, of Vladimir, 190, 197
Dimitrii Vasiliivich, 234-235
Dimitrii, First Pretender, 319, 326-335, 337, 340, 347, 349, 360-361, 437 f-438 f
Dimitrii, Second Pretender, 319-320, 336-343, 347-350, 360-361, 438 f
Dionisii, Abbot, 345
Dionisii of Ferapont, 281
Dionisii, Metropolitan, 322
Dir, 52, 138-139
Dobrynia, 76
Dombrovsky, A., 422 f
Doroshenko, D., 8-9
Dostoyevskii, F., XIII

Edigay, 172, 222-223
Ediger, Simeon, 304
Elizabeth, of England, 310-311, 437 f
Engels, F., 25
Eric, of Sweden, 309, 311
Esugay-Bagatur, 155-156

Fedotov, Yu., 10
Filotei (Philotei), 243, 251, 277 432 f
Fiodor I, 319-327, 335, 347, 349, 354, 359-360, 381
Fiodor, see Godunov
Fiodor, imposter, 335
Fletcher, G., 174, 327, 441 f
Florinsky, M., XV, 64, 73, 97, 287, 289, 335, 344, 362, 421 f, 424 f
Fotii, see Photius
Fra Angelico, 281

Gardie, Magnus, de la, 338
Gedeonov, S., 51
Gedymin, of Lithuania, 221, 264, 292, 300
Gelasii, Metropolitan, 323
Genghis-Khan, XIII, 9, 154-157, 159, 161, 171, 176, 428 f
George (Yurii), of Galicia, 148
George (Yurii) -Boleslav, of Galicia, 148
Gleb, 169
Glinskii, Helen, 239, 286-287, 296
Glinskii, the, 287, 296
Godunov, Boris, Czar, 285, 319-333, 338, 347, 349, 351, 359-361, 381-383, 388-389, 395, 400, 401, 437 f - 439 f
Godunov, Fiodor, Czar, 329, 331, 333-334.
Godunov, Irene, 320-324
Godunov, Ksenia, 329
Godunovs, the, 321-322
Gogol (Hohol), N., 429 f
Golitsin, V., 341, 347, 349, 439 f
Golitsins, the, 329, 340, 343
Golovins, the, 320, 322
Golubiev, S., 9
Gostomysl, 41, 48
Grekov, B., 173, 428 f
Grot, Ya., 400
Guyuk, 158, 166

Han dynasty, the, 154
Hapsburgs, the 49, 346-347, 421 f
Hastings, M., 292, 311

Haxthausen, A., 419 f
Heidelberg man, the, 21
Helen, Princess, 233
Herberstein (Gerberstein), S., 397, 432 f, 441 f
Herman, Metropolitan, 290
Hermogen, Patriarch, 333, 342-343, 345, 438 f
Herodotus, 134
Hlib (Gleb), 75
Hlinsky, M., 239
Hohenstaufens, the, 147
Homer, 132
Homo Sapiens, 22
Hrushevsky, M., 9, 51, 420 f, 438 f
Hulagu, 168

Ibn-Dasta 44, 418 f- 419 f
Ibn-Fadlan, 44, 418 f-419 f
Ibn-Hawkal, 418 f
Ibn-Khordadbeh, 419 f
Ibn-Yakub, 418 f
Ignatii, Patriarch, 333
Ihor (Igor), of Kiev, 50, 52, 75, 139-141
Ihor, son of Yaroslav, 145, 423 f
Ihor, son of Sviatoslav, 152
Ilarion, Metropolitan, 151
Ilovaiskii, D., 51
Iona, Metropolitan, 224
Isidore, Metropolitan, 227
Ivan I, Kalita (Moneybag), 167, 170, 176, 186-187, 199, 201, 204-208, 210, 218-219, 227, 254, 275, 430 f
Ivan II, 205, 209-211
Ivan III, the Great, 59, 201, 218, 227-236, 238-239, 244-247, 250-251, 253, 256, 258, 260, 263, 266-267, 274, 277-278, 285-286, 294, 312, 404, 424 f, 432 f
Ivan IV, the Terrible, the Dread, XIII, XV, 12, 98, 173, 176, 224, 239, 263, 284-314, 316, 318, 320, 324, 332, 348, 353, 354, 359-367, 369-370, 376-377, 379-380, 383,
400-403, 435 f-436 f, 439 f-440 f
Ivan, son of Ivan IV, 293
Ivan, Pretender's son, 343, 346-347
Iziaslav, of Kiev, 77, 145, 423 f

Jagatay, 157-159
Jagiello, see Yagailo
Janibeg, 170-171, 211
Job, see Yov
John III, of Sweden, 311, 349
Jordanis, 30, 418 f
Juchi, 157-159, 161, 171, 427 f

Kabul, 155
Kaidu, 159
Karamzin, N., 173-174, 428 f-429 f
Kasim, 225-226
Kazimierz, of Poland, 172, 227, 229, 232
Keenan, E., 436 f
Khara-Davan, E., 428 f
Kholmskii, V., 239
Khor, deity, 43
Khoryv, 37, 41, 136, 138
Khrushchev, N., 13, 285
Khvorostinin, I., 334
Kluchevsky (Kliuchevskii), V., 7-8, 39, 94-95, 112, 173, 198, 200, 218, 299, 303, 347, 367, 372, 390, 420 f, 428 f, 430 f
Kostomarov, N., 94, 174, 428 f
Kosygin, A., 13
Kotian, 163
Kubilay, 158-160, 168
Kulpa, 171
Kulski, W., XII
Kurbskii, A., 293, 295-296, 298, 301, 363, 366, 403, 435 f, 440 f
Kuzhil, U., XIV
Kyi, 37, 41, 136, 138

Lamanskii, V., 51
Lavrentii, imposter, 335
Lebed, 38, 136
Lekh, 37
Lenin, N. (Ulianov, V.), 13, 302
Leonid, Archbishop, 291

445

Leontovich, F., 428 f
Lev I, of Galicia, 148
Lev II, of Galicia, 148
Liapunov, P., 342, 344-345
Lisowski, A., 337
Lyashchenko, P., XV, 20, 351, 393, 419 f

Makarii, Metropolitan, 290-291, 294-295, 297, 366, 379-380, 400, 402
Mal, 41
Maliuta-Skuratov, G., 292, 301
Maliuta-Skuratov, Maria, 329
Mamai, 171, 214-216
Mangu-Temir, 168-169, 182, 189-190, 196
Maria, of Twer, 234
Martinka, imposter, 335
Mauricius, 418 f, 420 f
Maxim, Metropolitan, 206
Maxim, hermit, 279
Mendog, of Lithuania, 221
Mengli-Girey, 245
Mikhail, of Vladimir, 190-191
Mikhail, of Twer and Moscow, 202-204, 206
Mikhail of Twer, 212, 214, 219, 231
Mikhail of Veria, 230
Mikhail (Romanov), Czar, 12-13, 319, 347-349, 360, 362, 439 f
Minin-Sokhoruk, K., 345-346
Mniszek, Jerzy, 328
Mniszek, Marina, 328, 330, 332, 340, 343
Mohamed-Girey, 245, 432 f
Moisei, Archbishop, 132
Mokosh, deity, 43
Mongka, 158-159, 163, 166-167, 194
Morozovs, the, 396
Mozhaiskii, I., 225
Mstislav, of Novgorod, 55-56, 78
Mstislavskii, F., 322, 342, 344
Mstyslav, of Kiev, 147
Mstyslav, Prince, 148
Mueller, G., 49

Nagoi, Maria, 293, 322-323
Nagois, the, 322
Nasonov., A., 194
Neanderthal man, 21-22
Nestor, chronicler, 31, 151
Nevruz, 171
Nicholas I, 13, 286
Nicholas II, 13
Nogay, 169-170

Obolenskii, I., 287, 296
Obolenskii, S., 224
Olearius, 441 f
Oleh (Oleg), of Kiev, 50, 52, 75, 139-140
Oleh, of Chernihiv, 78
Olgierd, of Lithuania, 211, 221
Olha (Olga), of Kiev, 141
Ordinskii, P., 169
Ostrozhsky, C., 238
Otrepiev, G., see Dimitrii, First Pretender
Ovchina-Telepniev-Obolenskii, I., 286, 296

Pares, B., XIV, 274
Patrikiev, I., 253, 256
Paul I, 12-13, 300
Pavlov, I., XIII
Peresvietov, I., 363, 402-403
Perun, deity, 43-44
Peter I, the Great, XII, 12-13, 151, 176, 285-286, 435 f-436 f, 439 f
Peter, Metropolitan, 206-207, 212, 283
Peter, imposter, 335
Peter, Vasilii's lieutenant, 432 f
Philaret (Filaret), Patriarch, 324-325, 328, 331, 333, 340-341, 343, 347-348
Philip, Metropolitan, 291, 301
Philip, Prince, 350
Photius (Fotii), Metropolitan, 220, 223, 282
Plato, 132
Platonov, S., 7, 79-80, 90, 200, 210, 239, 313, 368, 420 f 438 f

446

Pogodin, M., XII, 9-10, 94
Pokrovskii, M., 7, 9
Possevinus, Jesuit, 308
Pozharskii, D., 345-347
Presniakov, A., 94, 200
Procopius, 30, 39, 418 f, 420 f
Prussus, 241, 293
Pugachov, E., 356

Radim, 31, 37, 41
Riasanovsky, N., 58, 404, 428 f
Riazin, S., 356
Roman, of Galicia, 147-148
Roman, of Smolensk, 132
Romanov, N., 320
Romanov, F., see Philaret
Romanovs, the, 12-13, 284-285, 321, 325, 328, 333, 348, 351, 385
Roric of Jutland, see Rurik
Rostislav, of Rostov, 78
Rostyslav, of Galicia, 145
Różynski, R., 337
Rublev, A., 281
Rurik, 48-52, 75, 96, 139, 241, 264
Rurik house, the, 76-78, 82, 84, 91, 94-96, 102, 112, 118, 140, 145-146, 149-150, 161, 186, 198, 232, 282, 285, 292, 300, 321, 332, 347, 360-361
Rus, 37
Rybakov, B., 10, 137

Saburov, S., 239
Saltykov, I., 341-342
Sanin, Joseph, of Volokolam, 242, 277, 290, 379, 402
Sapieha, Jan, 337
Sartak, 167, 194
Saxo Gramaticus, 27
Schloezer, A., 49
Serapion, Bishop, 282
Sergei, Abbot, 215
Sergeievich, V., 424 f, 428 f
Serpukhov, V., 224
Shakhmatov, M., 9, 130
Shakhovskoi, G., 334-335

Shchek, 37, 41, 136, 138
Shelekhov, G., 352
Shelukhin, S., 77
Sheremietiev, 439 f
Shuiskii, Dimitrii, 341-342, 345
Shuiskii, Vasilii, 285, 301, 322-323, 327, 329-342, 345, 347, 349-350, 361, 364, 374, 378, 437 f - 438 f
Shuiskiis, the, 287, 296-297, 320, 329, 340
Shulgine, B., 10
Sigismund III, of Poland, 337, 339-343, 345-346, 349, 438 f
Sigismund August, of Poland, 311
Simeon, the Proud, 167, 186, 205, 209-211, 218
Simeon, of Kaluga, 236
Simeon, imposter, 335
Sitskiis, the, 301
Skopins, the, 301
Skopin-Shuiskii, M., 335, 338-339, 341
Smirnov., P., 46
Smolatych, C., Metropolitan, 151
Sobolevskii, A., XII, 9, 10
Soloviov, S., 94, 173, 239, 428 f
Sophia Paleologue, 228, 234-235, 244
Sorskii, Nil, 278-279
Spiridon, Metropolitan, 241-242, 251, 277
Spitsin, A., 130
Stalin, J., 13, 285-286, 302, 429 f, 435 f
Stribog, deity, 43
Striga-Obolenskii, I., 224
Stroganovs, the, 316, 352, 396, 403-404
Struve, P., 7, 8
Subudey, 162-163
Svarog, deity, 43-44
Sviatopolk, the Sinner, 144, 426 f
Sviatoslav, of Kiev, 75-76, 141-142
Sviatoslav, of Novgorod Siversky, 199
Sviatoslav, Prince, 77, 145, 423 f
Sviatoslav, of Vladimir, 189, 191
Sylvester, priest, 292-293, 295-298, 306, 363, 366, 403

Tamerlane (Timur Lane), 160,
    171-172, 188, 222, 354
Tatishchev, V., 48
Tele-Buga, 169
Temudzhin, see Genghis-Khan
Theodosius, of Pechera, 151
Theognost, Metropolitan, 207, 212
Theophilus, Archbishop, 59
Thor, deity, 43
Tikhomirov, M., 46
Timur, see Tamerlane
Timur-Melik, 171
Tinibeg, 170
Tkachov, P., 419 f
Tokhmatish, 171-172, 216, 261
Tokhta, 169-170
Tretiak-Dalmatov, V., 239
Tretiakov, P., 10, 137
Trubetskoi, D., 344, 346
Trubetskoi, N., philologist, 9, 129,
    174, 428 f
Trubetskois, the, 301
Tuda-Mangu, 169
Tuluy, 157-159
Turakina, 158

Ugedey, 157-161, 163-164
Ulagchi, 167-168, 194
Ulianov, see Lenin
Ulu-Mahmed, 225
Urus-Khan, 171
Uzbeg, 170, 176, 430 f

Vasilii I, 180, 218-219, 222-223,
    227
Vasilii II, 58-59, 201, 218-220,
    223-228, 231, 234, 260, 275,
    285
Vasilii III, 218, 227, 233, 235-239,
    244-247, 250-251, 256, 266,
    277-278, 285-287, 294, 296,
    402, 404, 428 f, 432 f
Vasilii, imposter, 335
Vasilii, of Vladimir, 190, 195, 197
Vasilii, Yuriivich, 223
Vasilii, Archbishop, 132
Vassian, monk, (Patrikiev), 239,
    279, 402
Veliaminov, V., 99

Vernadsky, G., XV, 8-9, 44, 95,
    126, 134, 152, 155-156, 158,
    173-174, 195, 252, 428 f,
    432 f
Viacheslav, 145, 423 f
Viatko, 31, 37, 41
Viazemskii, A., 292, 301
Vitovt, of Lithuania, 220,
    222-223, 225
Vladimir, of Novgorod, 54, 145,
    242
Vladimirskii-Budanov, M., 9, 173,
    428 f
Volodymyr (Vladimir), the Great,
    50, 52-53, 75-76, 105, 127,
    142-143, 150
Volodymyr (Vladimir) Monomakh,
    77-78, 95, 146, 150-151, 176
Volodymyr, of Volhinia, 148
Volos, deity, 43-44
Vorotynskii, I., 305
Vorotynskiis, the, 320
Vsevolod, of Kiev, 77-78, 91,
    145, 423 f
Vsievolod, of Novgorod, 54
Vsievolod III, Big Nest, 55, 83-84,
    86, 88-90, 92-93, 95-98, 110,
    129, 132, 147, 189, 198, 236,
    421 f, 423 f, 440 f
Vuiefast, 76

Wallace, D., 419 f
Welfs, the, 147
Wladyslaw, of Poland, 320,
    340-343, 346, 349-350, 360,
    362, 438 f - 439 f

Yagailo (Jagiello), of Poland,
    214-215
Yakim, deacon, 431 f
Yakub, 225-226
Yaroslav, the Wise, 50, 52-54, 69
    76-77, 79, 91-92, 95, 105,
    132, 143-146, 150, 152, 426 f
Yaroslav, of Vladimir, 166,
    189-191, 282
Yaroslav II, of Vladimir, 190,
    195-197
Yeremiah, Patriarch, 382
Yermak, 316-317, 351

Yoasaf (Joasaph), Metropolitan, 287
Yov, Patriarch, 324-325, 330, 382
Yuan dynasty, the, 159-160
Yurii I, Dolgorukii, 50, 54, 79, 81-89, 92, 95, 98, 106, 110, 147, 199, 236
Yurii I, of Moscow, 190, 199, 202-204, 206
Yurii II, of Vladimir, 90, 162, 185, 189-190

Yurii Dimitrovich, 220, 223
Yurii Ivanovich, 236
Yurii, son of Vasilii II, 229
Yurii, son of Vasilii III, 239

Zagoskin, N., 428 f
Zakharin, R., 297
Zarutskii, I., 338, 344, 346
Zólkiewski, S., 341-342